DEATH CAB FOR CUTIE AUTUMN DE WILDE

CHRONICLE BOOKS
SAN FRANCISCO

o1151999

the DEATH CAB FOR CUTIE wish list
(or, OF BEARS AND MOTORCYCLES: TO SWOOP OR SWIPE?)

INTRODUCTION: These are the things that we have collectively decided would be of much importance to us in the event of a "record deal." We do, in fact, feel strongly about many of these things. Strong like professional wrestlers. Some of them we feel slightly less strongly about; say, perhaps as strongly as a small alligator, or a sick bear. There's always dinner.

LEGAL PART: This document is in no way to be interpreted as a binding contract of any sort. That's because it's not a legally binding contract. It's just not. Onward...

THE LIST:

1) We don't want to wear silver pants. But if we decide to wear silver pants, it would have to be legally/contractually acceptable (though still morally questionable.)

2) Non-exclusivity, to a reasonable degree. We don't expect to have the freedom to put full length records out on multiple labels, but we very much expect that calling a third party in to put out vinyl (if contract label chooses not to... so sad!) would be acceptable. We also expect that putting out 7"s on other labels would be okay. We're all aware that it's not 1963, and that 7"s don't interfere with record sales.

3) MUSIC. That's what this is all about, no? Yes. So...
   a) We write the songs, as we see fit. By Ben, or Nick, or one of Nathan's dogs. No label interference.
   b) No demos to label (unless we choose to send them, Which is entirely possible, if the label actually trusts us and is genuinely excited about what we're doing.).
   c) We get to choose the song order & track list.
   d) Our choice of studio/house/walkman/whatever.
   e) Our choice of producer (band members inclusive).
   f) Picking singles.

   Ultimately, This part of the contract would define what we feel the band/label experience should be: We make records, label releases and promotes them. In an ideal situation, it's more than that; it's a trust and a respect that develops between artist and label mutually.

   We anticipate recording ourselves for some period of time to come, which translates to relatively small recording budgets, Which get spent on equipment that we use and keep and maintain, and can record subsequent projects on. In all honesty, none of us understand how it's possible or why it's necessary to spend $1ook on an album, particularly when you don't get to keep the studio.

4) We want to reserve the right to choose where the record is mastered, and who by. (don't worry, none of us personally want to do it).

5) We want health insurance.

6) We want to be guaranteed three records. If label decides to drop us, label would ultimately have to buy its way out of

the contract. We don't know the legal name of this clause, but we know what it does. Artist development... hello? Hello??

7) We reserve the right to be snide, as demonstrated by the end of item #6.

8) A van. A new one. In which to tour. Not frilly, only utilitarian and reliable, so we can maintain our reputation for being the single most notoriously early band in rock & roll today, so we can see the sun rise over the Siskiyous as we drive over them, rather than as we wait for AAA. Oh... yes, AAA too. And a gas card.

9) An advance that would allow us to live comfortably for a year or so. Without working at Starbucks. Not absurdly or lavishly -- just comfortably.

10) No mandatory videos. We can be swayed, but only if the label foots the bill and we get the creative control.

11) Final call on all art direction, layouts, photoes andrelated publicity.

12) Tour support (per deims & hotel rooms). The van could play heavily into this. Heavy like lead.

13) We will tour. We want to tour. But we want to be able to make the final calls on touring, as well (surprise). For example: We will always say no to a tour that ends in Mississippi on 12/23 with Matchbox 20. If it was Mercury Rev or Talk Talk, however, it could be a different story.

14) Movie soundtracks... possibly very lucrative, but usually as morally questionable as silver pants. We want the option, but again, don't want to end up on a hip alterna-kid soundtrack.

15) In the event of a massive company personnell change or restructuring, or downsizing (all = people get fired), we want the ability to back out of our contract without any legal or financial repercussions. If we sign a contract, it will be because there's a balance of what's on this list that's been okayed and drafted by a group of people who we want to develop a lasting professional relationship with, and who we have a gut feeling about. People who are predictable, but not necessarily always safe... willing to go out on a limb, musically or otherwise... But people who we can trust, who we know aren't out to screw us. Speaking of which...

16) We ABSOLUTELY MUST own the rights to our own songs. Not negotiable.

17) It would be nice to each get a greeting card from the president of the label on the holidays of our individual choices.

That's all for now. We're not ruling out more. Now... put this gibberish down and go back to your Kafka.

Love, DEATH CAB FOR CUTIE.

THIS BOOK IS DEDICATED

TO MY PARENTS WHO TOOK CARE OF ARROW WHILE I WAS ON THE ROAD.
TO ROB WHO BOUGHT ME A PLANE TICKET TO SEATTLE.
TO BEN, NICK, CHRIS, AND JASON, WHO TOOK A CHANCE THAT FIRST NIGHT AT THE GLASS HOUSE.

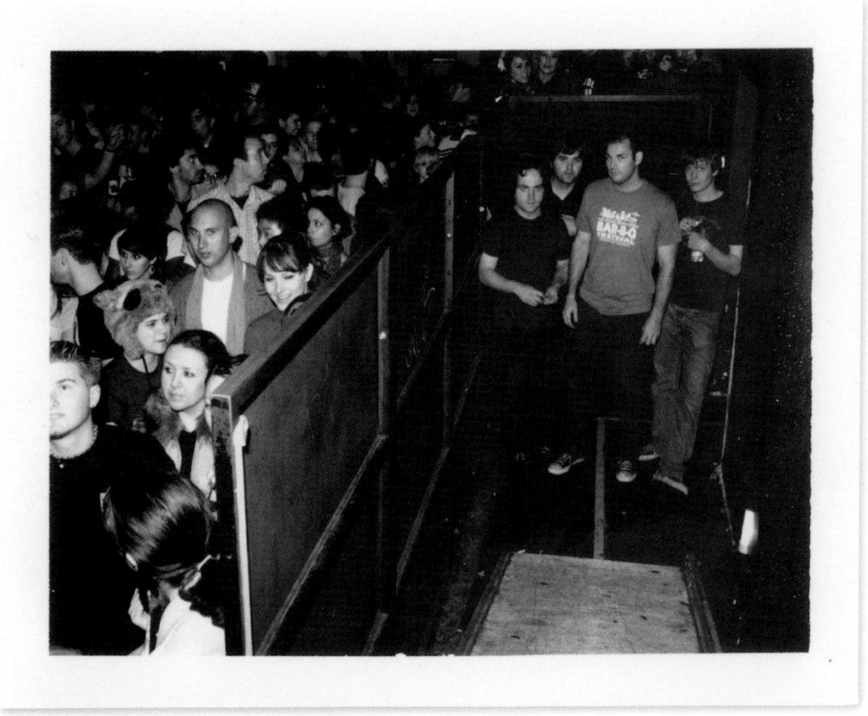

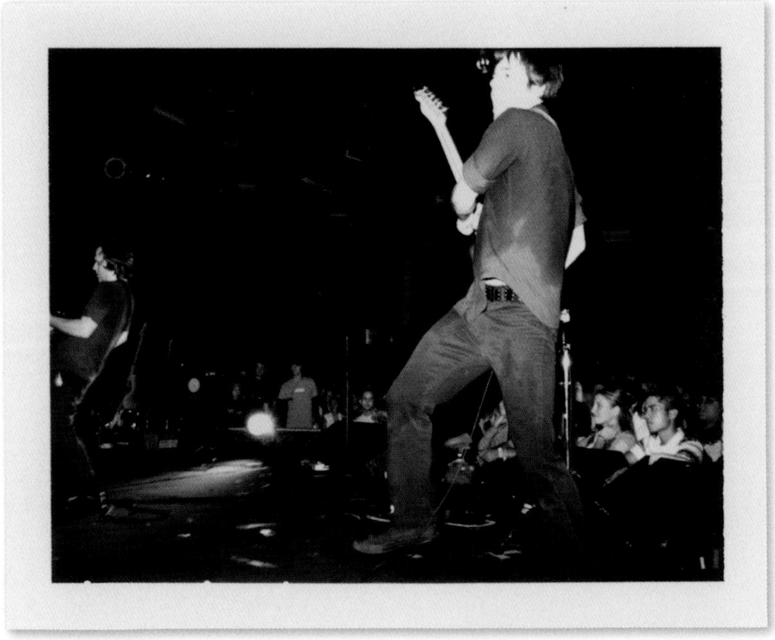

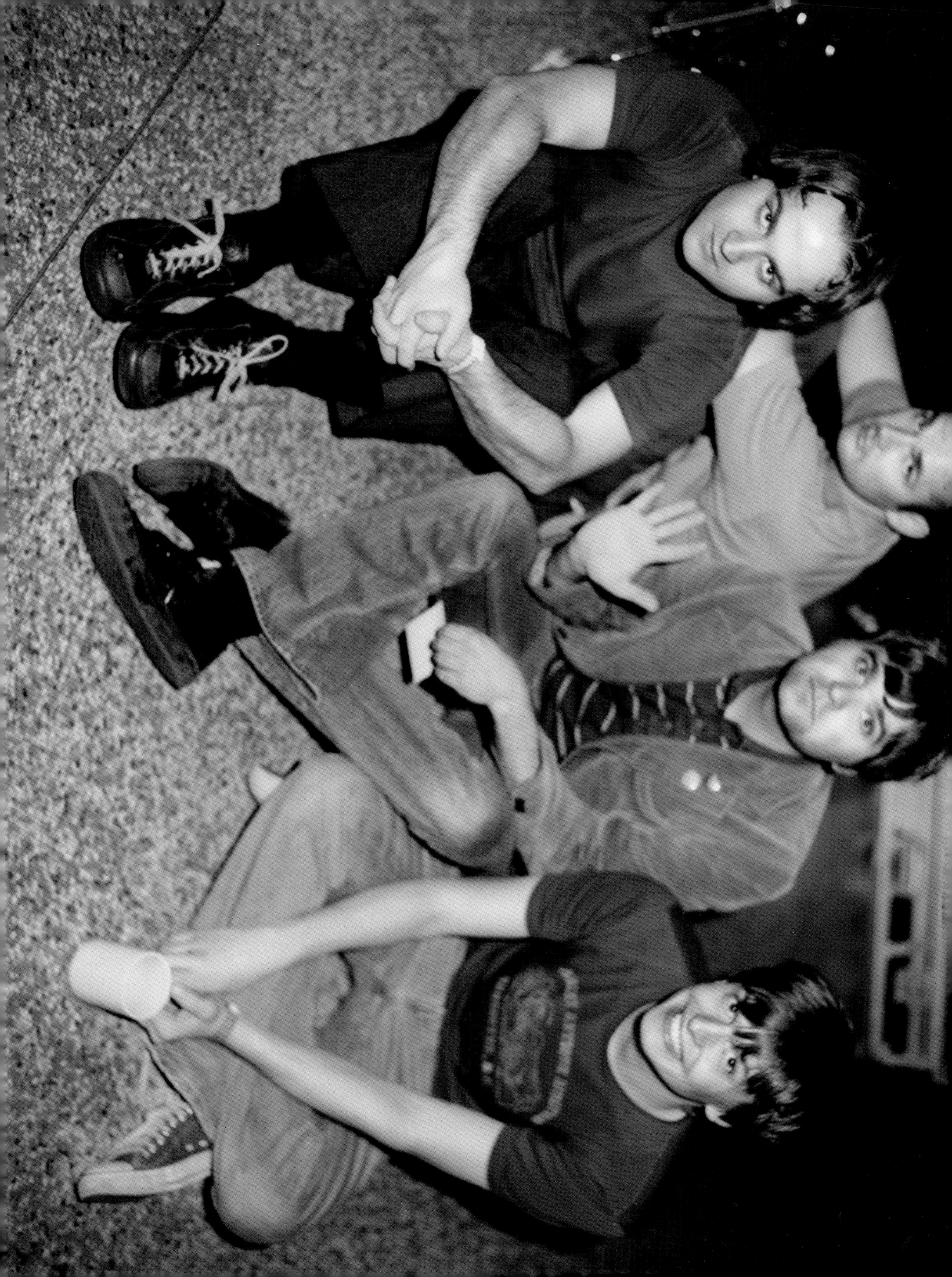

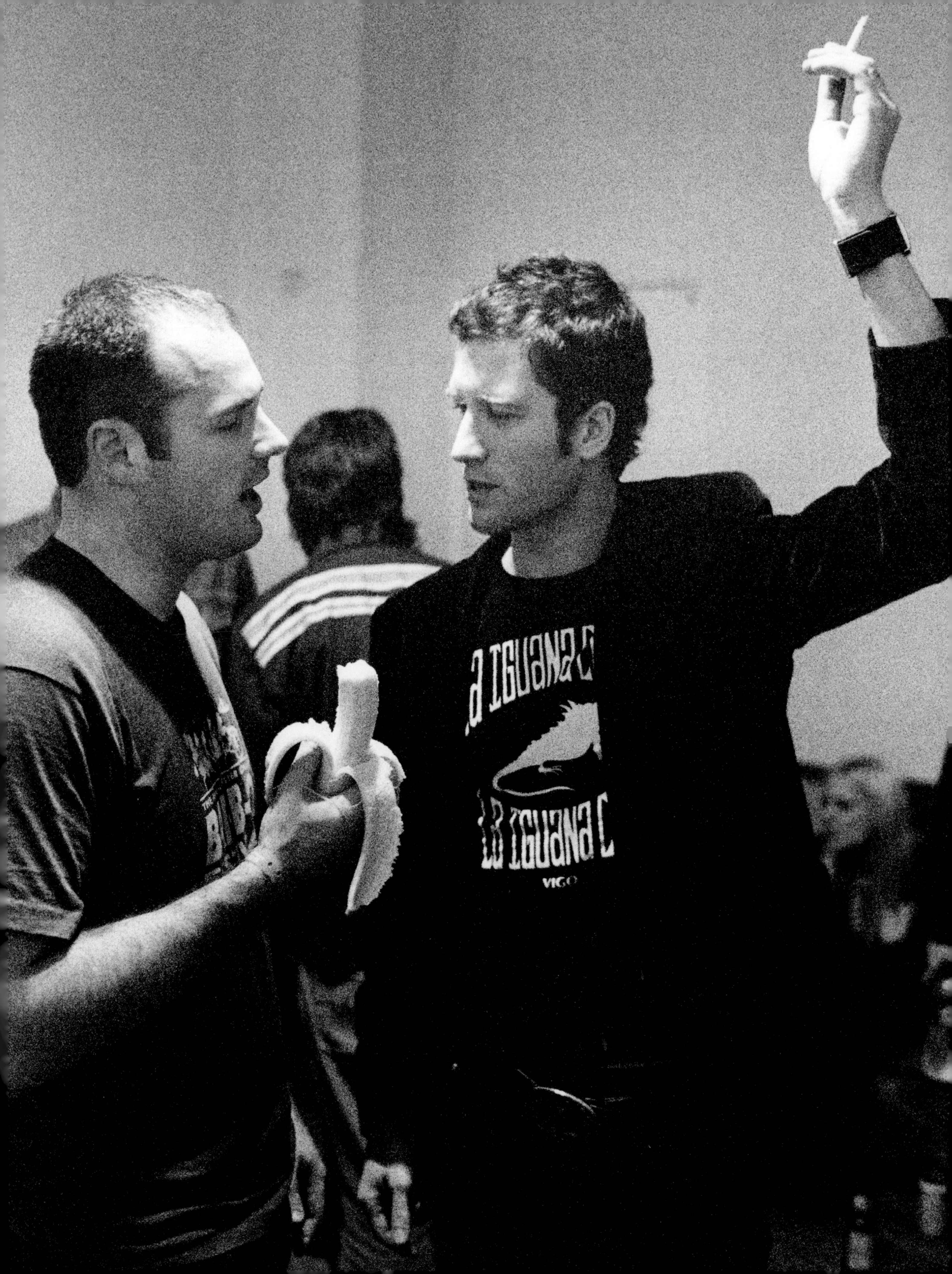
IGUANA
IGUANA
VIGO

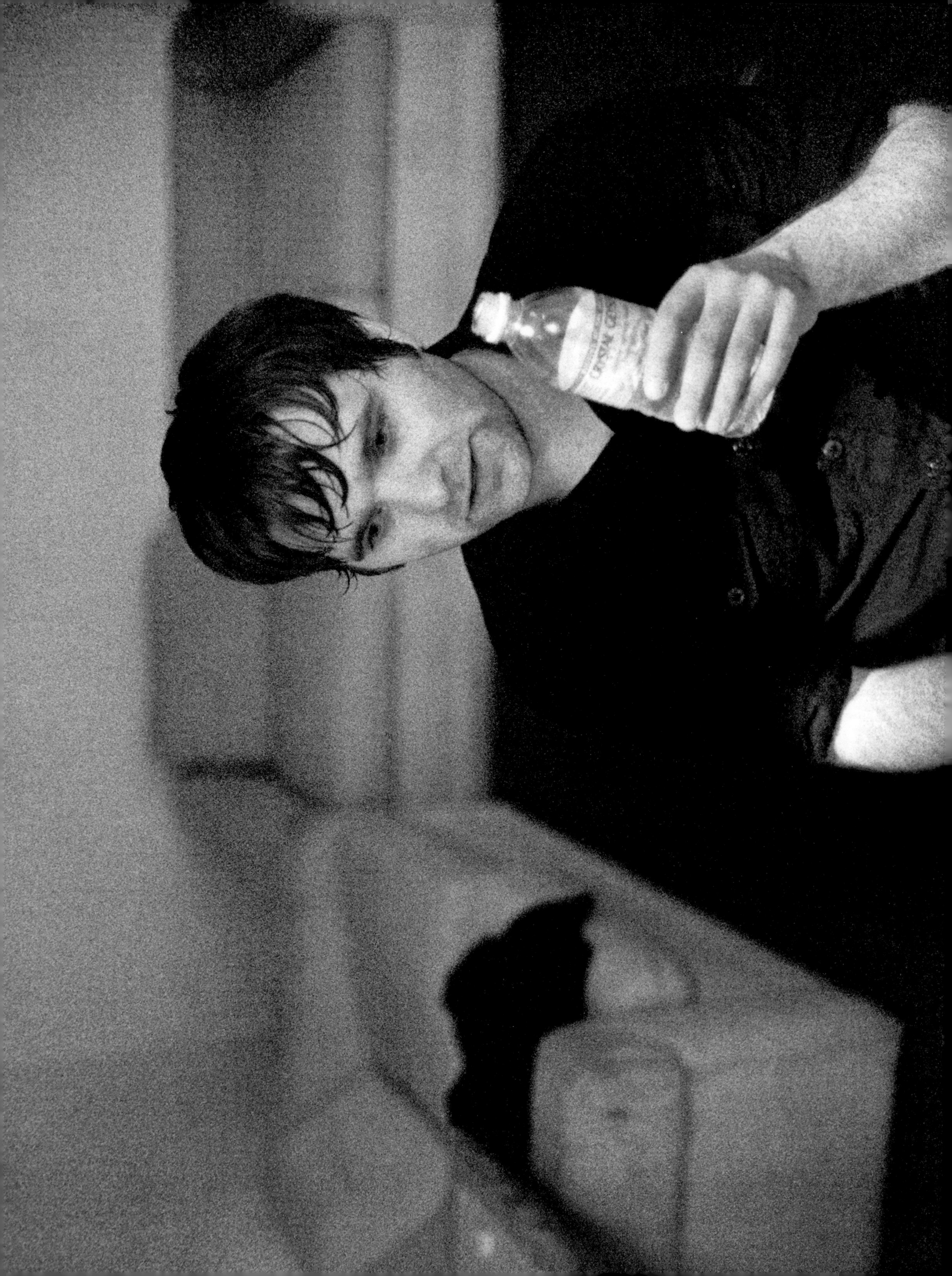

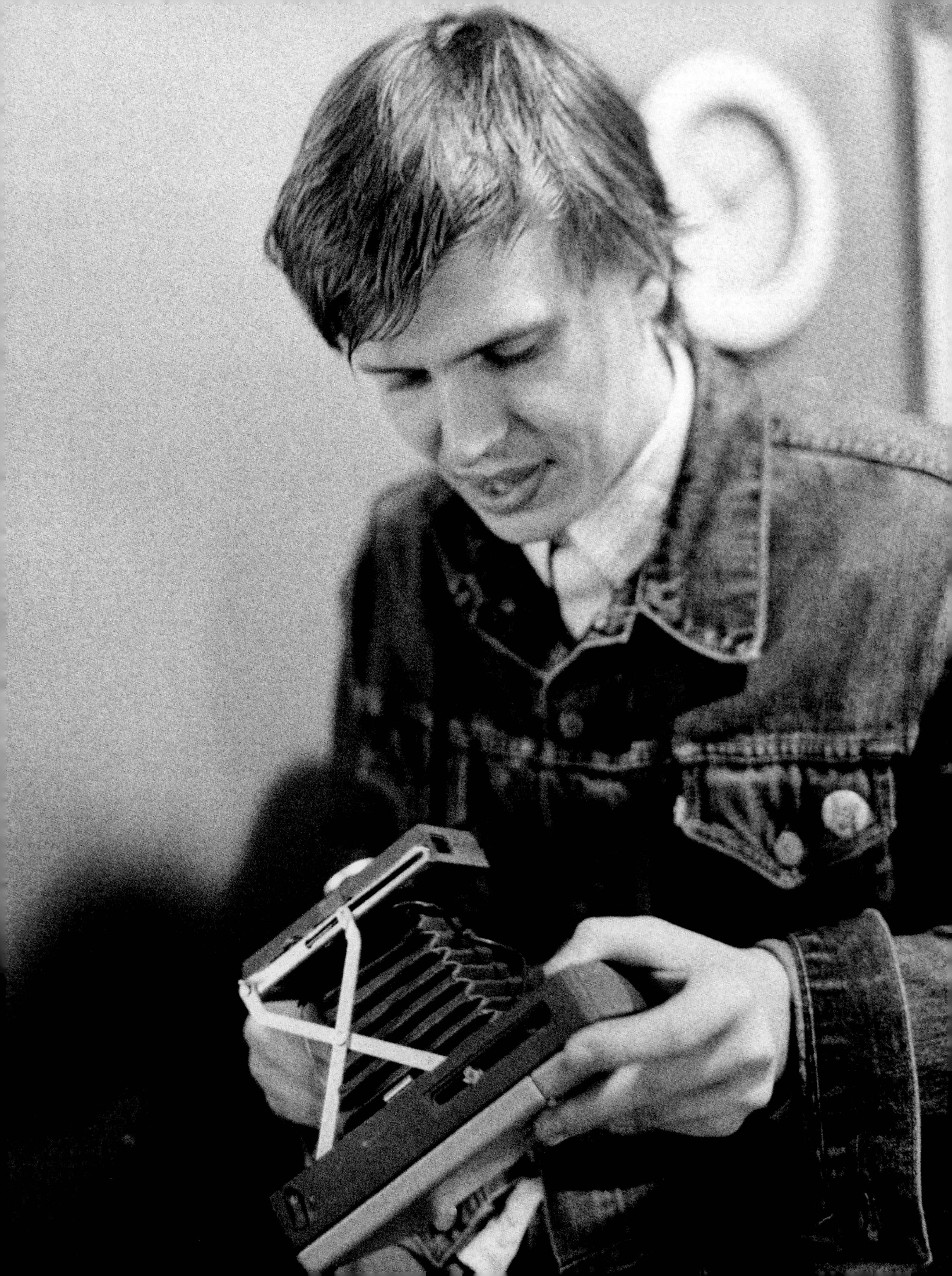

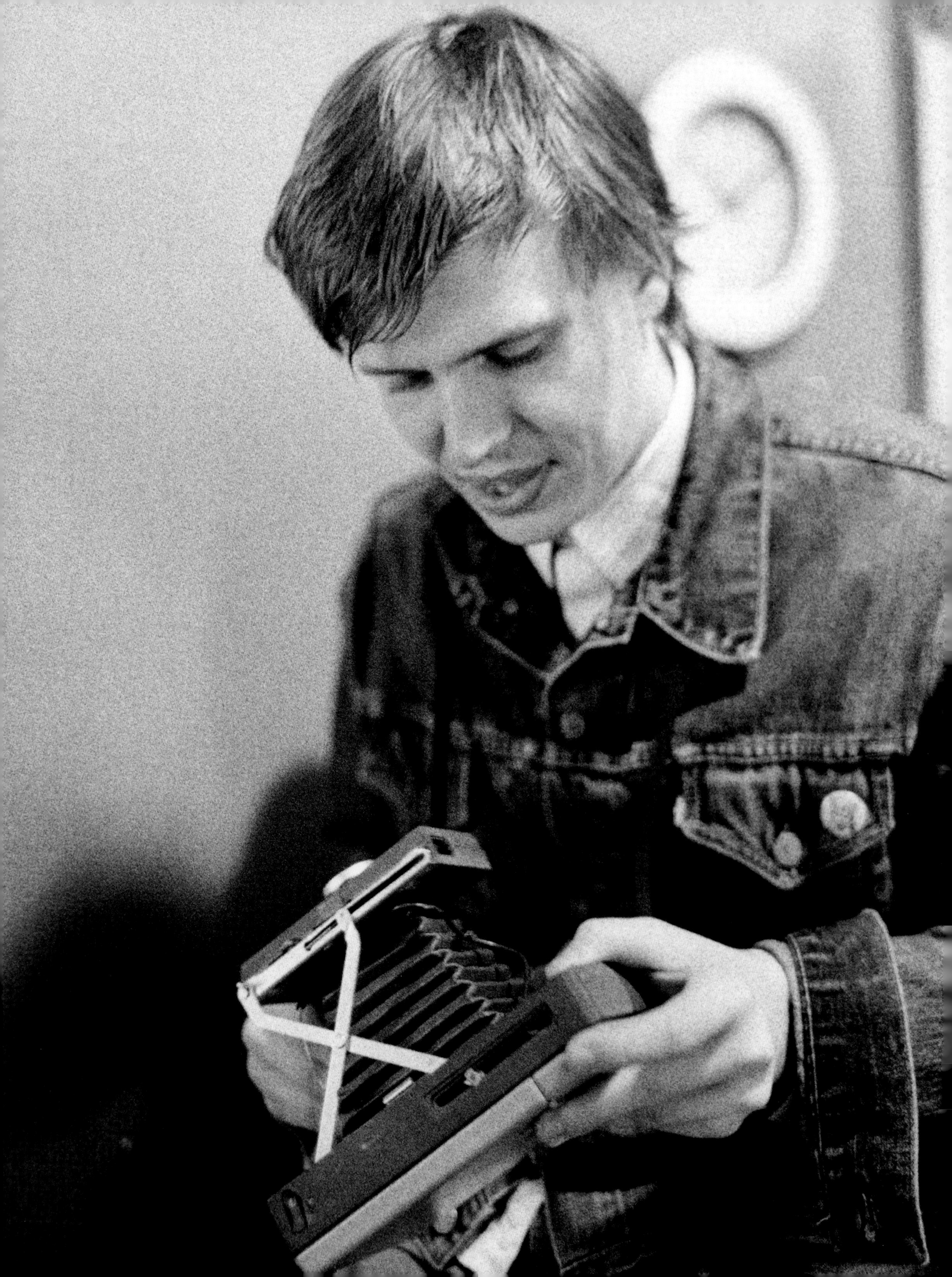

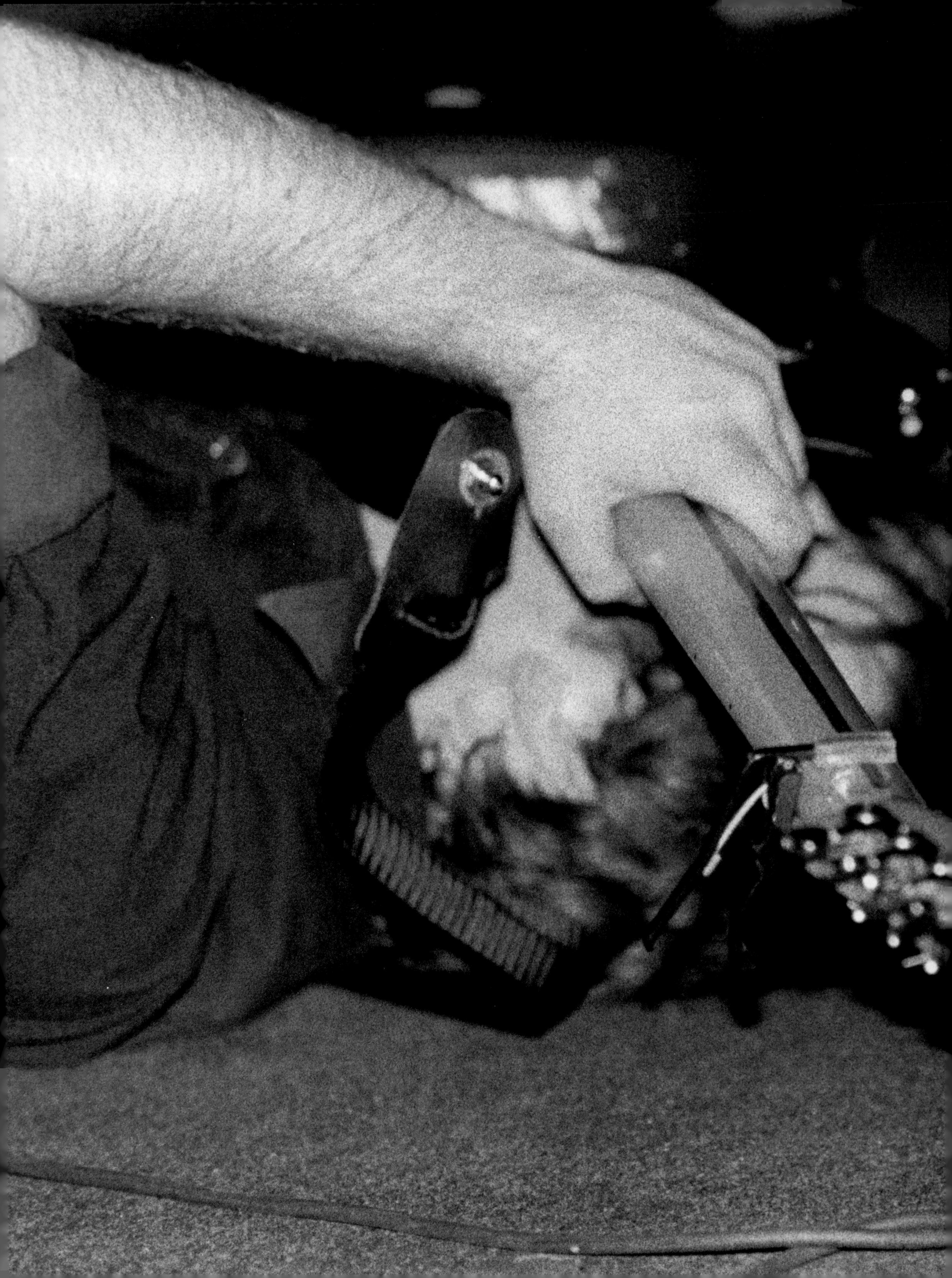

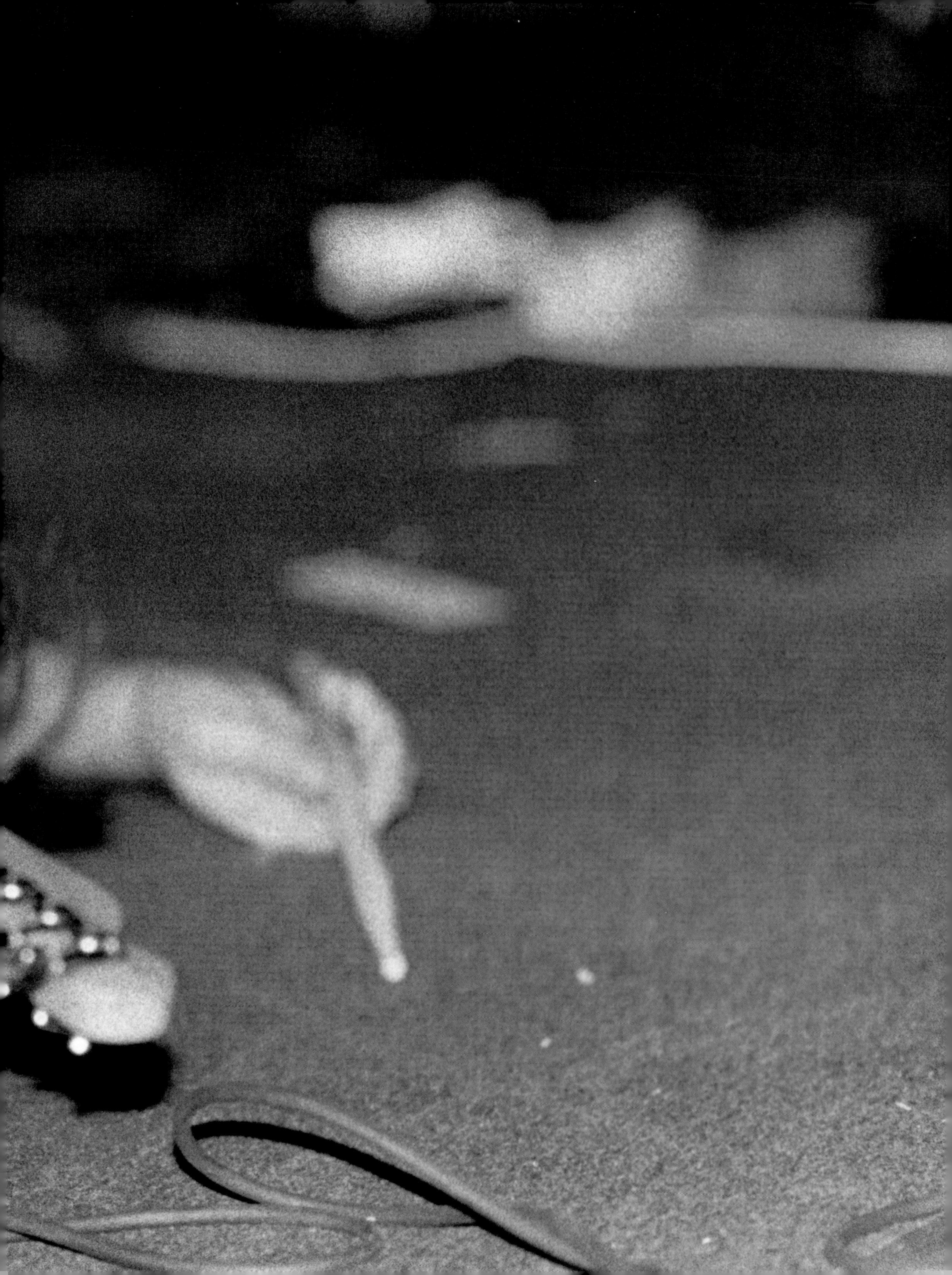

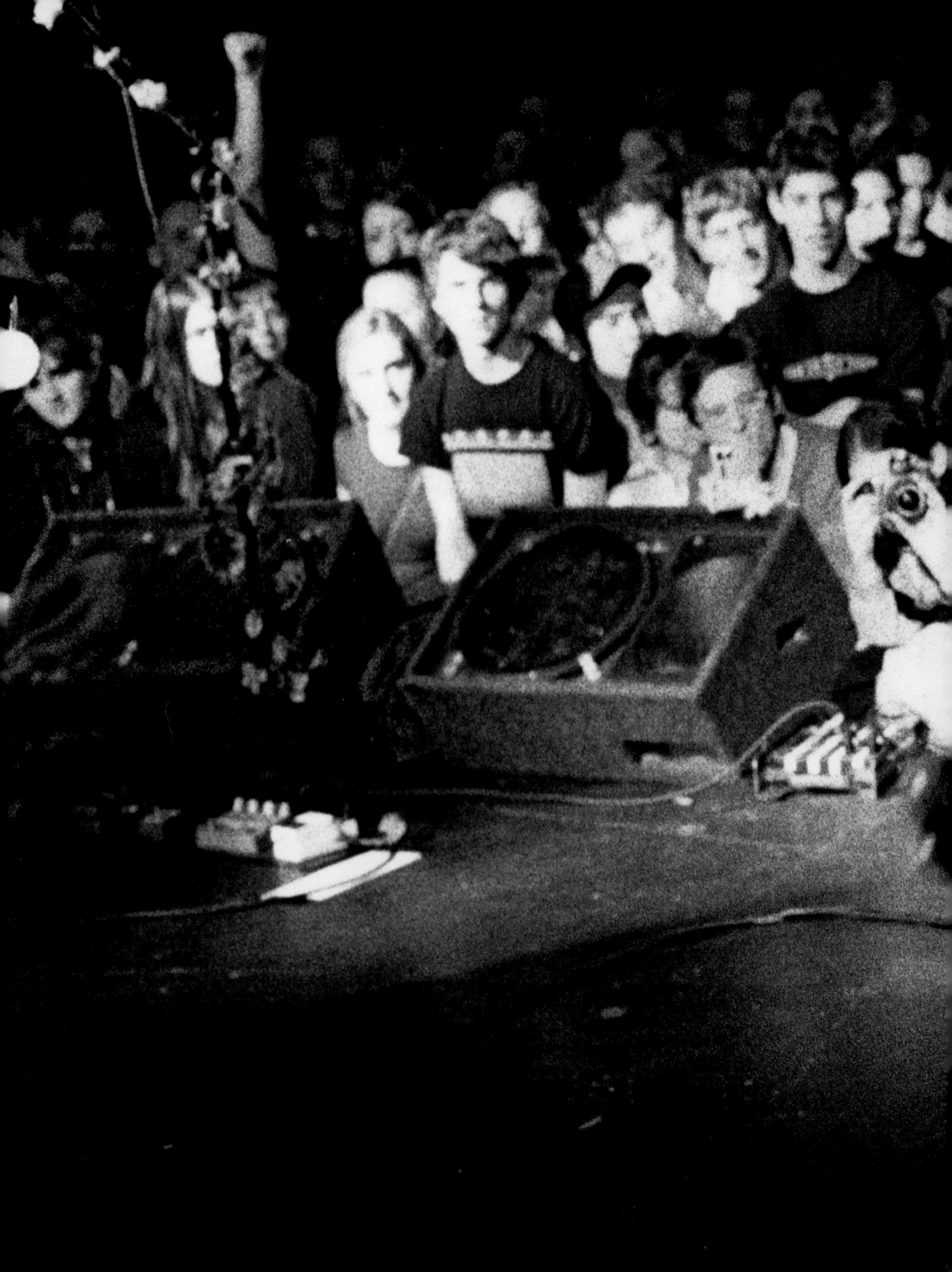

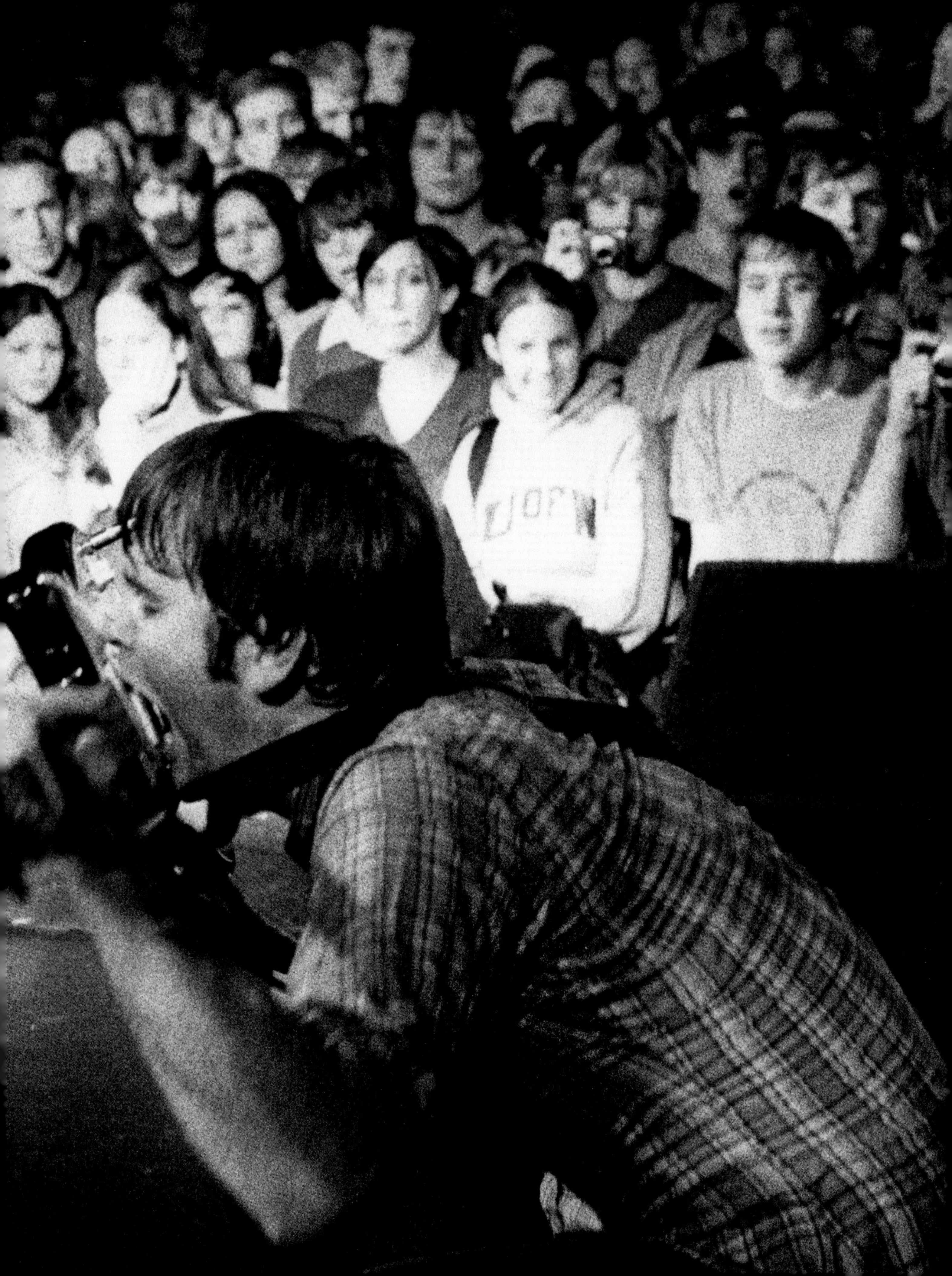

HALL OF JUSTICE

AUTUMN: I wanted to ask about the history of the Hall of Justice and what records were made there.

WALLA: The Hall of Justice is wherever it decides to be.

AUTUMN: The first Hall of Justice was where?

WALLA: It was at 1138 Ellis Street in Bellingham.

AUTUMN: Which was where you and Ben lived?

WALLA: All four of us lived there at different points.

BEN: I was in a band called Pinwheel, and one of my bandmates lived there. When they left that house, I took over the lease with Nick, and [to Nick] who was the third roommate?

NICK: It was Arman.

AUTUMN: Did you say "Our mom"?

NICK: Yeah, [laughing] our mom moved in with us first.

BEN: Then you moved in?

AUTUMN: How old were you?

NICK: Twenty.

AUTUMN: Are you guys all the same age?

NICK: No, I'm two years older.

WALLA: I'm somewhere in between.

BEN: I moved in there when I was nineteen.

NICK: Ben and I lived together on did Indian Street, and then Ellis Street, and then I moved out.

AUTUMN: Is it true that Walla threw out all the dishes?

WALLA: No, that would've been Ben.

NICK: He didn't throw them away; he hid them.

WALLA: That was a particularly toxic group of people.

BEN: It was a group house. Over the course of five years, people brought in coffee cups and dishes whenever they moved in and never took them out.

WALLA: There were probably a good twenty to thirty complete place-settings.

BEN: There were twenty to thirty place-settings, and there were three people living there. There was no dining room. Basically, nobody had to do dishes, ever, and it got to the point where there were fucking shitloads of dishes coming out of the sink. So I boxed up all of the dishes except for three of each type and put them in the garage. "Now we'll only have to wash these three sets of dishes." Then our third roommate, Brian Enslow, came back and said, "What if we have a dinner guest?!" To which I said, "When have we ever had a dinner guest here?!" Enslow was really pissed. [to Walla] I think you were pissed about it, too, but didn't say much about it.

If it's <u>Sunny</u> Day Real

Elliott Smith will take us an

<u>Jr. High</u> school for a ride do

for Cutie. We can bring som

canteen of Pink <u>Martini</u>. But

anything, or Elliot will <u>Murd</u>

Amused? Confused? Then listen

Tours, Mondays 4-6 on KLC, w

their neighbors

It will give you that old

WALLA: I was pissed. I just didn't say much about it.

BEN: So I brought them back in the house, and the problem persisted.

WALLA: That was a bad house, but it sounded really good.
[to Autumn] That was the first Hall of Justice.

AUTUMN: Were you called Death Cab for Cutie yet?

BEN: Well, yes, but Pinwheel was still going strong. Walla had songs, and I had songs, and I would play drums or whatever. . . . We would do covers and stuff.

AUTUMN: What were you recording on?

WALLA: Most of that stuff got done on a cassette 8-track machine.

AUTUMN: How long after that did your first release come out?

WALLA: That stuff we recorded? I think that only four of them came out. Those are on *You Can Play These Songs with Chords*.

BEN: We were mixing the cassette around my twenty-first birthday. When did we started calling stuff Death Cab?

WALLA: It was shortly after I moved to Bellingham.

AUTUMN: So for those who don't know, what is the reason you called yourselves Death Cab for Cutie?

BEN: Well, at the time, it wasn't meant to be more than a side project that I was doing away from Pinwheel. I had all these songs, I had just met Walla in Bellingham amongst our friends, and we had this kind of insular indie scene, with *everyone* releasing side projects on cassette. Everyone had their own side projects. It just fell in line with that kind of aesthetic.

WALLA: Like The Somewhat Legend, and Magnetic Bicycle Craft? [laughing]. My other band was Martin Youth Auxiliary. Ben was watching *Magical Mystery Tour*. He stood up and made a grand proclamation: "My next band will be called Death Cab for Cutie."

AUTUMN: And it came from . . .

WALLA: Yes, a scene in *Magical Mystery Tour*.

NICK: You know, that band with John Lennon, Ringo Starr, George Harrison . . .

WALLA: . . . Paul McCartney. [laughing] There's a scene towards the end of the film, the Beatles are high out of their minds, a burlesque show is going on and a band called the Bonzo Dog Doo Dah Band is on stage playing a song called "Death Cab for Cutie." Those are the initial beginnings.

JASON: Meanwhile, Nick and I were across town in a tiny little practice space working on prog rock together.

NAIVE

AUTUMN: Even though this happened before I started photographing you, I want to hear the story about you guys touring in a van in Spain and nearly starving to death.

NICK: And inadvertently running drugs through the country?

BEN: When we took this tour, I don't know why, in hindsight you wonder why you did anything, but it was like ten days, right?

NICK: Yeah, we crisscrossed, we were in Bilbao, La Coruna . . .

WALLA: The map, I mean it looked like a Chinese checkers board, the routing for the tour. We crossed Spain from end to end and side to side like five times.

AUTUMN: So basically they took a bunch of red tacks and threw them against the map?

WALLA: Pretty much, and then used as much yarn as they possibly could to wind between them.

BEN: You had to do it if you were gonna run a bunch of drugs all over, inadvertently.

NICK: We had this guy who sort of magically showed up in the van, supposedly because the driver didn't speak the dialect of northern Spain. Suddenly, our routing changed, and we were stopping at *a lot* of bus stations. We would sit in the van while this guy would run in and come back out with, literally, like a package wrapped up in string. [laughing] At first we were like, oh, I guess he's just making a quick stop for some merchandise.

WALLA: Oh, he's a cheese dealer.

NICK: And then it happened with enough frequency that we realized what was actually going on, that there was some kind of illicit operation or "distribution" happening, and he was using our tour to facilitate his clients' needs. [laughing]

VEGETARIANS VS. SPAIN

AUTUMN: So, you were starving in Spain . . .

NICK: The food got substantially better on that coast run. Those last three shows, finally we got grilled vegetables.

BEN: Once we got to the south of Spain, after Walla left in Madrid. We were there [in Madrid] for two days milling around, just bummed and depressed.

NICK: Well, Walla was the only one keeping you guys alive because you [to Walla] figured out how to make hummus.

AUTUMN: You were vegan, or vegetarian?

WALLA: Vegetarian. Yeah, I figured out how to mash it up in the back of the van.

NICK: [to Walla] I remember that when you left it was sad times, because you were our main supply for food in the van. He would stop at grocery stores and buy garbanzo beans while our "translator" was buying drugs. It was a smooth operation.

BEN: Walla had to leave because his grandmother died, so me and Nick were bumming around because we were worried about him. We were homesick and stuck in this shitty hotel in Madrid.

WALLA: That was a dark hotel.

BEN: It was a dark hotel. I spent the entire day figuring out how I could order codeine cough syrup at a pharmacy, in Spanish, and then just spent the day drinking it and listening to the Flaming Lips.

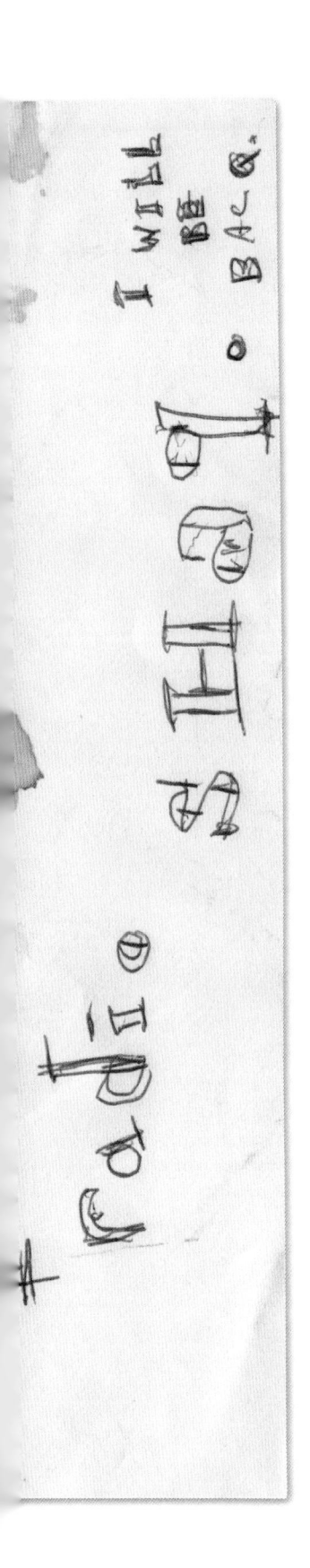

NICK: We were doing laundry in the bathtub.

BEN: Then we drove down to the south of Spain for those two shows that Walla couldn't be there for, and they were glorious. Actually the shows weren't glorious, but the . . .

NICK: The food.

BEN: We were in the south with all the Moorish influence, with great hummuses and falafels.

NICK: The first time they brought out a platter of grilled vegetables, I remember we just sat there looking at it in all its glory. Previously, any time we had made efforts to order vegetarian food, I remember . . .

WALLA: . . . in Vigo, those grilled cheese sandwiches . . .

NICK: No, it was in Bilbao. We went out to this restaurant, you ordered "sin carne," no meat, and the family running the restaurant thought that we were just poor. They thought we didn't have enough money for the meat, so they hid it underneath the vegetables for these guys [Walla and Ben], and they didn't find it until they were deep into their meals.

BEN: Was that the restaurant with the cured meat hanging from the ceiling?

WALLA: That's where Michael [Schorr, previous DCFC drummer] ordered the fish that had apparently eaten the ham. He thought he was just ordering the fish, but then there was the ham he discovered inside the fish, once he had already started to eat it.

NICK: It was wild.

AUTUMN: This was during the tour for *The Photo Album*?

BEN: Yeah.

AUTUMN: When did Jason join the band?

JASON: October of 2002, just before preproduction for *Transatlanticism*, so, like at the end of the year we basically just did a little rehearsing.

AUTUMN: [to Nick] But you had played with Jason in a different band?

NICK: First, well we had been in a band together before Death Cab. It was called Eureka Farm.

AUTUMN: When I first met you guys, you were on your first U.S. tour for *Transatlanticism*. Nada Surf was opening.

BEN: Yeah, they did the last half of the tour.

NICK: We met you for the first time backstage at the Henry Fonda [Theater, in Los Angeles].

AUTUMN: Right. And then you invited me to shoot your next show at the Glass House [concert venue in Pomona, California]. Walla and I bonded over our mutual obsession with Polaroid Land cameras and peel-apart film.

WALLA: 665 . . . yum.

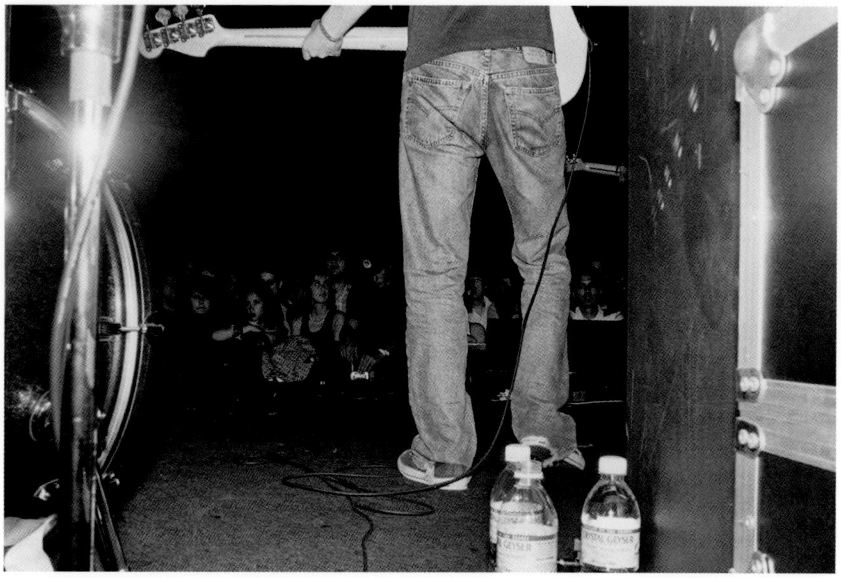

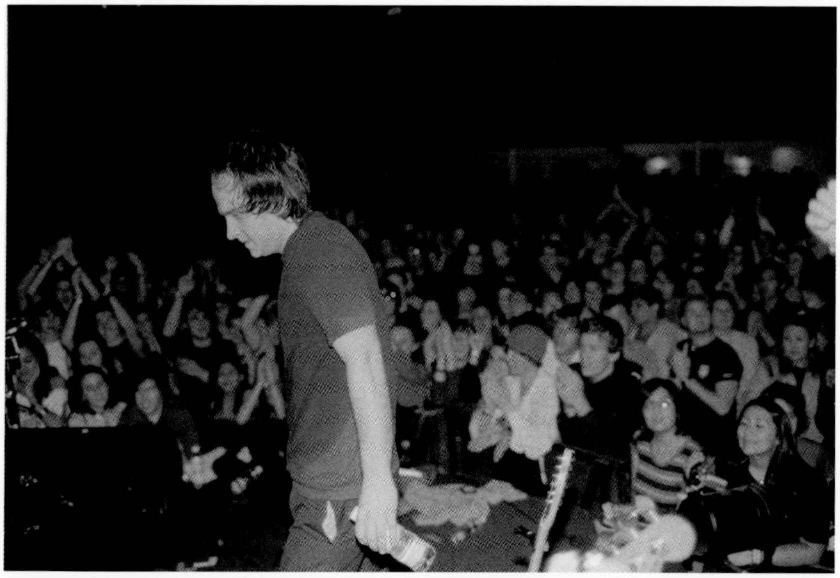

THE ANNUAL CHESTER COUNTY
BAR-B-Q
FESTIVAL
HENDERSON, TENNESSEE

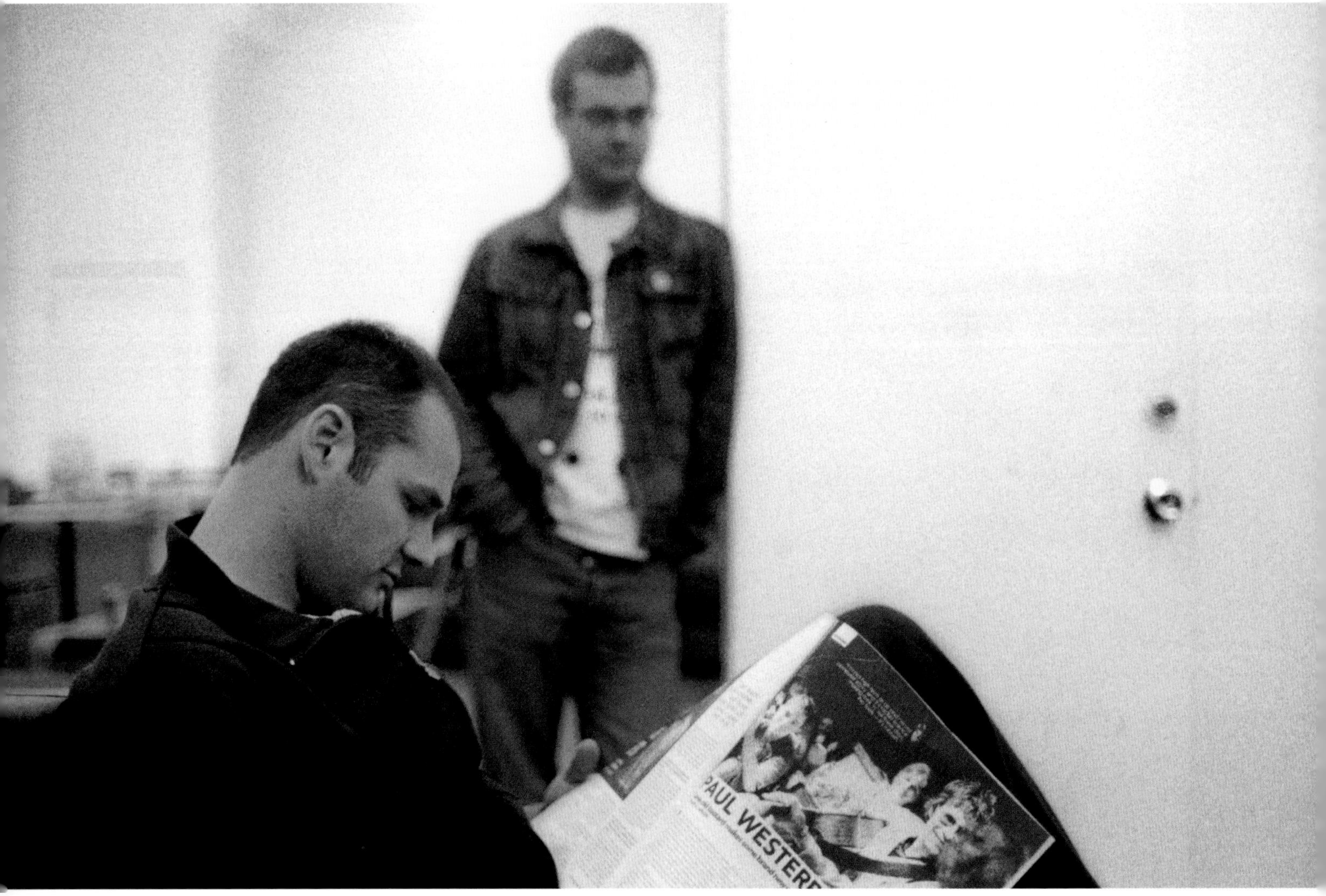
PAUL WESTER

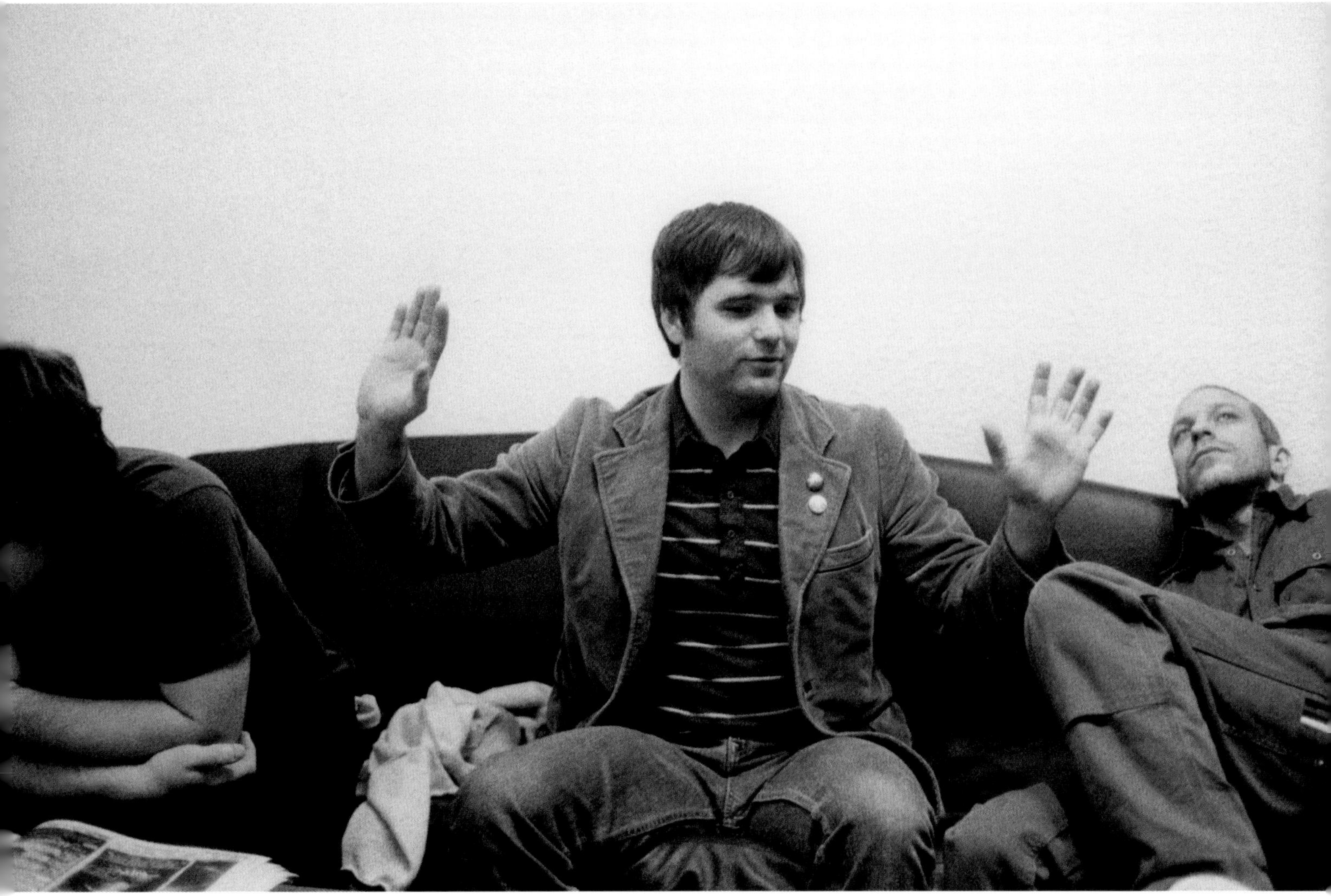

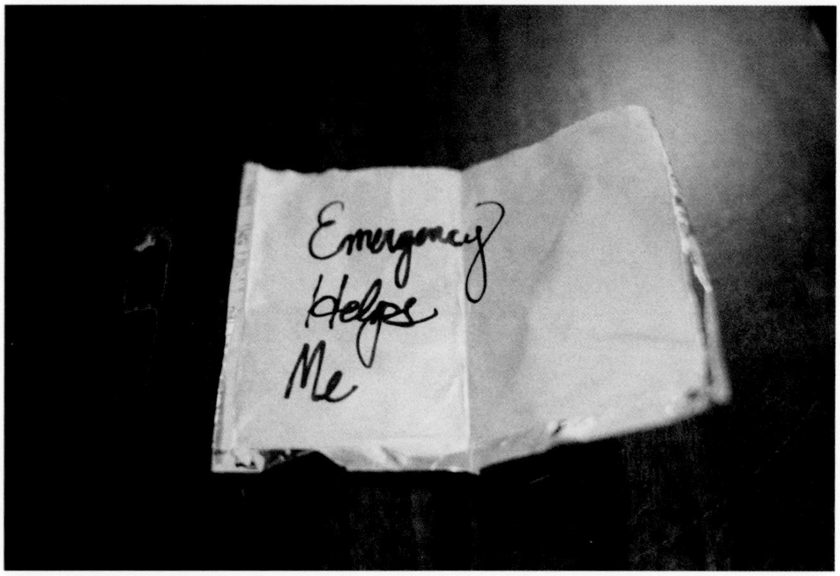
Emergency
Helps
Me

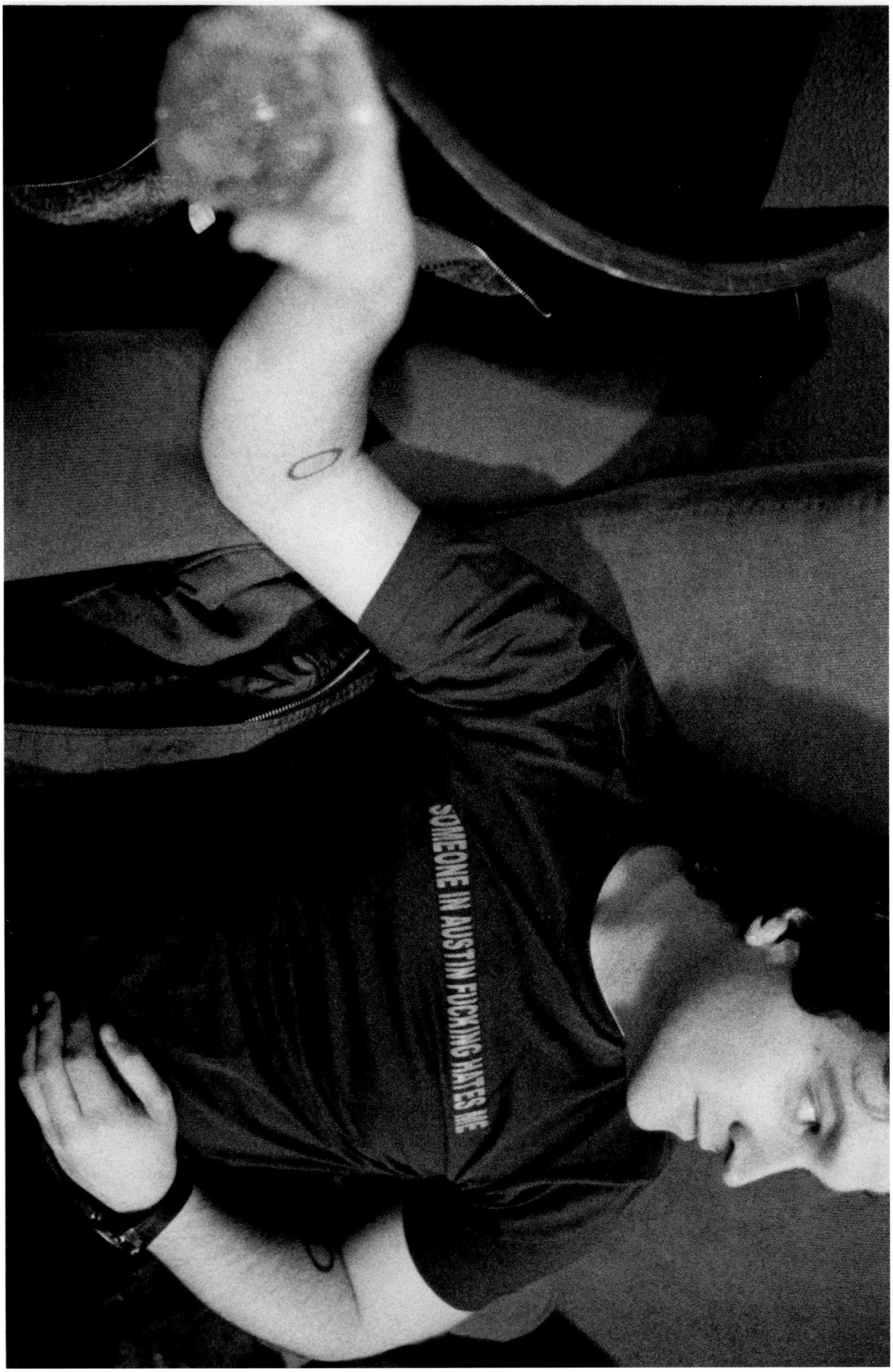
SOMEONE IN AUSTIN FUCKING HATES ME

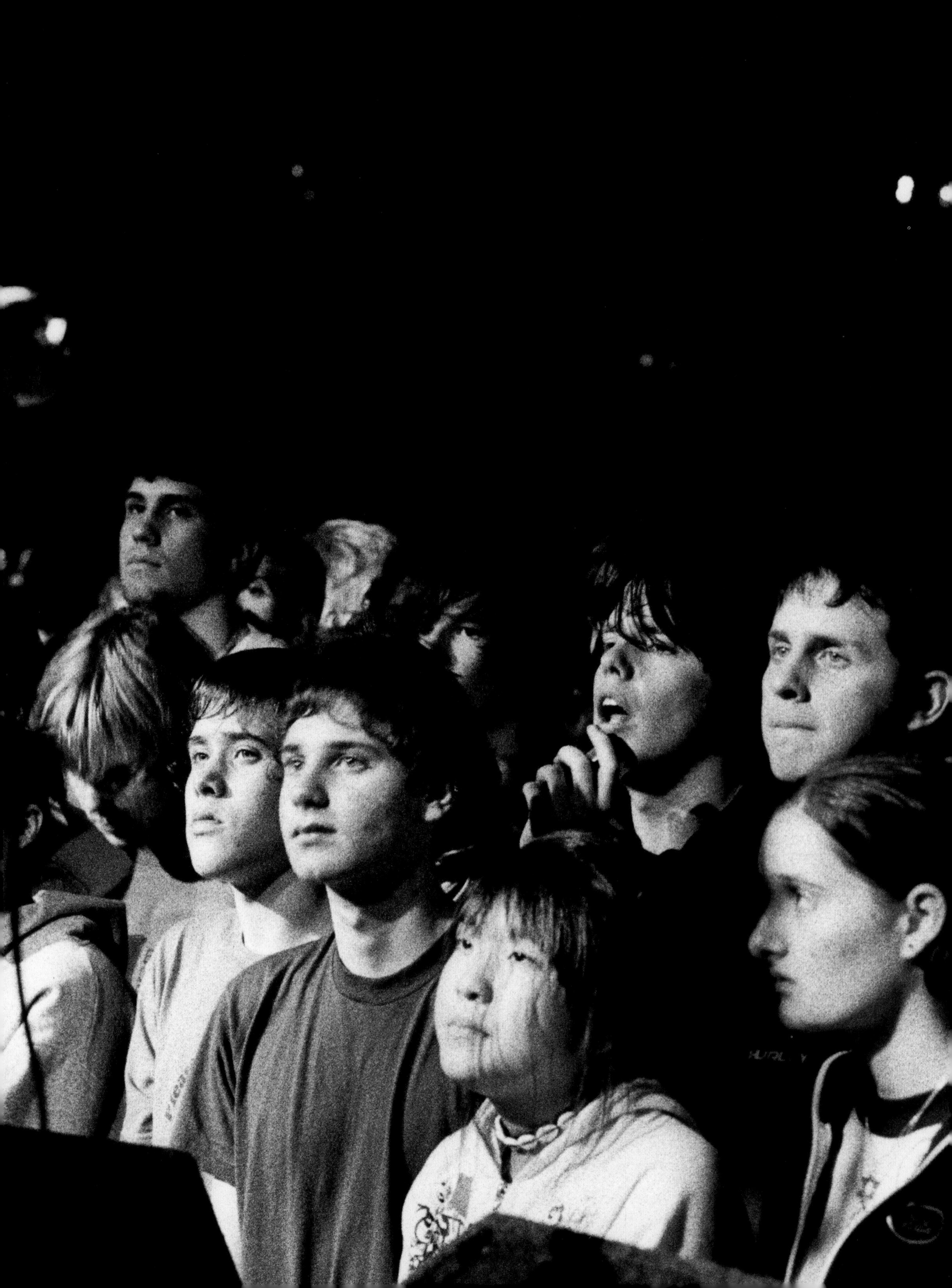

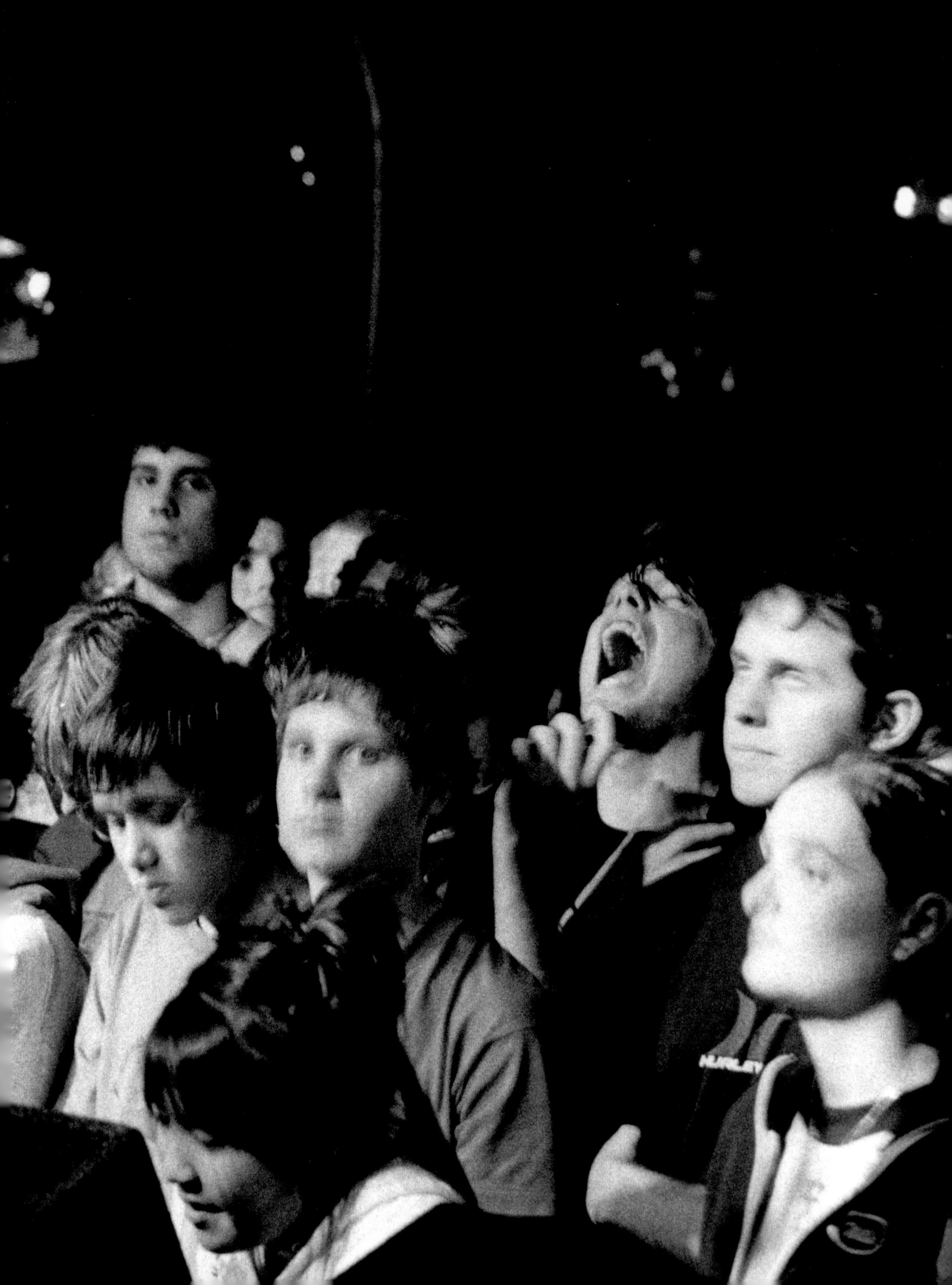

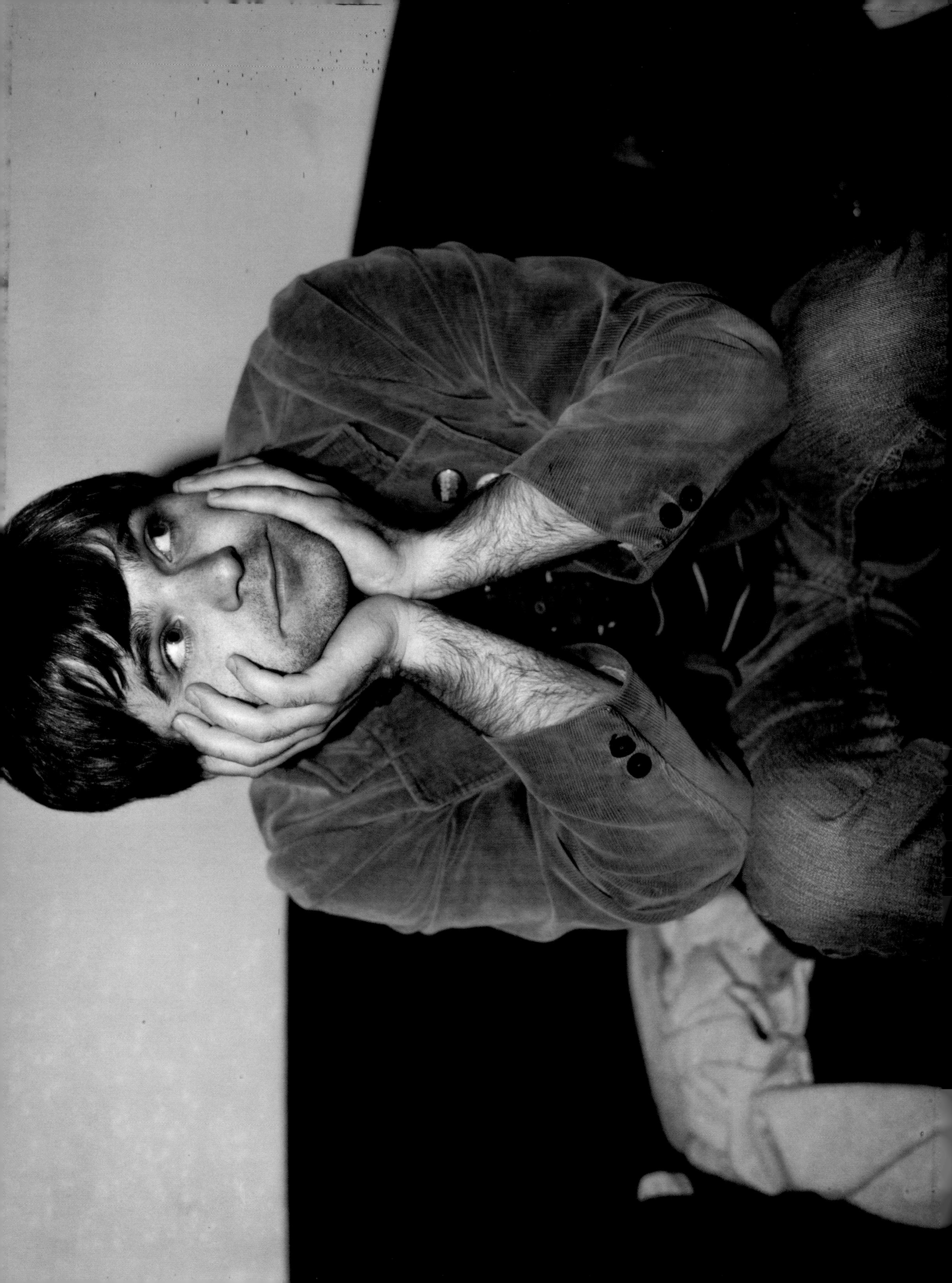

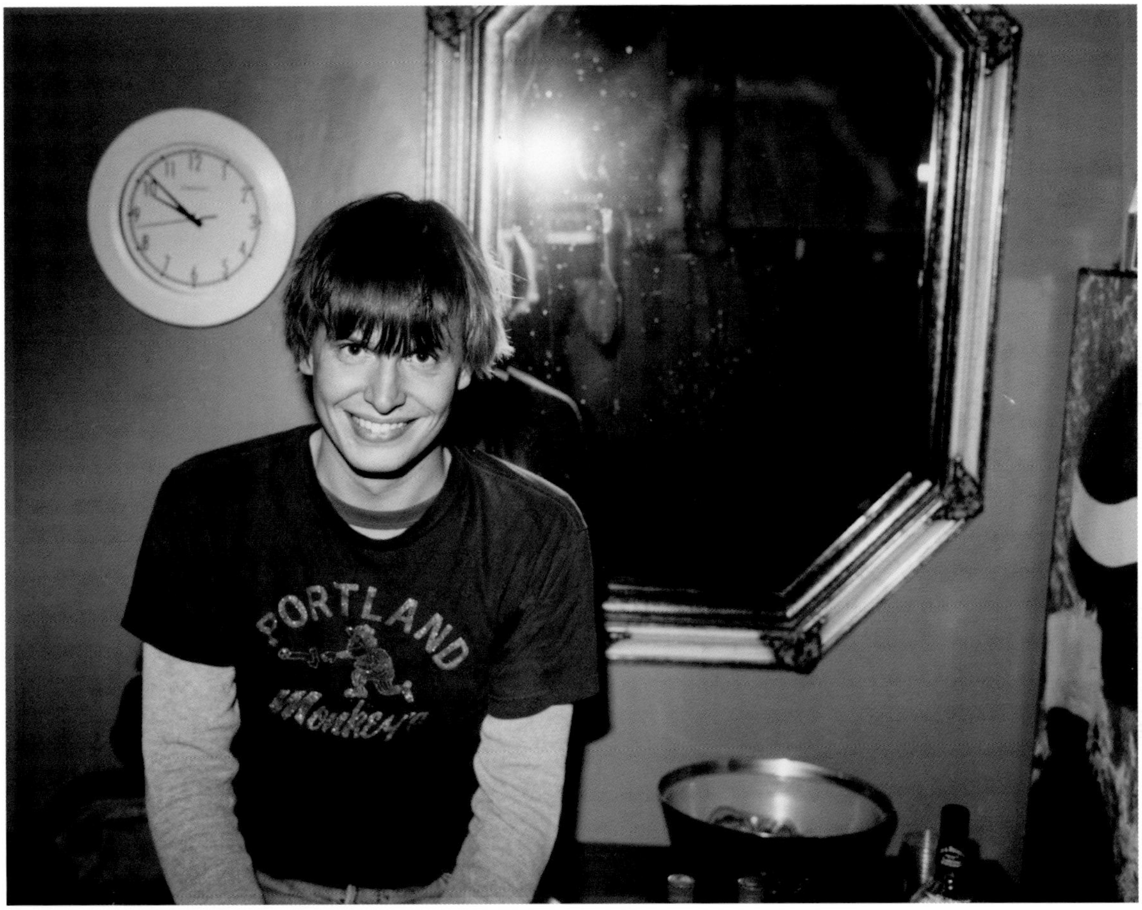
PORTLAND
Monkeys

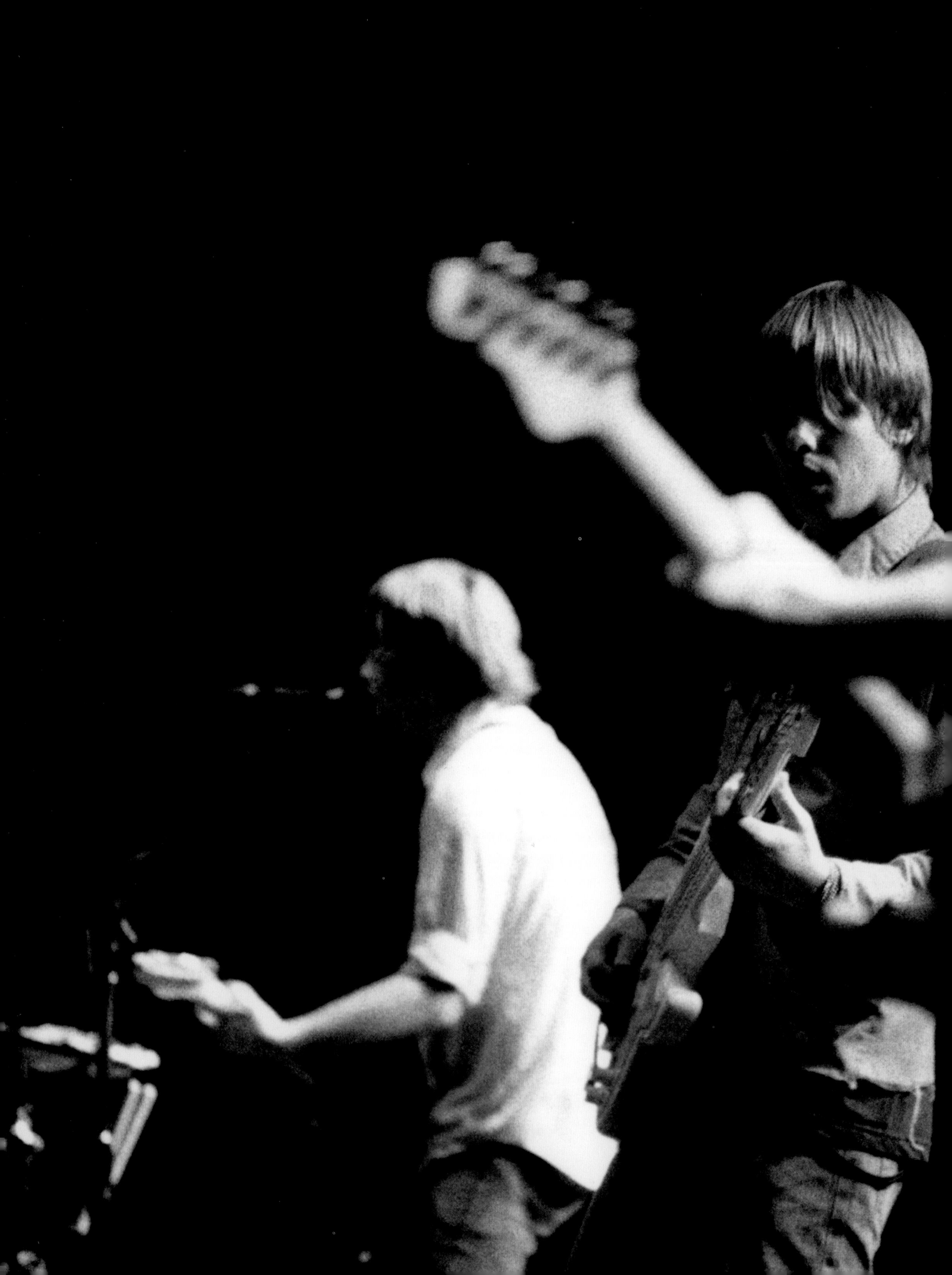

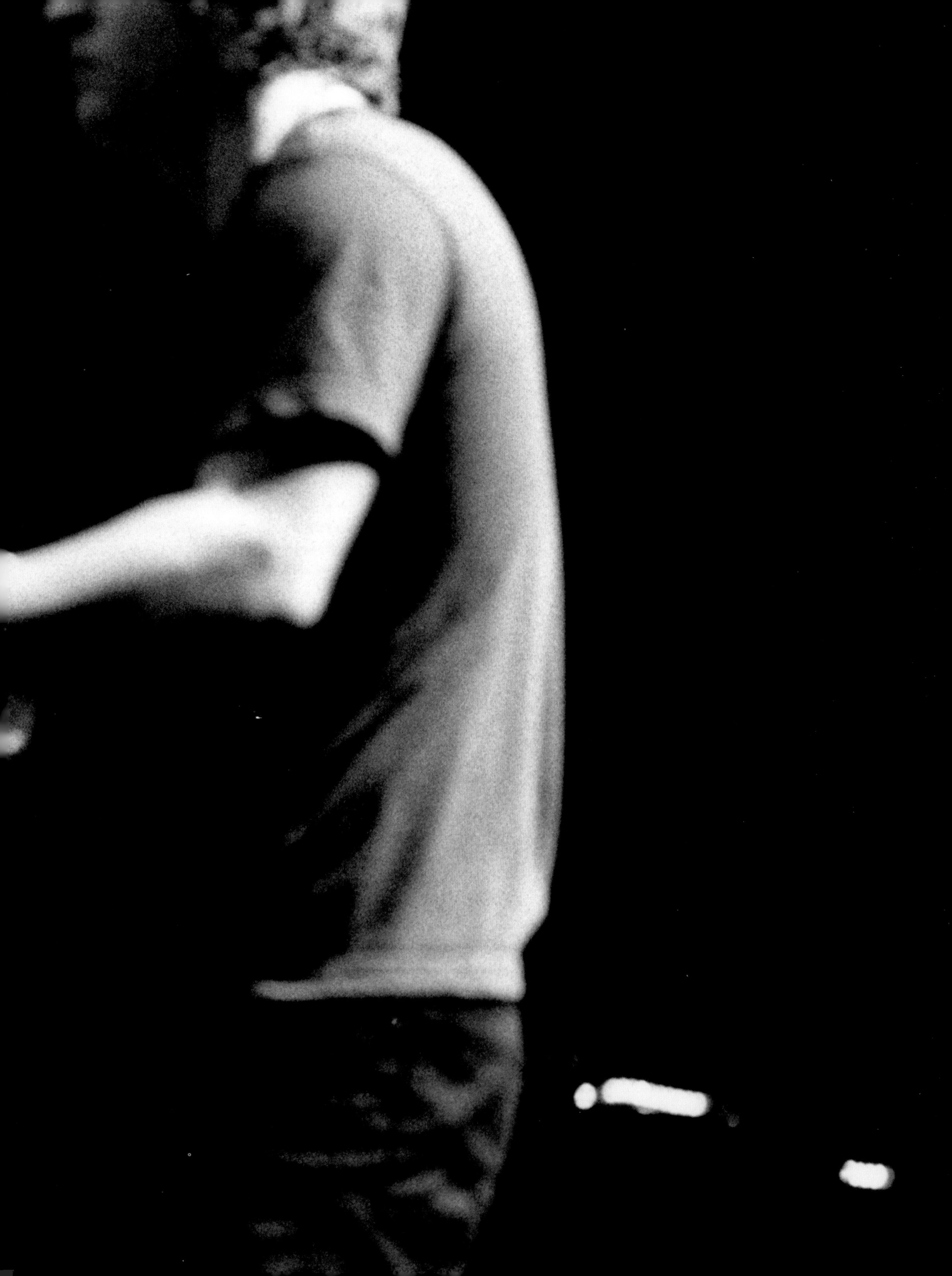

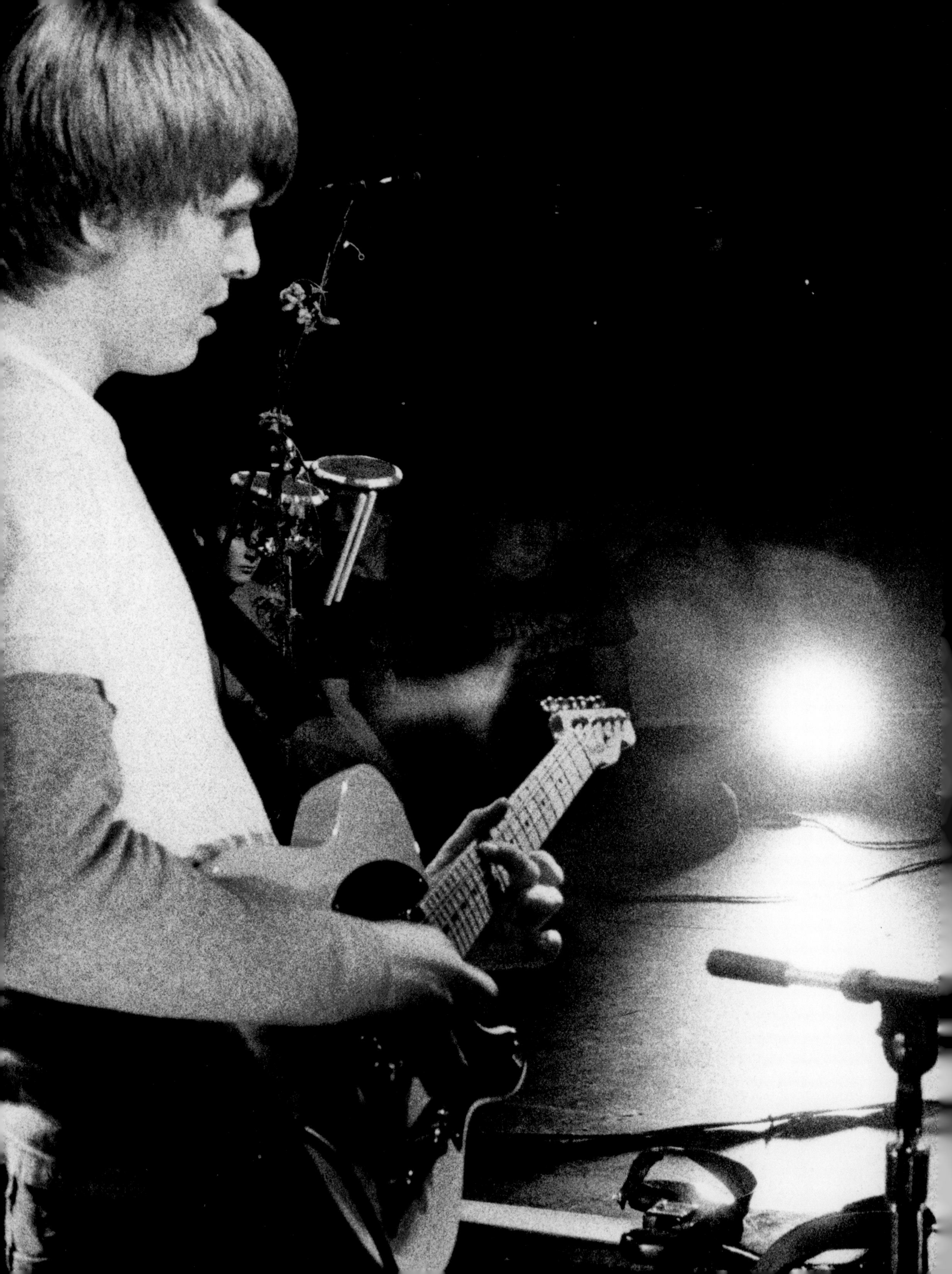

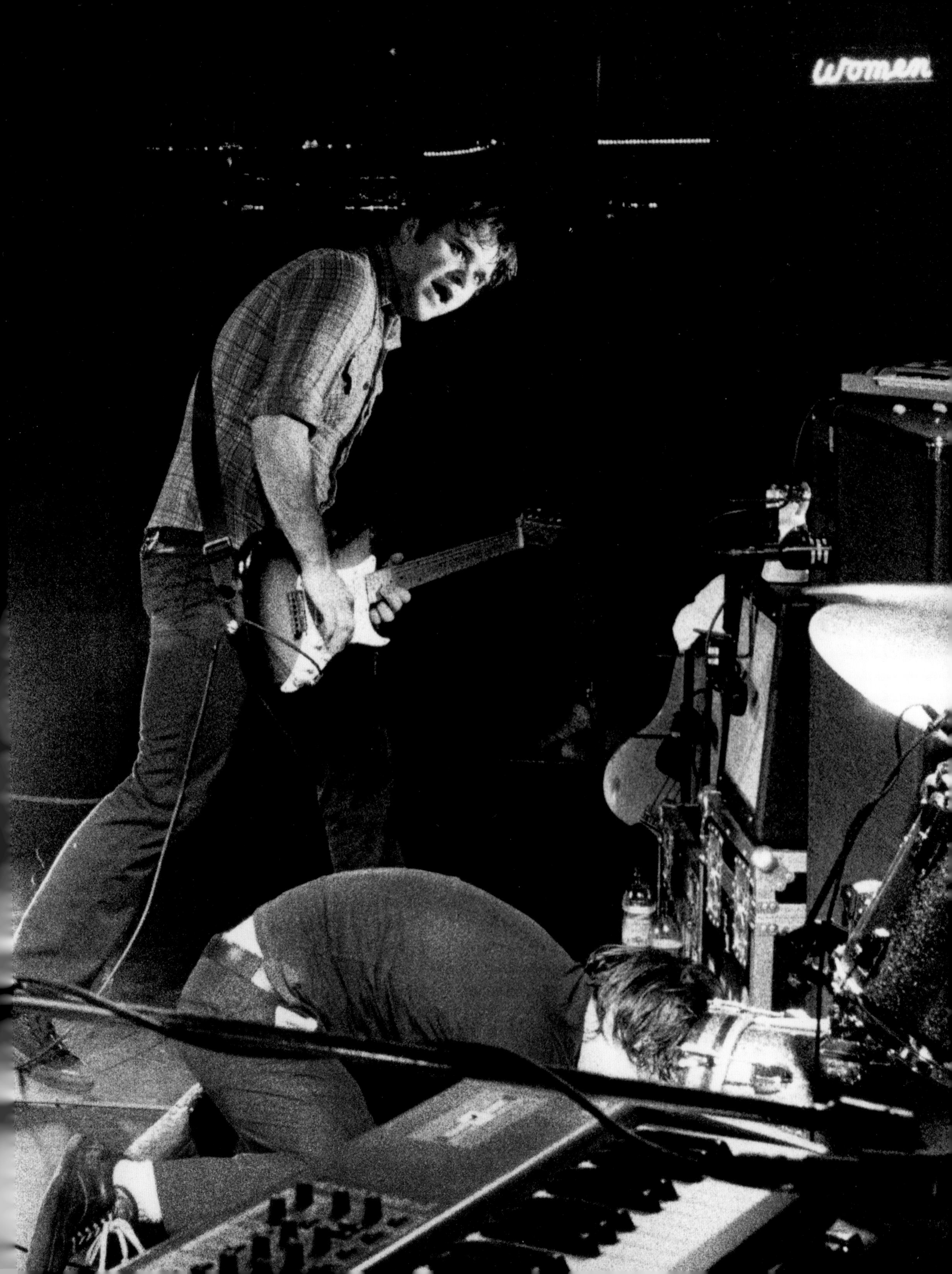
women

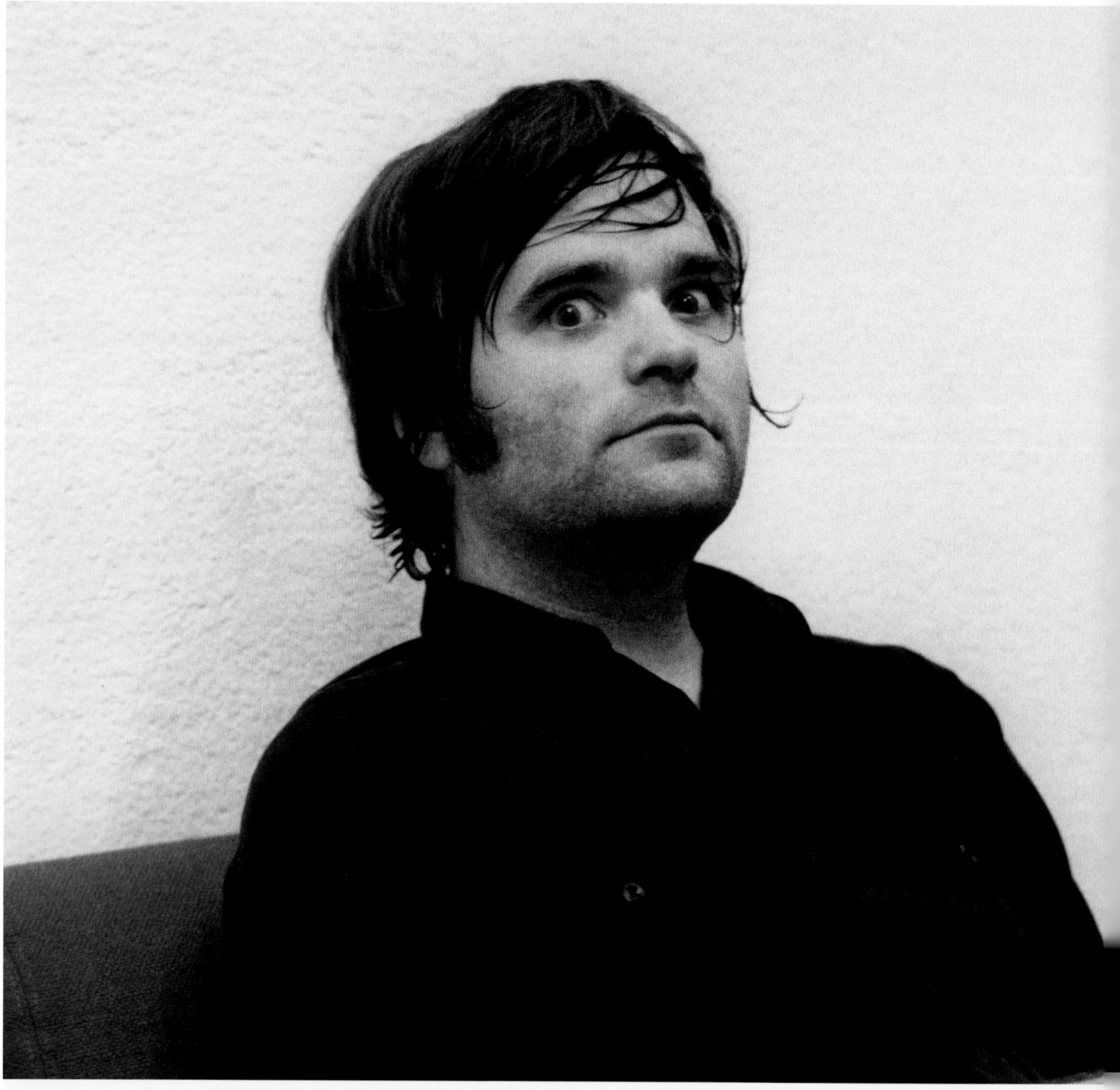

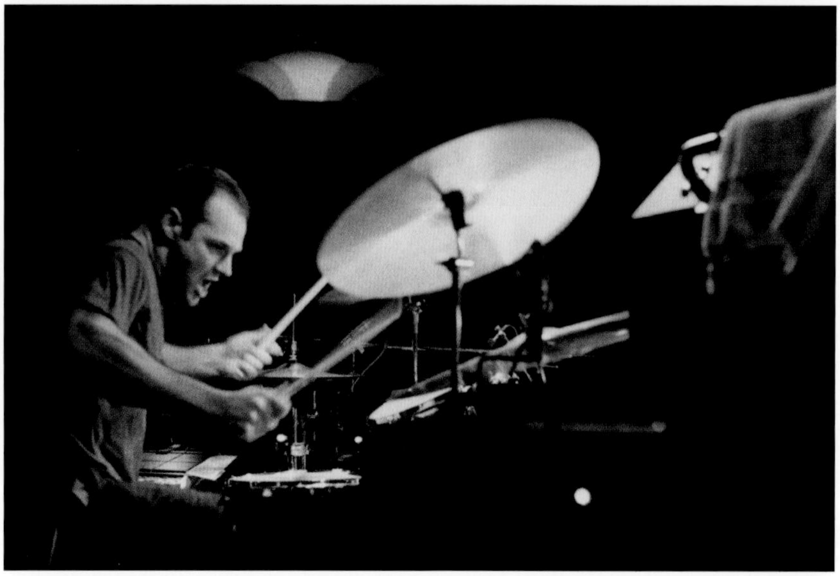

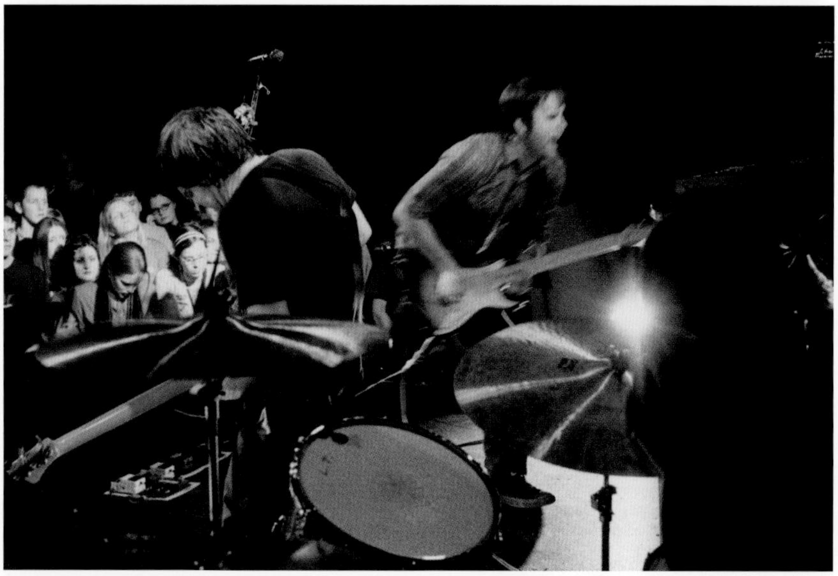

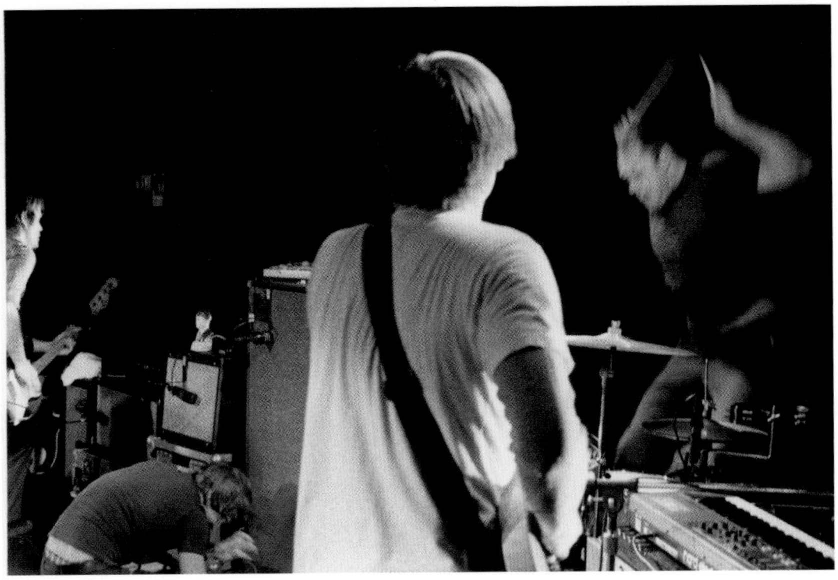

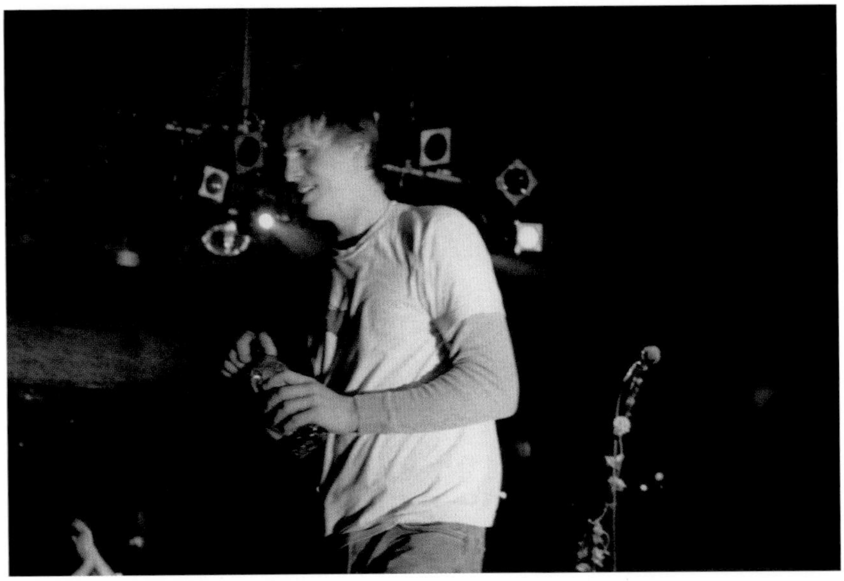

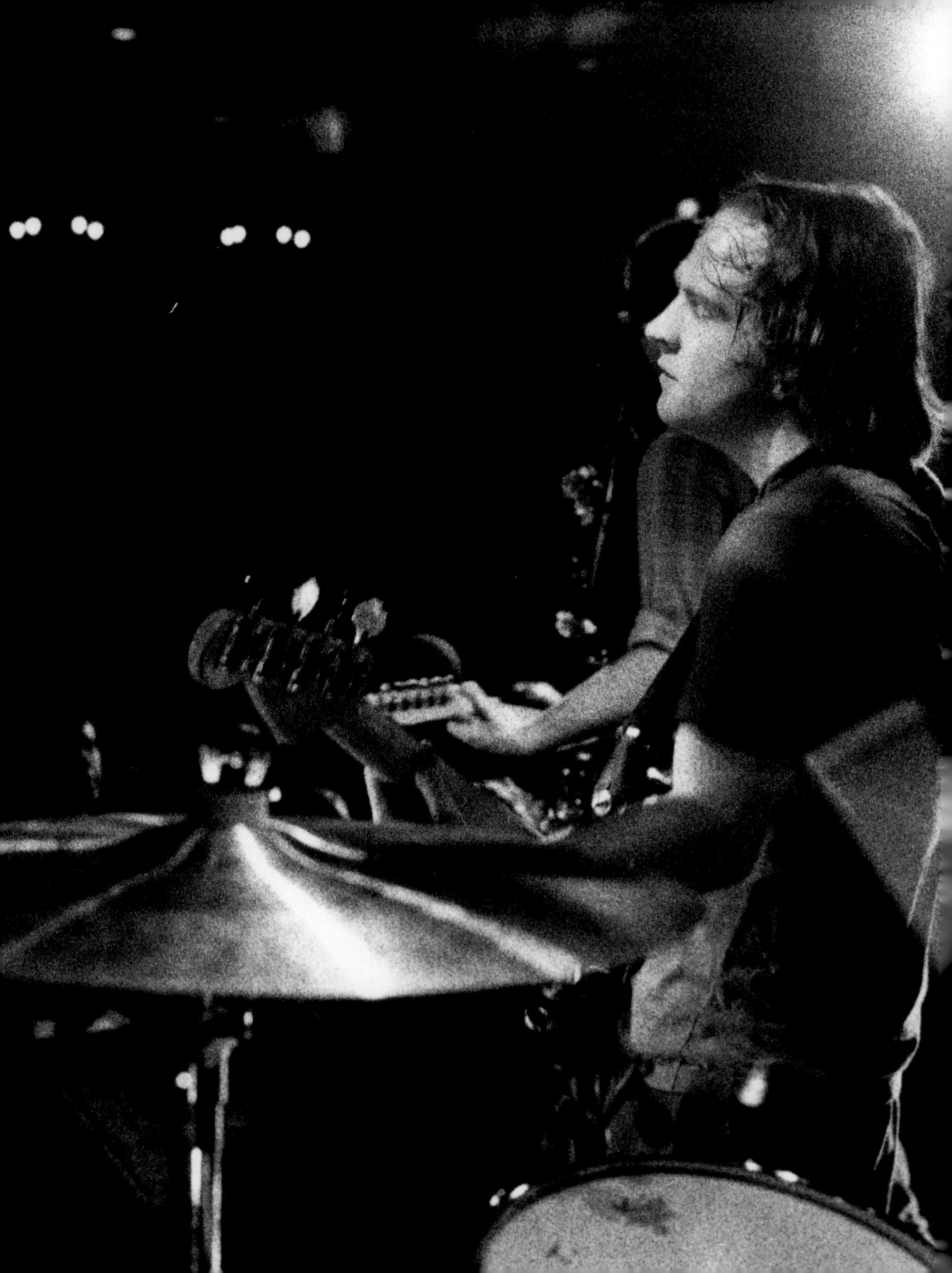

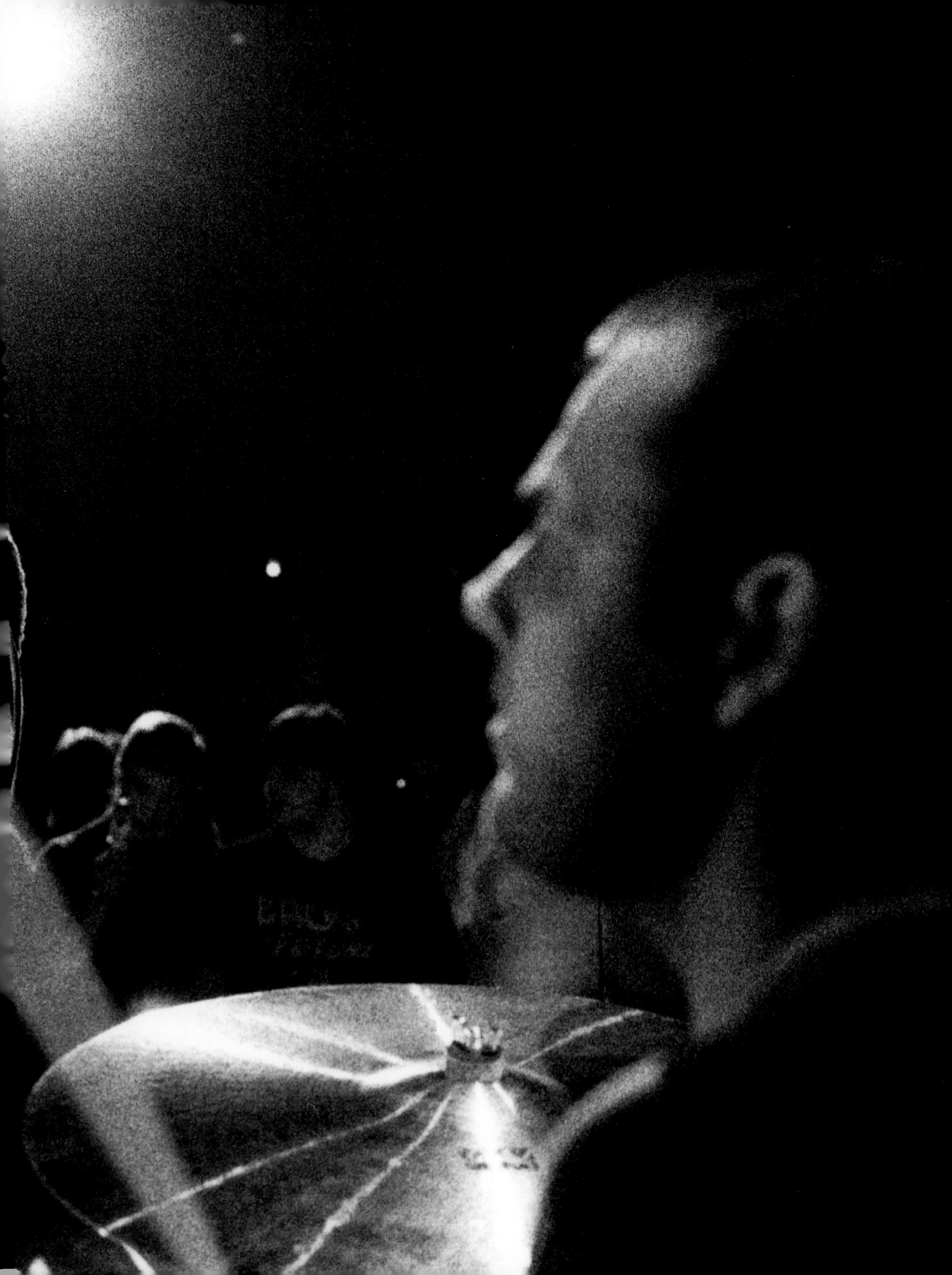

ROOM 5
DEATH CAB FOR CUTIE
FUNK NIGHT
TIC-X
ATTIC
FUNK NIGHT

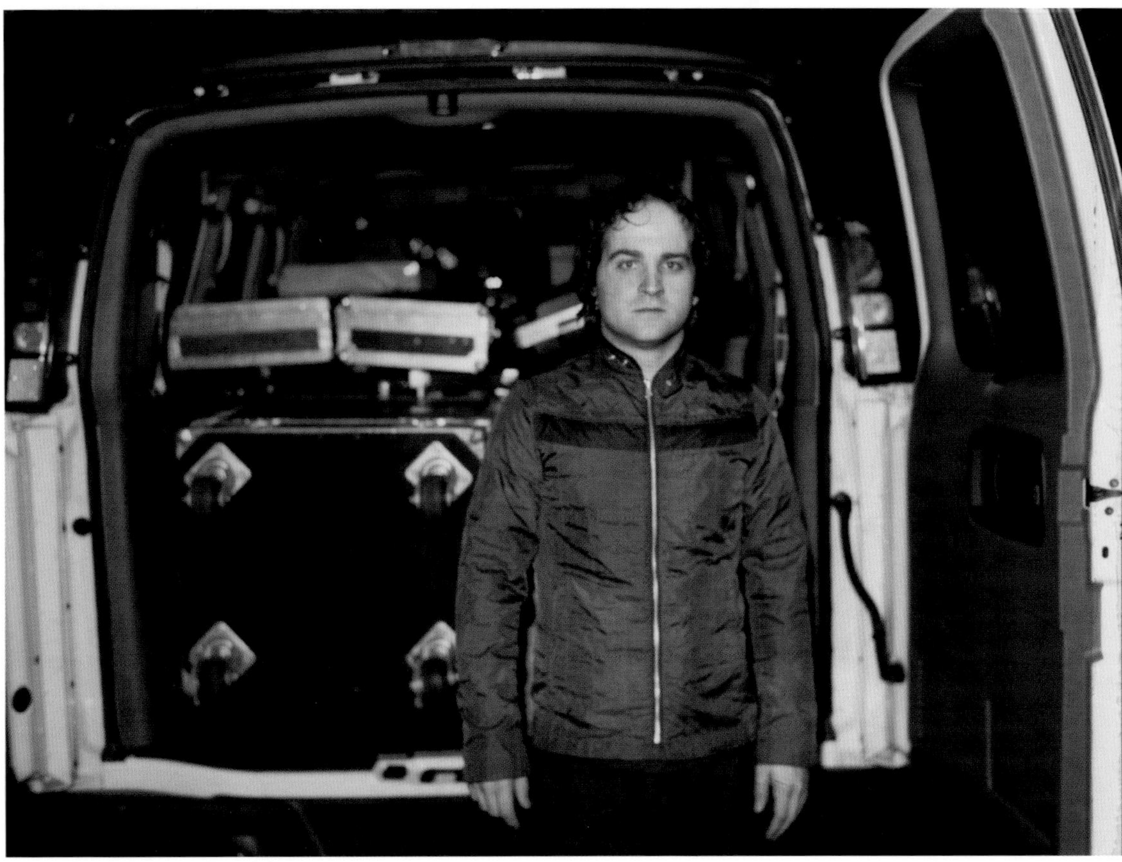

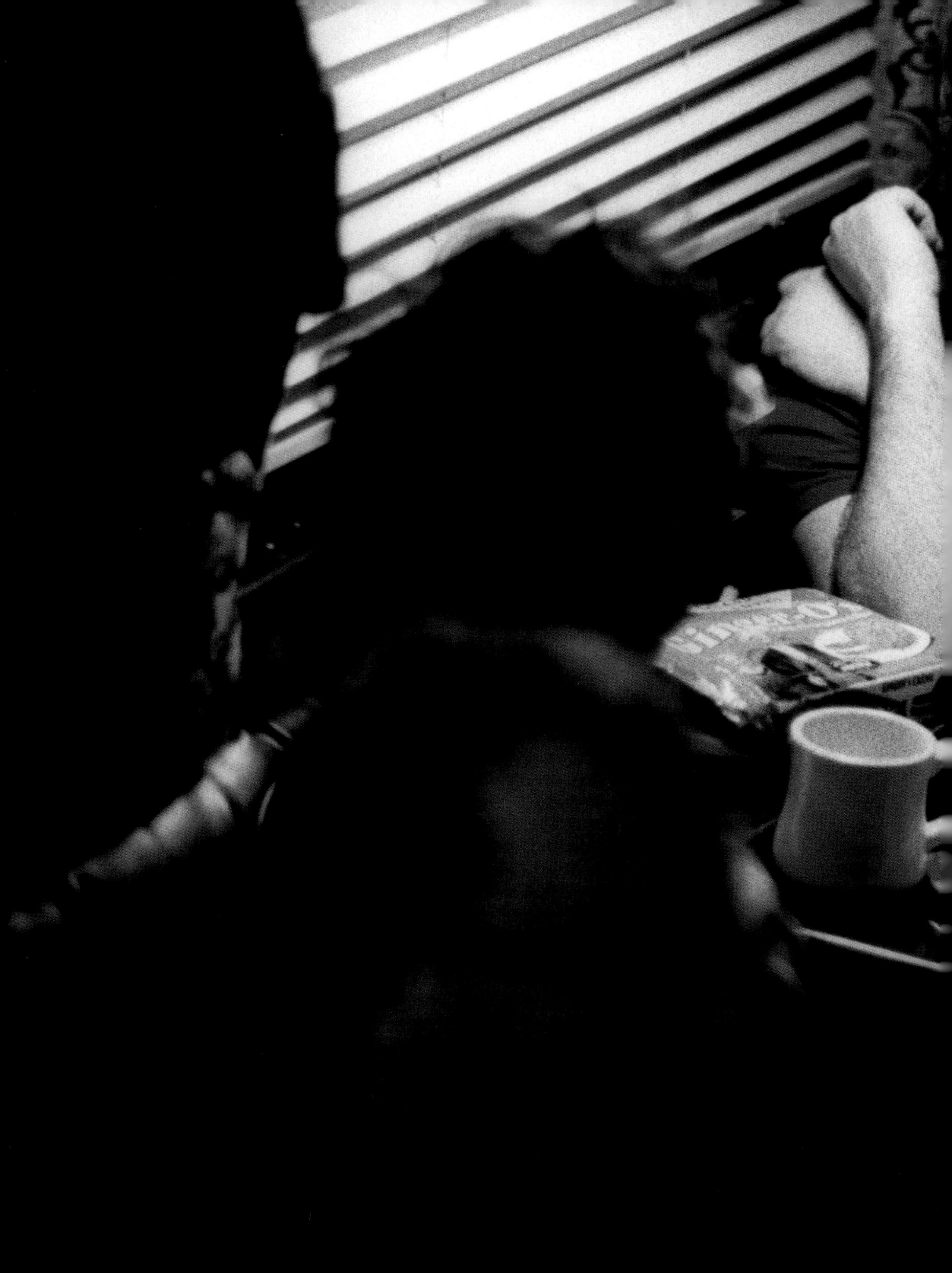

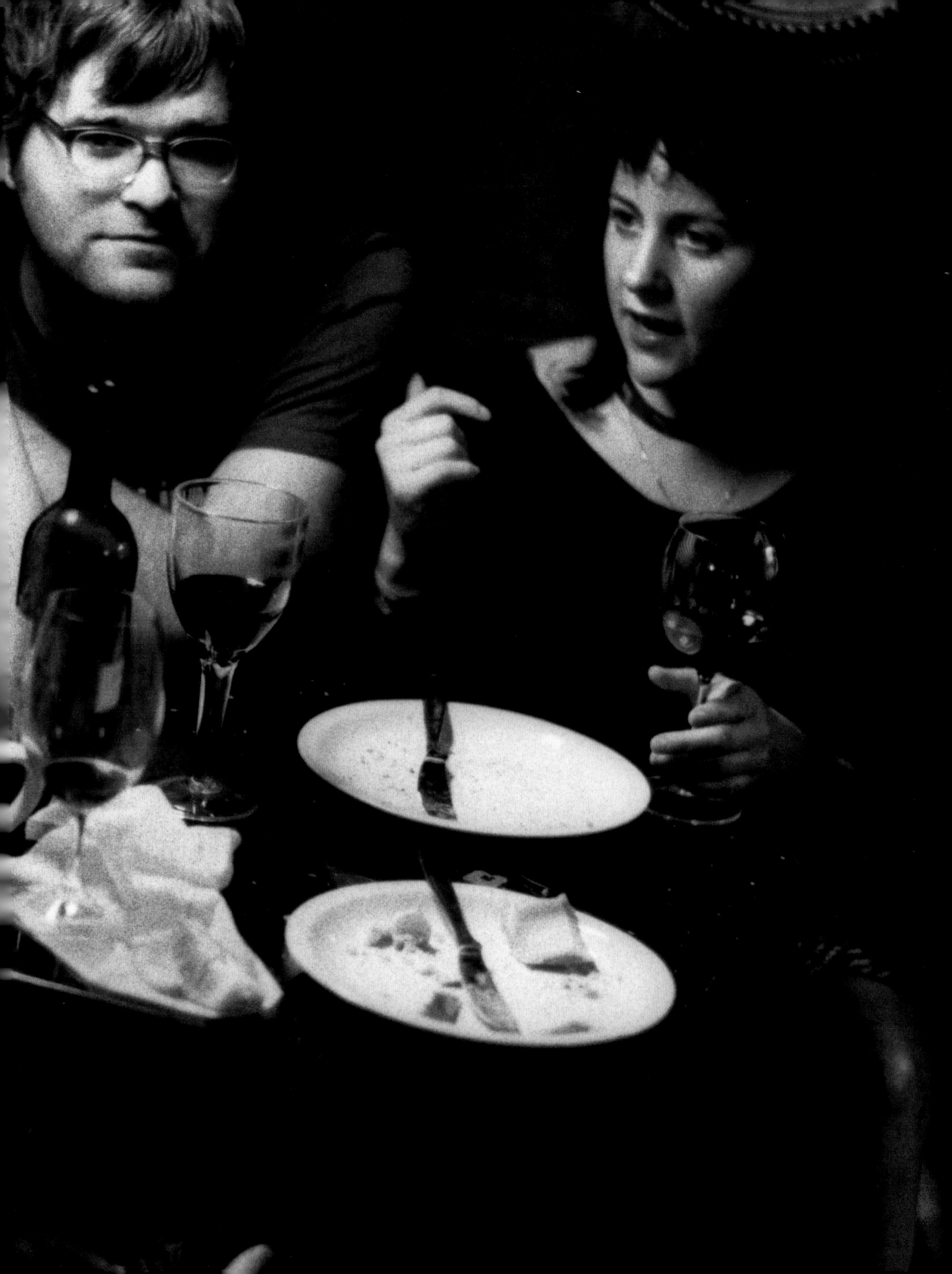

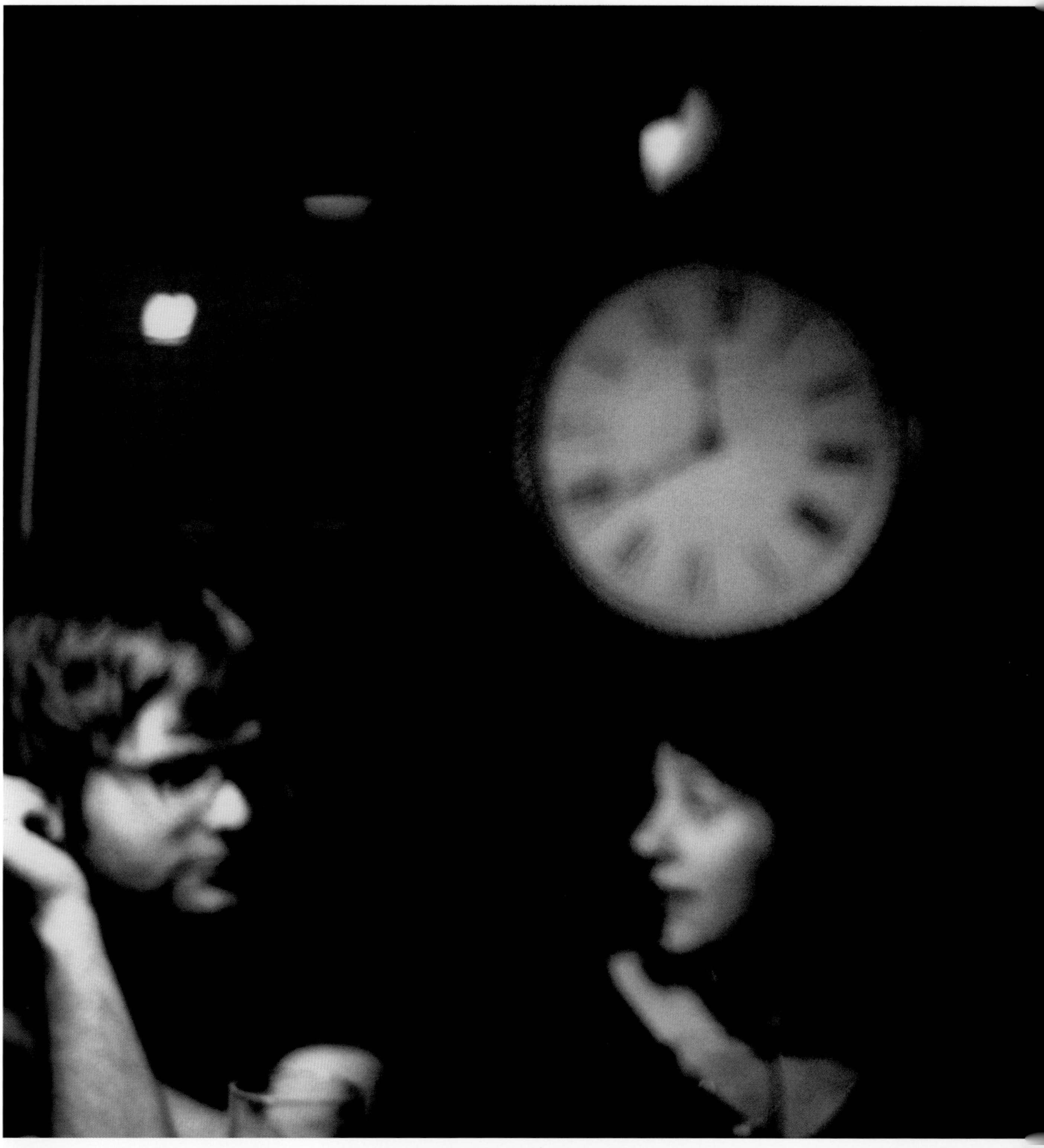

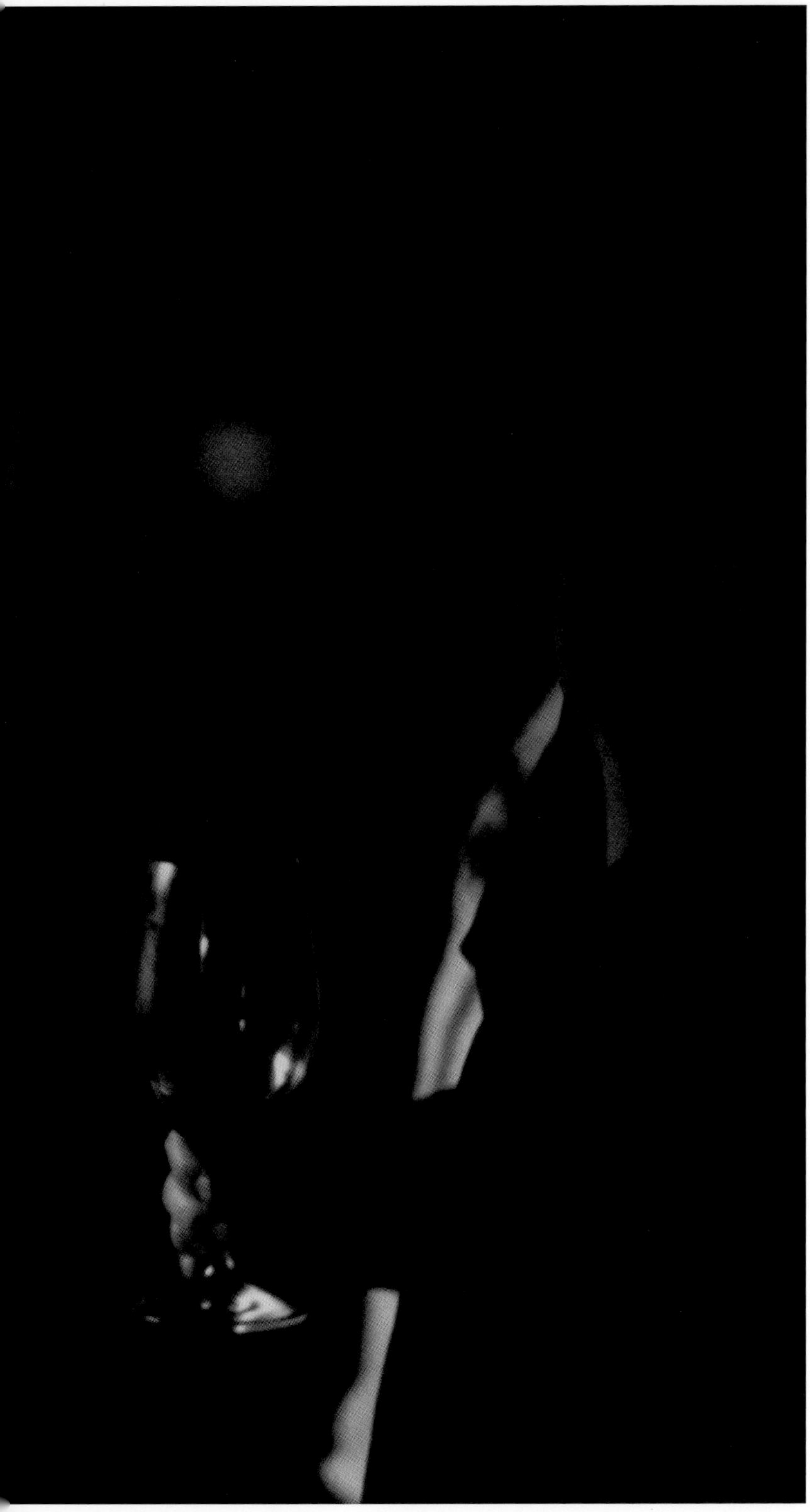

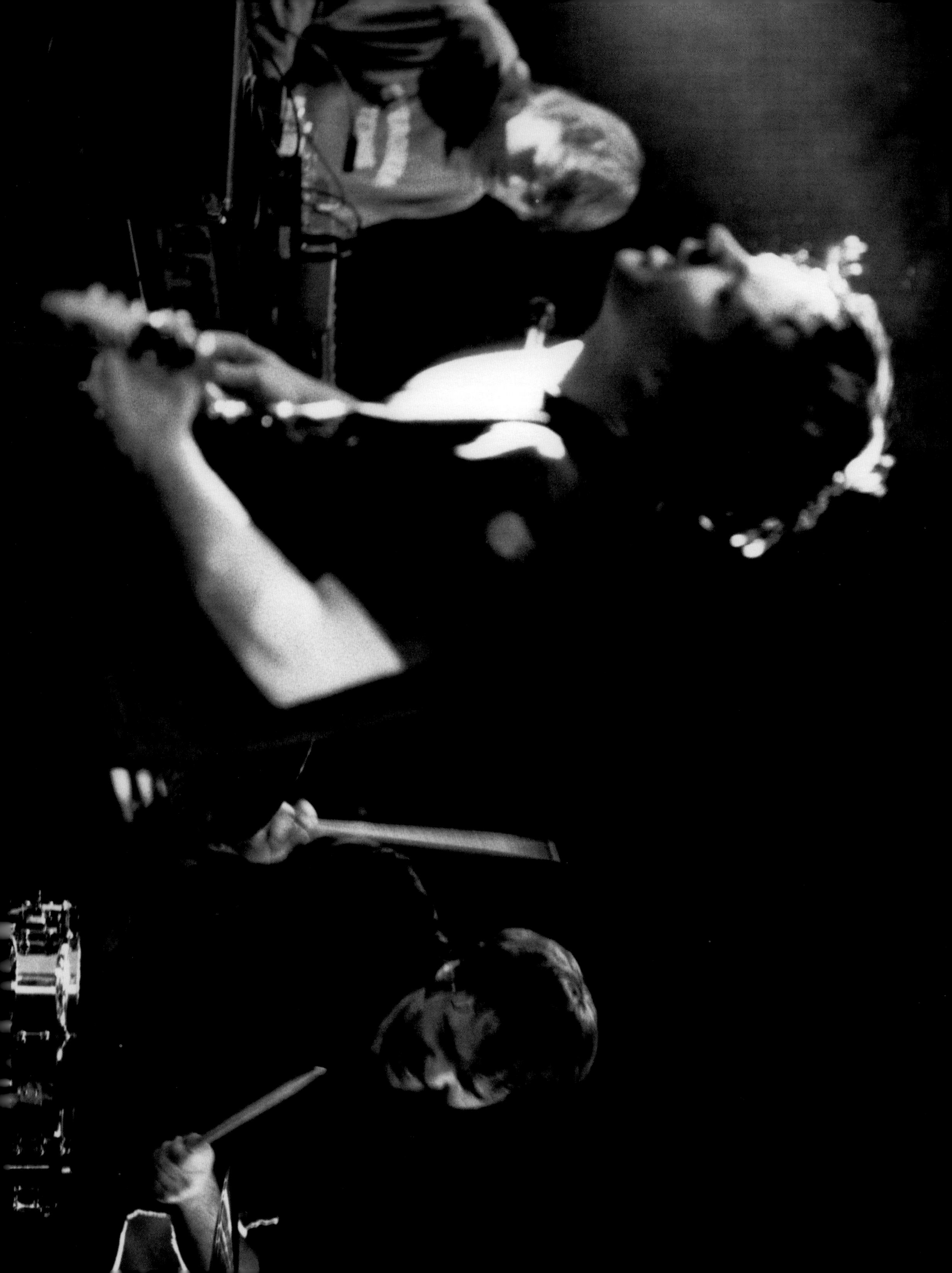

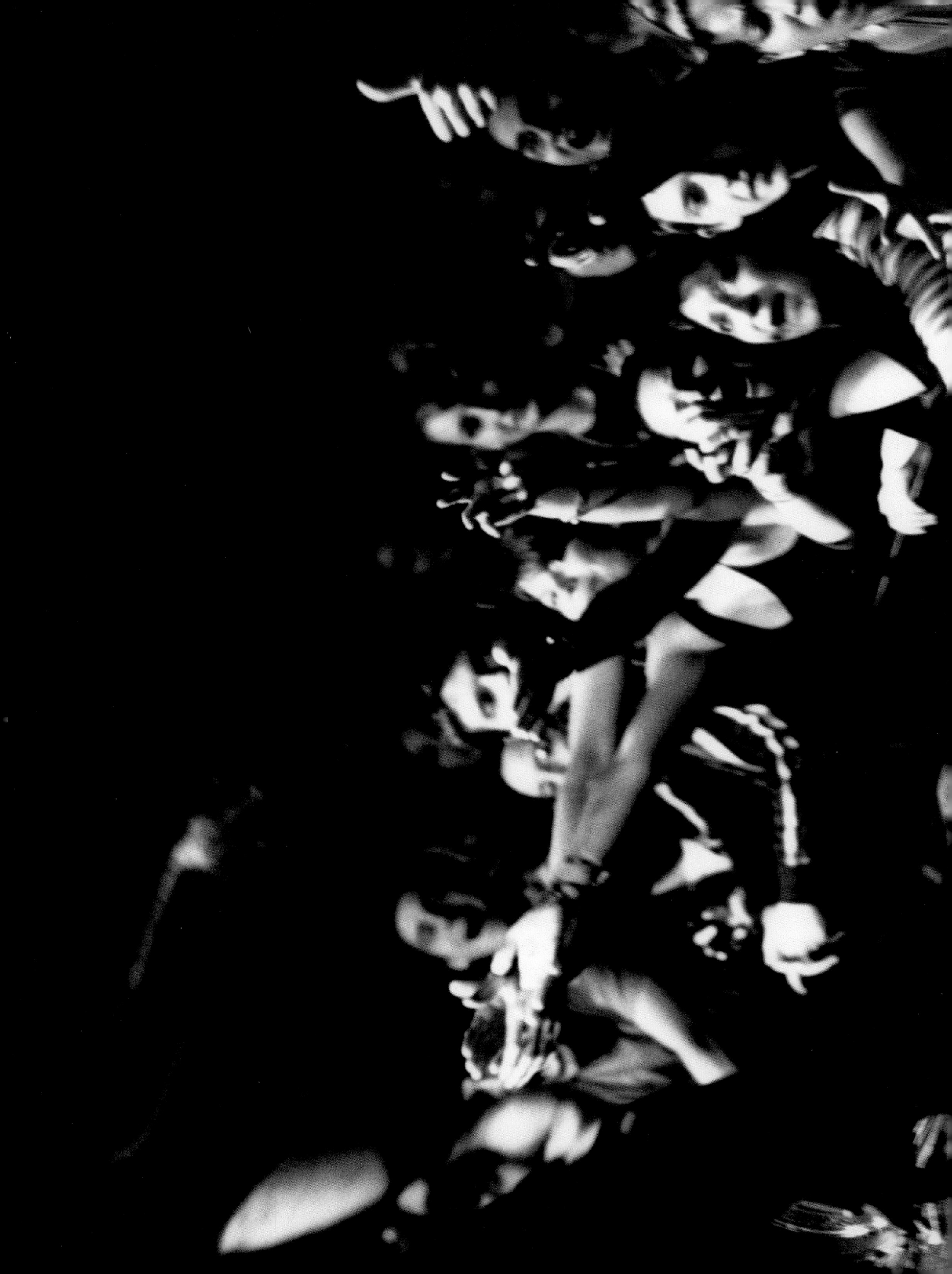

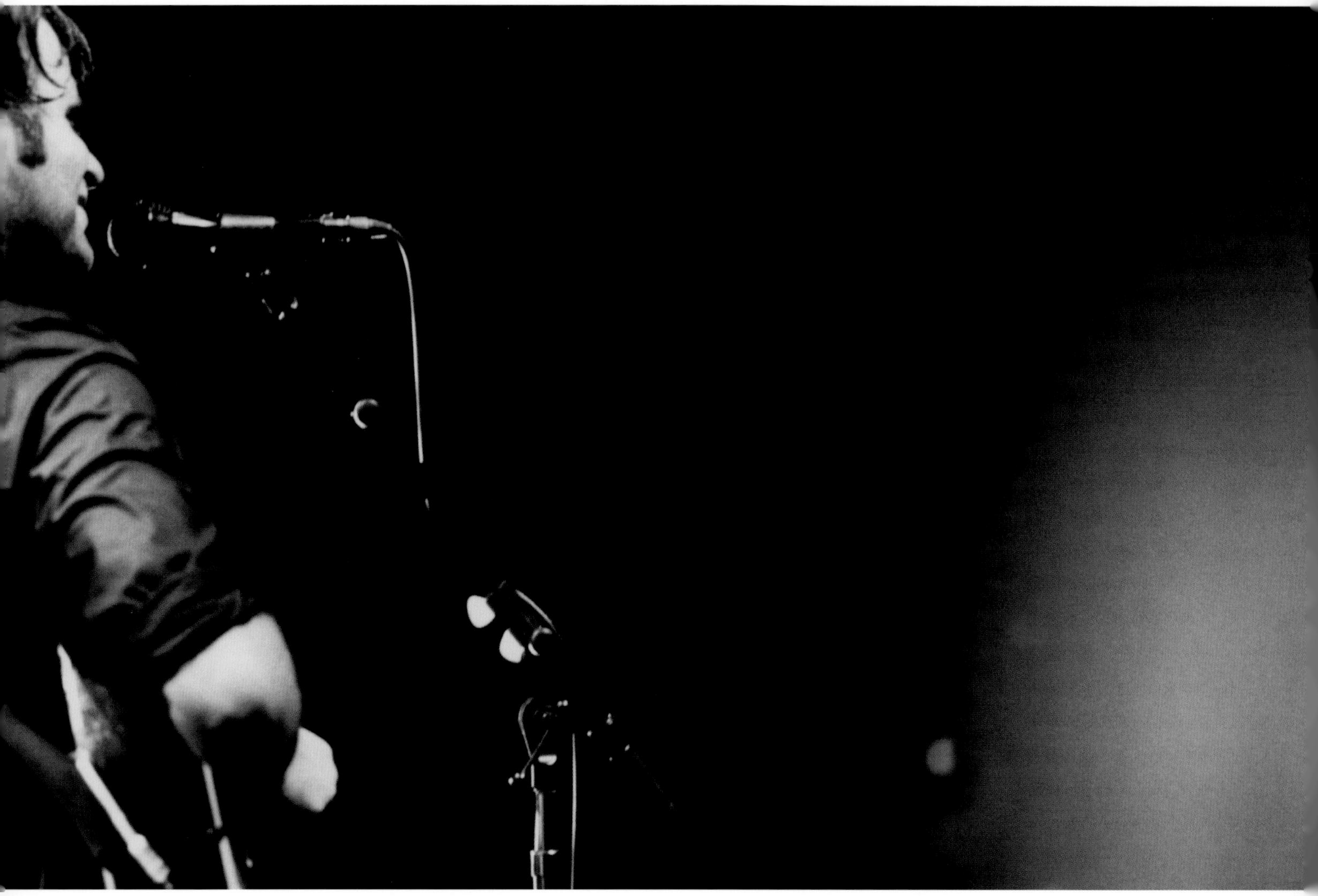

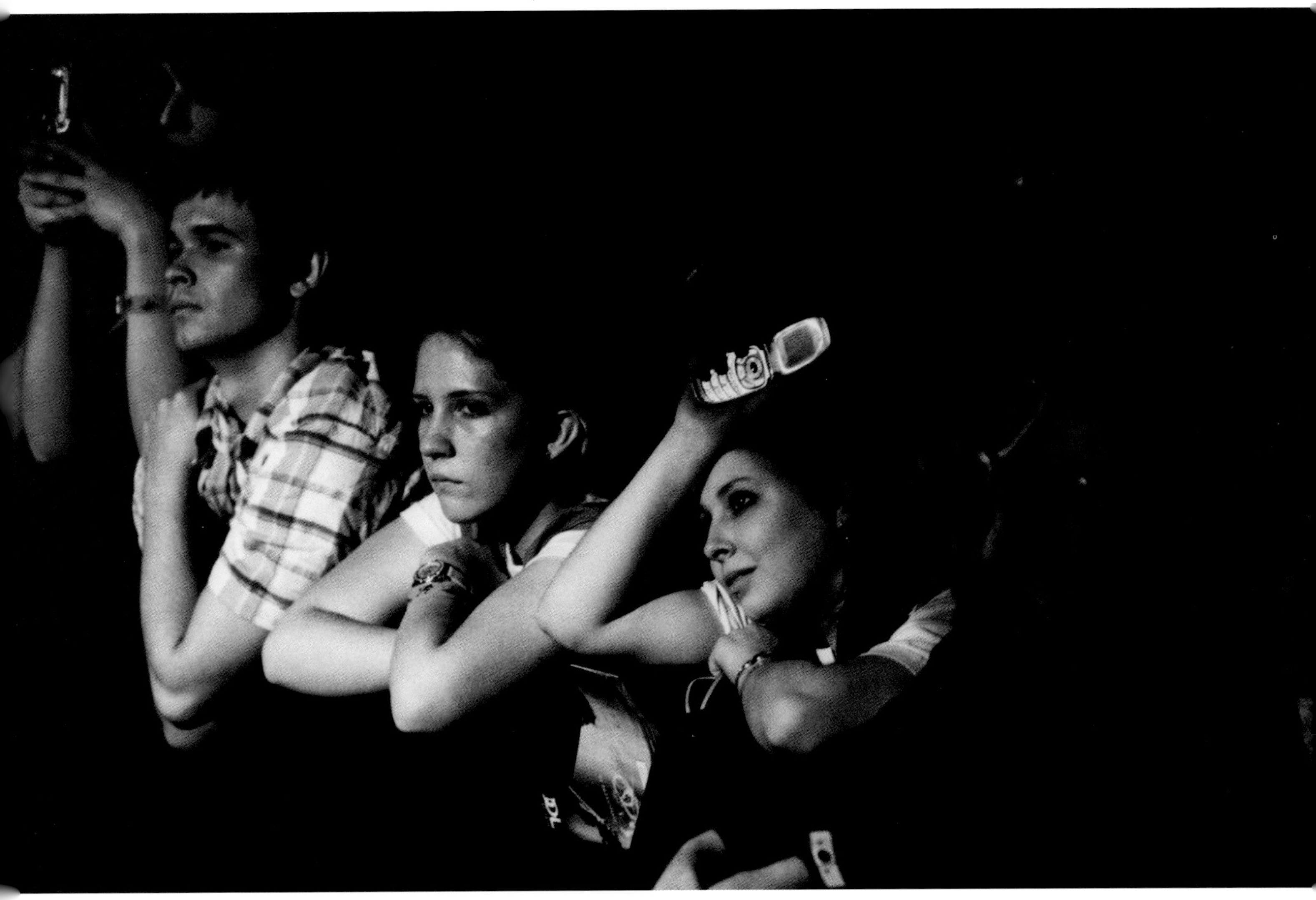

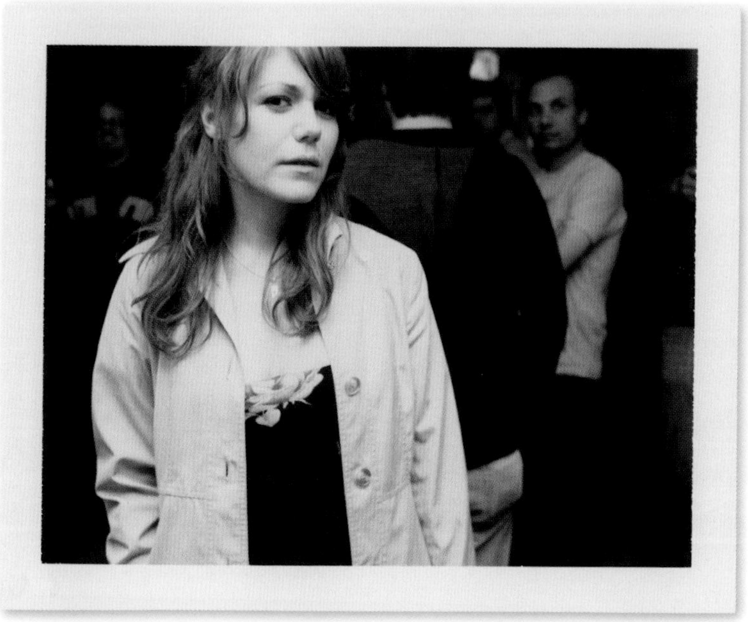

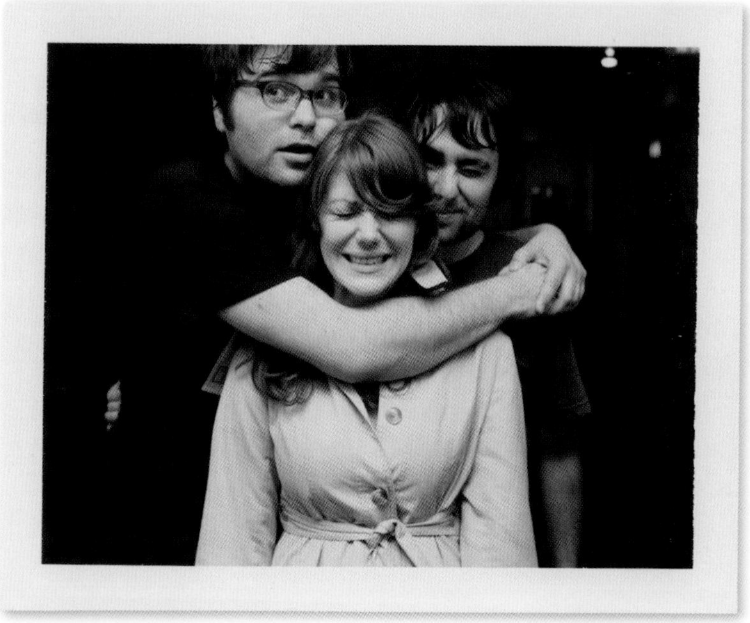

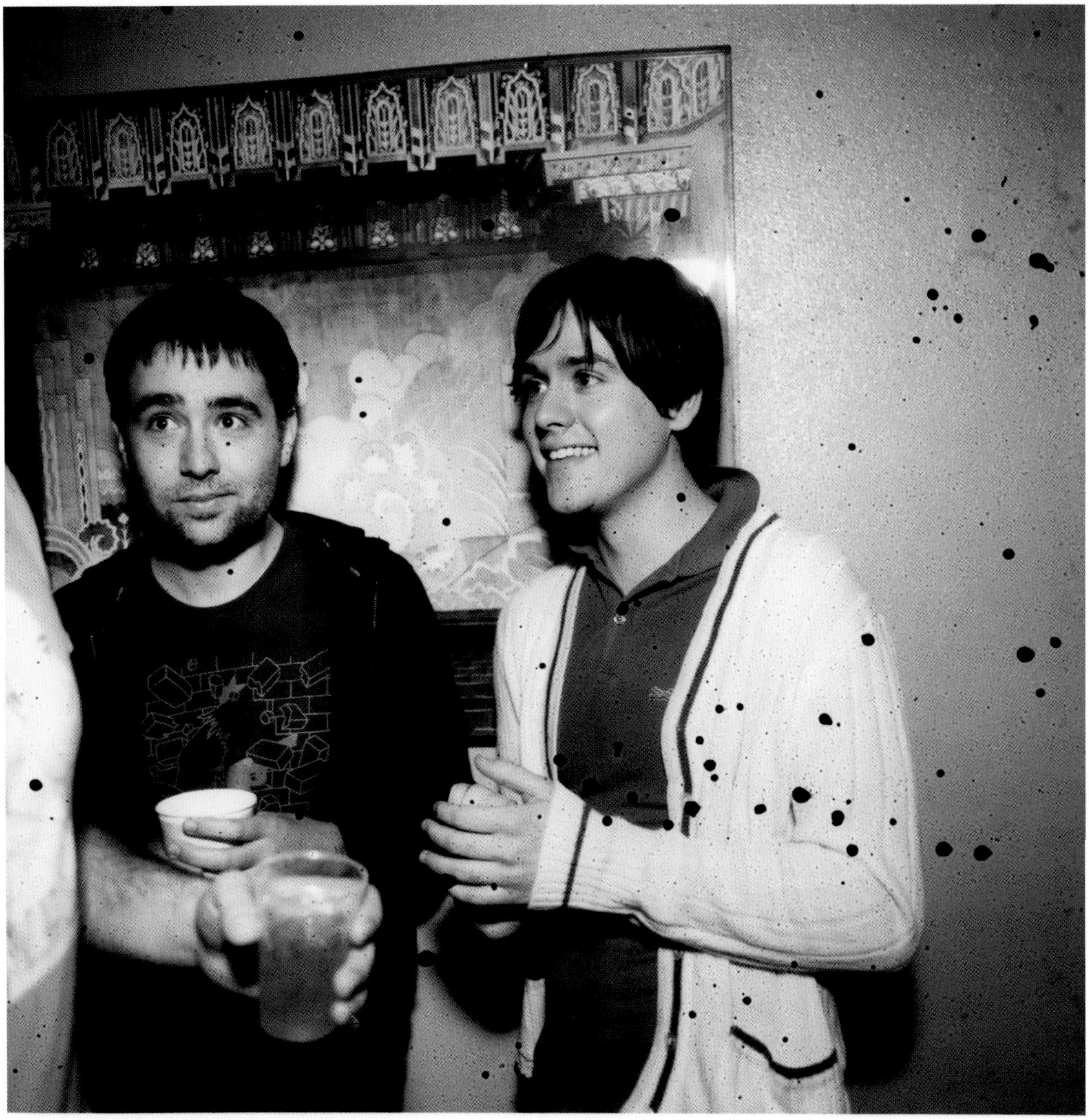

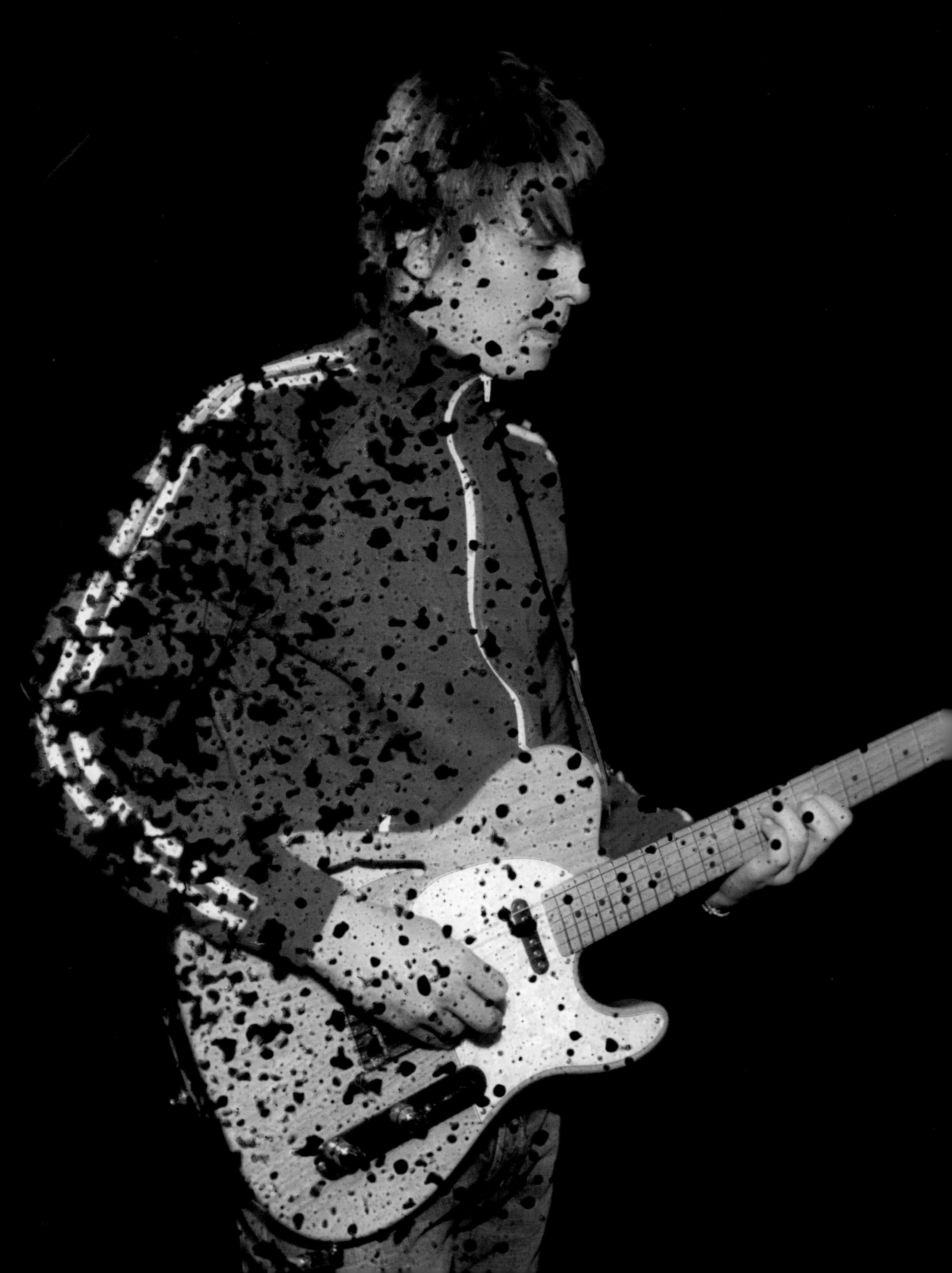

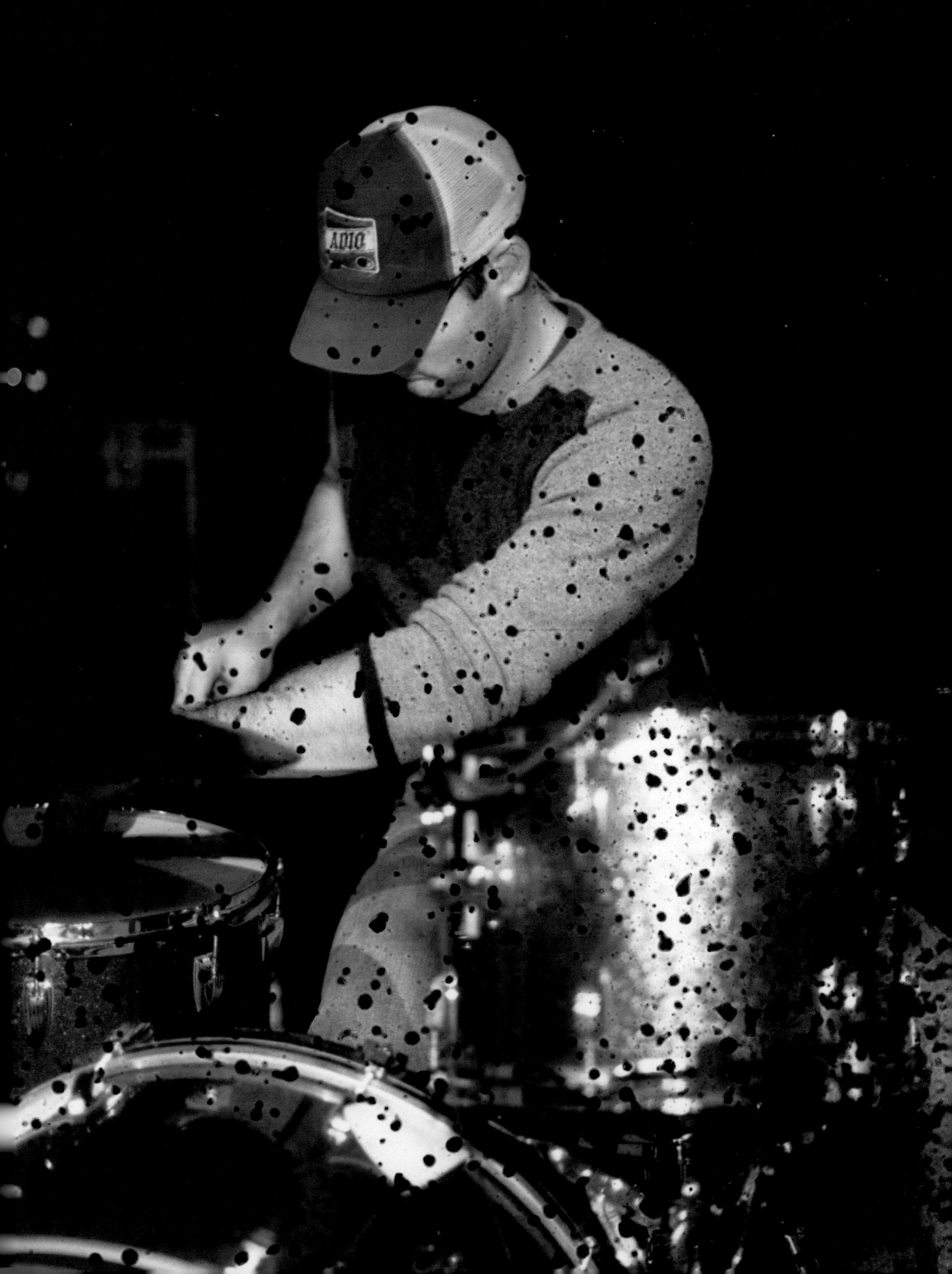
ADIO

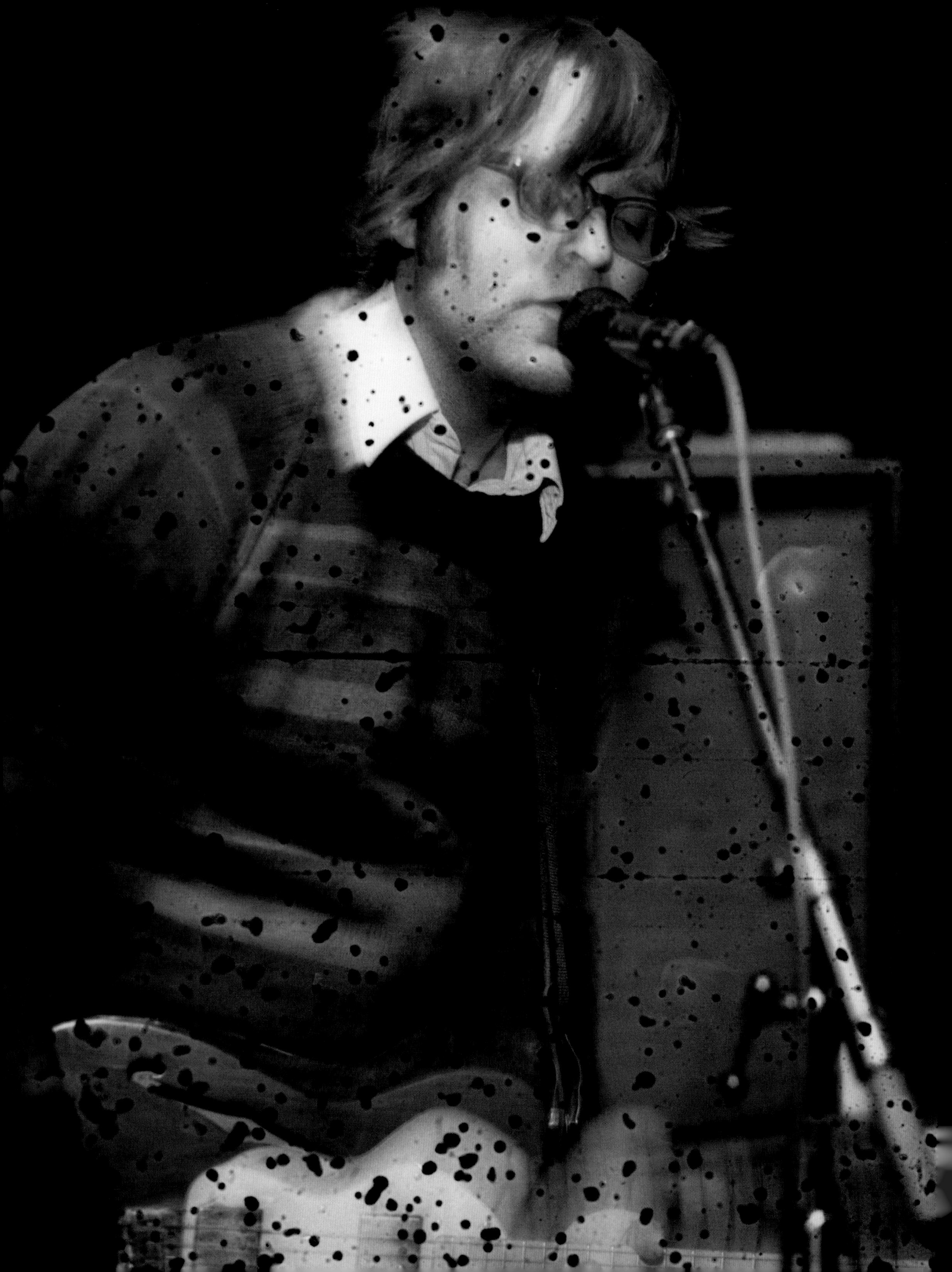

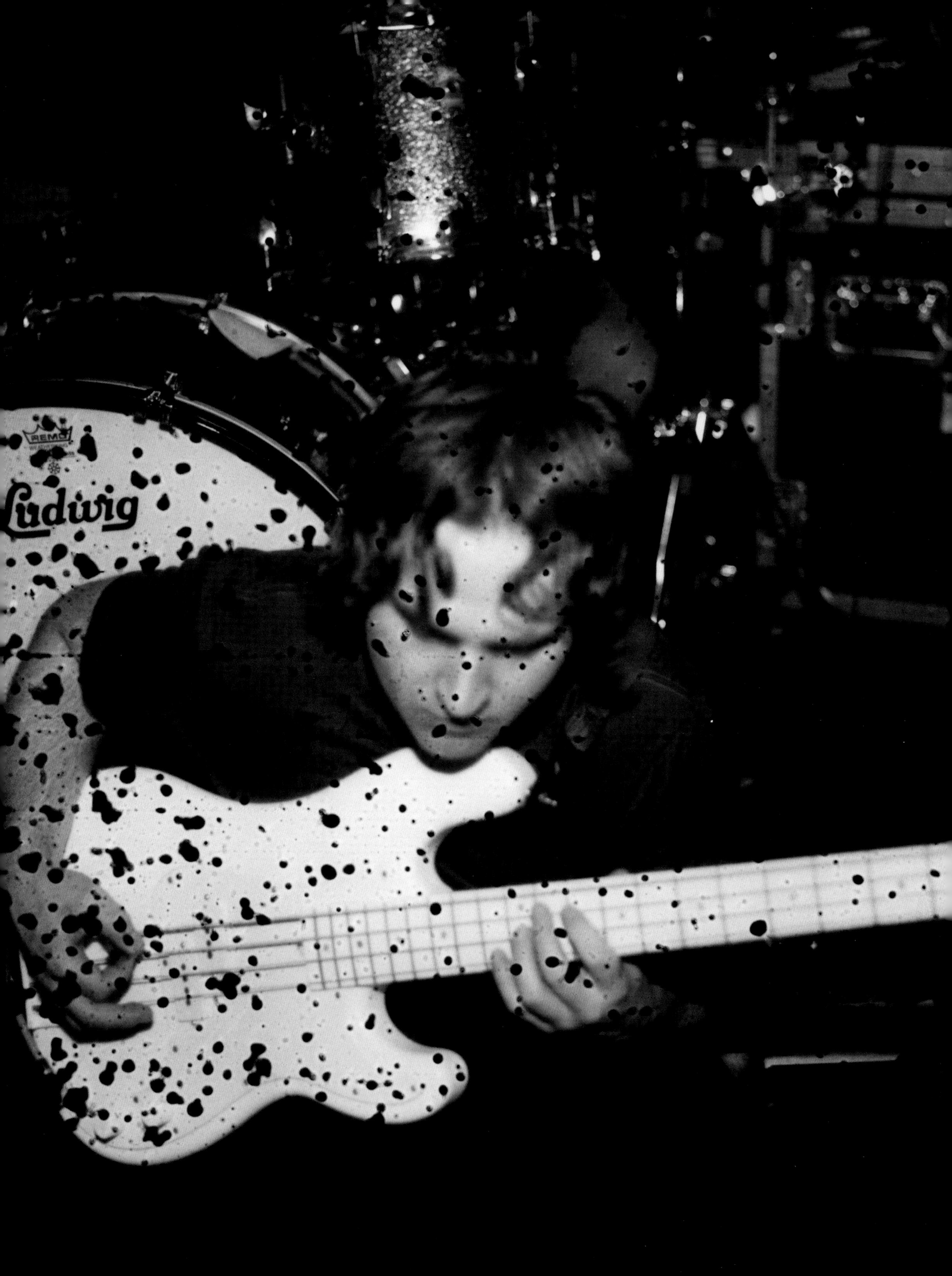
REMO
Ludwig

LONG VIEW

AUTUMN: Why did you decide to record *Plans* out in Massachusetts at Long View Farm Studios?

WALLA: [long pause] Sorry guys.

[ALL LAUGH]

BEN: Well, we all went *willingly*.

JASON: Yeah, we all went willingly.

WALLA: I went out to Long View. John Goodmanson [Seattle-based producer and engineer] had been doing a bunch of work out there, and he was really digging it. I went out there on two different occasions when we were playing shows in and around Boston, and I really, really enjoyed it. I liked the barn a lot. I liked the people out there a lot. And it felt, at the time, after having toured a bunch of studios in L.A. and thinking about maybe doing it in a studio—a proper *studio* studio in Seattle—it seemed like getting away . . . from families and record labels . . .

AUTUMN: Isolating yourself a little bit.

WALLA: . . . isolating ourselves just a little bit would be a good thing to do. And I still think it was, to a degree. I just think that, as we have a long history of doing in this band, we did it for a little bit too long. I think that had it been a two-week experience, it would have been really super-perfect.

AUTUMN: How long was it? I forgot. I think I was there for a week with you guys.

WALLA: We were there for thirty days.

BEN: We were all really excited about it. I think we realized when we got out there that the material that we were recording didn't necessarily lend itself to us recording at the same time, or really interacting musically, so we ended up with one person in front of a microphone for hours upon hours upon hours. All of the material we were recording involved samples, and trying to figure out how to get a sequence out of RADAR [a digital audio recorder] and into another keyboard so we could play the end of the song. It was far more of a construction project of an album than . . . certainly than *Narrow Stairs*. I think that if we had rehearsed these songs and we were going to get in a room and record them . . .

JASON: There wasn't a space to set up as a band and isolate your instrument while tracking. In retrospect, it probably would have worked better if we'd approached it the way we did *Narrow Stairs*, playing together and bleeding through each others' microphones, because you could hear everything in every room in the barn.

BEN: I think that we all kind of knew this about ourselves, but we as individuals all have our own thresholds for how long we can push ourselves in one place before we need a break. It was perfect for you [to Walla], because you love to get in and just work work work work work, and not really take breaks. Just go in and do it. And for me, personally, I have about four or five productive hours in the day, and then I just shut down. So being stuck in a place where there's recording happening and there's a record being made, but there's literally nowhere to go that's not in a place where you're aware there's a record being made . . . I'm really glad we went out there. I think that we learned something about what works and doesn't work with this band. Once we got there, we were all really excited.

NICK: I wouldn't even say . . . I only went kind of nuts that last five days. It was all that snow and everything else. Two weeks would have been fine. I think by that final week was when I was like, "Okay, I don't know exactly what else I need to be here for."

AUTUMN: It turned out you couldn't do vocals there, right?

JASON: There were a lot of things that we were having problems with. We didn't really count on the fact that the big barn didn't keep heat very well.

WALLA: Yeah, there was no central heating. All of our guitars sort of fell apart out there.

JASON: There was a giant wood-burning stove, like huge, and the barn was thirty feet high by a hundred feet long, a hundred years old, and no insulation. They would shovel wood into this giant stove all day long, and it would get to eighty degrees.

NICK: Yeah, it would fluctuate by thirty degrees.

JASON: At night it would be fifty or forty-five.

BEN: And it was that dry, East Coast cold.

AUTUMN: We were all sniffling because you'd have to walk through the horses and the hay.

NICK: All that wood just soaked all the moisture out of the air.

BEN: The longer you're in a place, the more you start getting annoyed by little things that didn't necessarily bother you at first. Like, I started getting annoyed with the flies near the coffee pot, or having to duck down because of the low hallway on the way to my room, things that weren't even issues the first week I was there. We were just there for a little bit too long. We certainly got a lot of work done there. I think that we were all into the romance about what it meant, for the first time to go out into the woods, to an isolated location where we wouldn't be bothered, and that we could solely concentrate on the record. But we also learned that we're the kind of people, and that we're the kind of band, that we don't have a hard time focusing. We may focus in different ways, like some of us may want to stay in the studio for twenty hours a day, the way Walla does sometimes. [to Walla] You never left the barn, the grounds, for thirty days.

NICK: It was not as much to get us to focus out there as it was to keep people from interrupting us.

WALLA: That's true.

NICK: Why we nixed L.A. is so we could keep random people from stopping in saying, "Hey! You guys are making a record! Oh, cool, I want to hang out!" We're that social, too, so that people would feel comfortable calling us up and saying, "Hey, I want to drop in," and we would not necessarily be good at saying, "Don't come."

WALLA: I think that that was really a delicate time, too. Because we were all really sensitive about the whole new label thing, and we weren't quite sure how much interaction was actually going to happen and how much we were going to be expected to share, or not share.

AUTUMN: And how much security you needed at the borders.

NICK: Totally.

WALLA: In that regard, it worked out really well. There is kind of a moat around North Brookfield, Massachusetts.

JASON: Yeah, there is.

WALLA: It's definitely a great place to go get lost in a record. I think that we did need that, at that point. And I think that we probably don't need that again. I feel that there was . . . it was funny. I was really into the idea of just everybody going someplace and . . .

AUTUMN: That wasn't home or familiar to anyone.

WALLA: Right.

AUTUMN: And that was also the first time you had a budget to do something with, too, right?

WALLA: That's true. Yeah.

JASON: And most of that budget was used to ship all our gear out there, which we barely used.

WALLA: Yeah, we barely used any of it because of the guitars.

BEN: We used all that money setting the guitars up.

NICK: In hindsight, we could have probably done it for about half as much as we did then, knowing what we know about shipping now.

WALLA: It was crazy. It was, like, thirty-eight cases. We could have taken five amps and five guitars and been totally cool.

BEN: Well, we were bringing stuff, like . . . I brought a classical-style guitar, like *we may need this*! But it's never been out of its case, do you know what I mean? We brought it *in case* we needed something.

BEN: It was totally understandable. We were going to the middle of nowhere. Why wouldn't we take everything we'd ever owned?

WALLA: The other thing that was a real bummer was that there wasn't really any junk out there. I've really come to realize how important that is. How the one shitty guitar that has one string on it that makes one amazing noise saves you when you're in that moment when you're searching for something that isn't in your arsenal. You need this one flavor, and there's a bunch of stuff around to play with. That's what I love about recording at Tiny Telephone, the particular quality of the junk that JV [John Vanderslice, studio owner/songwriter] has accumulated there. But what we actually got there [at Long View], just in sheer nuts and bolts in terms of what was there, it was really pretty fairly priced, actually.

NICK: It came with horses.

BEN: For me, it came with ten pounds and all that rich food for a month.

JASON: It came with a great sled run, and it came with Tin Can Alley.

AUTUMN: What's Tin Can Alley?

NICK: That's where Jason and I would wander off to.

JASON: When we were bored and you guys [to Ben and Walla] were working on the record, there was a little old toolshed down by the pond, and Nick and I had picked up two plastic, P-9 . . .

NICK: Pellet guns.

```
DEATH CAB FOR CUTIE


Death Cab For Cutie


death cab for cutie


DEATH CAB for CUTIE



f    for
```

JASON: And we would stash our coats full of pop cans, set them up, close the door and take turns with a stopwatch and see how many cans we could take out in a sixty-second run.

NICK: We thought we were so tough.

JASON: The whole experience culminates in knight costumes and pellet guns. I remember waking up early in the morning, having the sun come in the back glass, and recording drums. I think that that stuff came through in that record. The amount of space that we were surrounded with, the depth of the snow. There's space in the notes of the recording, and there's an ambiance that resonates in the record that was very much a product of our environment in our isolation.

NICK: Remember that night we were all drinking and going crazy and making a racket for no good reason? I mean, we were *banging* on stuff. [to Walla] You were doing that weird drum thing when you're just freaked out, hitting the drums.

AUTUMN: You were singing that Band song over and over.

BEN: I think we were probably singing "The Weight."

NICK: Just pounding on stuff.

AUTUMN: I have photos of that, and I don't know how to explain what we were doing. We must have played that Band song fifty times.

NICK: I remember the next morning we woke up and the A&R guy who was recording with a band the in the next studio across the way came over and went up to Ben . . .

BEN: I was *hungover* as hell, and the guy comes up to me and says, "Hey man, I heard you guys working up there in the barn—sounded really great!" I was like, "Thanks, man!"

STORMING THE CASTLE

AUTUMN: So, you haven't seen these photos in a while . . .

NICK: [looking at a picture of himself in a knight costume on an exercise bike] Is this the Pavlov part, where you show us a picture and see how we react?

BEN: [looking at a photo of himself putting on a knight costume] This clearly showcases how much individual free time we all had.

JASON: [looking at a picture of himself in a knight costume, pumping iron] We went crazy out there, obviously. We were just stir crazy.

BEN: Saturdays were Walla's day. He stayed in the studio all day cleaning up stuff, and we had the day off, so we drove into Worcester, which is the closest city, still thirty miles away. And there was a mall and, inexplicably, a Halloween supply store.

NICK: A *giant* Halloween supply store. In February, the middle of winter.

BEN: And it was just full of those shitty, cheap costumes.

NICK: Fully stocked. Multiple employees. Strobe lights. So we bought these knight costumes.

AUTUMN: And I made sure we got one for everyone. And we pulled over . . .

BEN: We wanted to show up at the studio and surprise Walla and Jason, dressed up as knights.

NICK: To storm the castle.

BEN: Walla was in pure work mode and couldn't be bothered with the idiots.

NICK: We thought it was going to be a great and moment, and Walla would love it. [laughing]

BEN: [to Walla] You had all this shit going, heavy-duty sequencing, and pianos, and running things backwards. You were lost in Science World, and we just waltzed in: "We're dressed like *knights*!"

WALLA: I just did all the transfers for that record recently, for Atlantic.

JASON: How many piano tracks did you do?

WALLA: It's the fucking craziest shit ever.

NICK: I bet.

AUTUMN: I remember feeling a little deflated. The build-up . . . it was all for Walla.

BEN: And now, looking back, understandably, he was *working*.

[ALL LAUGH]

WALLA: I wasn't sad, but I didn't . . .

BEN: No, you were sad. You were shitty.

NICK: We got a knight costume for Walla, but he never put it on.

WALLA: I still have it. I pull it out for every record that I'm working on. To see if anybody wants to put it on.

NICK: Nobody does.

WALLA: I've never put it on myself.

BEN: [to Walla] You were just in a *very* different headspace than we were.

NICK: It's like that final scene from the movie version of *Lord of the Flies*, when the little kids are having all of these adult problems and getting crazy and society's falling apart and they're chasing Ralph out of the jungle and they fall in the sand at the feet of that soldier who's standing on the beach, and he looks down and says, "What are you kids doing?" And, suddenly, you realize they're just little kids playing. That's how it felt when Walla turned around, like *what are you kids doing*? I was thinking, *I'm a child. You're absolutely right. I should be reading Dostoyevsky. What am I doing in a knight costume with a plastic sword?* [laughing] Wow, I've come this far since college. It was a humbling moment.

BEN: There was this crazy thing about the space. Nobody could have known this before we went there, but the thing with Long View that after two or three weeks started to get *really* annoying was that there was nowhere you could go in that entire building to get away from the recording. The drums came through everything; it didn't matter where you were—in your bedroom, in the kitchen, in the TV room.

WALLA: It was an eternal soundcheck.

BEN: Yeah, exactly.

AUTUMN: It's interesting though, like you were saying, all of that added to the record. Like the tension and the beauty . . .

WALLA: I guess there are a few things that we did there that couldn't have happened anywhere else. I think that's true of every record. The way that "Soul Meets Body" came out had a lot to do with that building. Just being able to record in that building that way, with the mic close to Ben, and then further, and then further, and further, like all the way out to a half mile away.

NICK: "Different Names for the Same Thing."

WALLA: Yeah, "Different Names," because of the fire, and the microphone that I melted.

AUTUMN: Did you record a microphone melting in the fire, or did the microphone melt because you were close to the fire?

WALLA: The microphone went in the fireplace.

NICK: Other than RADAR, there was something so decidedly *undigital* about that entire place. We were in a barn doing this sort of more hybridized, analog-digital thing.

BEN: There's a little bit of, like a nervousness in some of the recordings, too. I guess "nervousness" is not the right word.

JASON: "Restlessness" is probably a good word.

BEN: For somebody like myself who has always been about the destination, it was really difficult for me to see the forest from the trees. We were recording little bits of *everything* for thirty days. There were very few moments when we finished anything.

NICK: Nothing was finished at Long View.

JASON: With the exception of "I Will Follow You into the Dark."

NICK: [to Ben] Which you got in one take.

WALLA: That's right. There's a quiet moment in every session where something like that can happen; the particular way that it comes about is of that place, really *of* that building.

BEN: I have really fond memories of that place, you know what I mean?

NICK: I have the fondest memories of the times in this band that have been the most tumultuous. There's just something about that that forces us to bind together a little tighter and rely on each other a little bit more to get out of the situation. I hardly remember some of the easy, long breaks. That week of shows when they were all awesome. I'm not even talking shit about Long View. It was a complex environment. There were as many good things as there were bad things.

BEN: I have never thought of myself as the kind of person who would be, "Oh yeah, I would just love to get out in the middle of nowhere. Just be alone with my thoughts." I'm not that guy. Honestly.

NICK: You're not that guy.

BEN: Too much time with my own thoughts is not healthy for me.

NICK: Which surprised, me when you were working on *Narrow Stairs*, that you wanted to go down to Bixby Canyon.

BEN: Well, you know me. I never learn. [laughing]

AUTUMN: What was the Bixby Canyon thing?

BEN: When I was finishing the songs for *Narrow Stairs*, I rented this cabin in Big Sur, the cabin that Kerouac had stayed in and was the setting of the book *Big Sur*. I went down there for two weeks. I'm glad I went, but as I grow older, I'm trying to understand what I like and what I don't like. When it comes time to finish the next record, I'm not going to go off somewhere for two weeks and try to finish the songs. I'll go to the office every day.

NICK: You like a change of environment.

BEN: Yeah. I do love a change of environment.

NICK: Exactly, it's just the isolation factor. Like, going out in the middle of nowhere.

BEN: Like I said before, I have about four or five productive hours in every day. And after those four or five hours, I'm just not going to get anything done.

NICK: Then the rest of that time . . .

BEN: I'm just sitting there waiting for something to happen that's not going to happen.

AUTUMN: I think you're really funny when you feel isolated and trapped, though. [laughing] I feel like, for me, as a documentarian . . . I mean from a photographer's point of view . . .

BEN: It's comical for you to be out there watching me losing my mind.

AUTUMN: Yeah, it was the best photo op I ever had, because you couldn't really wander off anywhere. I had you all in . . .

NICK: A cage? In an aquarium?

AUTUMN: You all had to interact with each another.

BEN: Like being stuck in the backseat during a roadtrip.

WALLA: It's really funny, my only memories of recording that record are really of recording that record.

JASON: Sitting down at that console?

WALLA: Because I never went into town, and I never went to the grocery store. I only know that grocery store from the photos that Autumn took. [laughing] It's really funny that so much of your documenting of this record is stuff . . .

AUTUMN: It actually informs of you what was going on around you.

WALLA: [laughing] Right. It was so *weird*.

COMPUTERHEAD

AUTUMN: It seems like when you made *Plans*, you were venturing into new territory. Had you set out to do things a little differently, or was is accidental?

NICK: *Plans* came right after Ben's Postal Service stuff, so he had been doing a lot of writing on his computer.

BEN: At the time, I was really inspired by this German wave of indie rockers who made electronic music that meshed with standard band arrangements.

AUTUMN: Melody driven.

BEN: Yeah. It's the reason a song like "Summer Skin" turned out the way it did. I had three chords that I kept looping, and it became an anchor for part of the song where the voice would come in. So much of the construction of the songs—with the exception of "I Will Follow You into the Dark," and "Crooked Teeth," and maybe a couple of other ones—they were all written in the computer. They came from relatively meager beginnings as far as having anything to really build a song around. I mean that in the best possible way. A lot of the structures of the songs are really open. There's not a verse-chorus-verse-chorus-bridge . . .

JASON: Would you say that there are more parts?

BEN: Well, I've noticed *fewer* parts. I feel like there's far more repetition on that album.

NICK: I remember a specific conversation I had with Walla, standing outside a restaurant in Seattle and waiting to go in. [to Ben] You had called me because you had sent out another round of demos and another bunch of songs that were all basically loops and digital stuff. [to Walla] You called and were like, "Where's the band in this? How are we going to be a band and do these songs?" And early on, I remember [to Ben] your concerns about how we were going to take all the digital stuff that you'd been writing and move that back toward analog and rock and roll and stuff that we could do and play. I remember having a conversation with you [to Walla] that was like, "I see all of the loops and the parts, but I don't understand what *we're* supposed to do yet. How do we get involved?"

WALLA: That's a version of paranoia that every drummer started to have at the point that the LinnDrum [drum machine] was introduced in 1980, and a version of the paranoia that every producer has about being completely outmoded and put out of a job because there are computers and machines now that do that stuff pretty good; a version of the paranoia that an auto worker has about being replaced by a robot. There's just some really . . . It's not a . . . I'm in this phase right now where I'm really enjoying all that stuff for the first time, and really finding creativity in it and realizing how interesting it can be to write around that kind of stuff.

NICK: I think that's what makes *Plans* unique in our catalog. It was all of that combined with pulling it *back* toward the band and sort of figuring out a way of basically approximating or re-creating anything you [Ben] had made digitally.

NICK: That's what makes those songs different in my mind, and in my ears, too. When we were touring those songs, we had a sampler breakdown on *Conan* [O'Brien], and we came back and we'd have these discussions where we were like, "Why do we have a sampler? We're not a sampler band!"

BEN: And I feel somewhat responsible for that. [laughing] What the fuck? This is my fault. I'm the one who brought all this shit in. And now it's fucking up on *Conan*, and it's my fault because I'm who decided that this song needed it.

NICK: That's so funny. I never would have put that on you. We all went in willingly, just like heading off to Long View. But I remember you [Jason] saying, "I just can't wait to be a *rock band*."

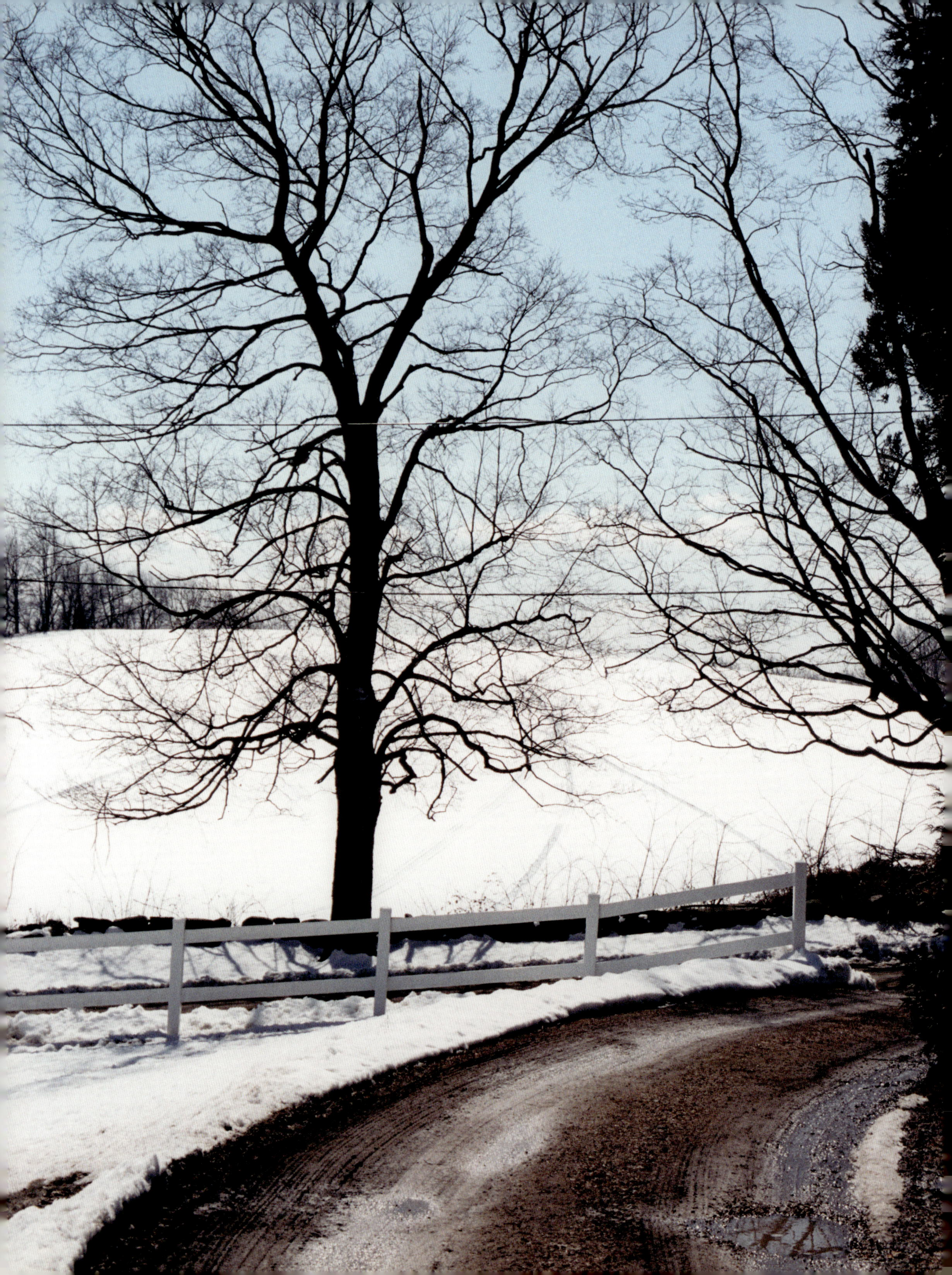

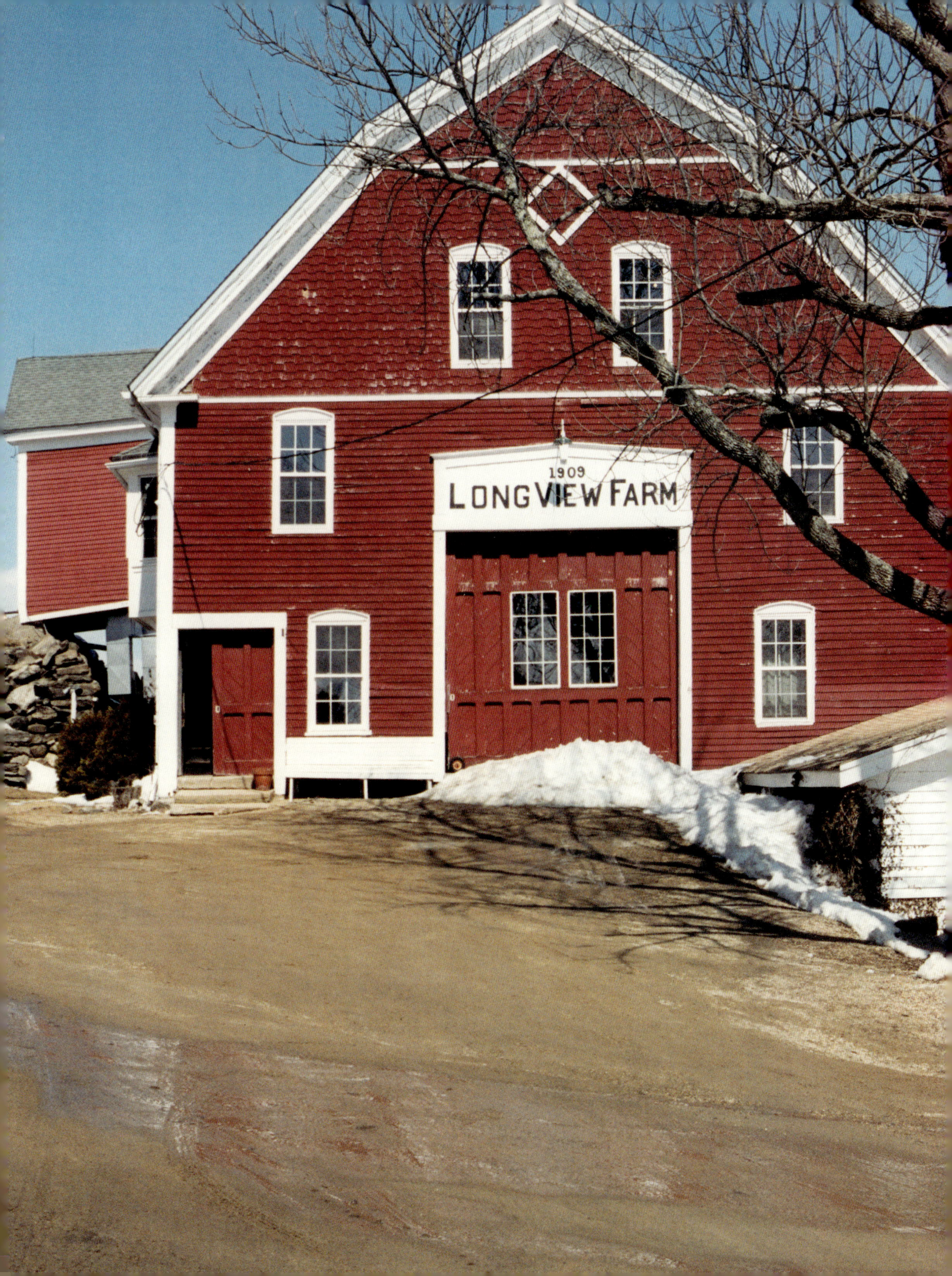
1909
LONGVIEW FARM

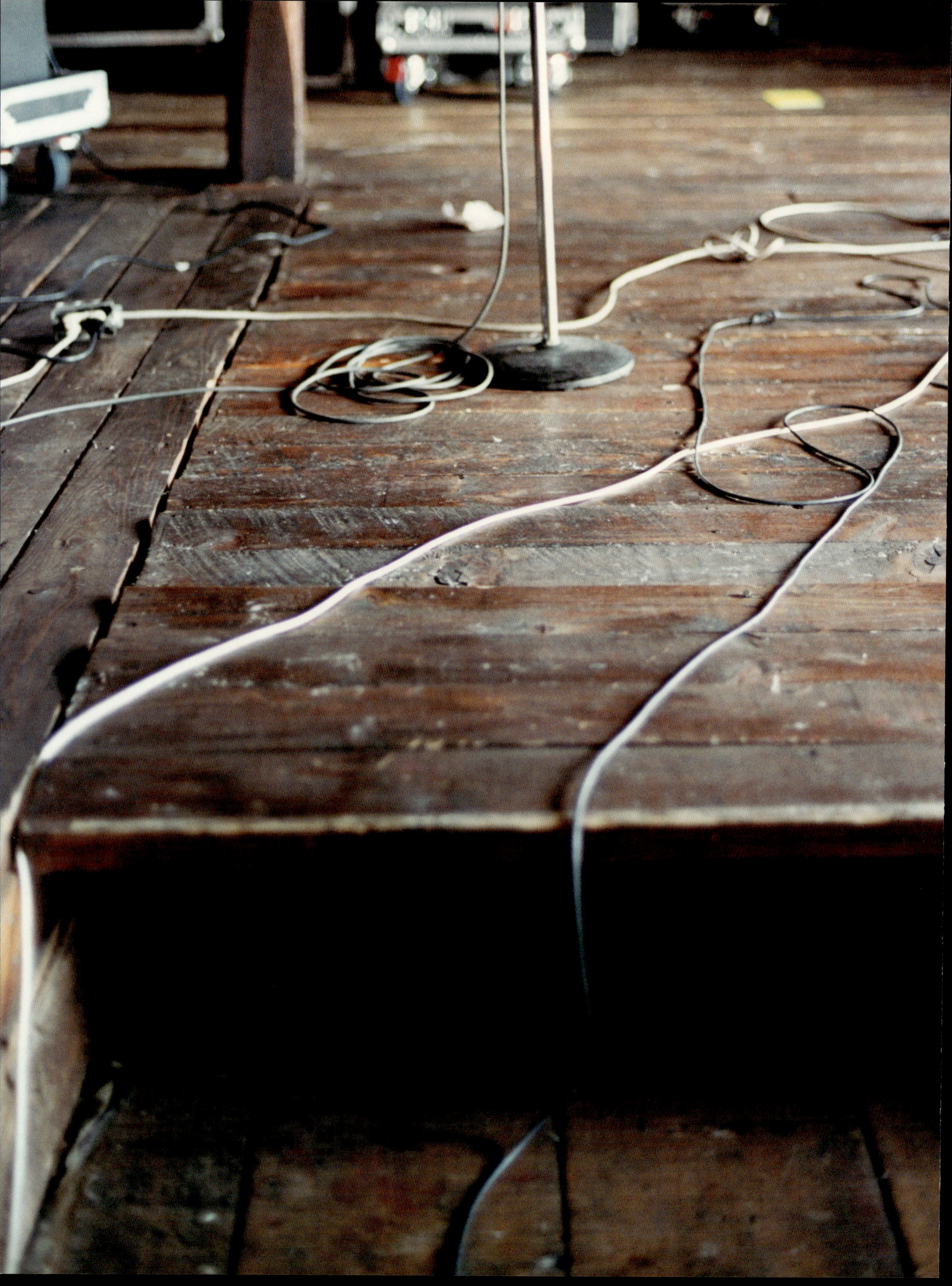

SESSION IN PROGRESS

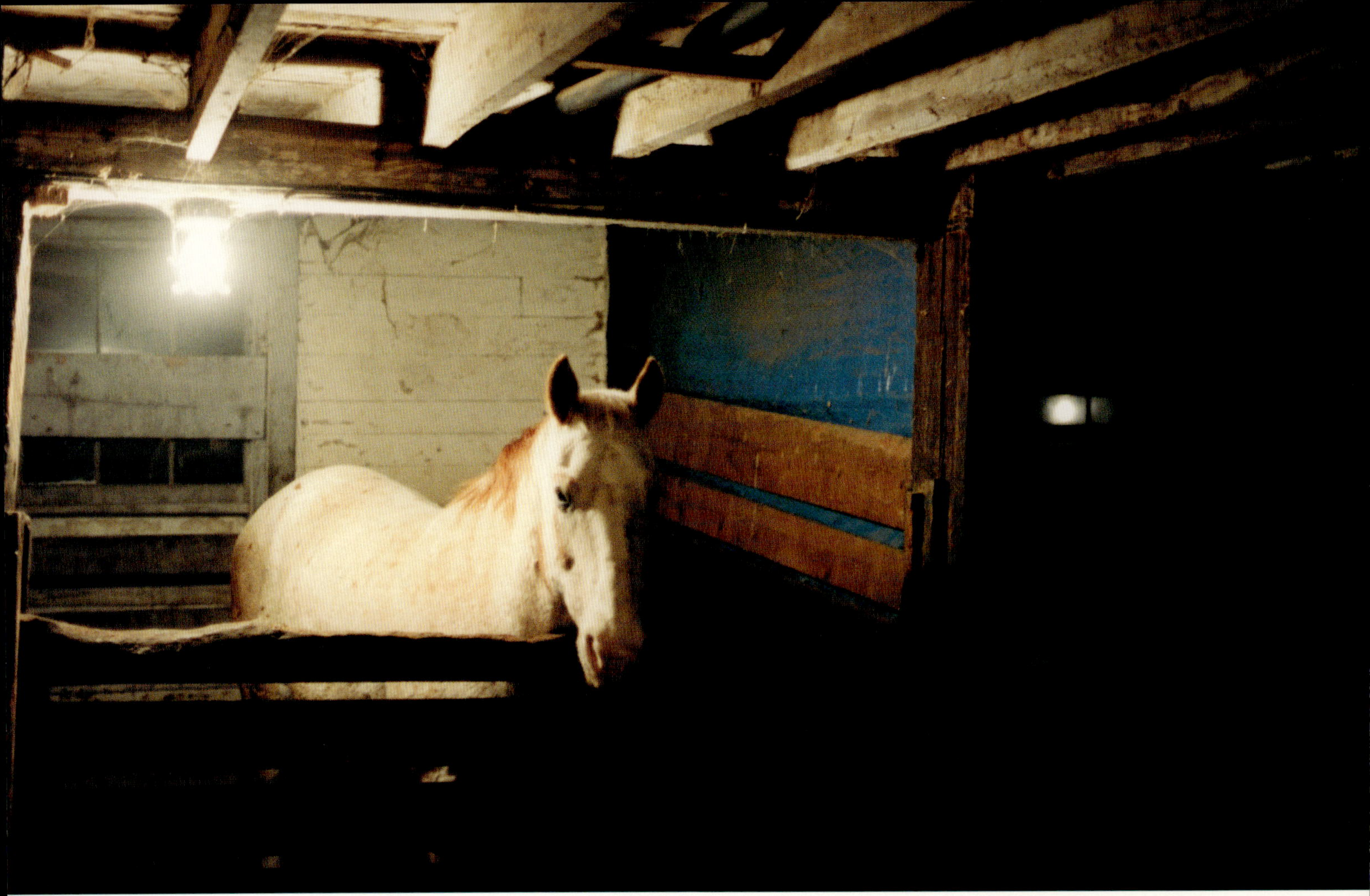

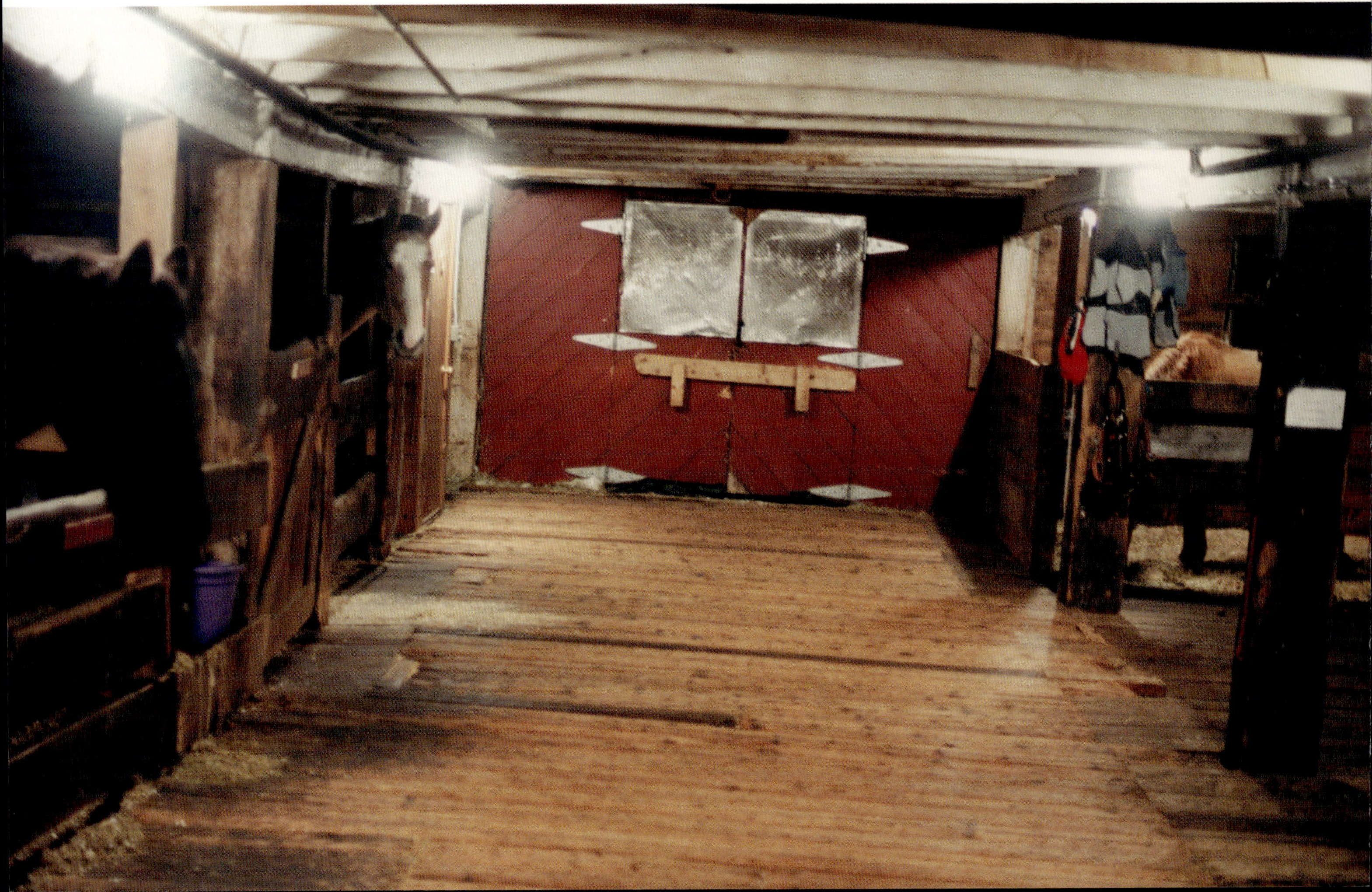

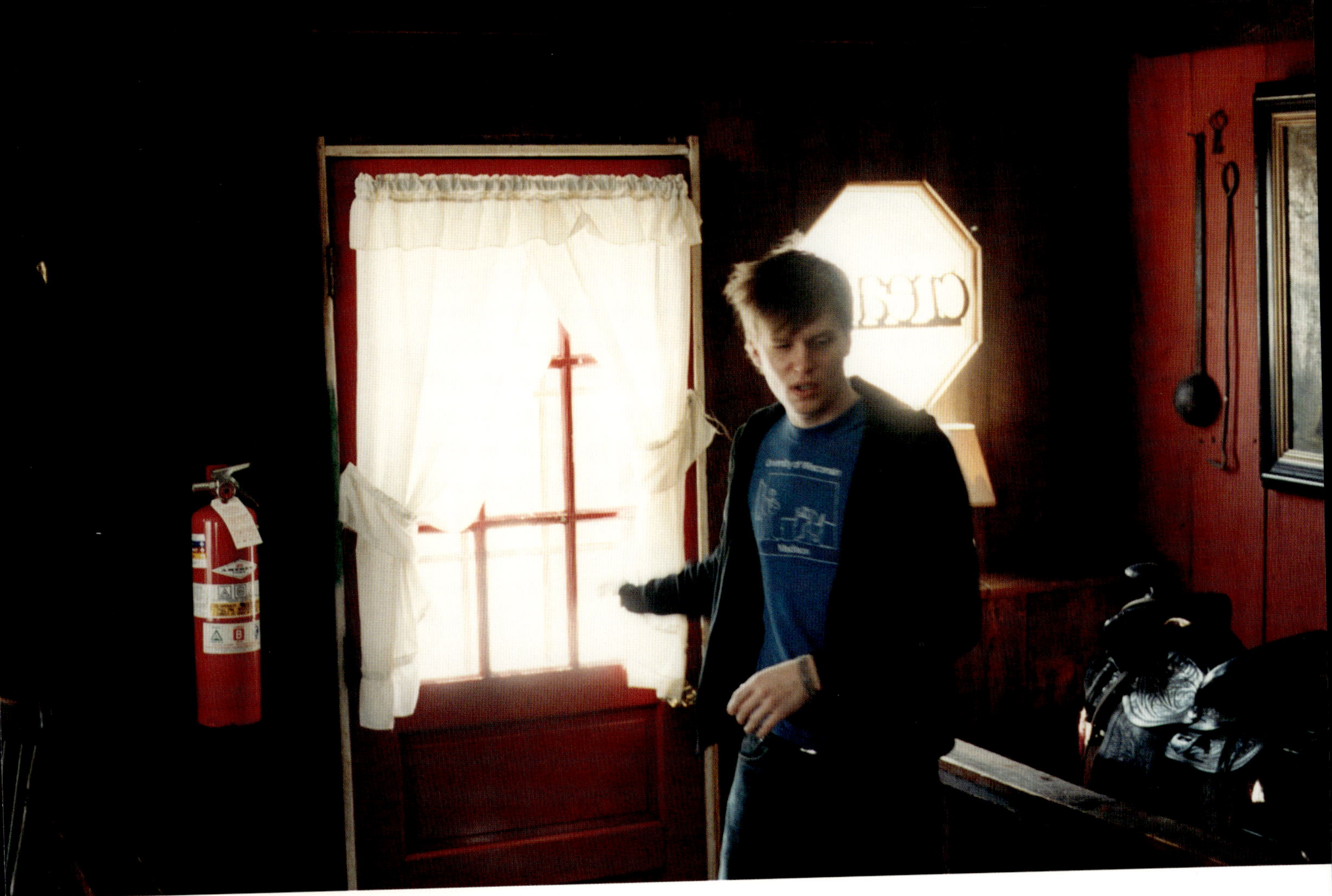

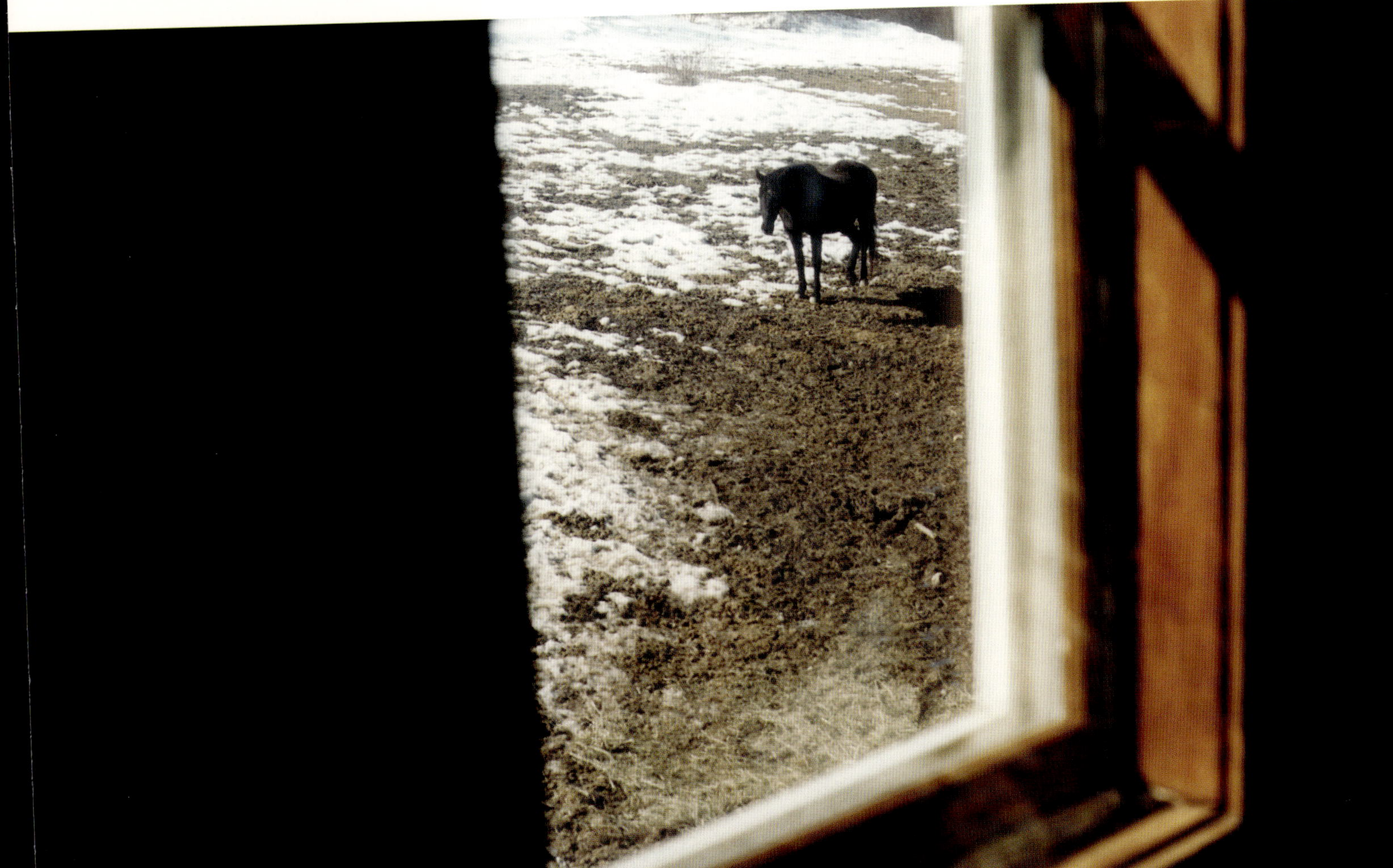

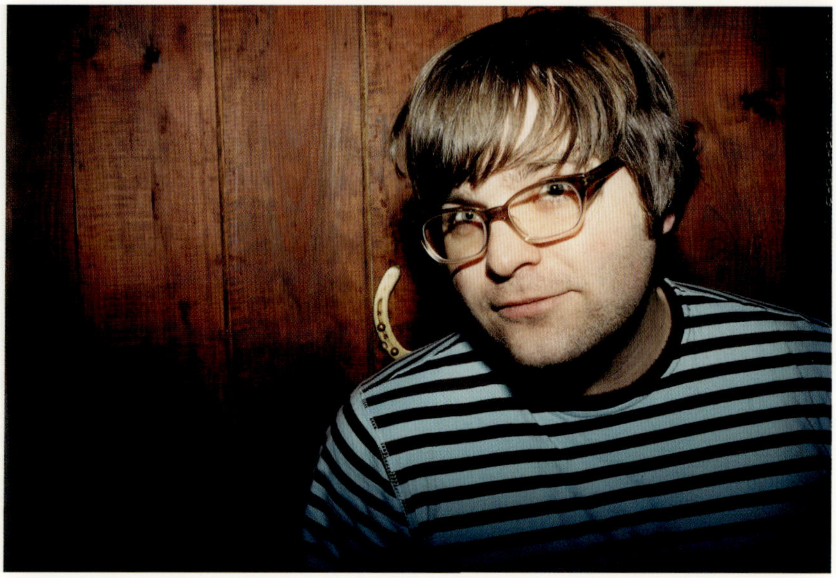

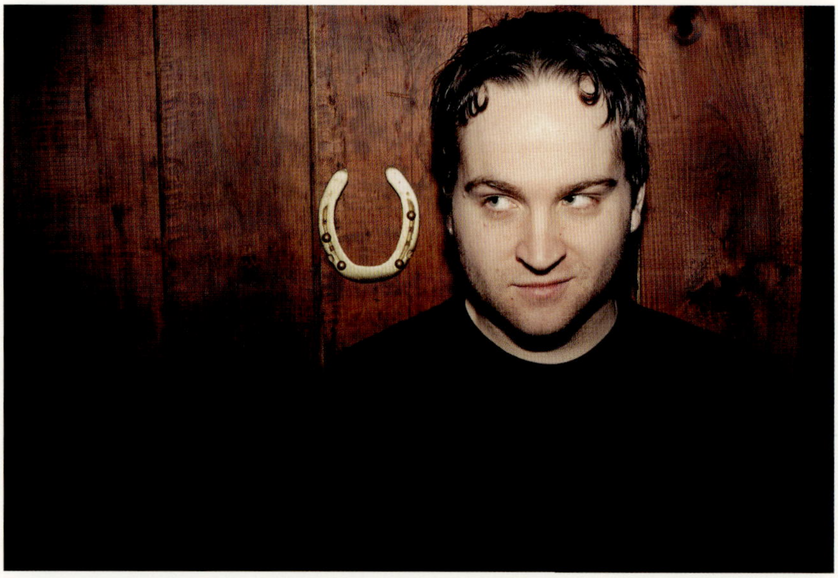

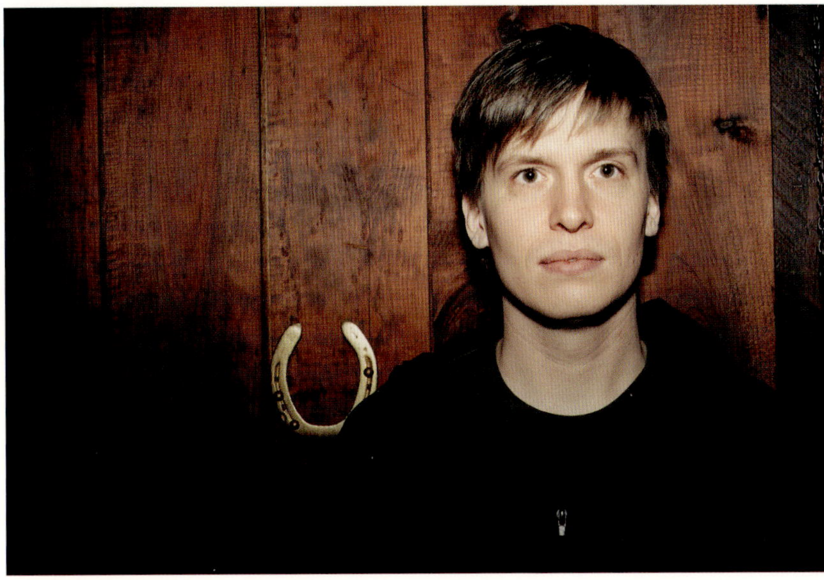

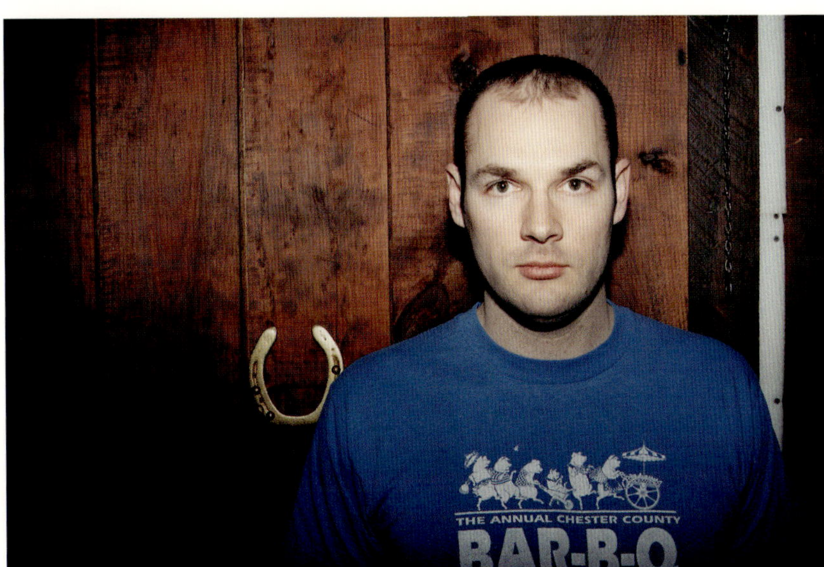
THE ANNUAL CHESTER COUNTY
BAR-B-Q

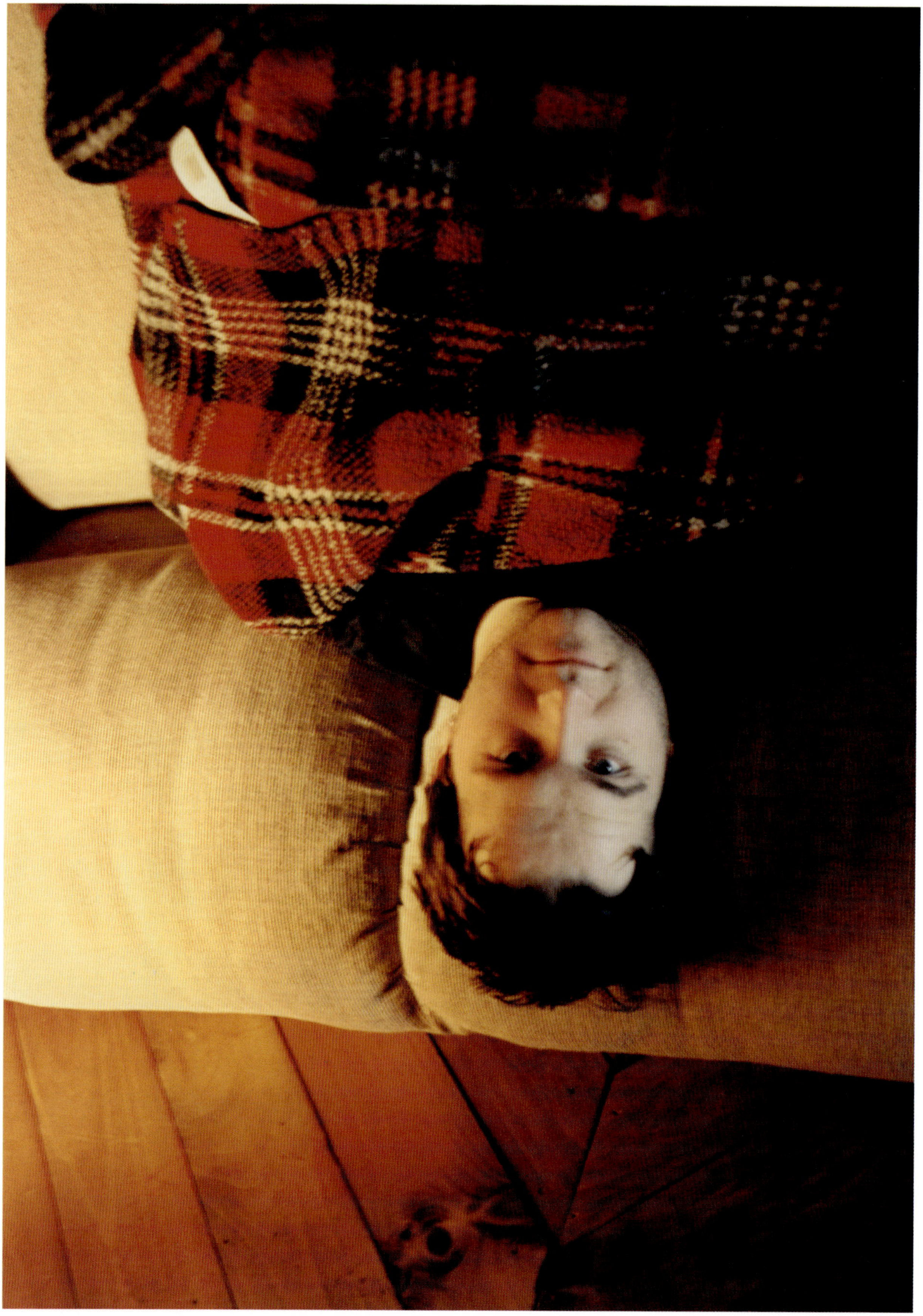

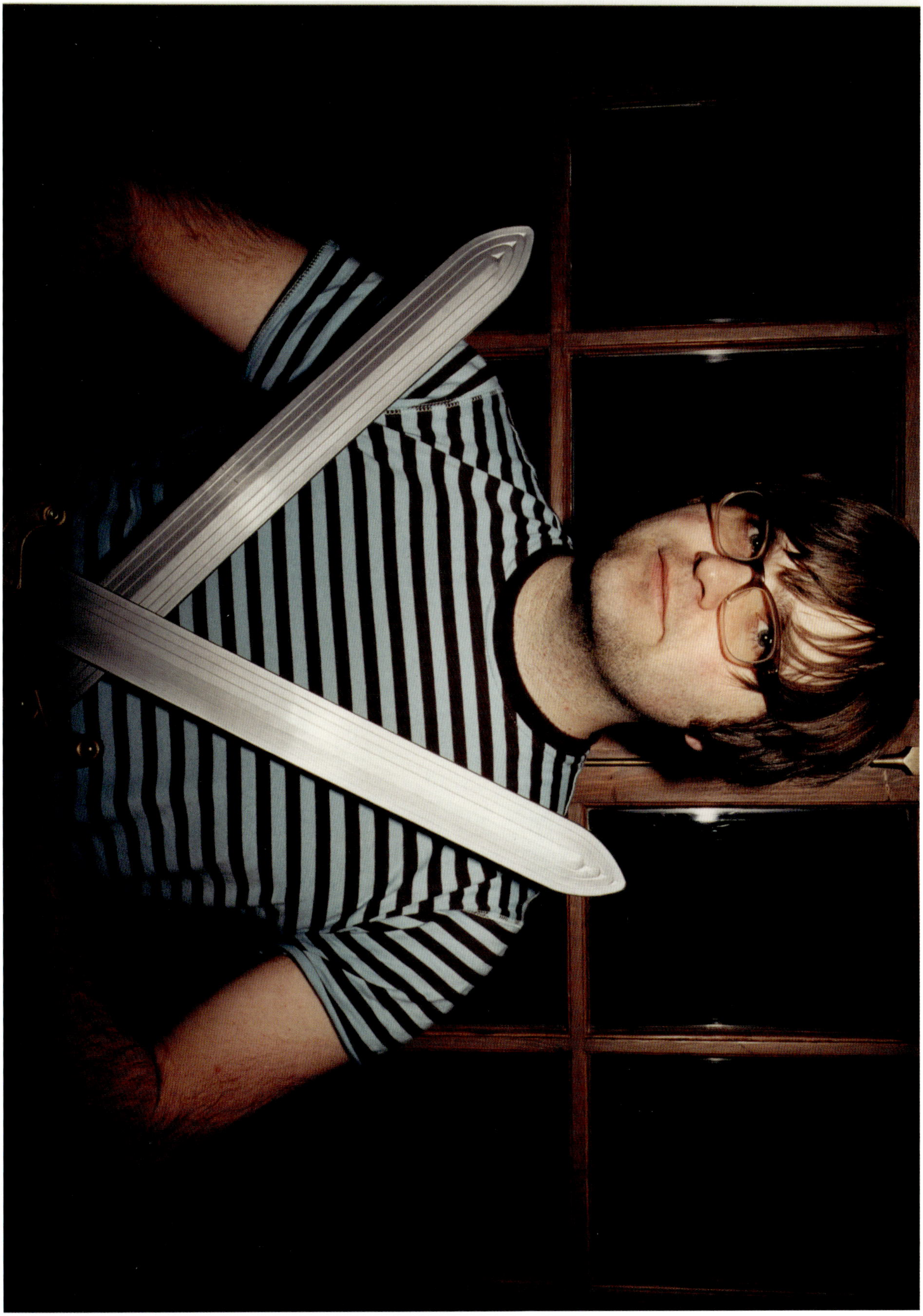

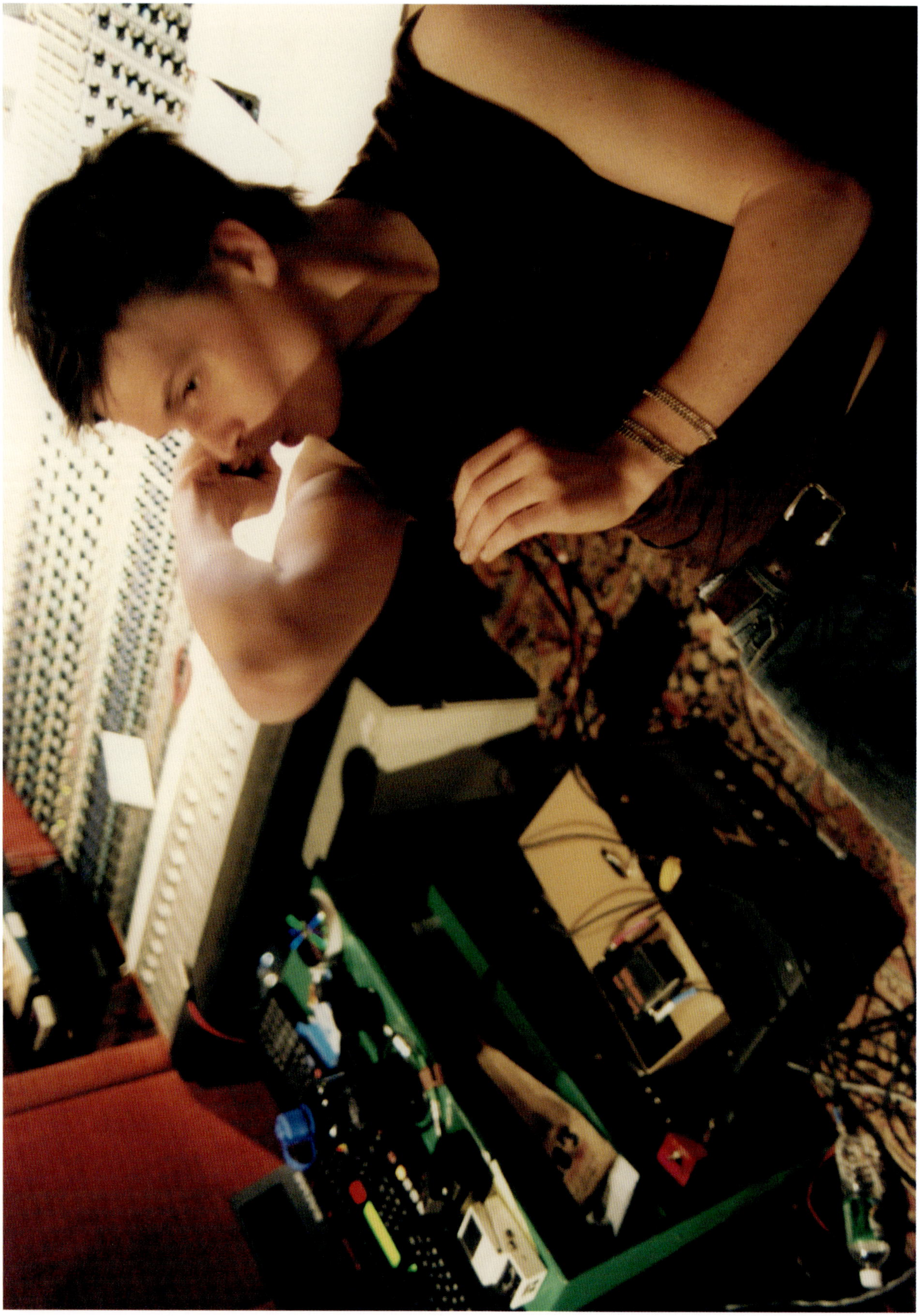

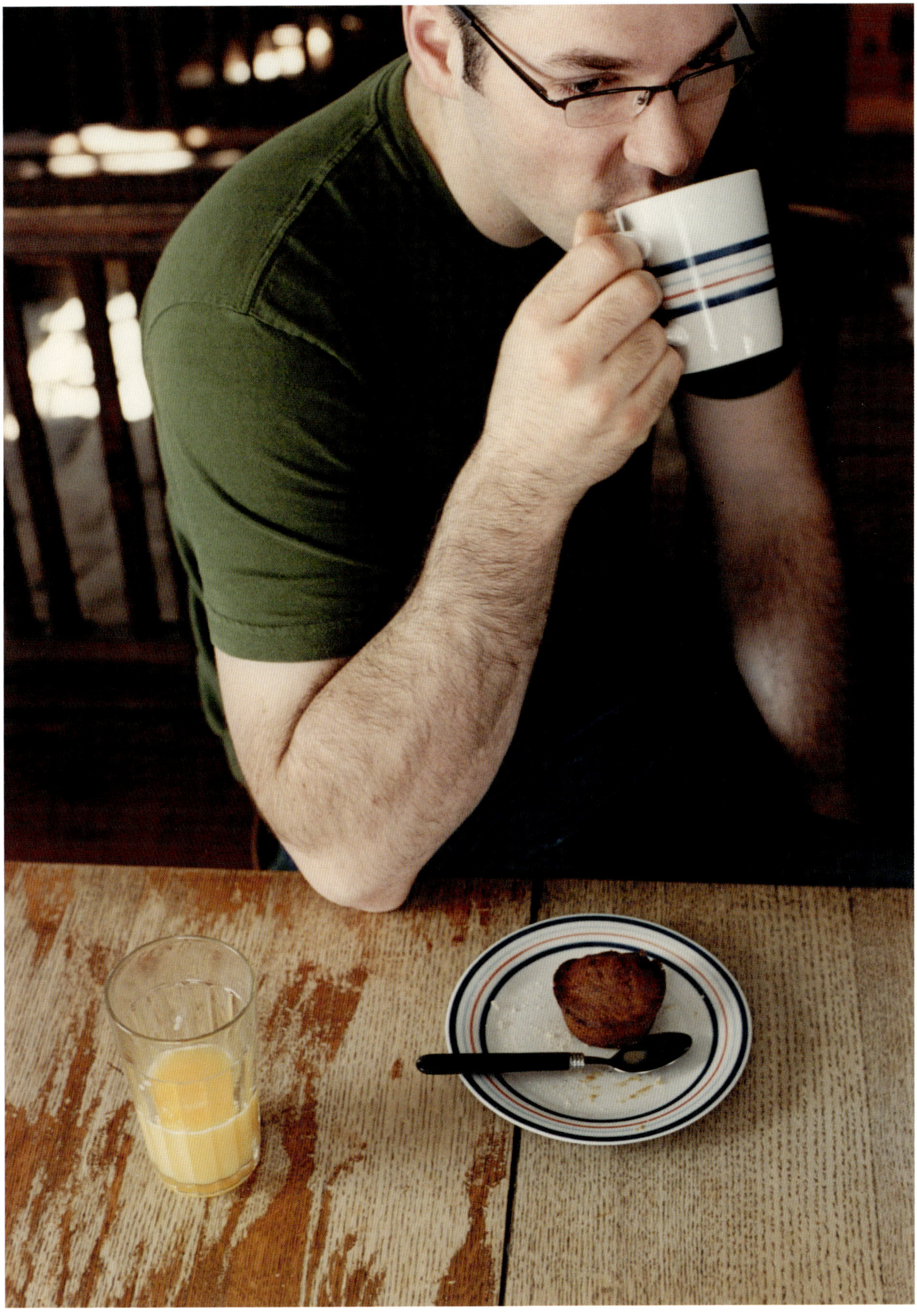

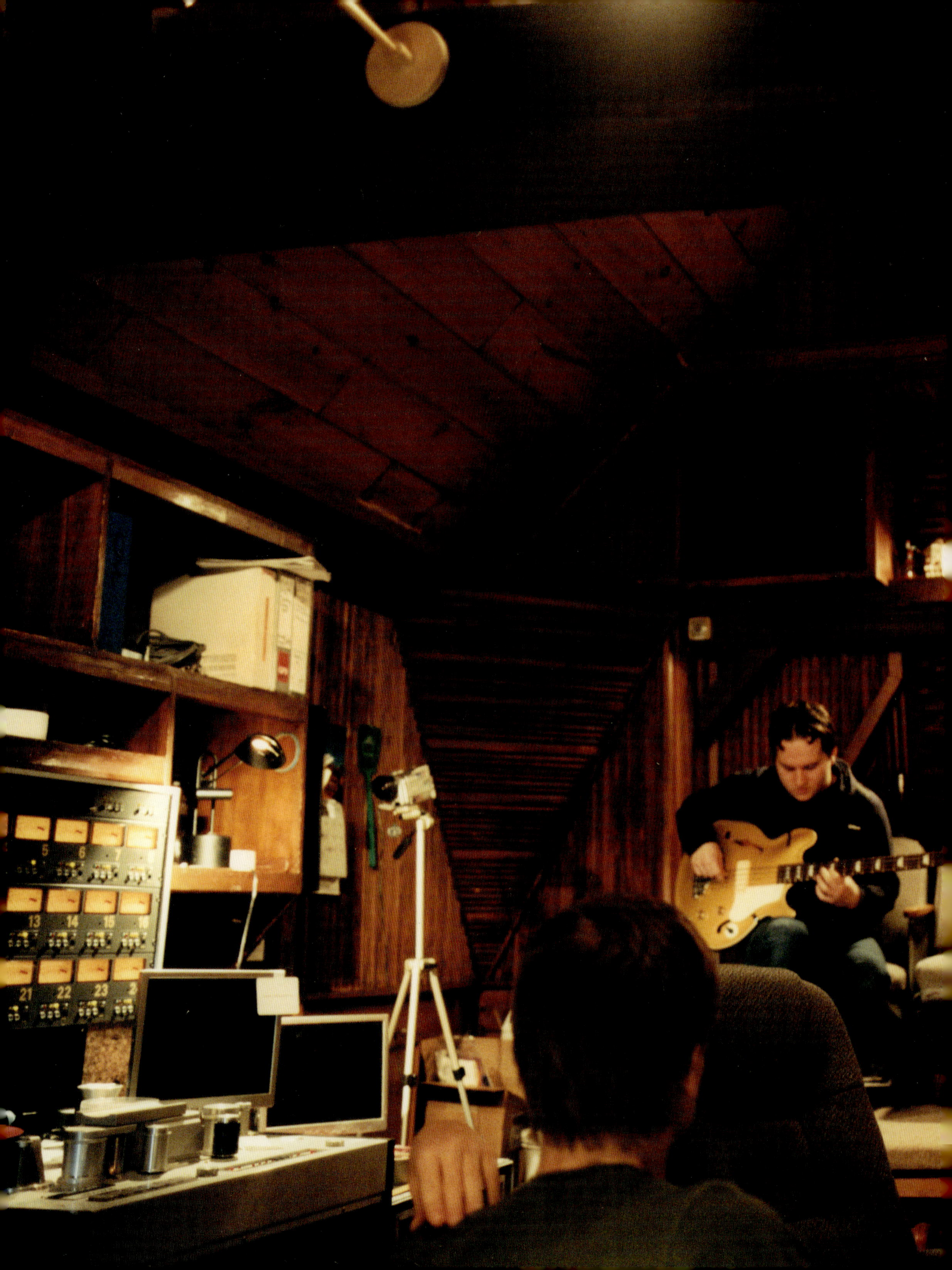
5 6 7
13 14 15 16
21 22 23

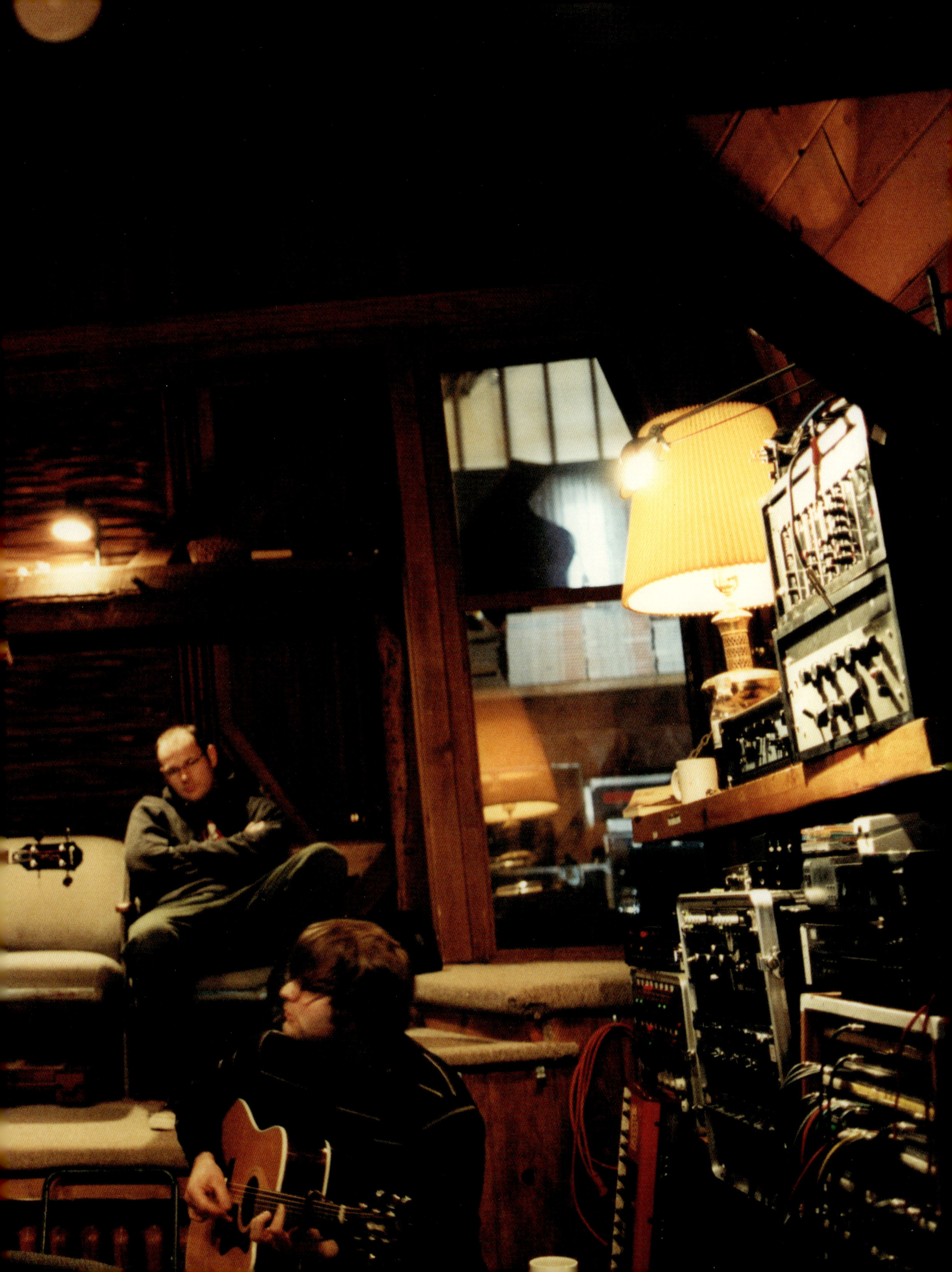

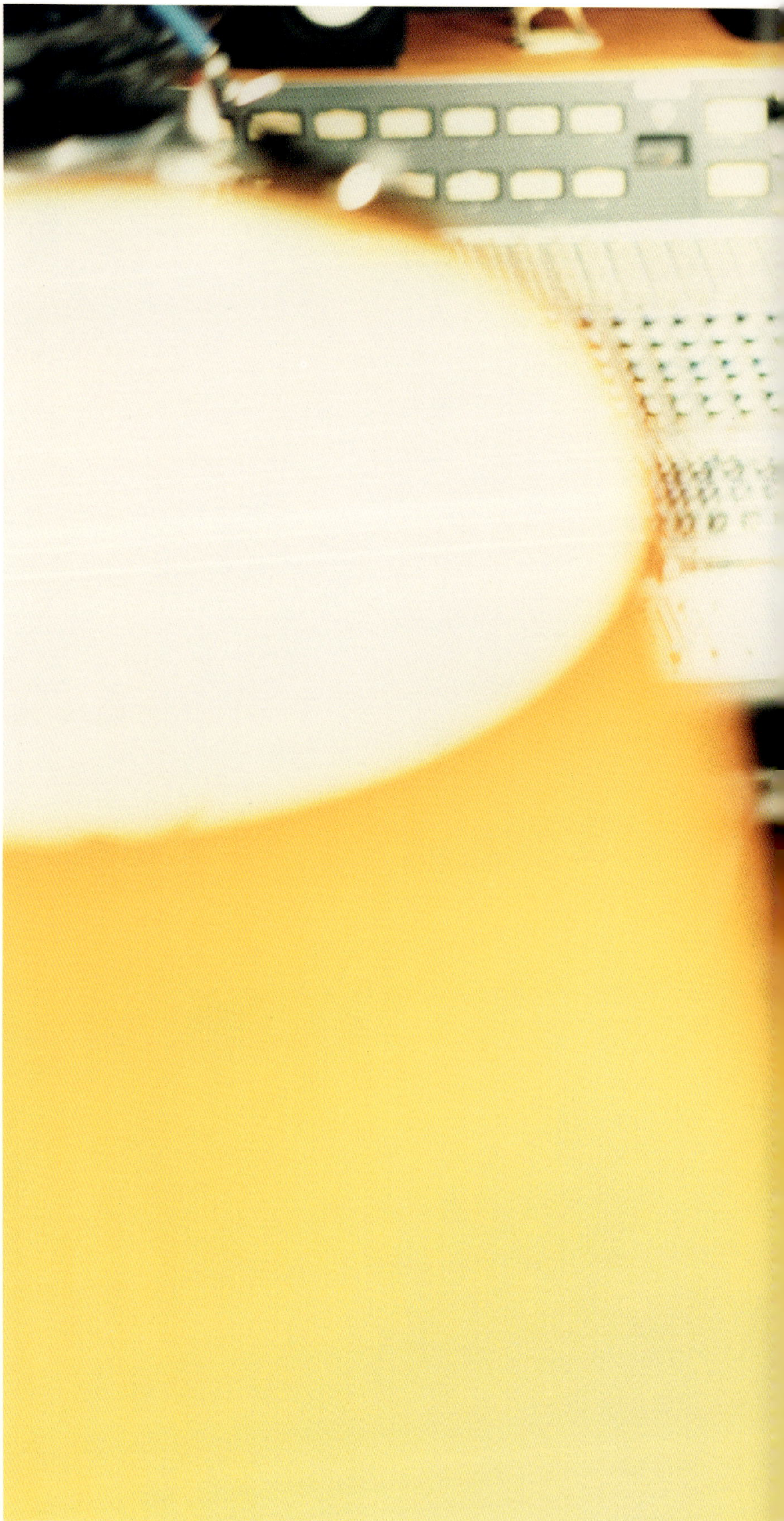

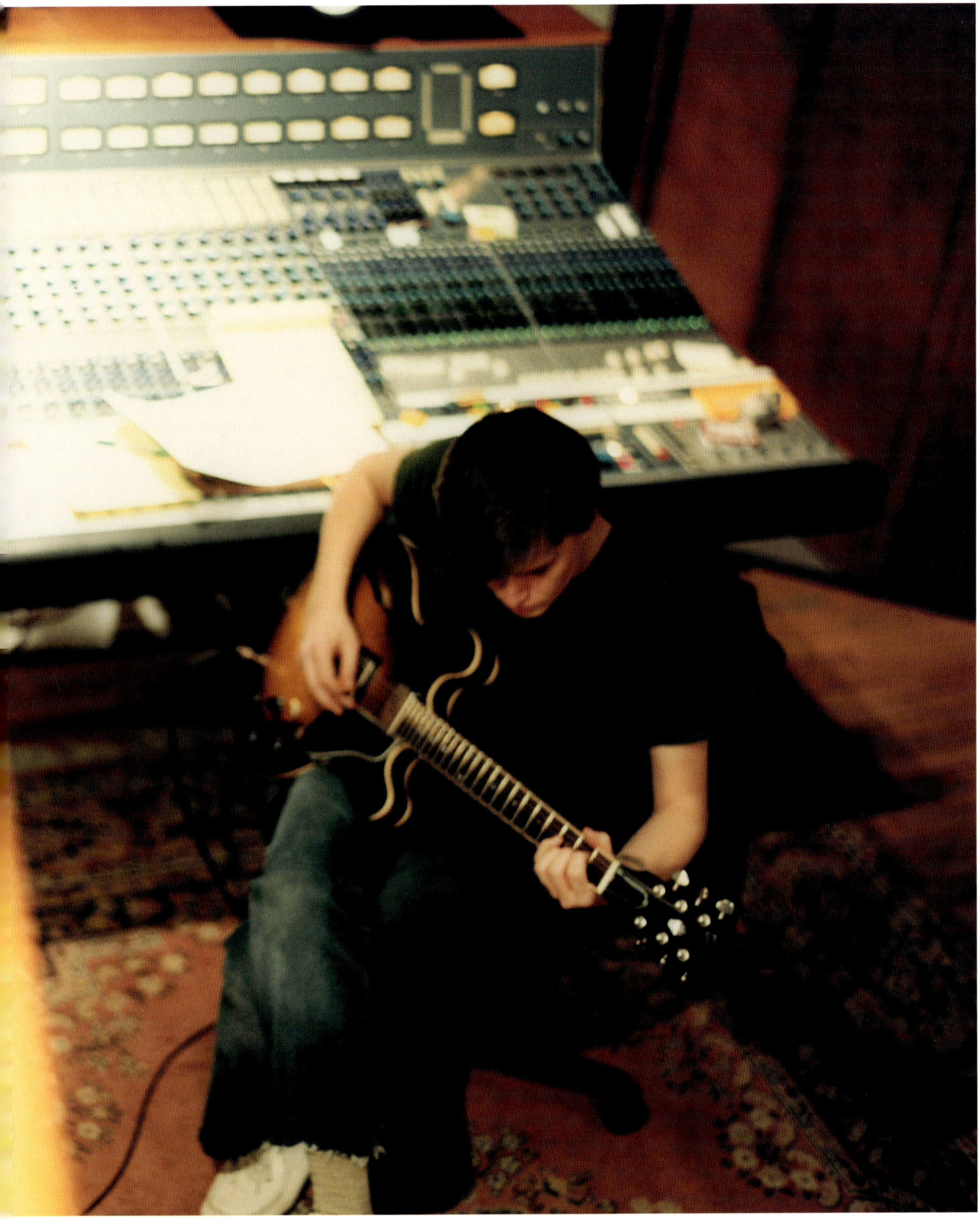

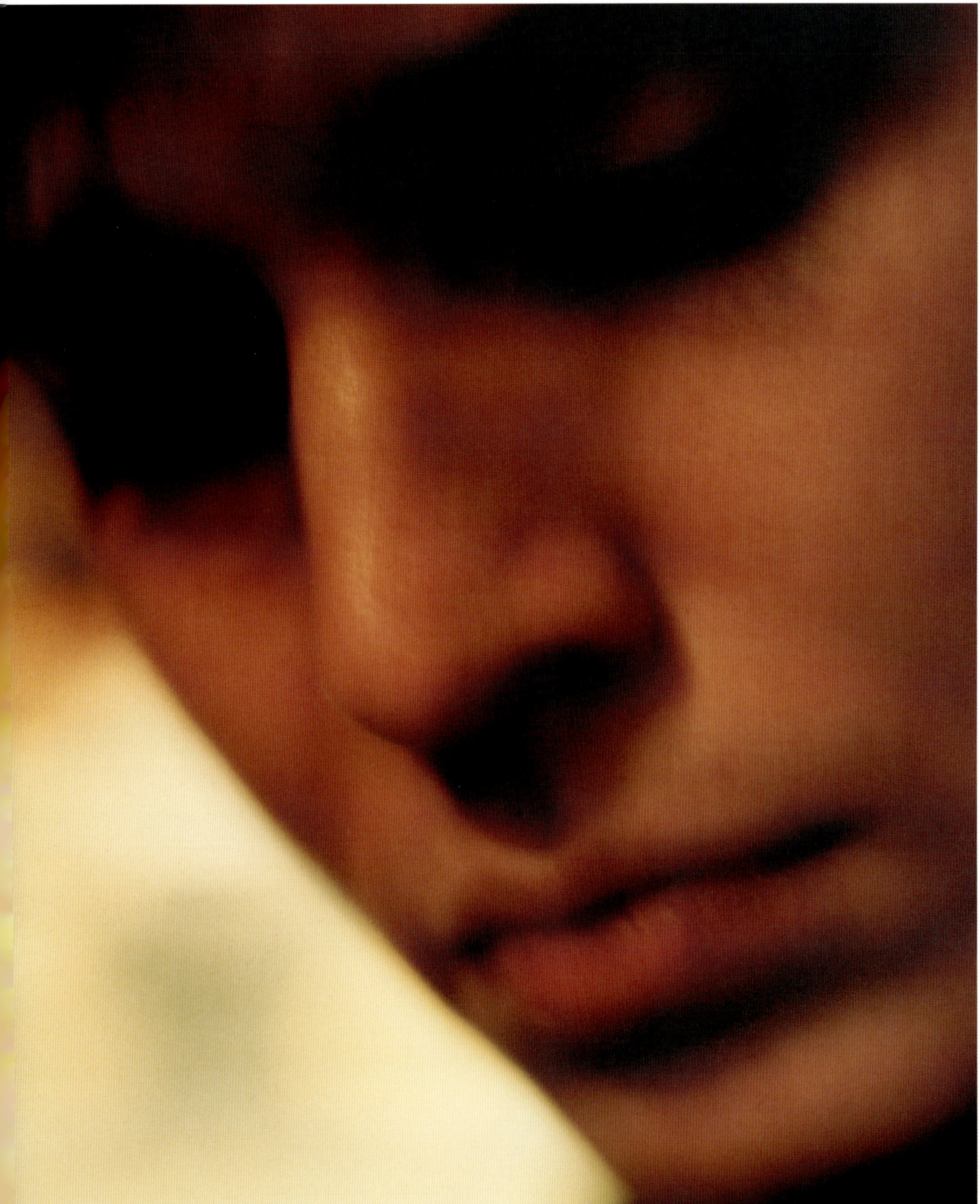

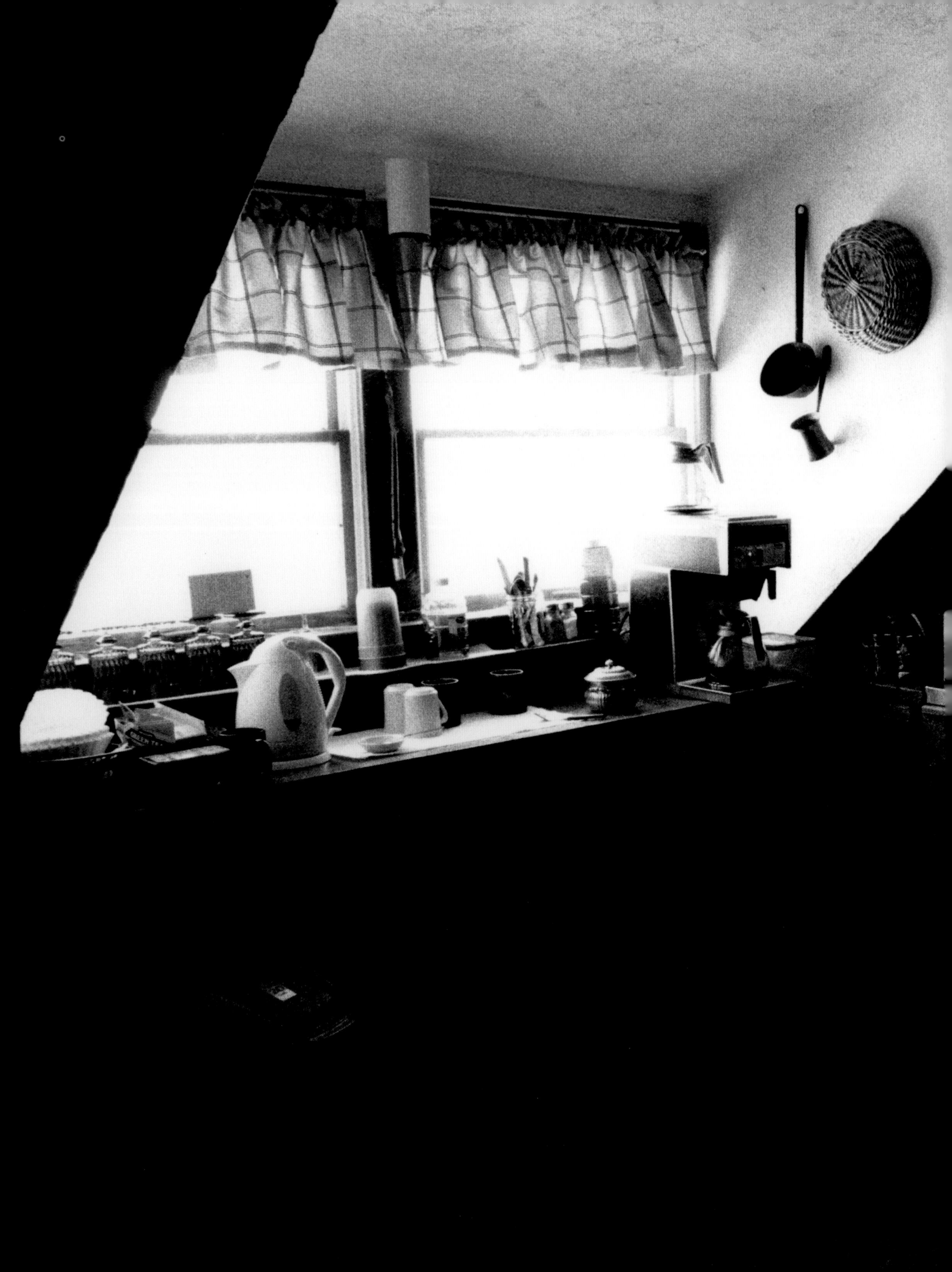

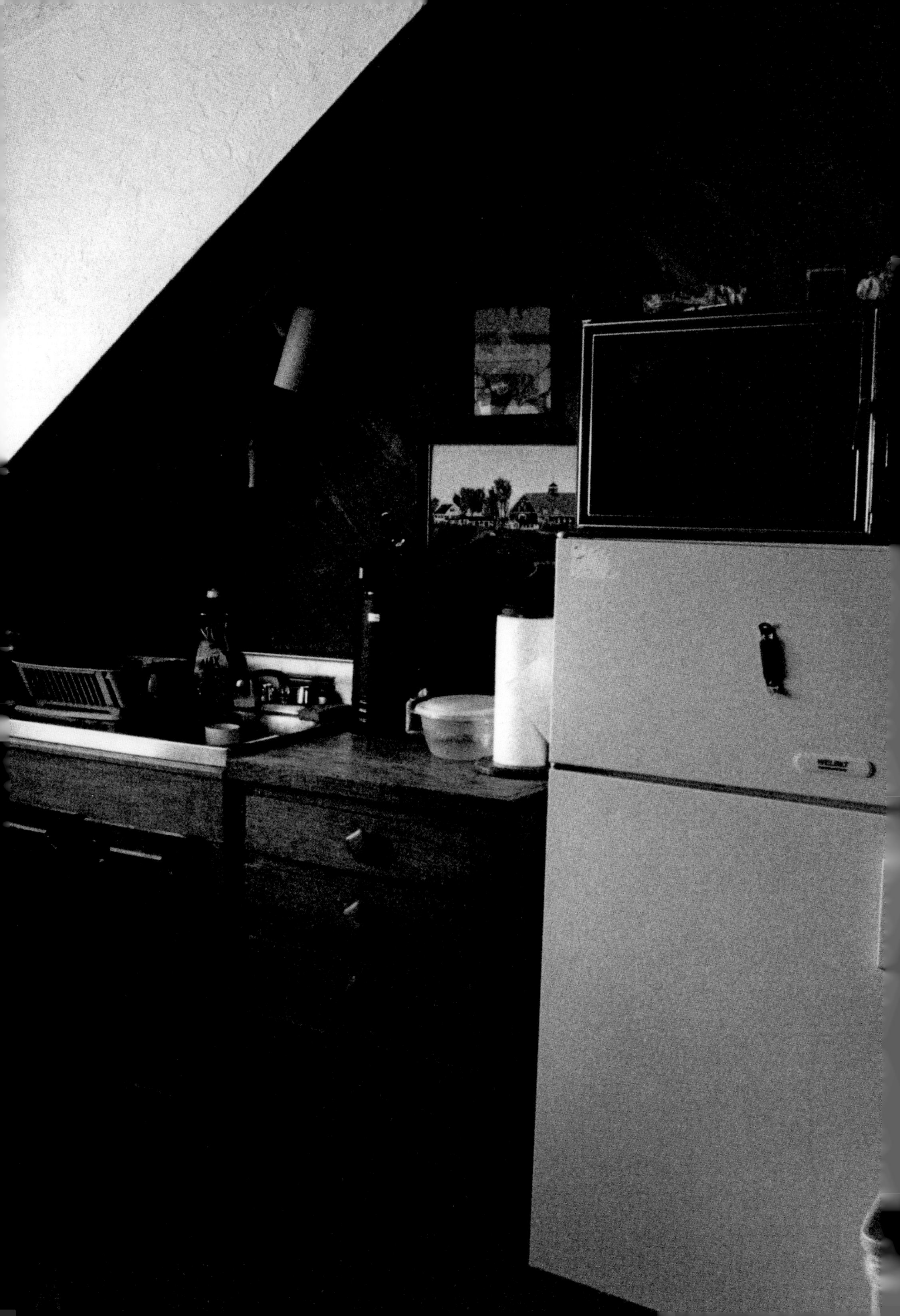

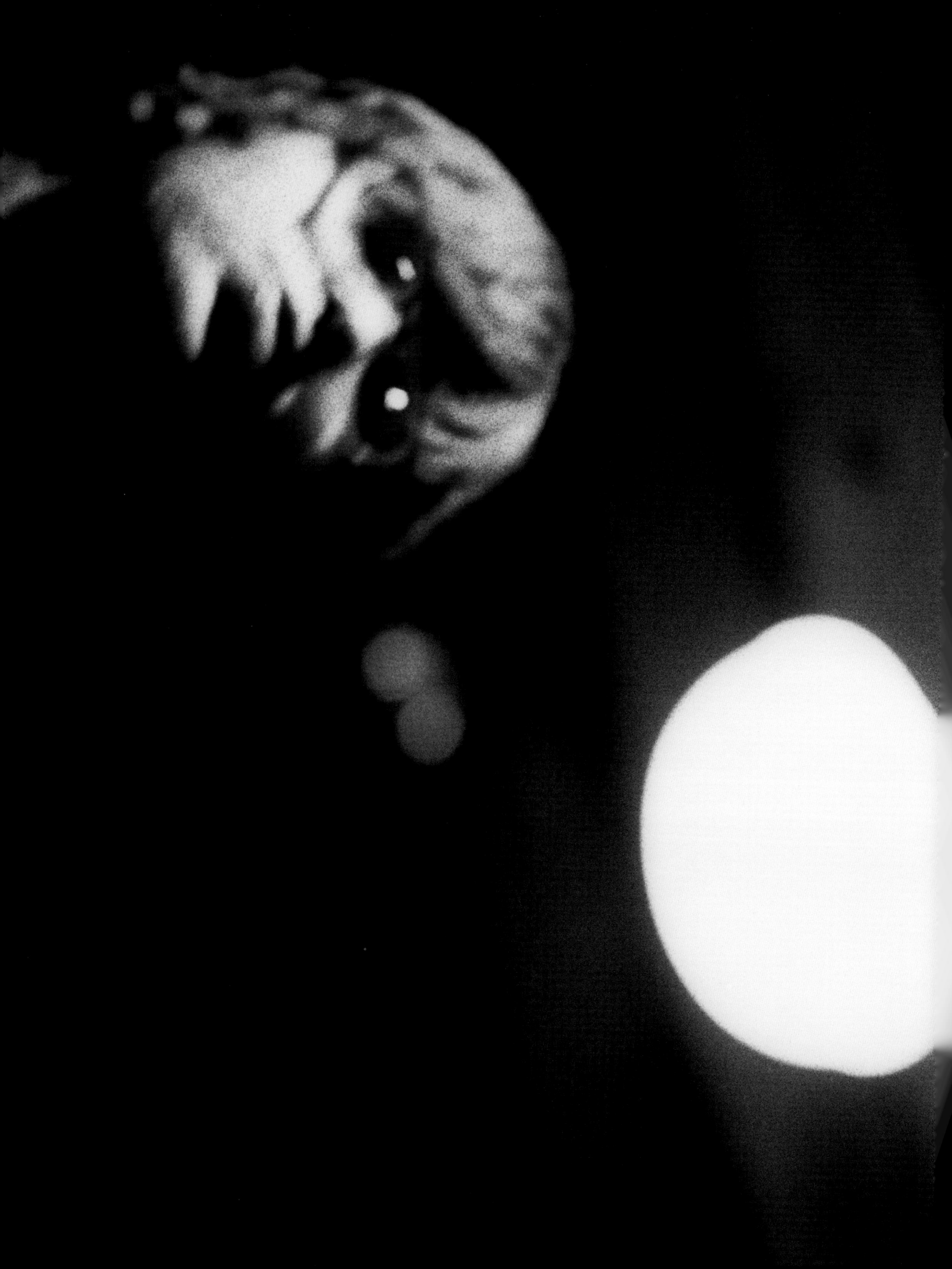

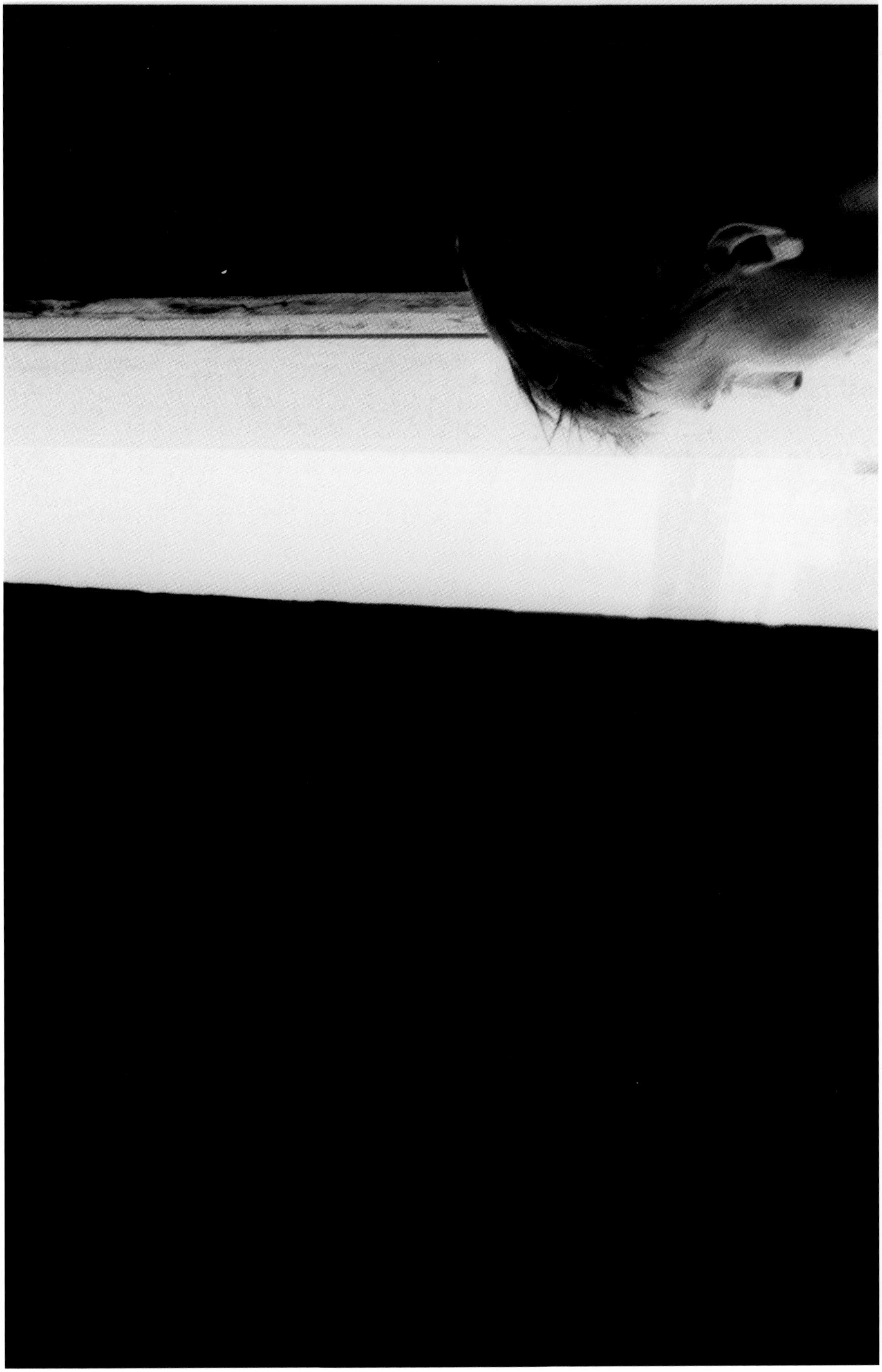

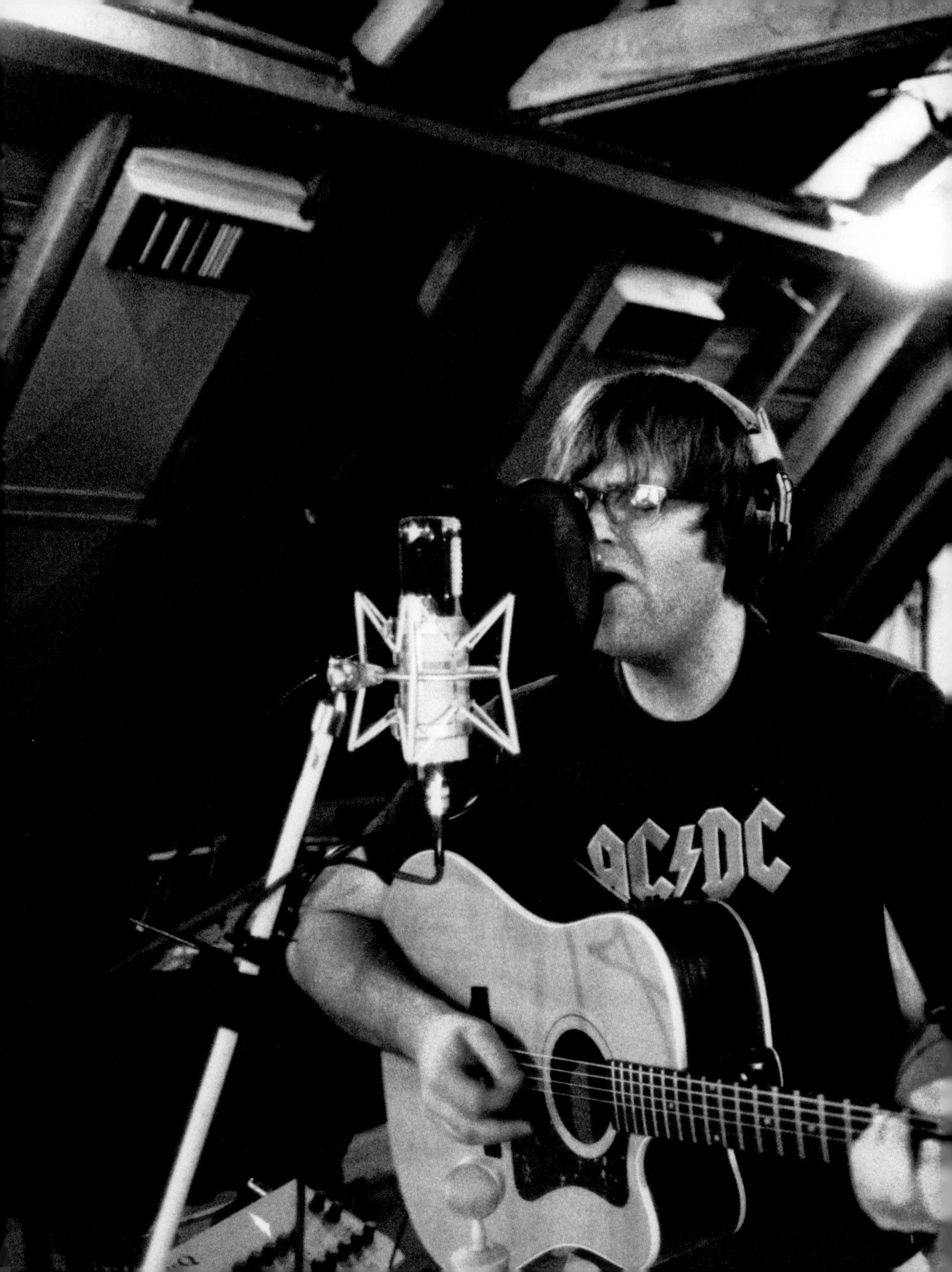
AC/DC

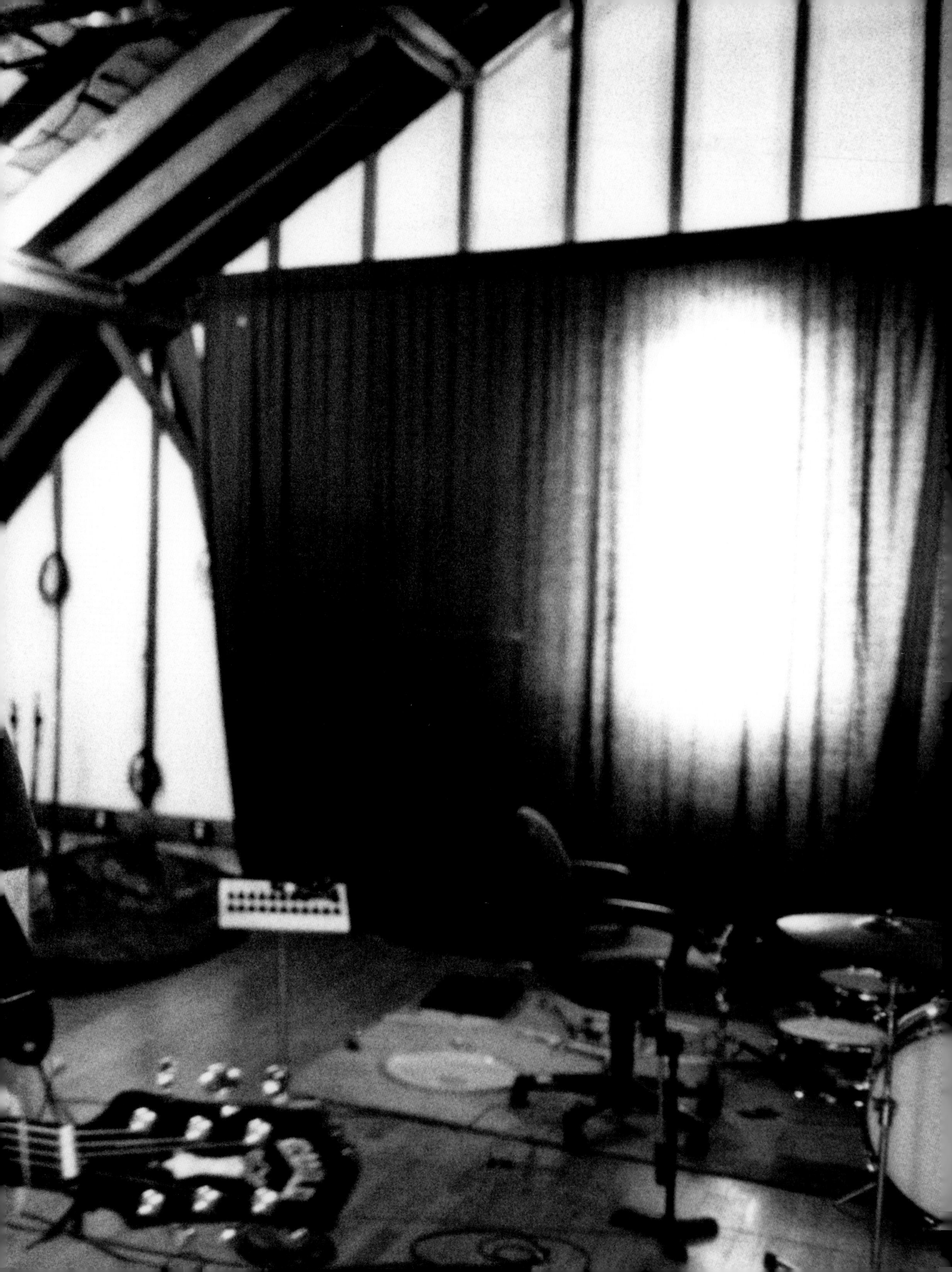

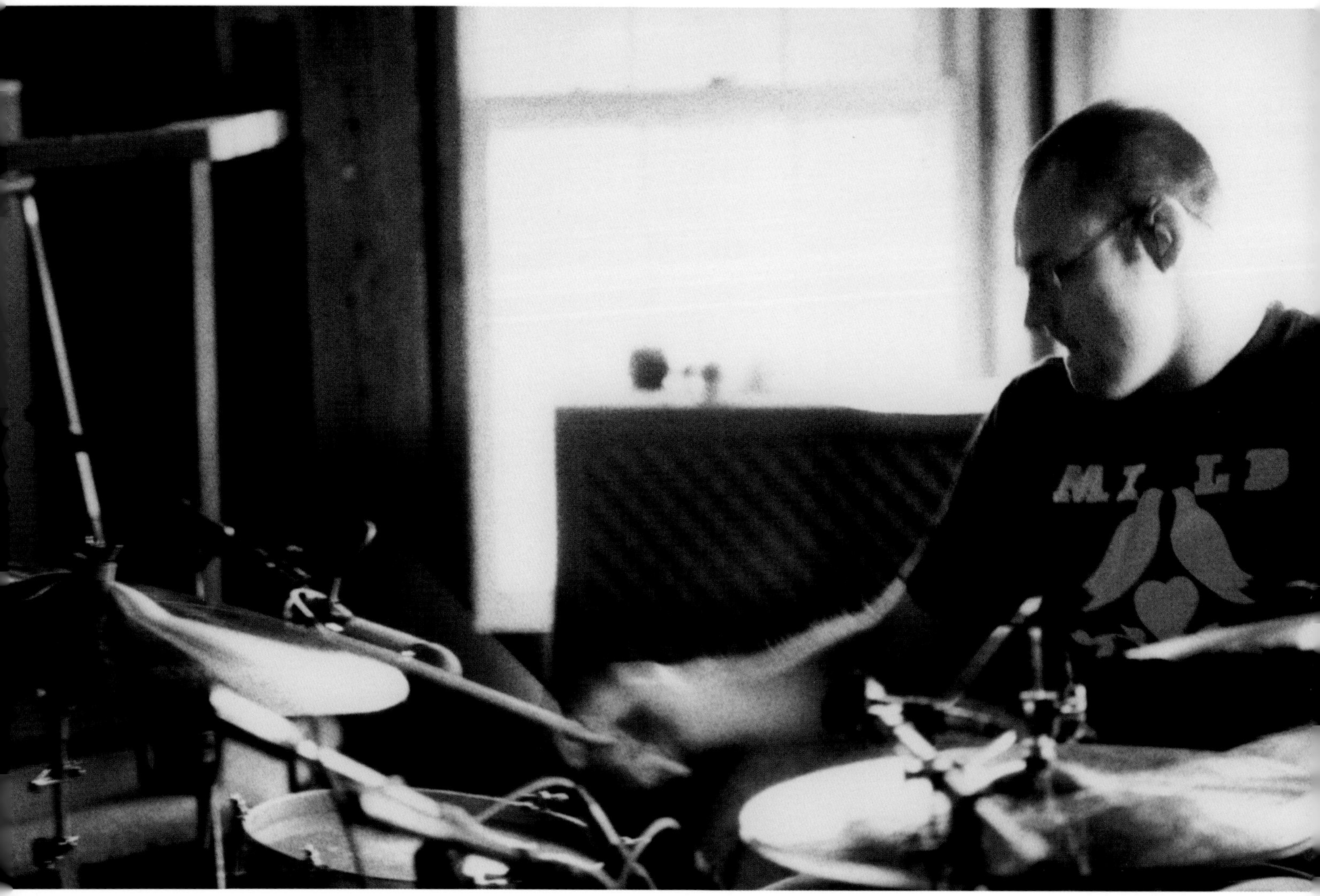

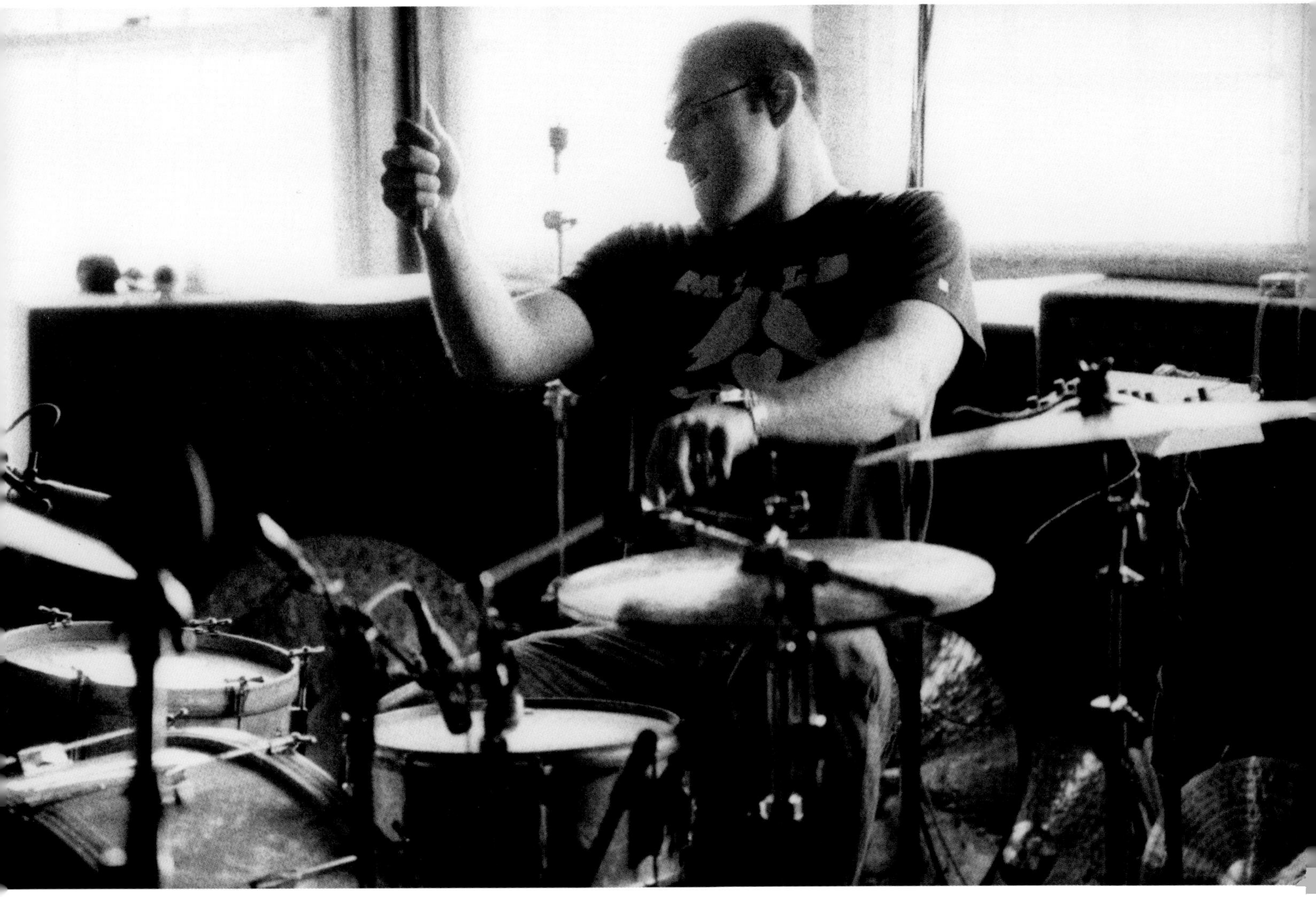

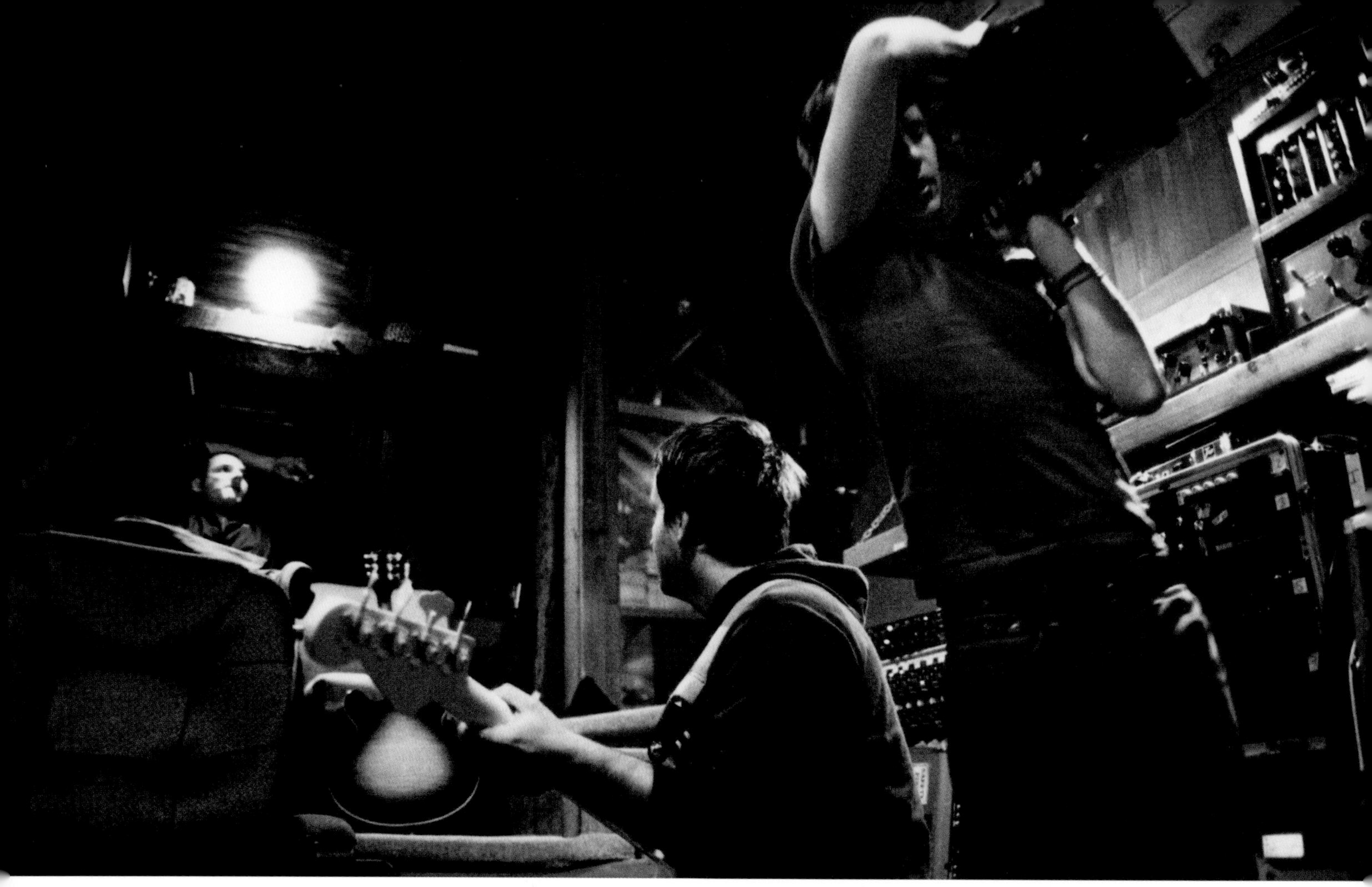

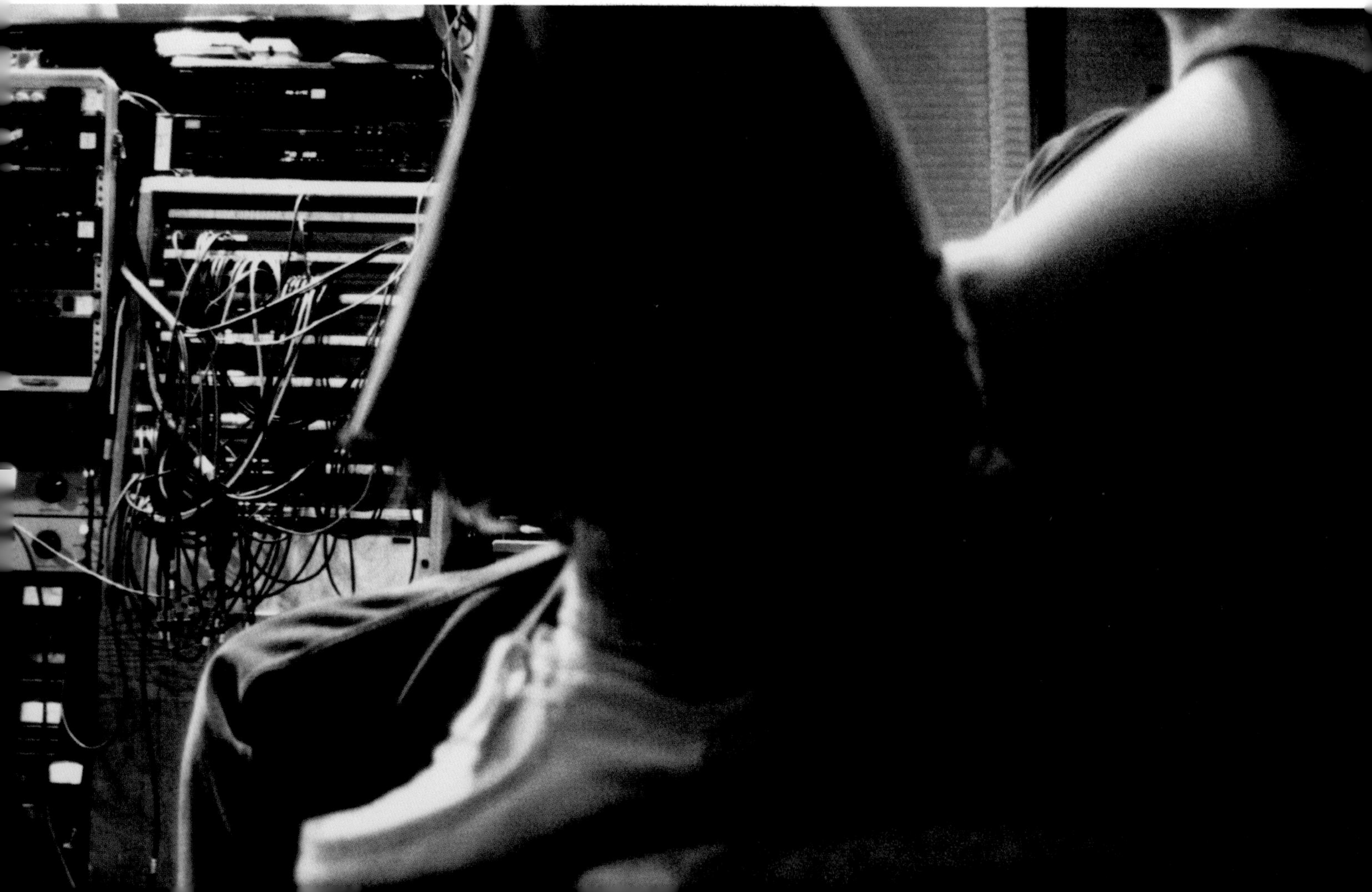

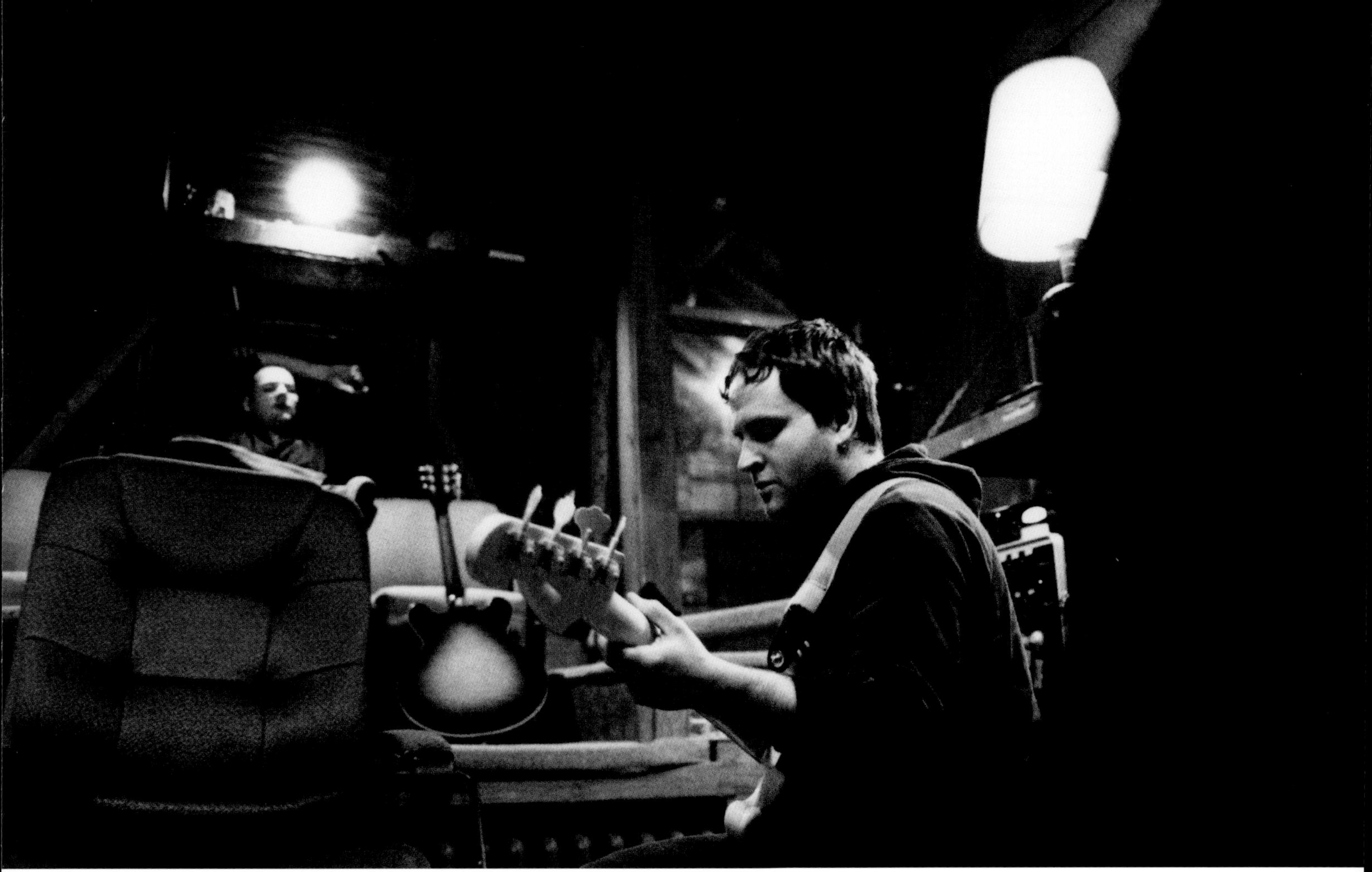

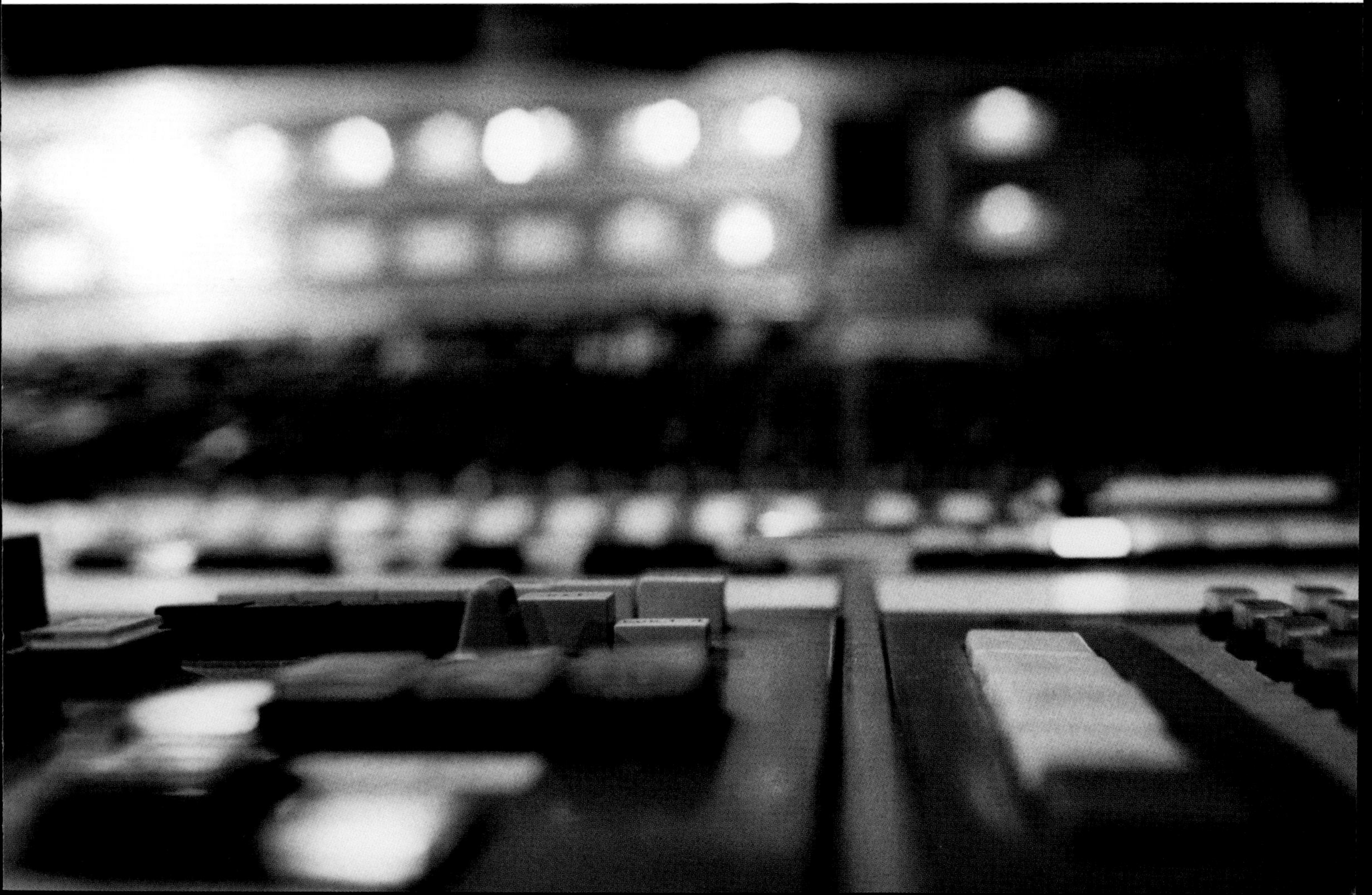

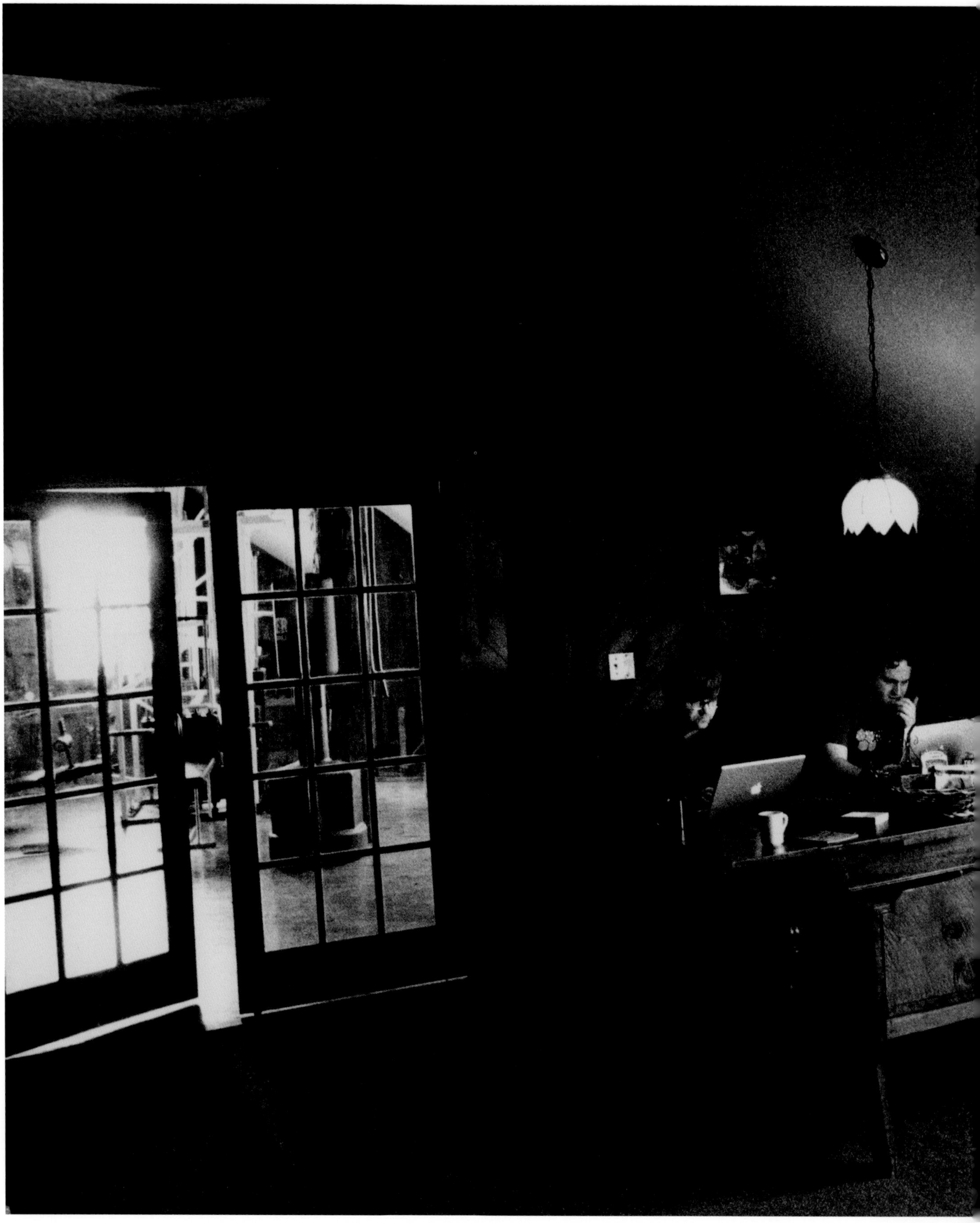

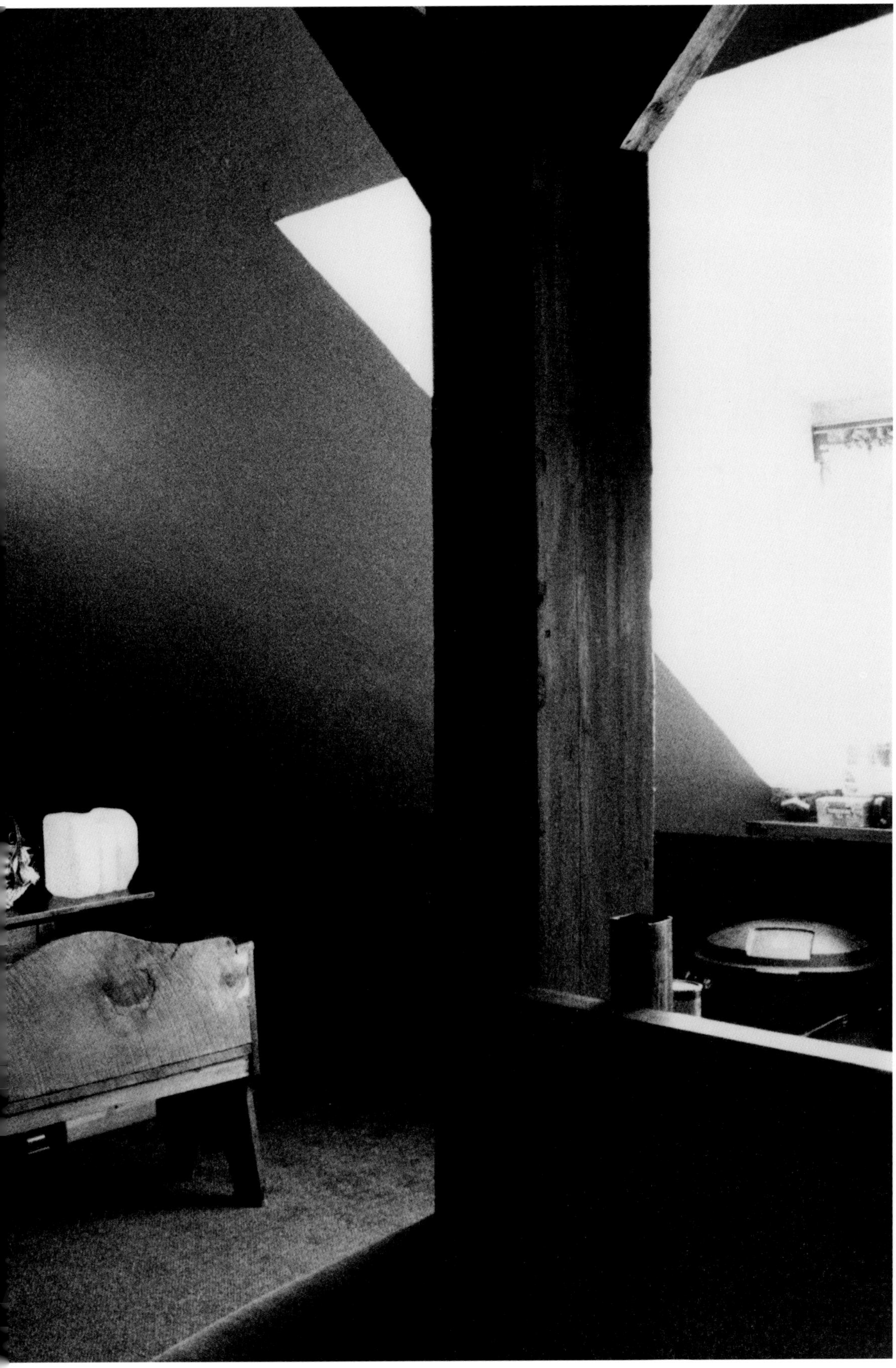

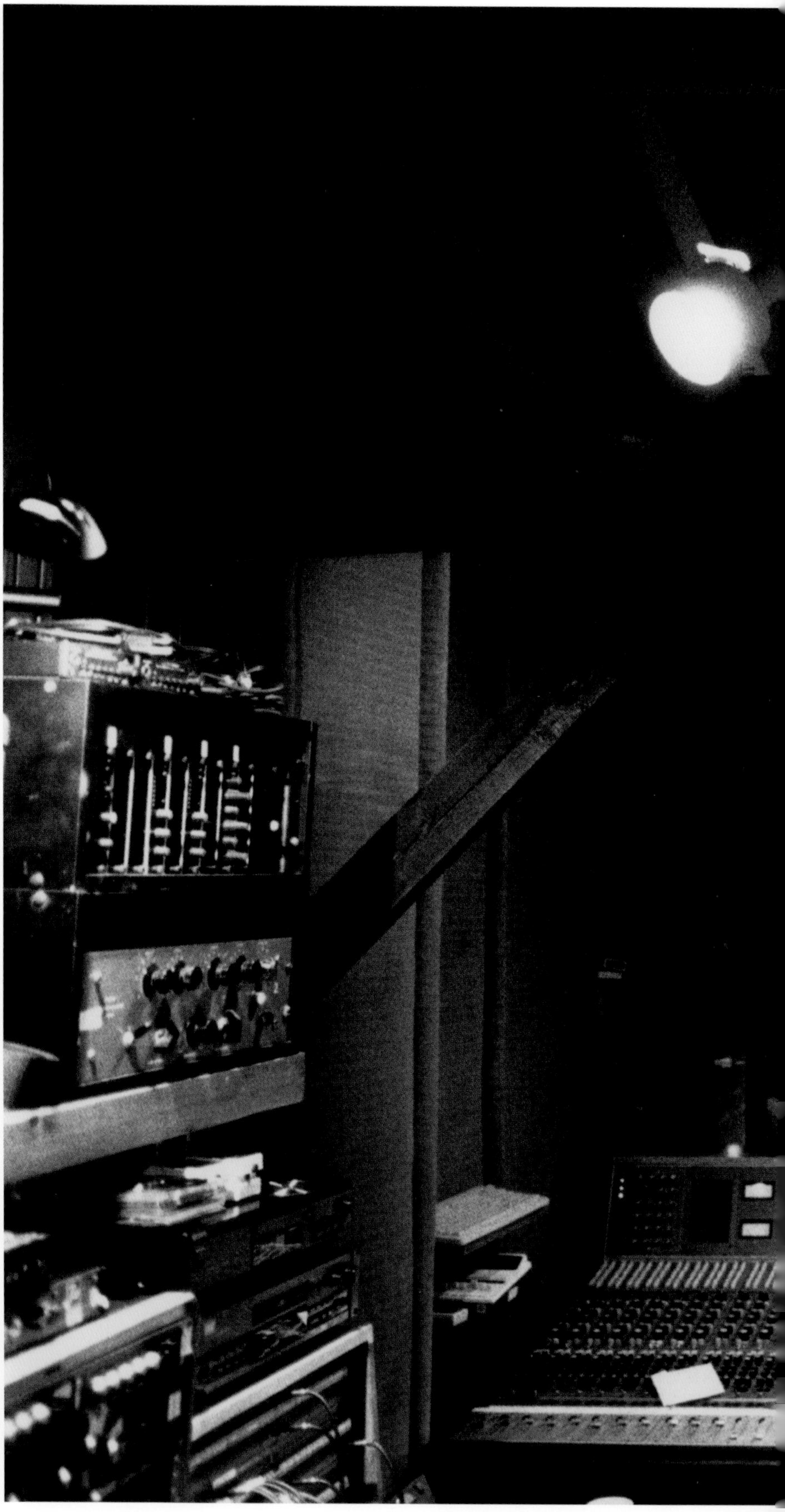

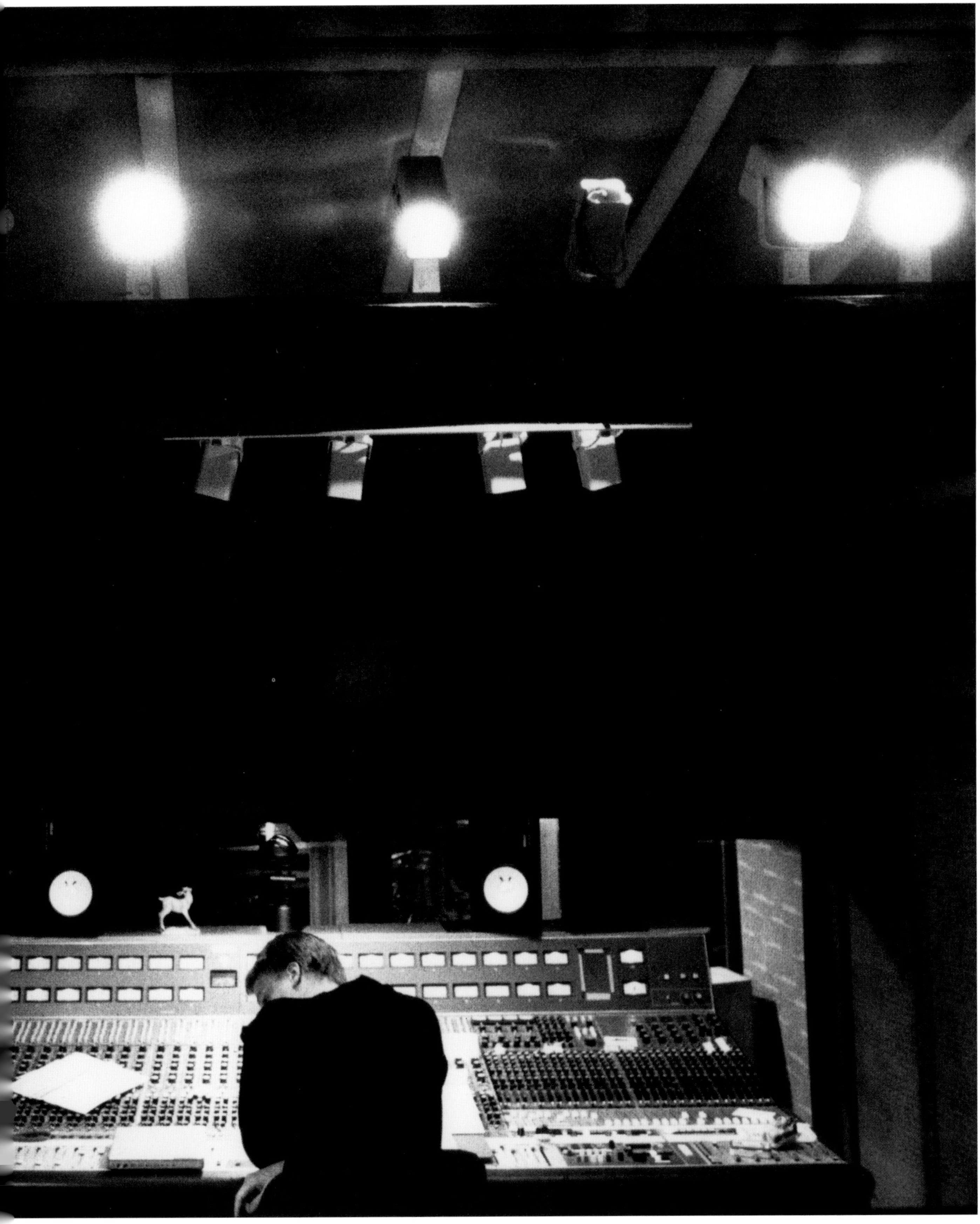

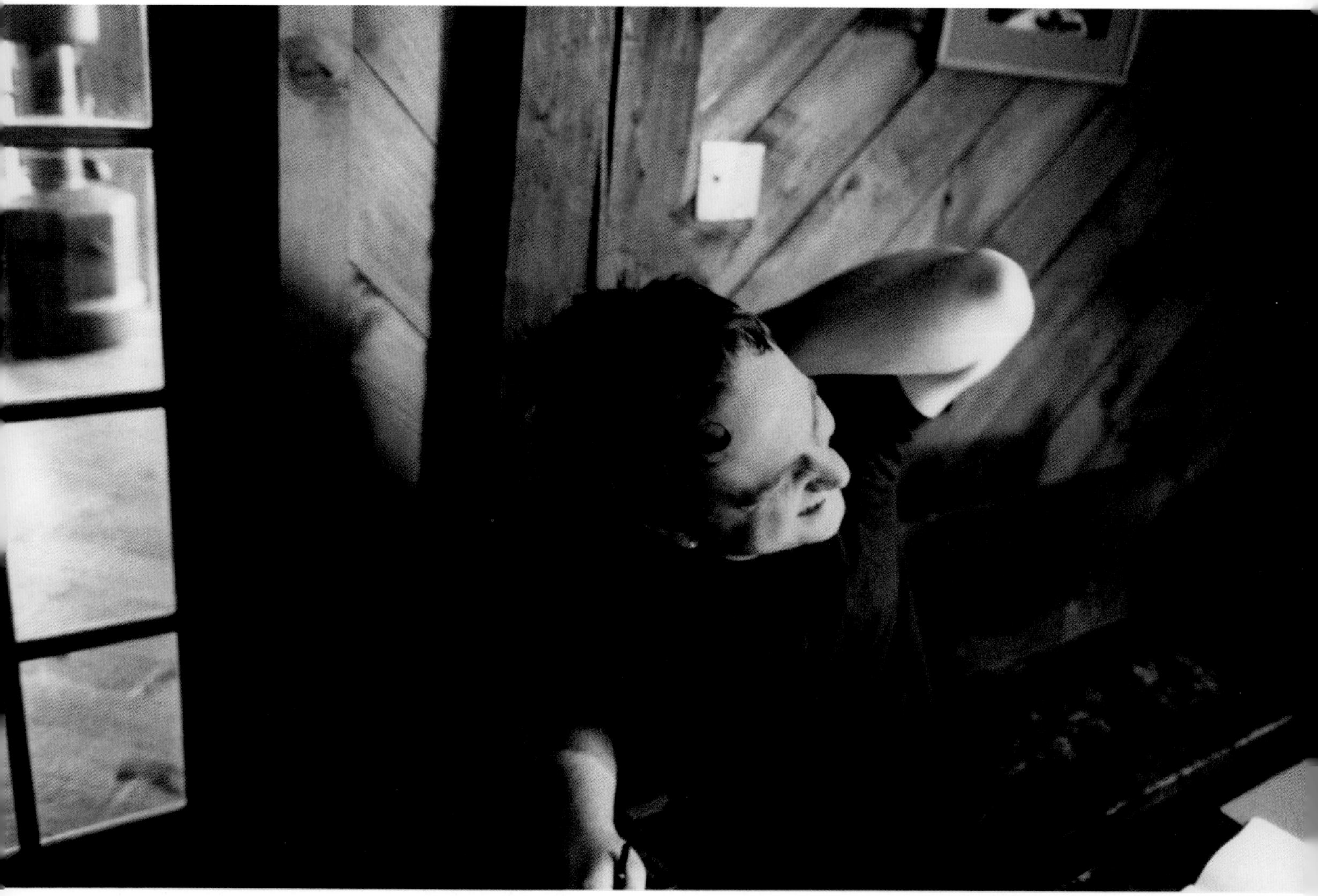

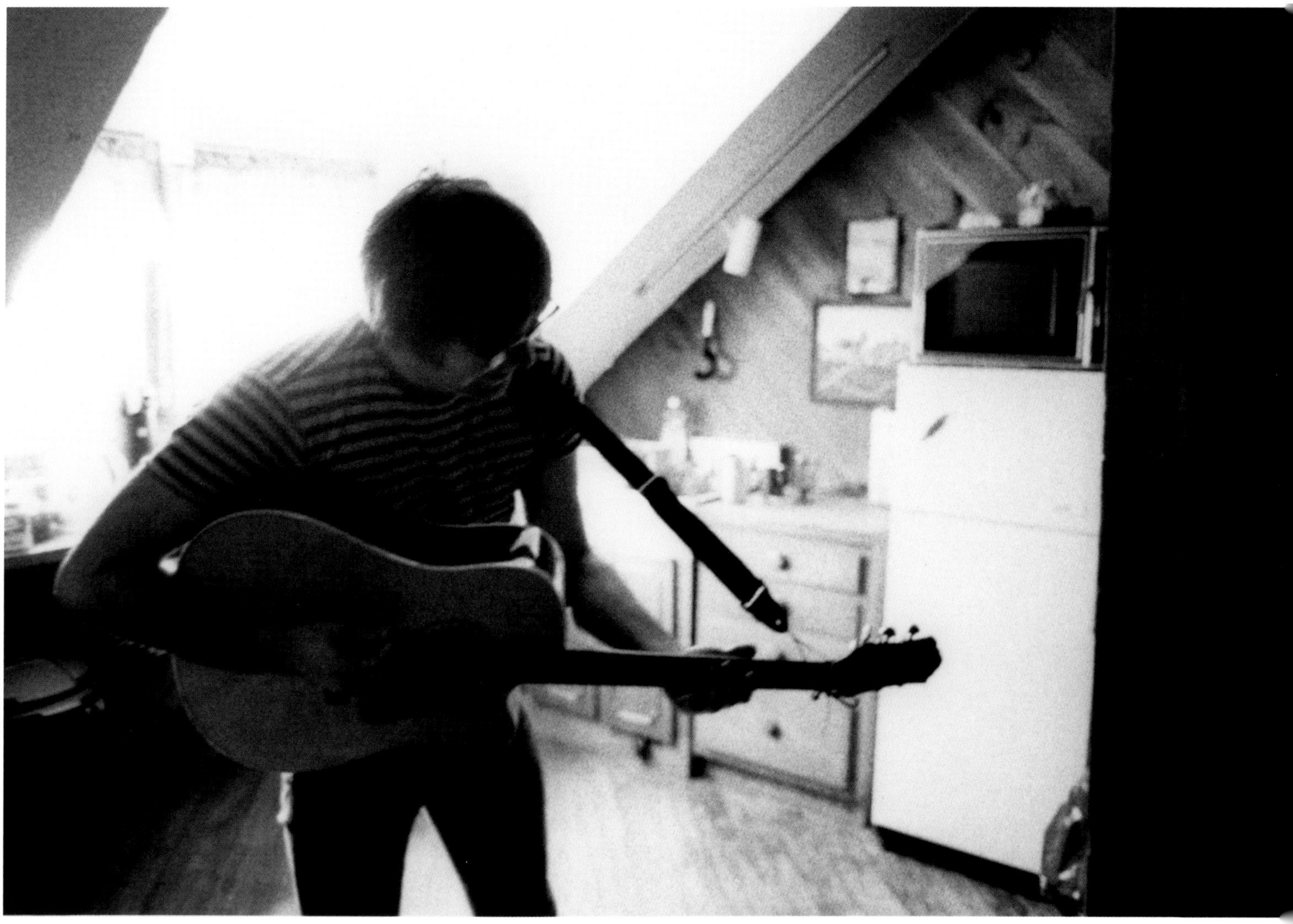

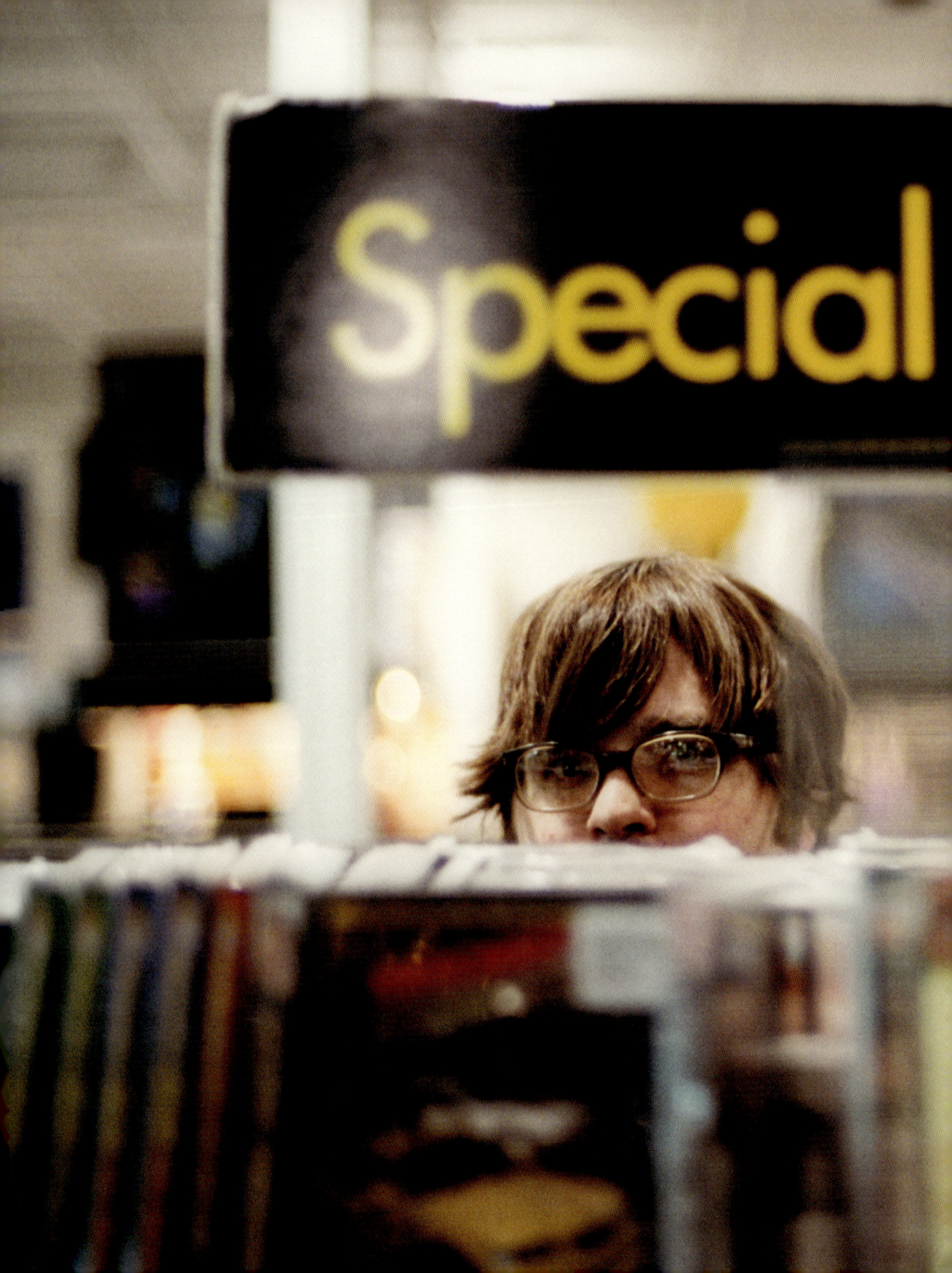
Special

Interest

$9.99 & Under

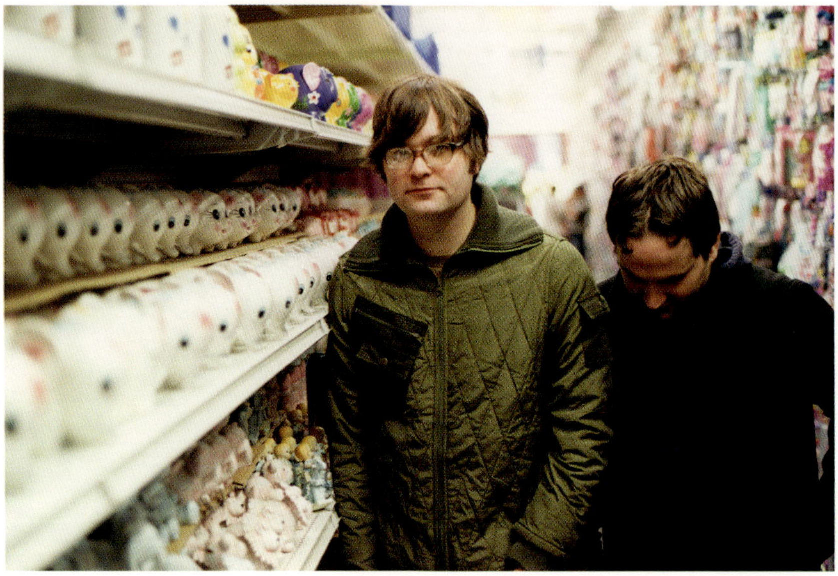

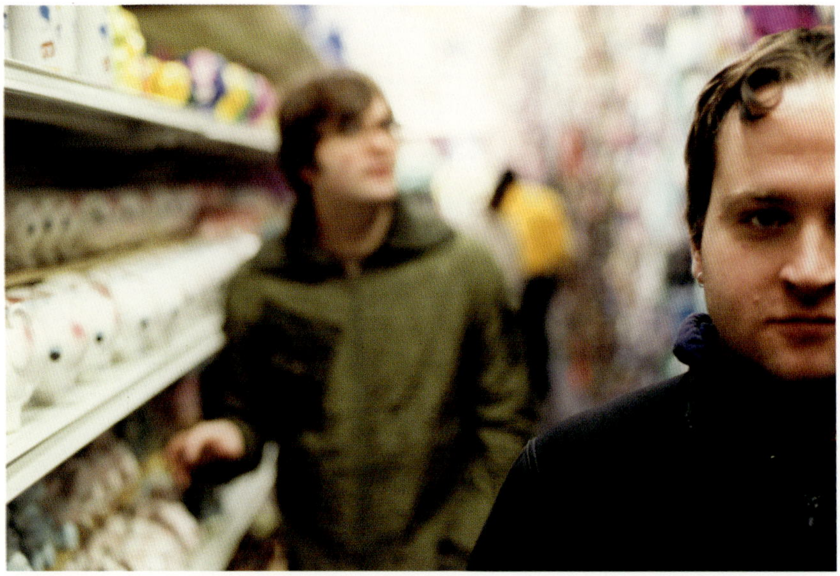

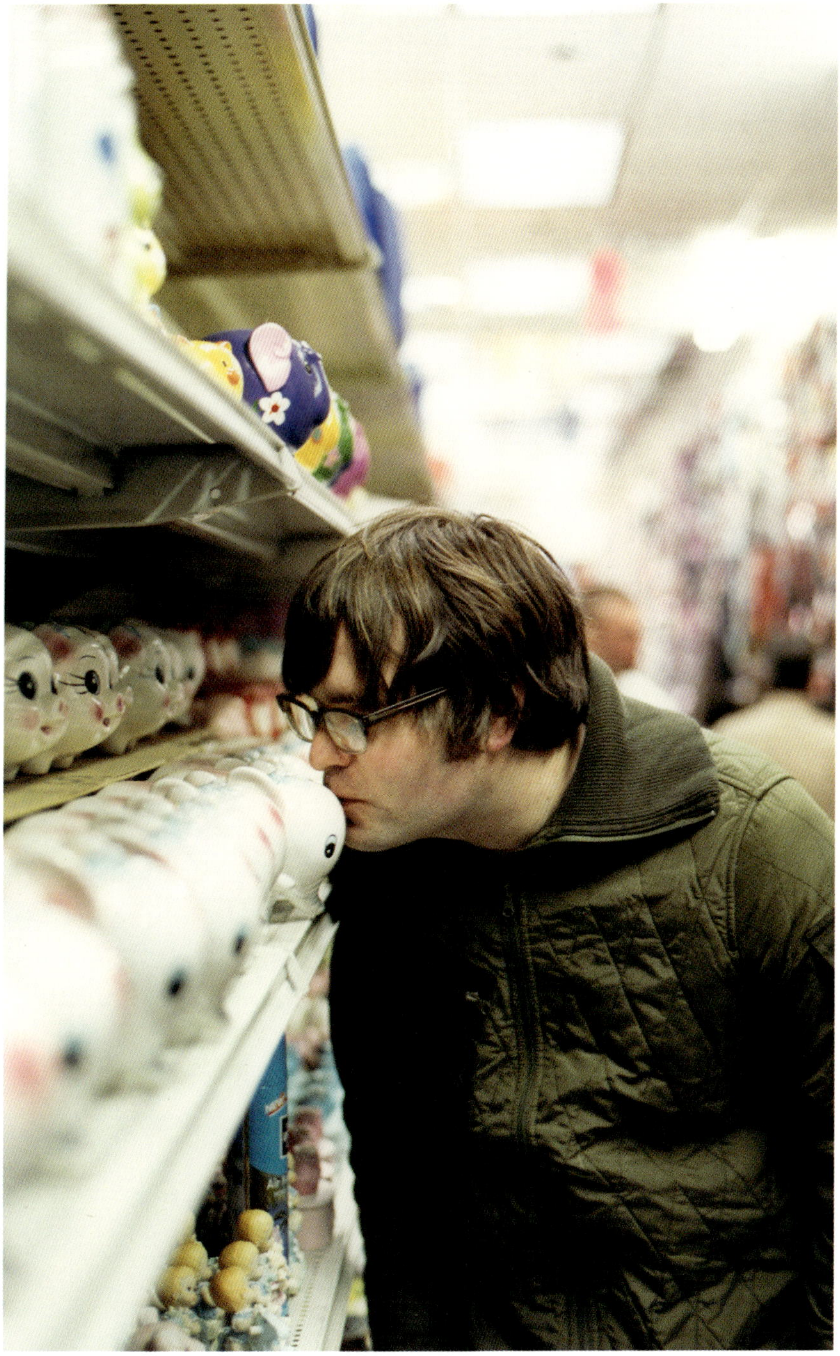

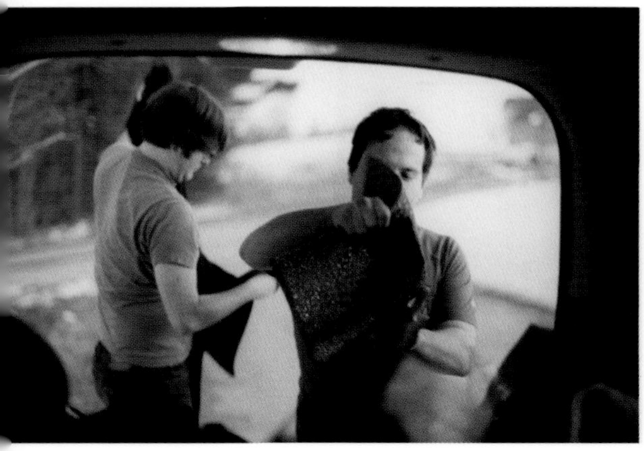
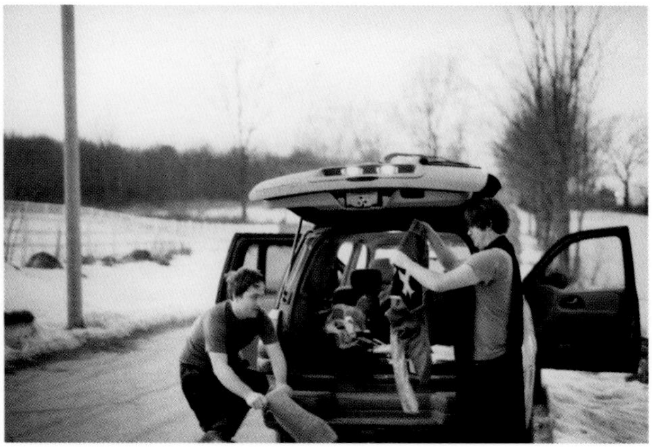
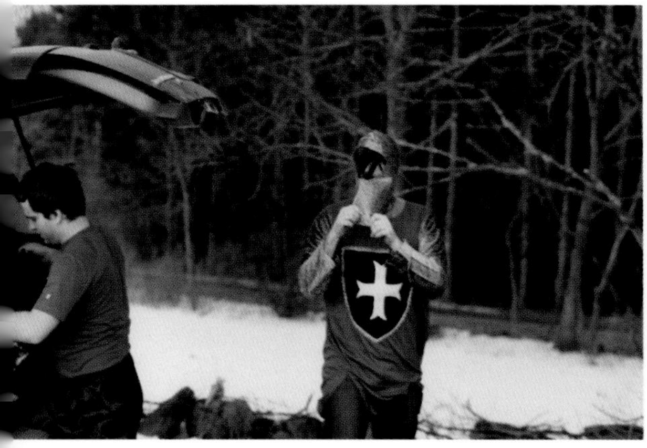
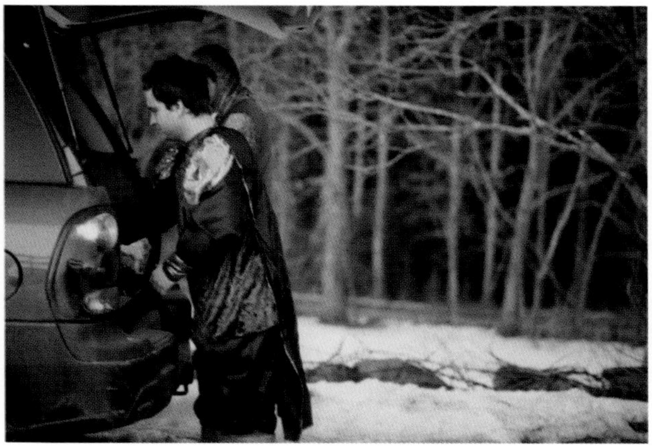
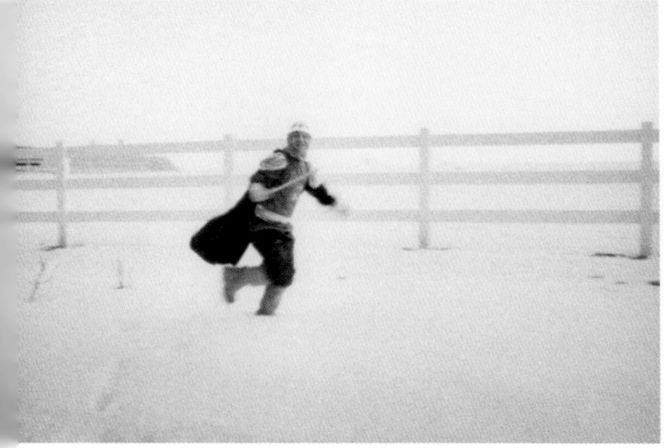
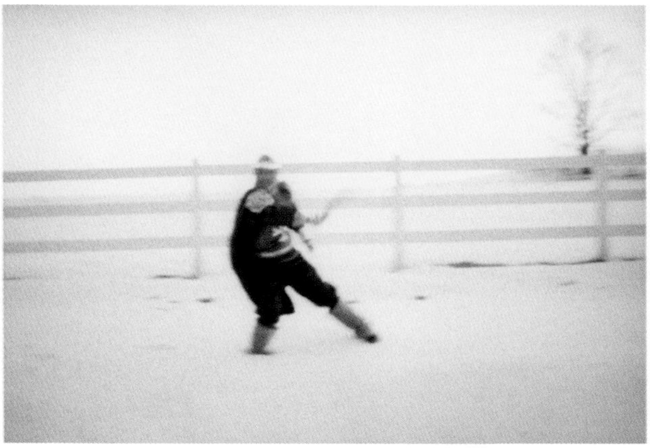

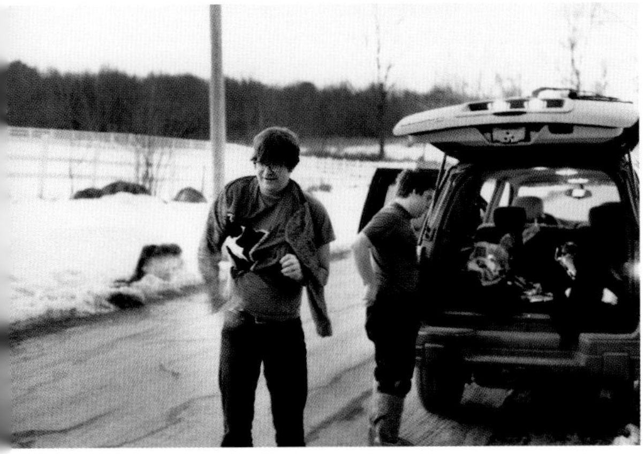
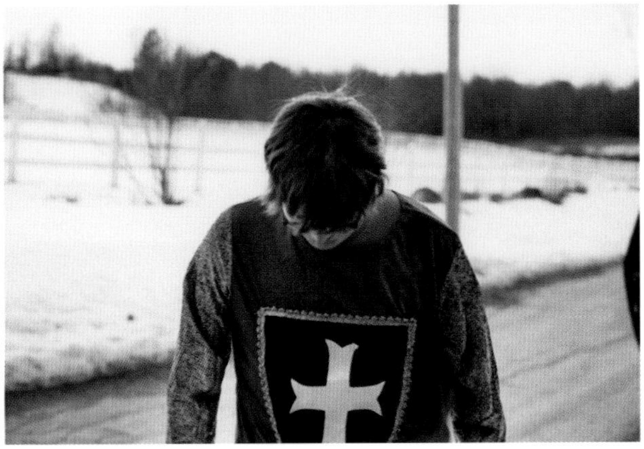
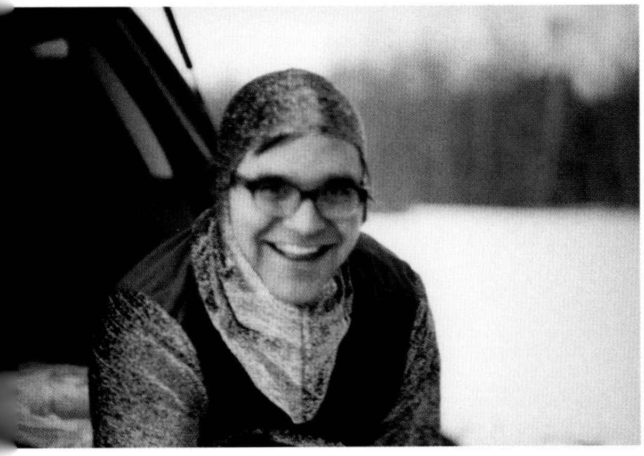
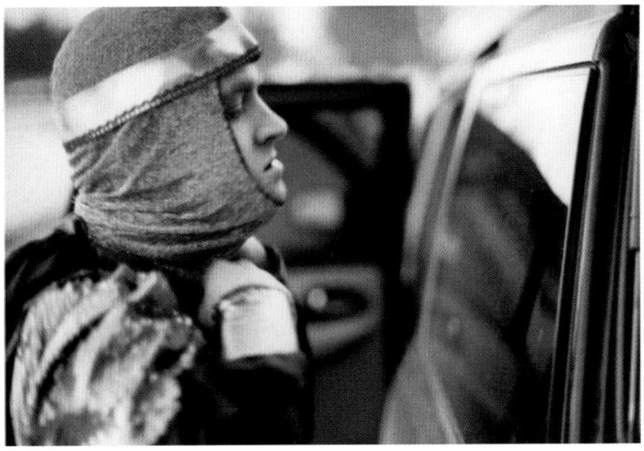
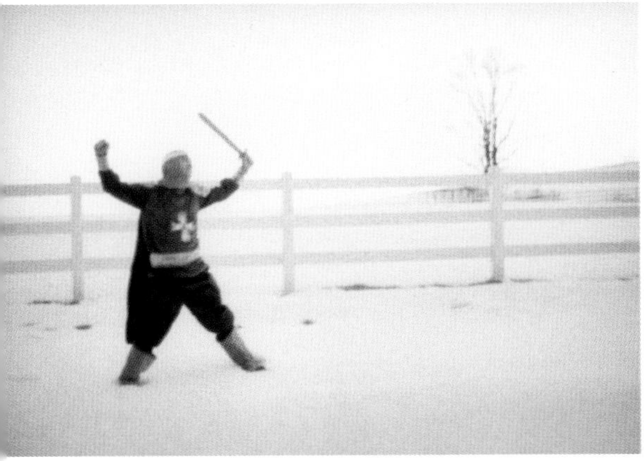
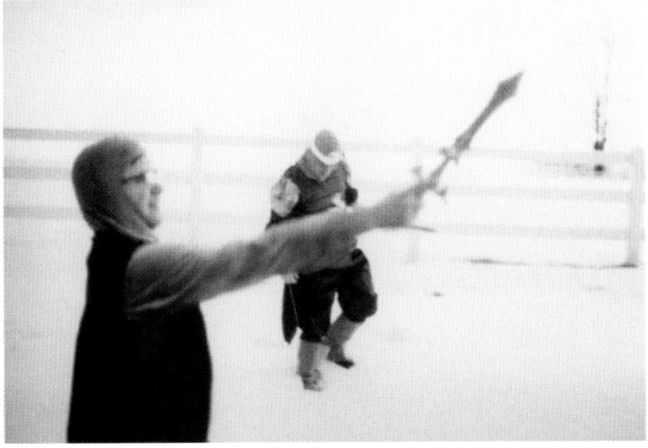

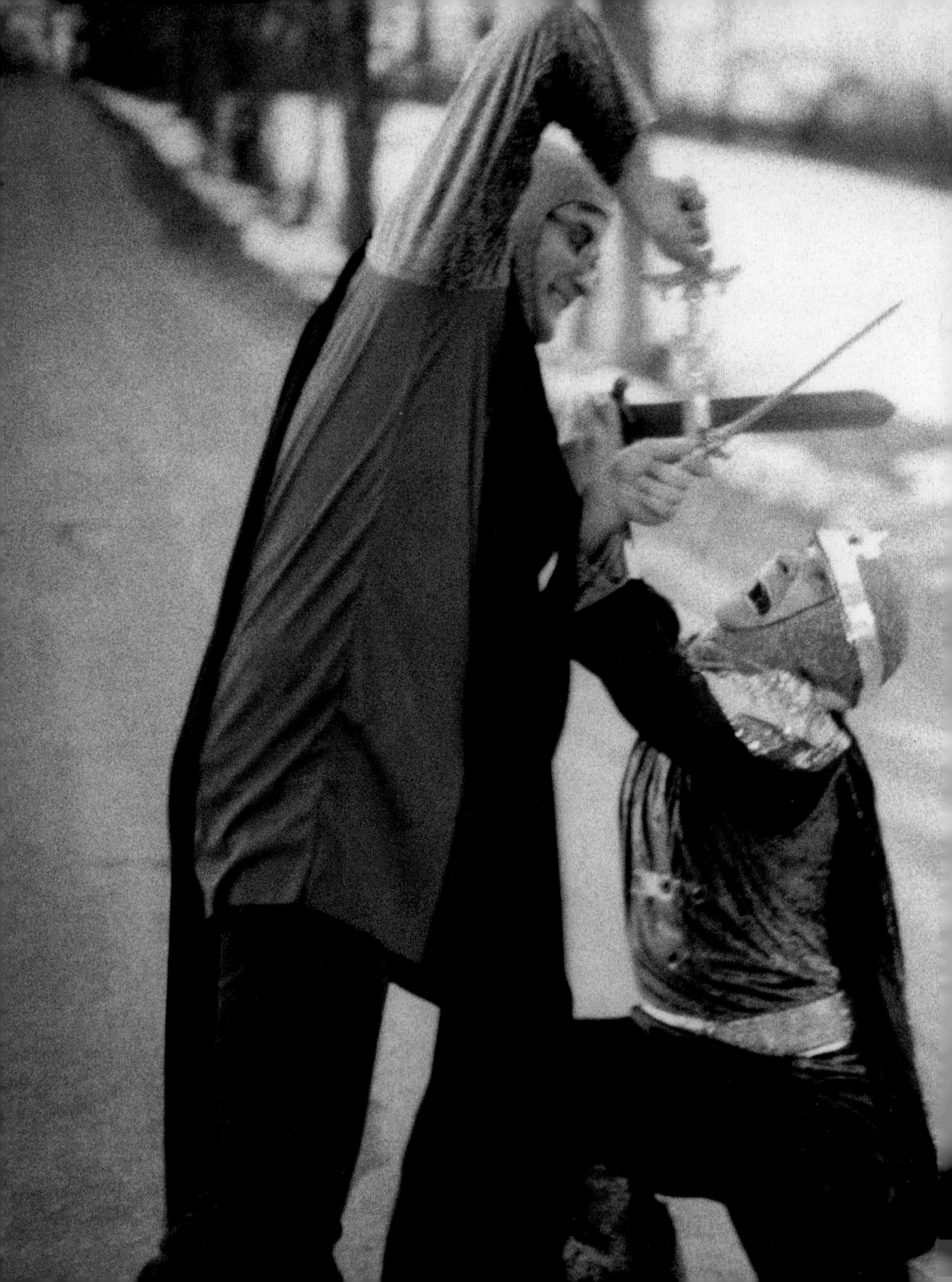

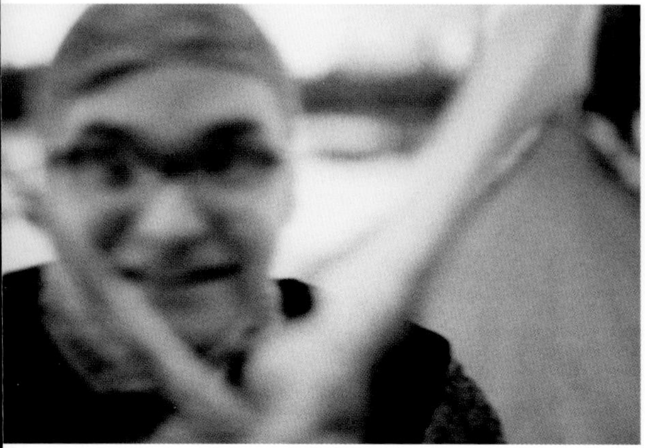
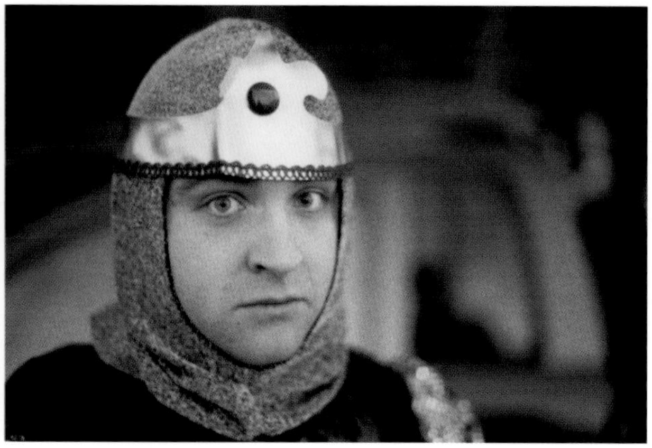
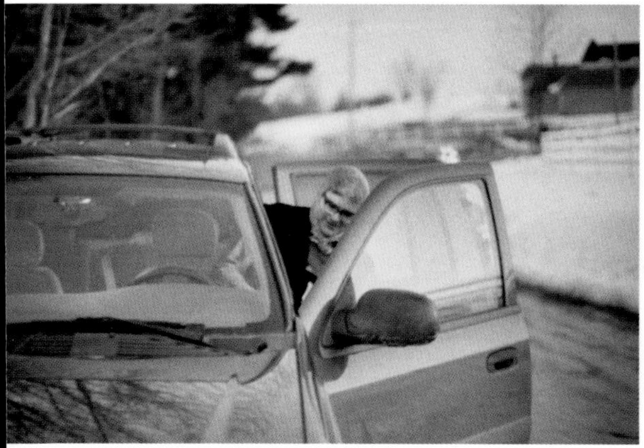
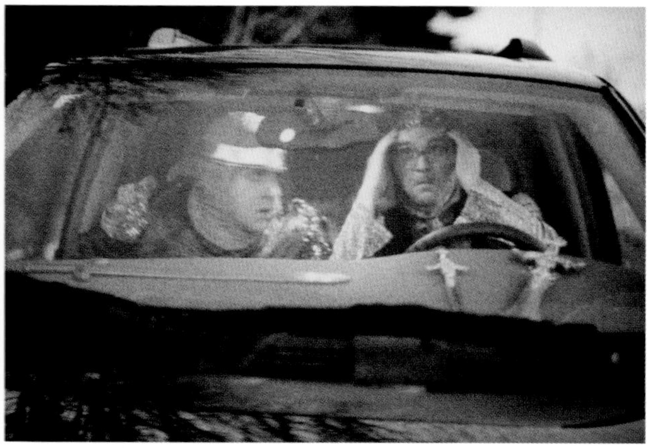
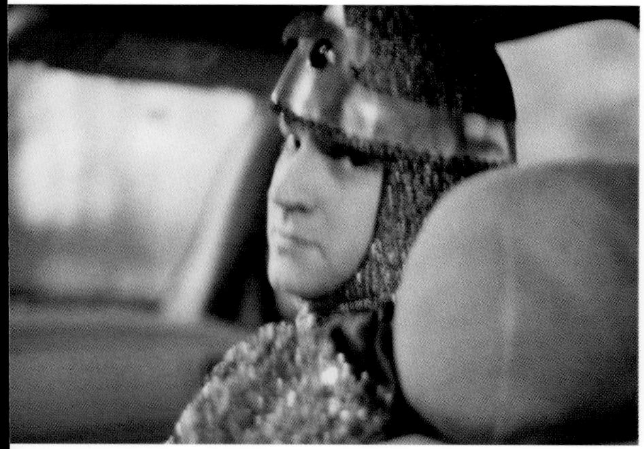
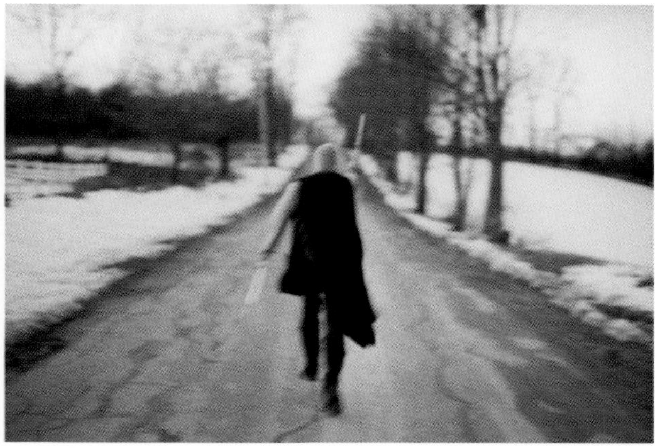

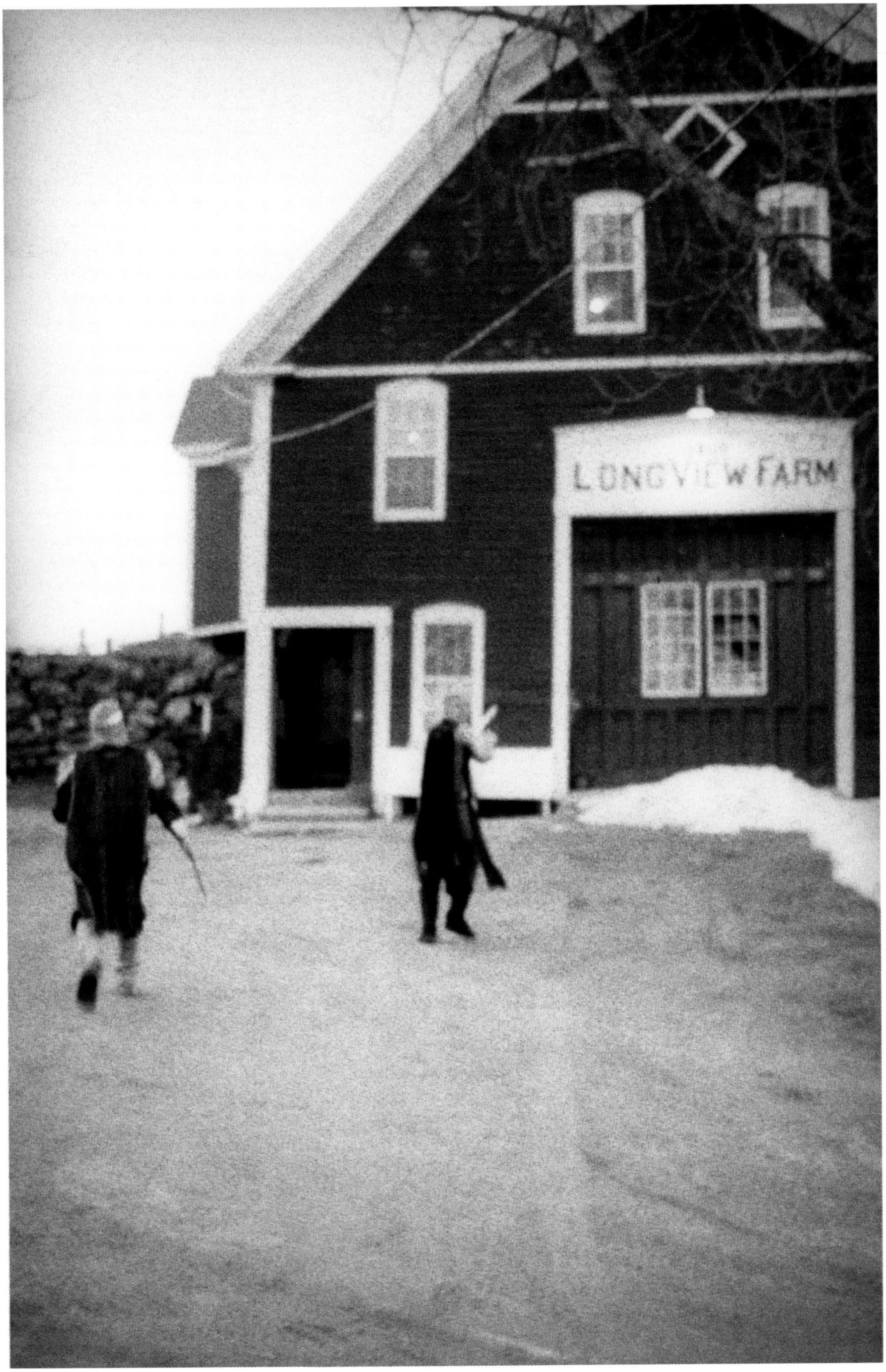
LONG VIEW FARM

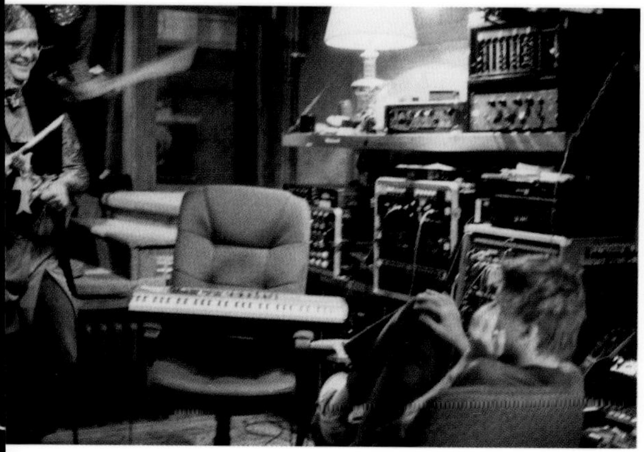
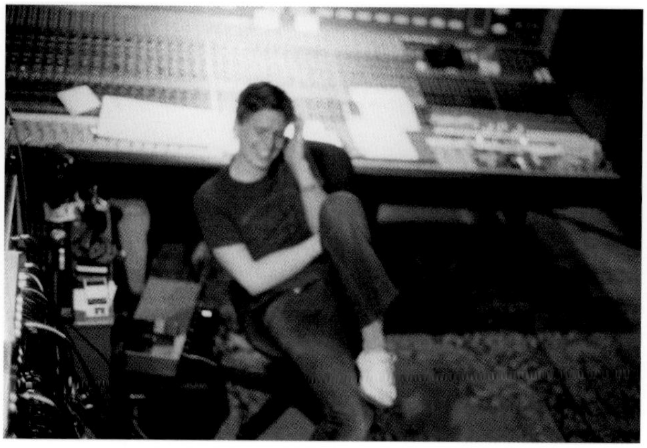
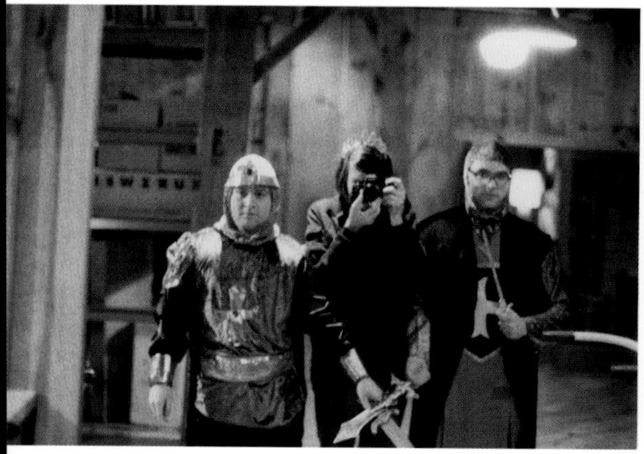
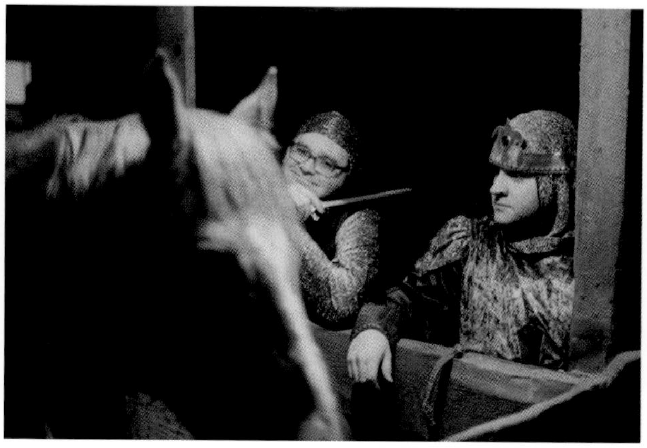
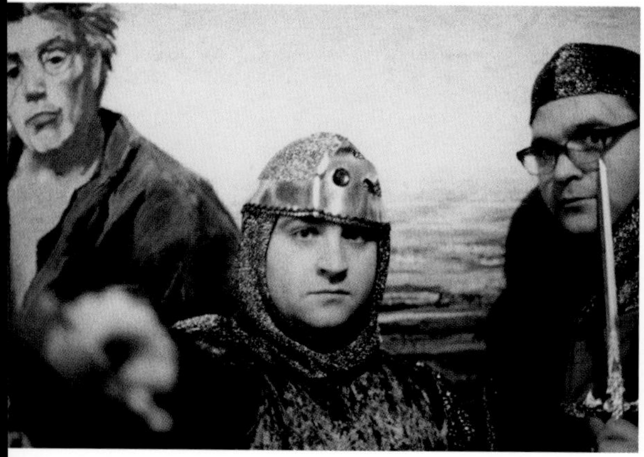
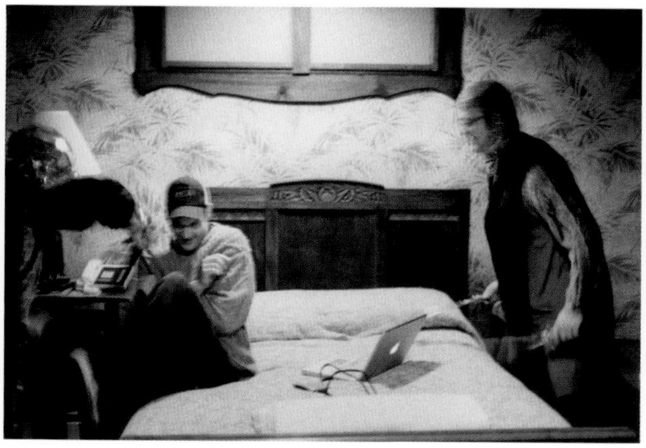

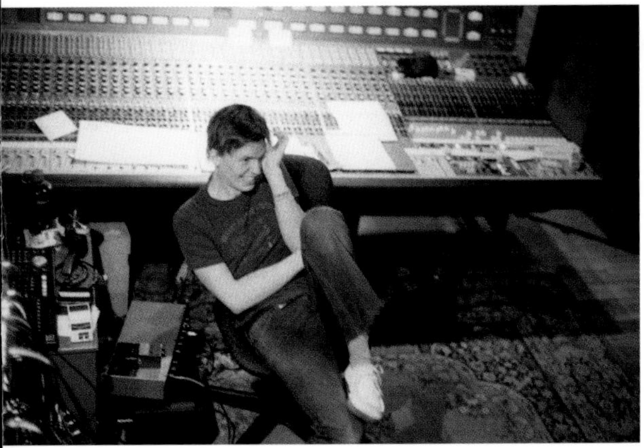

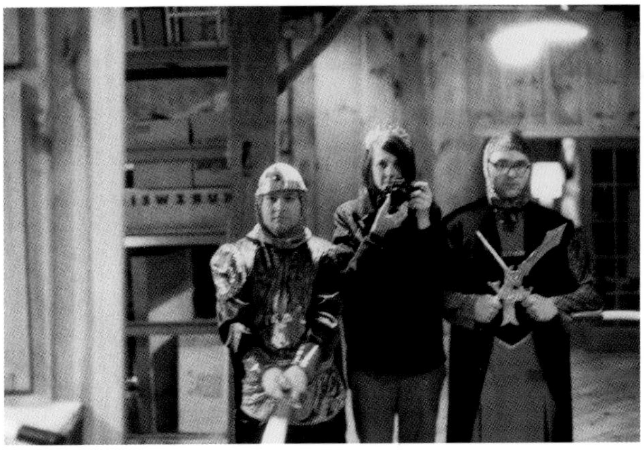

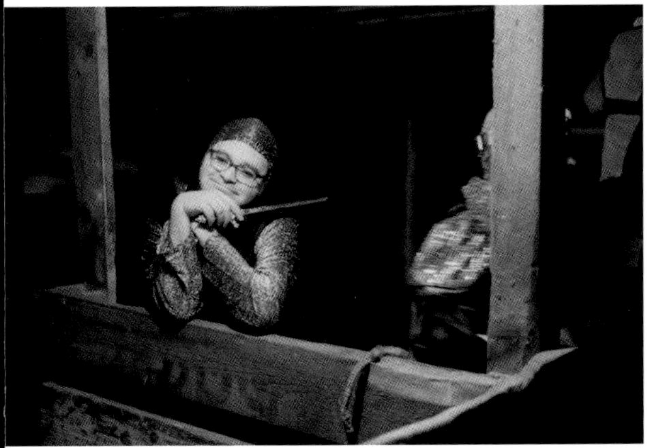

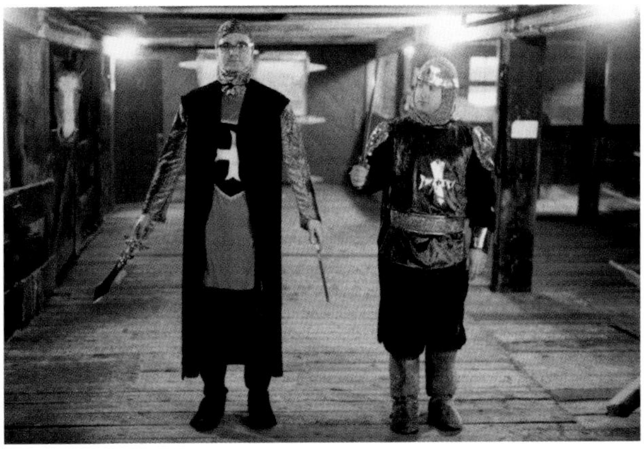

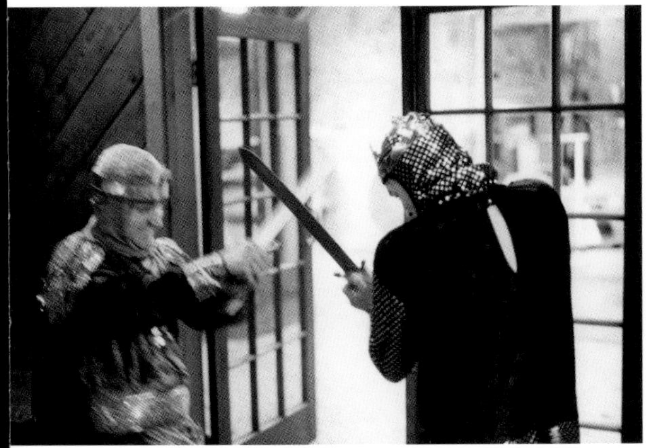

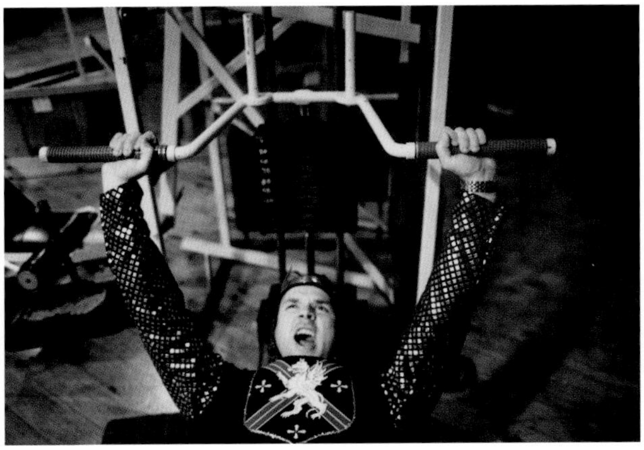

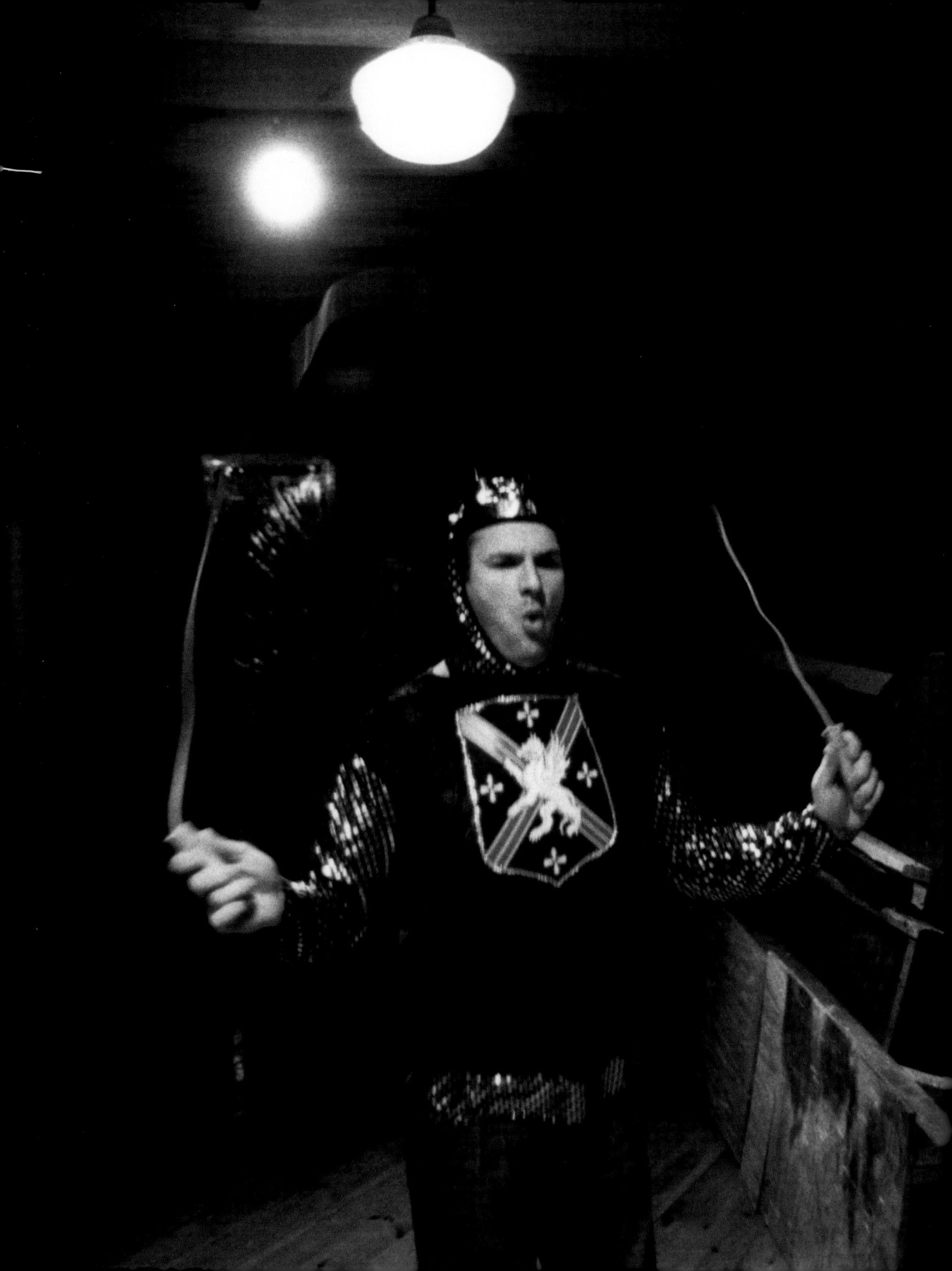

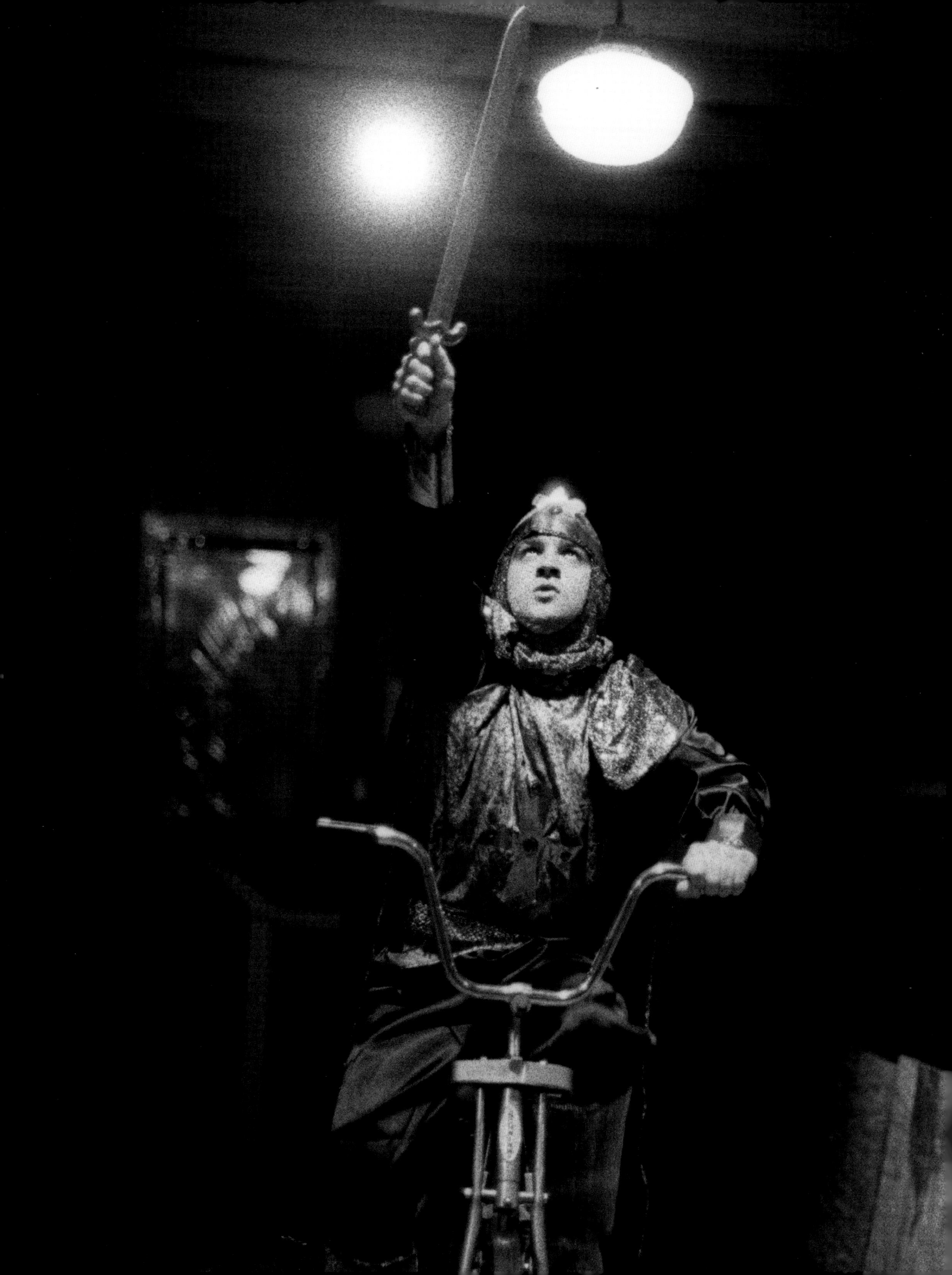

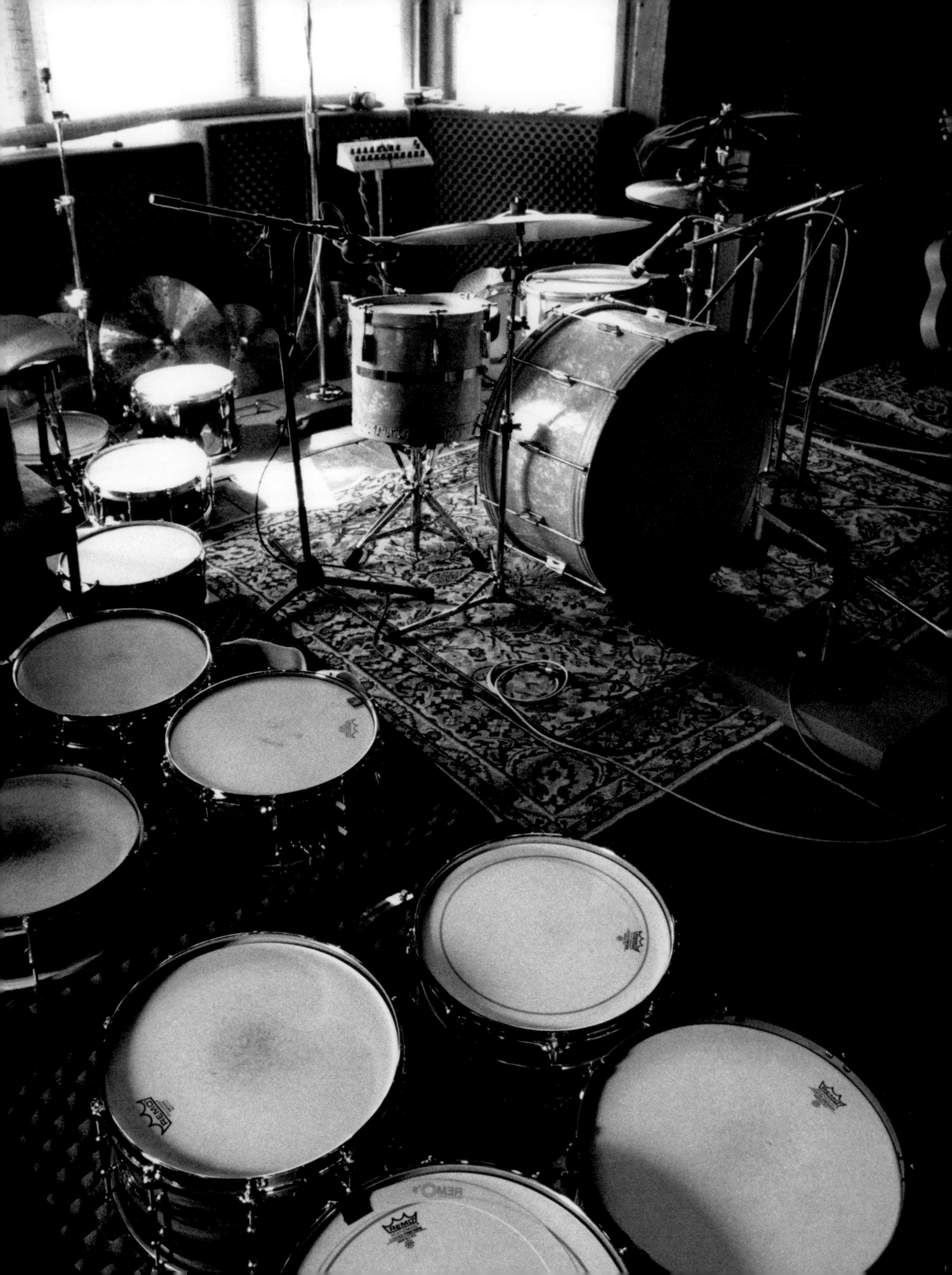
REMO

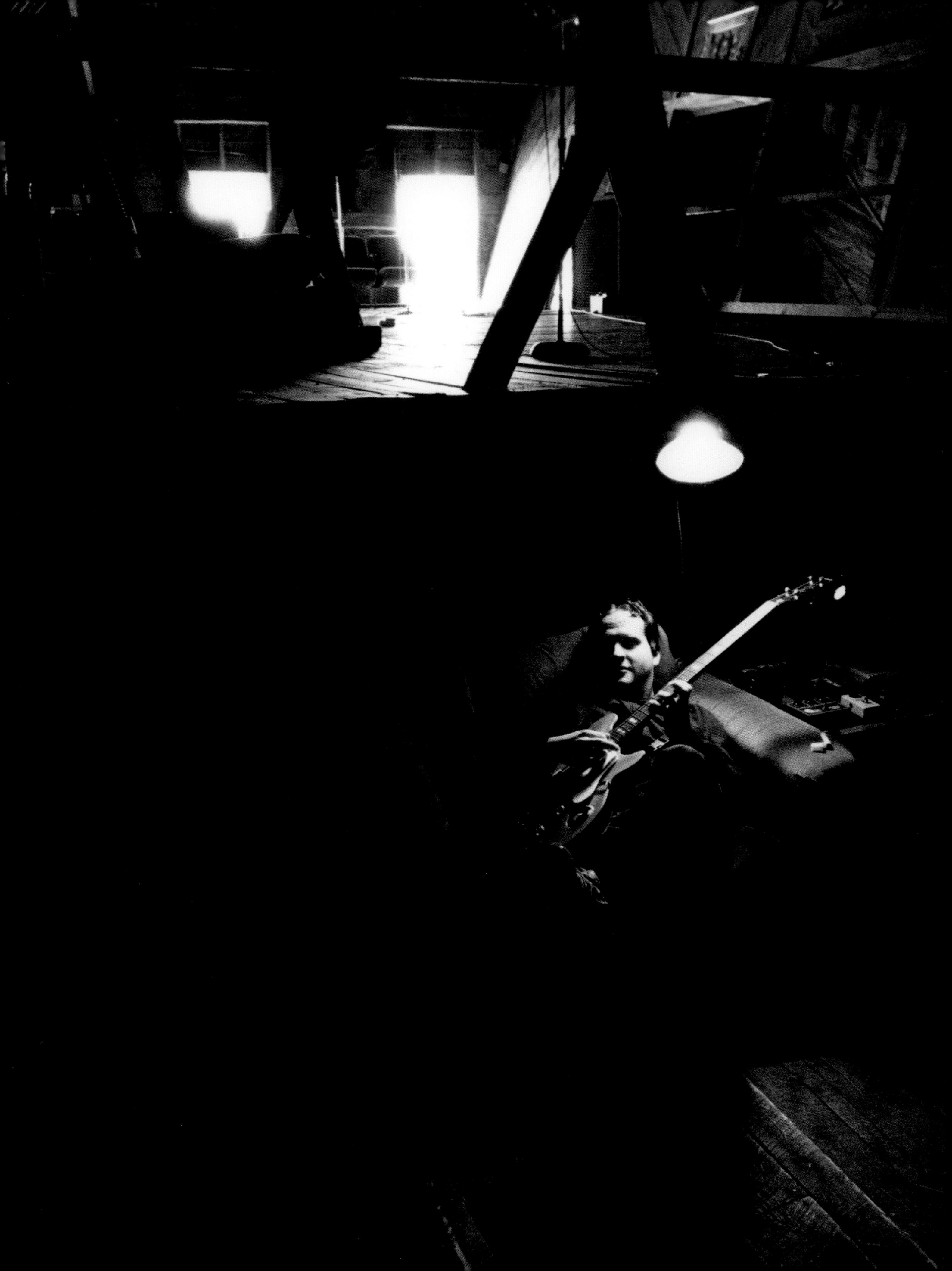

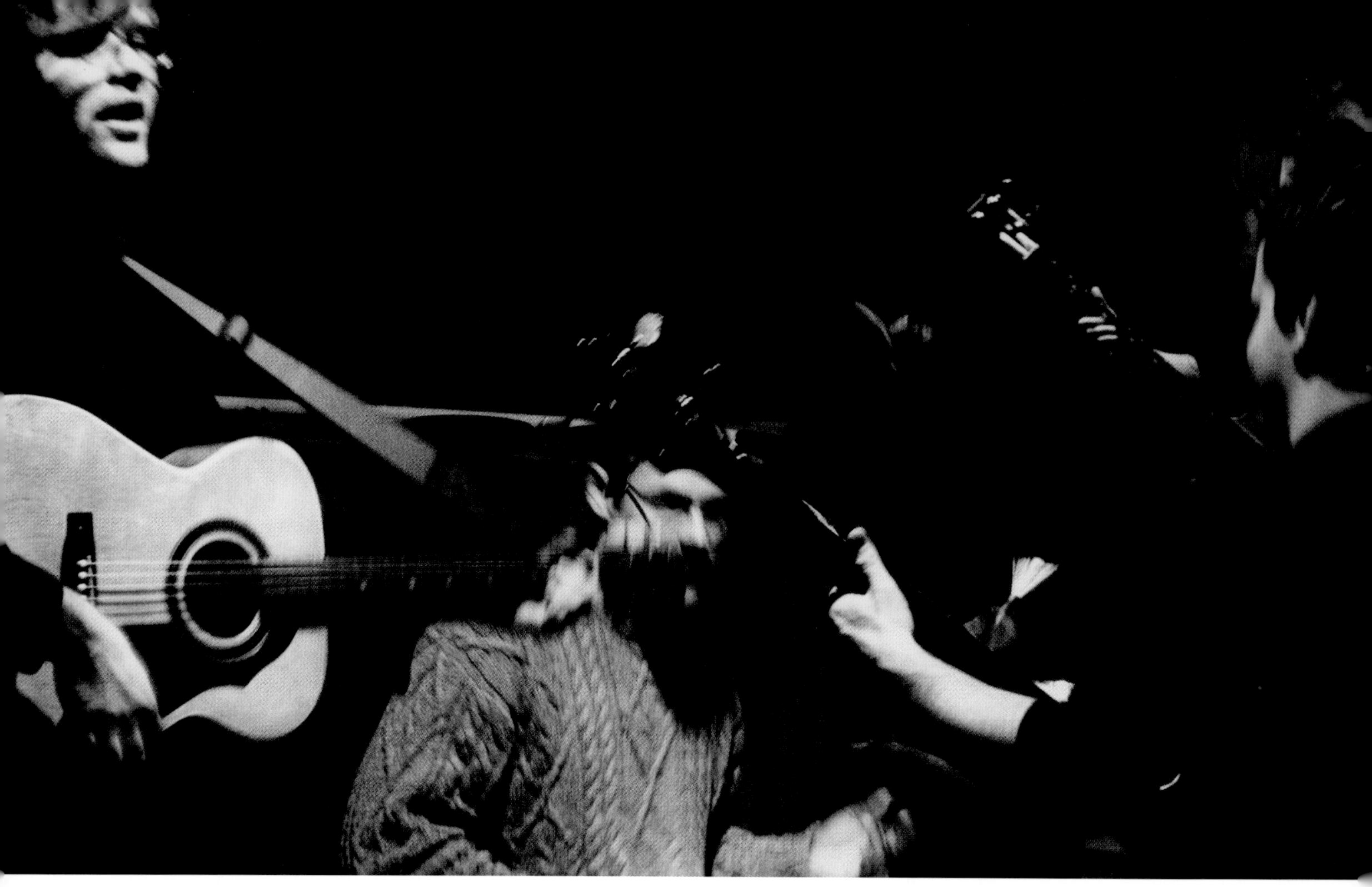

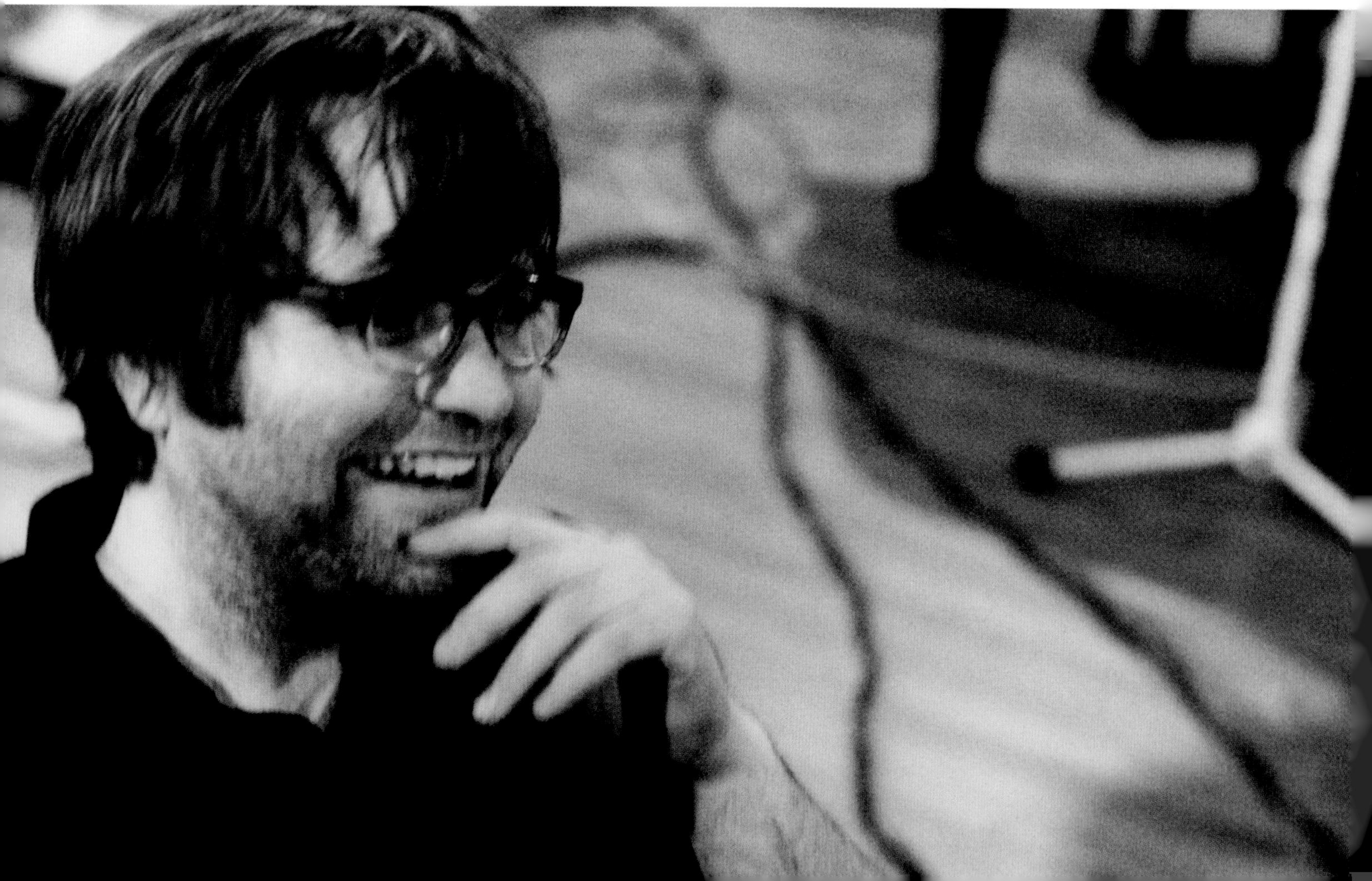

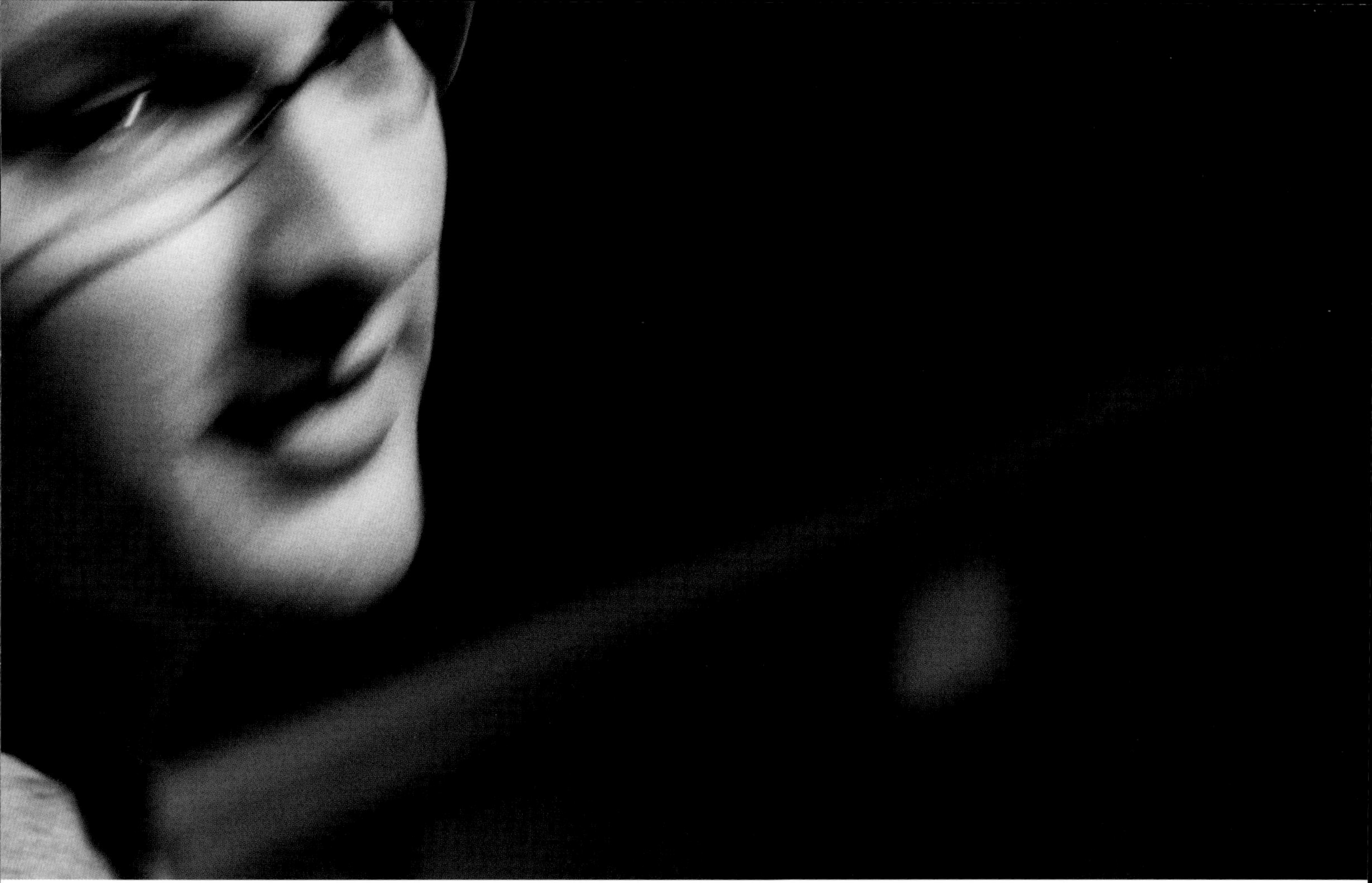

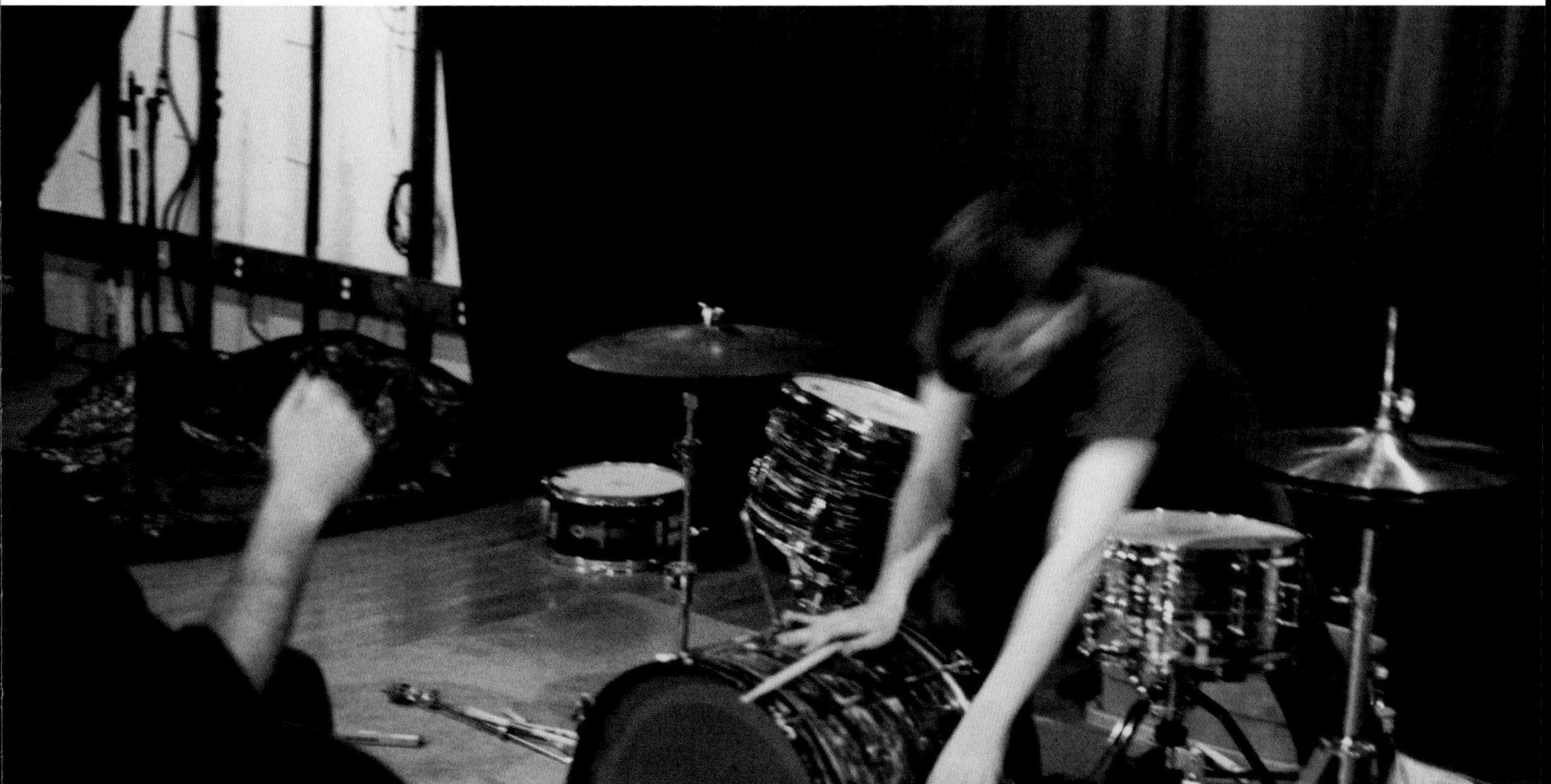

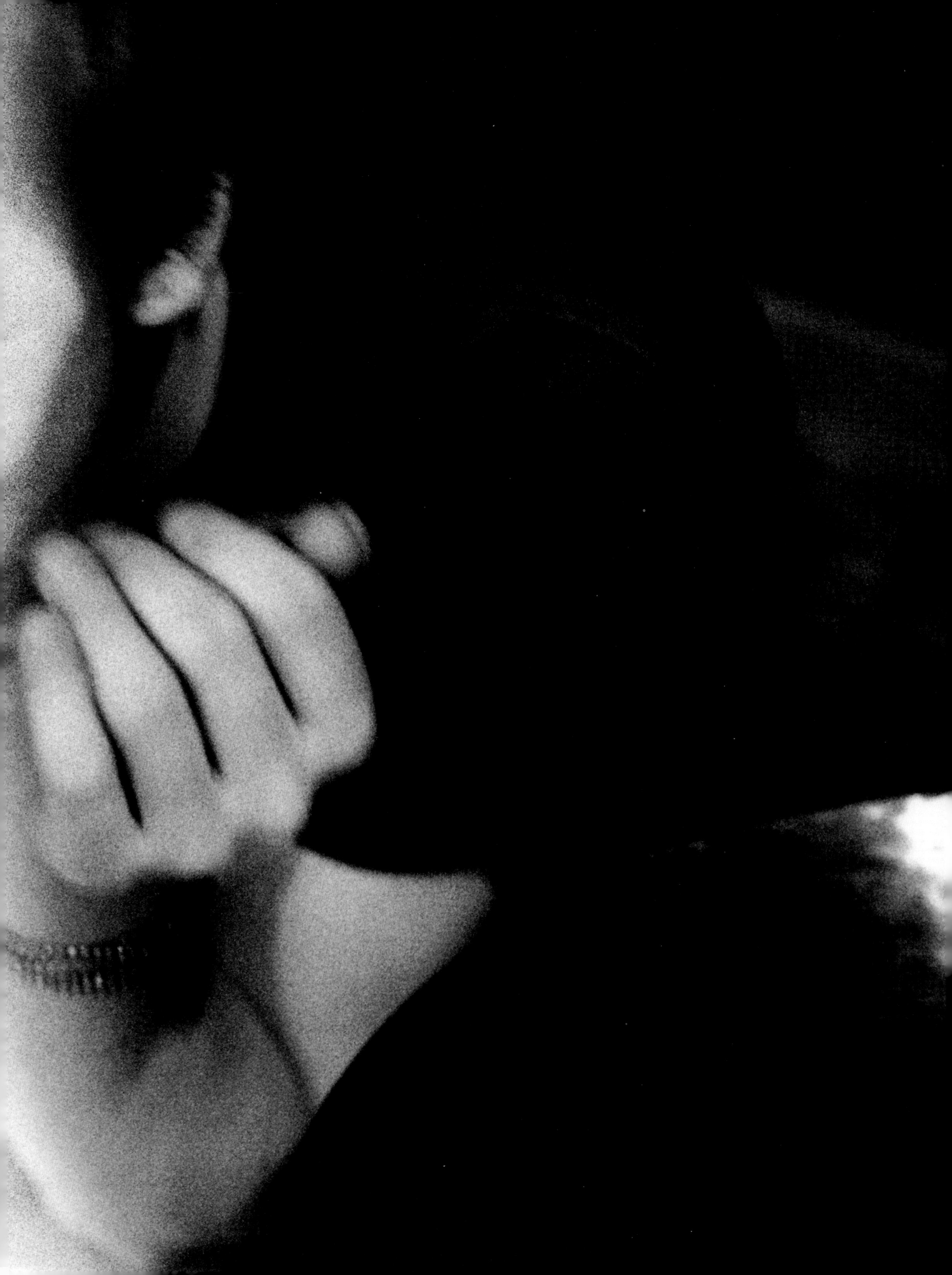

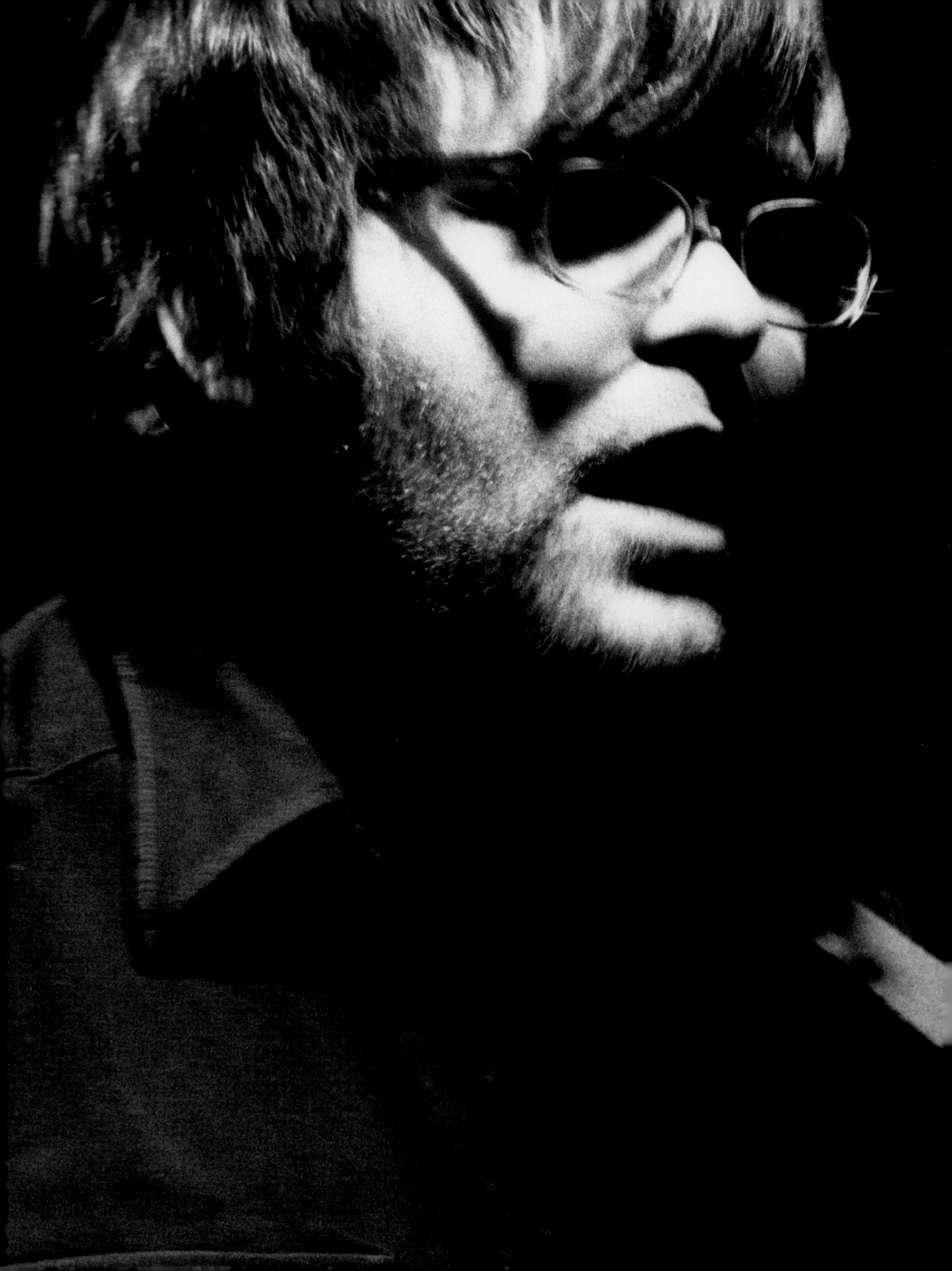

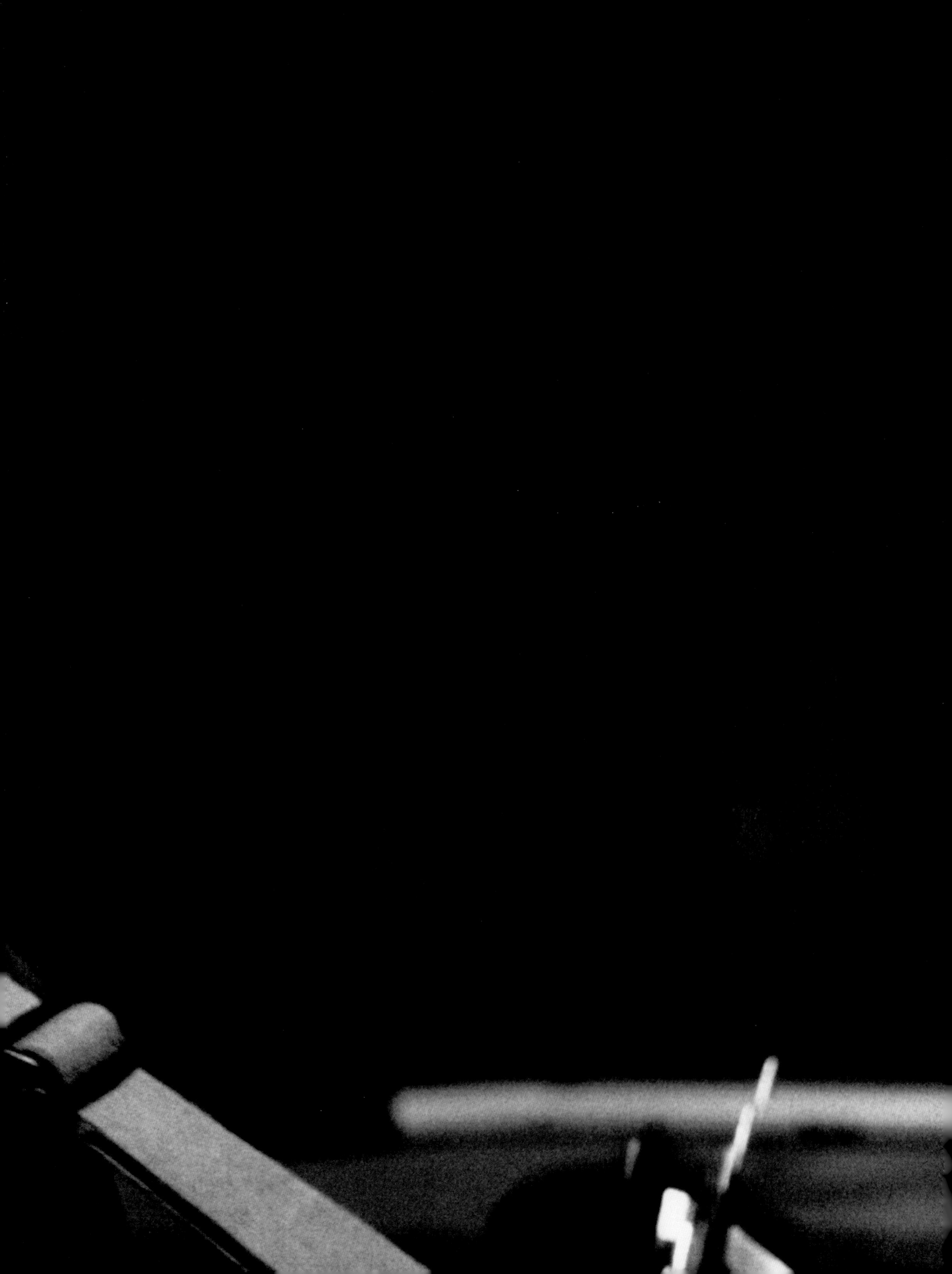

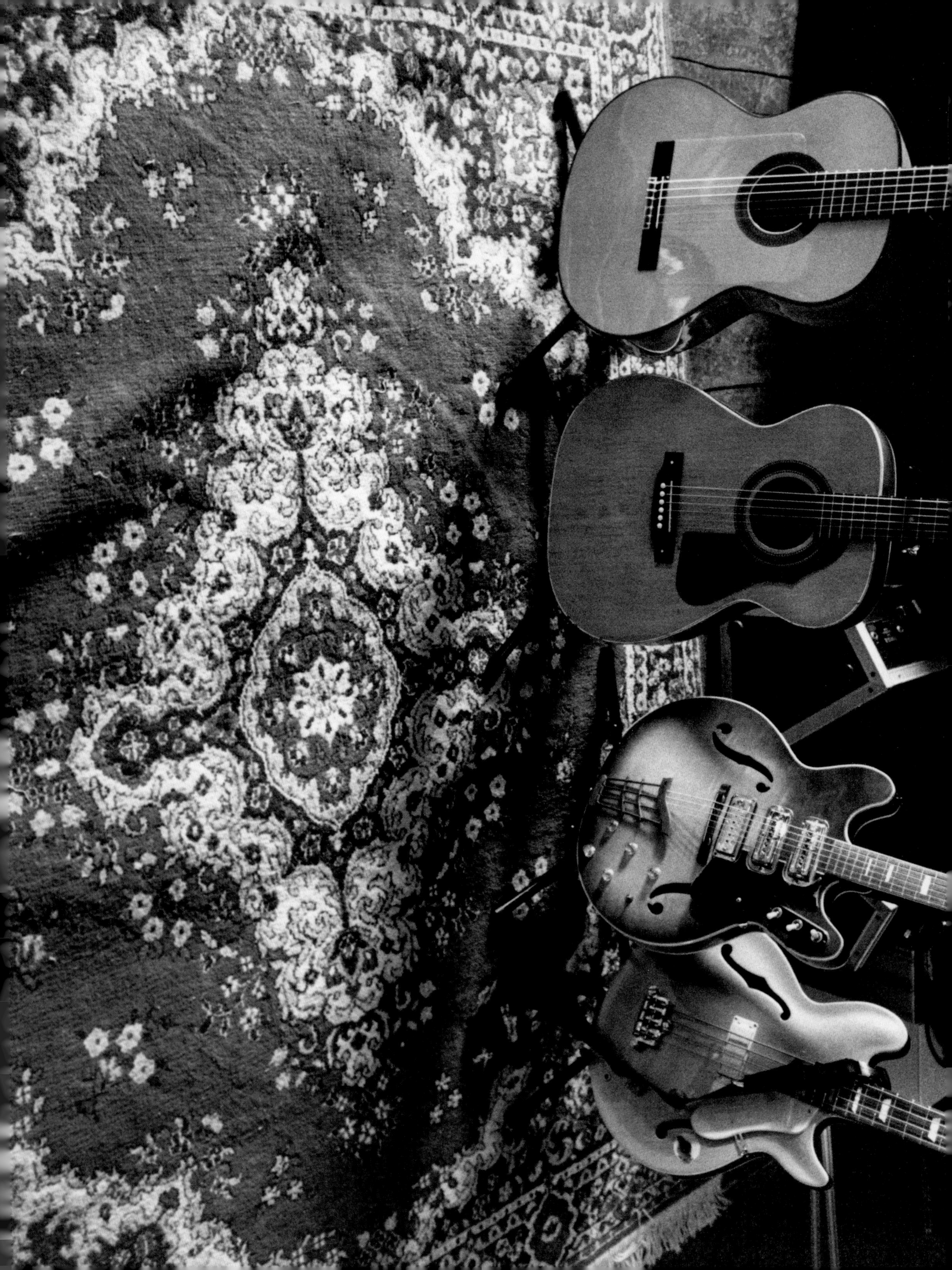

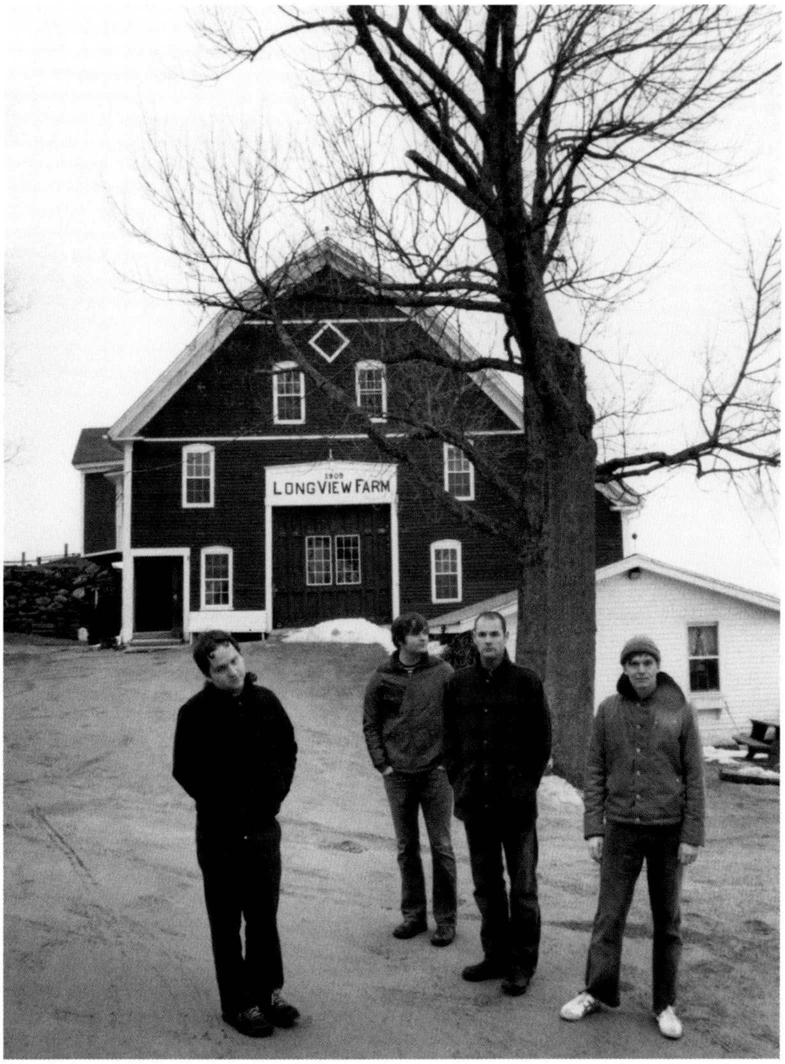
1909
LONGVIEW FARM

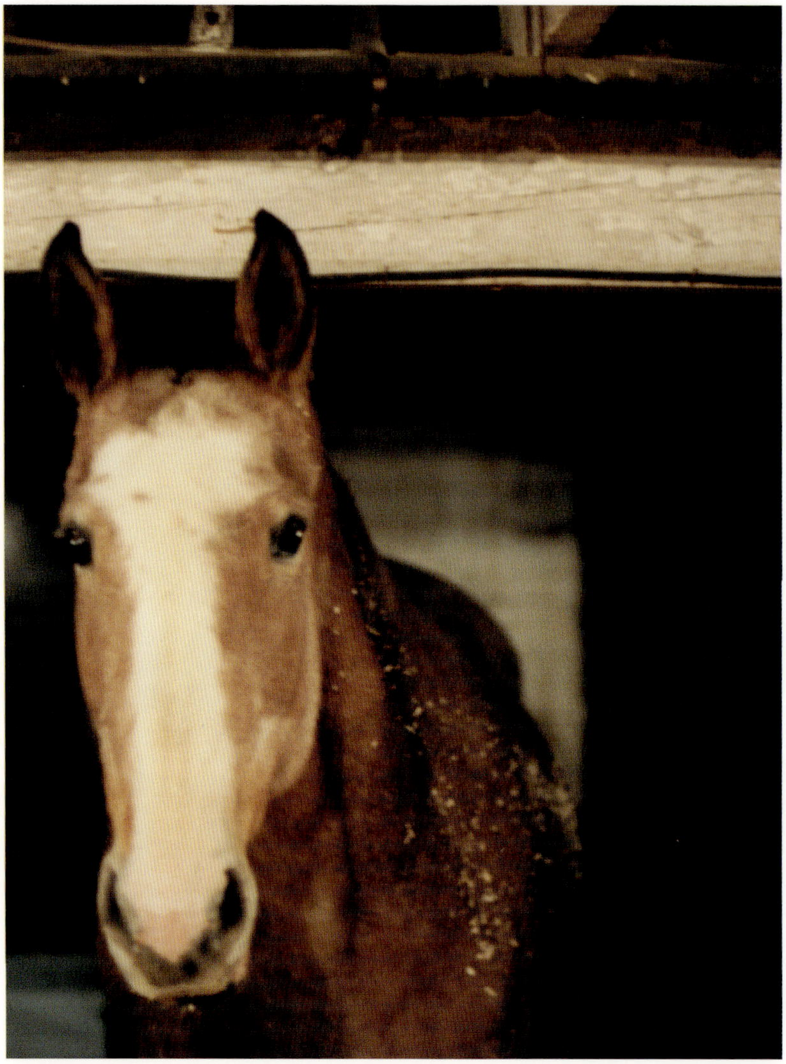

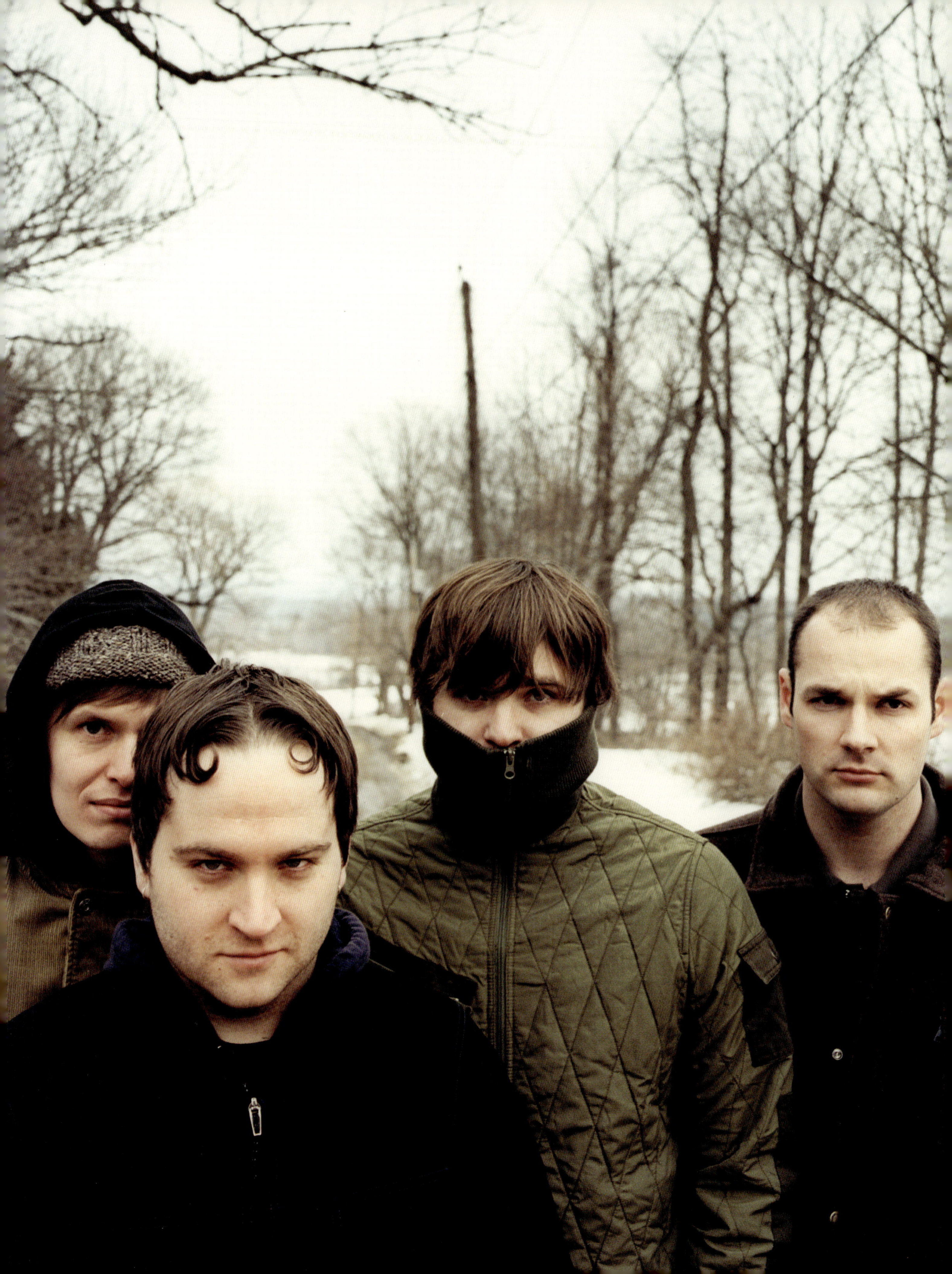

DANGER, WILL ROBINSON

WALLA: I didn't play a ton of guitar on *Plans* because by the time we tracked that record, I could only play guitar with three fingers.

AUTUMN: [to Walla] You had hurt your finger, right? Like really badly.

WALLA: [raises middle finger] This is the one I couldn't play with.

AUTUMN: [laughing] Fuck you, too!

WALLA: I removed about a dime-sized piece of my middle finger on my fretting hand, my left hand, with a razor blade.

JASON: You were cutting a little plastic tie, right?

WALLA: It was really bad. It was healing, but it was still tender as *fuck*. And it still is. I did some nerve damage. It's never gonna be fine, but I'm going to bitch about it. I was told at the hospital . . . the doctor said, "Okay, we have the obligation to inform you that you are now legally an amputee."

[ALL LAUGH]

WALLA: So, if I wanted to . . .

JASON: . . . get a parking pass . . .

WALLA: Yeah. I could *totally* get a handicapped parking pass. If there was any indication as to what's wrong with the health system in the United States, I'm it.

AUTUMN: Okay, cool, that was great. More injury stories! Ben, scorpion in your pants . . . go!

BEN: I'm Scorpion Man! [laughing] We were in San Diego with Neil Young, and I had these sweaty show clothes, because I perspire a lot, and after a show I hung them up in the back of the tour bus in the back closet. Then I drove separately down to San Diego, where we were opening for Neil. I took the clothes out of the back of the bus and took them inside and hung them in the dressing room to dry. Right before we're supposed to play, I put the pants on, and all of a sudden I felt like someone was jamming a needle into my left thigh, and I was like, "Ow! What the fuck? What the fuck?!!" I pulled my pants down and a fucking scorpion fell out, and it kind of started walking away. [laughing] Lucas was right there and he stomped on it.

AUTUMN: Did it come from the venue or was it your pants from another city? Hold on, great album title: *In Your Pants from Another City*. [laughing]

BEN: I don't know. It just climbed down somewhere and found a nice, slightly stinky and moist place to hang. As it fell out, I go, "There's a fucking scorpion in my pants!"

NICK: I thought it was going to be a joke. But no, there was really a scorpion.

JASON: I was out on the bus just talking on the phone, and I went in to the backstage area, and Walla came walking up and said, "Okay. Everything's fine, it's totally cool. Ben just got bit by a scorpion. It was in his pants. He's totally fine, though. The show's going to go on . . ." [laughing] And I say, "Oh, that's funny." I walked past him, and this paramedic walks by and says, "Excuse me." Then it's like: "Oh, you're not fucking lying, are you?"

BEN: We played the show, and it hurt really badly.

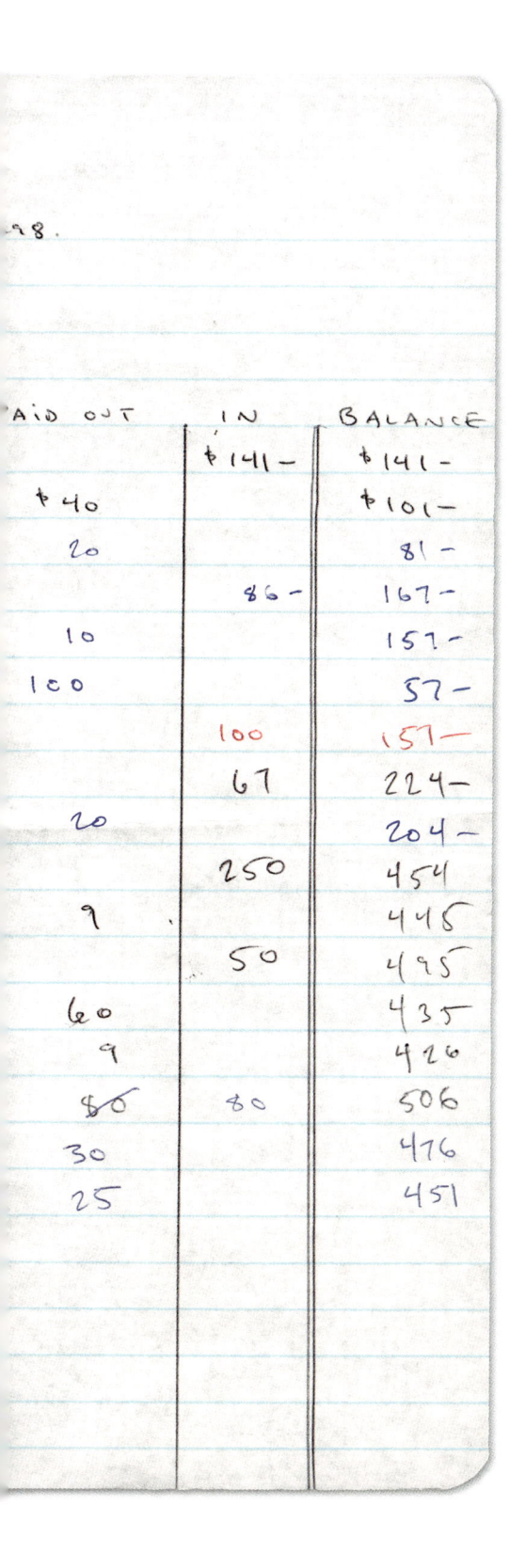

JASON: Then we let Ben drive, by himself, up to L.A. Up the dark highway that night.

BEN: I figured, we played for an hour...

NICK: You would have been dead by then, yeah.

BEN: I was jumping around and rocking out. If that would have moved through my body and been in a place where it would have done any real damage, I would have known by then.

AUTUMN: Were there any other strange injuries that have happened to the band?

NICK: There was the time when the three of us went down, in a row, that summer. It was me first. I went blind. I was out on a boat pulling an inner tube and a rope snapped and hit me and cut one of the eyes. I went blind in both eyes for the better part of a day and then my vision came back in. My pupils are different sizes because of that.

AUTUMN: Which I've noticed when I take your photo. Like David Bowie.

NICK: There you go. Ben, I think, was next. Ben got hit by a car on his bike and broke his arm. We had Bumbershoot coming up, and he had the cast put on so that he could still play guitar, kind of. Then you [to Walla] slipped and fell down the stairs and broke your foot, or a toe, or something like that.

WALLA: I was on crutches.

NICK: It was pretty bad; you've got to imagine: we're coming on stage for Bumbershoot. I'm wearing an eye patch... Michael was running like a 104-degree fever, fully delirious... I'm standing there, and I remember at one point I turned around and looked, and you [to Walla] had dropped the crutches and were standing on one foot, rocking out. Ben was playing guitar, but his arm was frozen in the cast right angle. I was just wondering, "Why are we playing this show?" We were so dedicated.

BEN: We needed the $900.

VAN VS. BUS

[ON THE PHONE WITH WALLA]

AUTUMN: I remember in the past, you said that you missed the van. Do you feel like you've come so far now that you couldn't go back into the van, or do you still miss it?

WALLA: I *love* driving, and I love seeing the country go by. There's no other way you can really get a sense of where you are and how the country works and how it all changes from place to place unless you are doing it in something that moves during the day in a terrestrial sort of way.

AUTUMN: And part of it is you driving and not being driven.

WALLA: Oh, definitely. I'm the driver. If I'm not the driver, it's not okay.

AUTUMN: So when you guys were touring in a van, you were driving?

WALLA: I think after about the first two or three tours, I was kind of the driver all the time. There was that one time that I took the TheraFlu in the blue box instead of the red box, and I probably *should* have let someone else drive. I didn't know what was happening. I just kind of got weird and tired, and then I looked at the box, and it was the nighttime kind, not the daytime kind. Because blue means "sad" and "sleep" and red means "angry" and "awake." And I was all sad and sleep. Somewhere in Texas, I think we were en route to Dallas. And unfortunately, I had to play a show after that.

AUTUMN: On the 'Flu.

WALLA: God . . . I probably got out of the van, drank six beers, and *then* played the show.

AUTUMN: Which records were "van" and which records were "bus"?

WALLA: The first three records were all van tour. Jason did one tour with us in a van, in 2003, while we were recording *Transatlanticism*.

AUTUMN: Right. When I met you, you guys were in a bus. Were you liking it at that point, or were you just thinking, "I hate this now, and I always will"?

WALLA: No, no. I really enjoyed it. I don't *dislike* the bus. I really enjoy the bus. I do dislike . . . um, if I get totally freaked out by the bus, and I need some time alone and I need to drive, I just rent a car. I have been known to just chase the bus for a day, or two days, or three days at a time.

AUTUMN: It's just a personal . . . wind in your hair . . . ?

WALLA: Kind of, yeah. On a bus, I always end up on vampire's schedule. Like I always end up staying up until seven or eight in the morning and sleeping until four in the afternoon. I can't not do that. It's difficult and weird.

AUTUMN: It's hard to know what time of day it is. Even if you know, the inside of the bus doesn't change enough to feel like it.

WALLA: It's really true. Yeah.

AUTUMN: It would be great to take the tinting off of one part of the bus, so there was a *For the Living Section*. Or you could use a *Vampire Bus*, or a *Mere Mortals Bus*.

WALLA: No one even likes it when I open the blinds. It's pretty vampiric in there.

AUTUMN: Did driving have anything to do with being the DJ?

WALLA: Well, okay . . . so, if I was driving, there was typically no music.

AUTUMN: [laughing] Oh, God!

WALLA: Well, I like it quiet! I love it when there's no music.

AUTUMN: Didn't that drive them crazy, though?

WALLA: [pause] They had headphones . . .

AUTUMN: [laughing] Was it like, when Death Cab started, everyone had Walkmans, and then by a certain record they were Discmans, and then . . .

WALLA: I think we had Disc*men* when we started, yeah.

AUTUMN: And cassette tapes in your van.

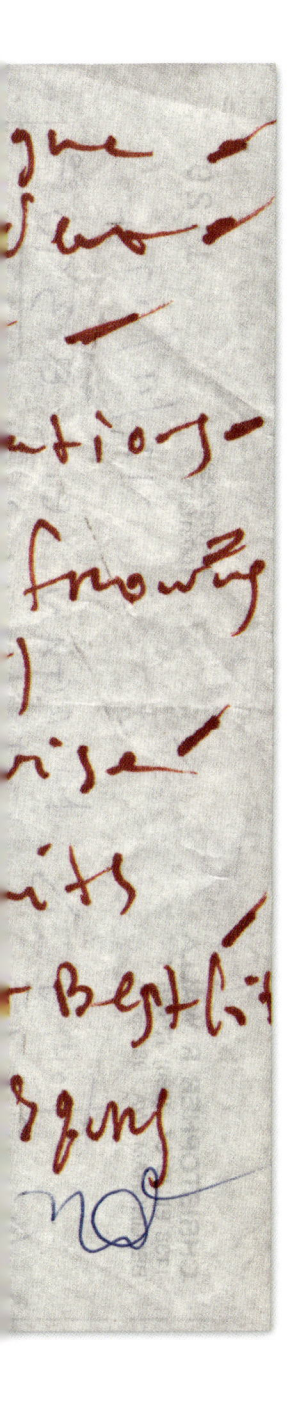

WALLA: Yeah. I still sort of enjoy the cassette tape in the vehicle. I think that's a good way to go.

AUTUMN: When you guys were touring in the van, was there a go-to record if you did play something.

WALLA: Yes, absolutely. It was *Between the Bridges* by Sloan.

AUTUMN: What record were you touring?

WALLA: It would have been *The Photo Album*.

AUTUMN: Was it your go-to record for a number of tours after that?

WALLA: It was my go-to record for *years*. It kind of still is.

AUTUMN: Are there other records that make you think of the early days? That doesn't really happen on a bus, where one record gets played and everybody listens to it, right?

WALLA: No, there's no music on the bus. That's why I also find that a little sad, too.

AUTUMN: You find it sad even though you didn't want music when you were driving? It's different?

WALLA: On the bus [sigh], what happens on the bus is that there's always a television on. Even if there's nothing on the television. Like the DirecTV logo is floating around the screen, and its illuminating the bus. It's this big, giant, stupid rectangle, and it drives me crazy. That's tough for me. I think that when we go out next, I'll be curious to see how it goes because everybody watches videos on their iPhones. And then there's also, there's more baseball now than I think there has ever been.

AUTUMN: Yeah, I've been noticing that.

WALLA: So, that will be a whole different thing.

AUTUMN: It'll be a sports bar bus without the bar.

WALLA: A sports bus. Yes. Hmmm ...

AUTUMN: Any other van or bus stories worth noting?

WALLA: Well, there was that time in the van when the windshield popped out.

AUTUMN: Oh my God. And then how did the windshield ... when ...?

WALLA: This was the only van tour that Jason did, for *Transatlanticism*. I sort of forget what happened; it just sort of popped loose. And then, on that same trip, this weird thing happened where the headlights didn't work. The brights worked, but they only worked in that temporary position where you're holding them back.

AUTUMN: So you had to manually hold your lights on?

WALLA: Yeah, for about seven hundred miles. It was really sad. I got a hand cramp. Boo.

AUTUMN: Did it affect your guitar solos?

WALLA: Probably.

BUS VS. VAN

[ON THE PHONE WITH BEN]

AUTUMN: I just talked to Walla about his love for the open road. So, okay, bus vs. van: Which one do you like better? Or do you like both for different reasons?

BEN: Bus is definitely a more awesome way to travel. There are elements of traveling in a van that I have nostalgia for. I got more reading done, and I listened to a lot more records. I was alone in my own thoughts a lot more in a van, when your circle of privacy is a pair of headphones stuck to your own head. But you can't climb off into a bunk and watch a movie or watch TV or something like that.

AUTUMN: You toured in a van for however many years so it must have been a big deal to switch over?

BEN: I think that as the band progressed and we were playing bigger and bigger shows, consequently we had to be at venues earlier and earlier, and at a certain point, it just didn't . . . the only reason you would stay in a van is if you had some complex about it, you know? Initially, the first week or so in the bus, I felt a little self-conscious because I was foolishly thinking that people were going to care . . . foolishly thinking that I should care or people *would* care whether we were rolling up in front in a bus or a van. Our job is to put on the best show we possibly can, given environmental circumstances, and a bus certainly makes for a better . . . for a band that's better rested, and is going to play better.

AUTUMN: I have toured with bands in a van and in a bus, and I remember the nostalgia of the van that follows after the experience, though during it, you do feel tortured. I think it's interesting that you feel like when you're all compressed into a small area, you have more alone time than on a bus.

BEN: That's true. There's a part of it that I like . . . when you're going to a job that you hate and daydreaming the whole time about going on tour and getting away, then climbing in a van and going on adventures is a very attractive alternative. It certainly was for me. I couldn't wait. Eventually, if you're lucky, those adventures become the center of your life, what you're doing, your job, and at a certain point you want to make adjustments to make it easier.

AUTUMN: Right, that's interesting.

BEN: I honestly think that people . . . that when you're on the indie rock circuit and playing the Bottlenecks and Crocodile Cafes of the world, you're playing to a crowd that goes out to a lot more shows. They're more forgiving of a raggedy group of dudes showing up and loading their gear right onto the stage. They're paying eight bucks to drink with their friends and kind of casually check out a band. We did some of our best shows under those circumstances. But at a certain point, when you're playing to people who are spending more money to come see you play and they go to less shows—in fact, they go to "concerts," not shows—I feel a responsibility to not show up on two hours of sleep and go right on stage without a sound check. An indie rock audience is more conditioned for that type and show and that kind of experience. You might still have a transcendent experience at a show like that, and I certainly do myself, but I think there's a different level of expectation built into it.

AUTUMN: I really like that about you guys, that even after years of touring, you still really care about the fact that the audience bought a ticket.

BEN: Exactly. And I really want to be clear that it's not that the more money you pay for a ticket, the better the show's going to be. We've played some of our best shows that I can remember to people who paid $3 to see us in a basement.

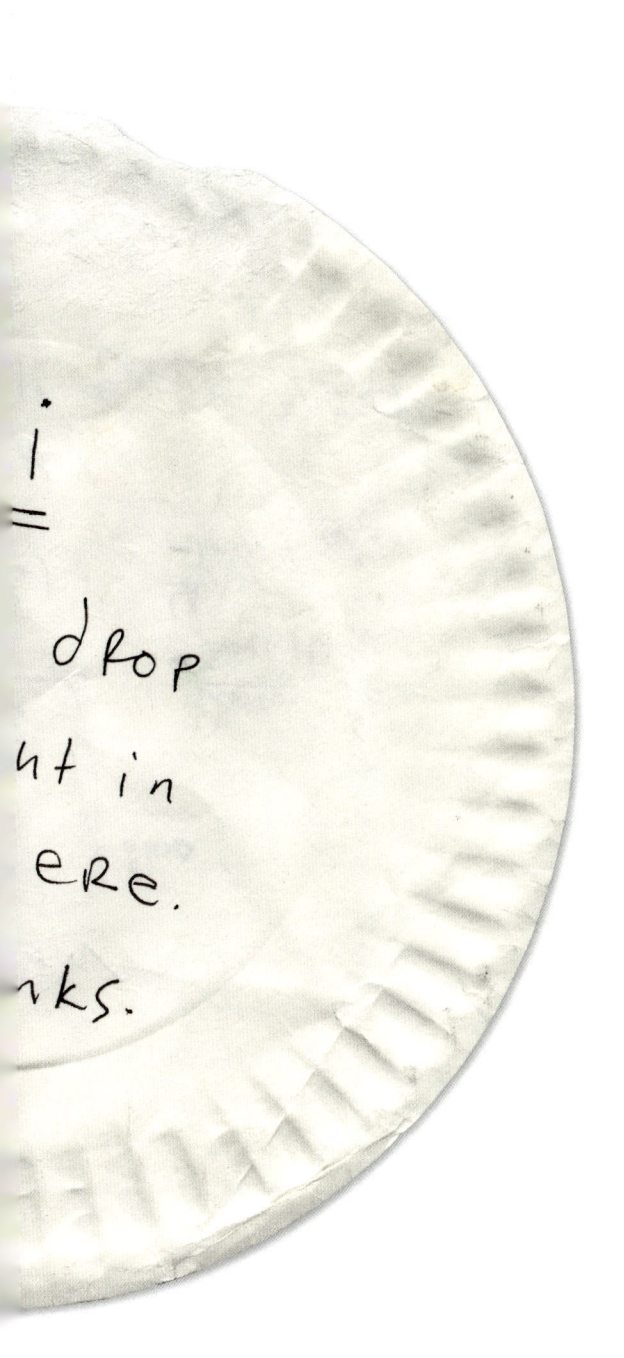

AUTUMN: Of course. As far as the band dynamics, were there any distinct changes between the four of you when you transitioned from the van to the bus. Walla said that he knew that you guys knew that he wouldn't get in the van if he wasn't driving.

BEN: Walla has always had issues with control. [laughing] I don't think he would even dispute that. I thinking shifting to the bus means everyone can be on their own schedule. When everybody has to wake up at 9 A.M. in a hotel and get everybody fed and coffeed and in the van and on the road in a decent amount of time because you have to make a show . . . [laughing] for example, Walla would *always* wake up at the very last second to hop in the shower. He was *always* the last one to get in the van. If he was the second person to get to the van, he would spin around and wander off somewhere else. He would never wait in the van until the two other people got there. Where that comes from, whether that comes from his sense of needing a level of control, of "We'll go when I'm ready to go," or . . .

AUTUMN: Or sense of adventure.

BEN: [laughing] Right, exactly.

AUTUMN: "One more person I can have a random conversation with by possibly buying mixed nuts."

BEN: I think it really has more to do with the fact the idea of, "Well I have to be in this can for eight hours today, I can squeeze . . . " I remember saying to him that there is no difference between getting up at eight thirty and getting up at eight forty-five, you know? There's no difference. Fifteen minutes of sleep just does not make or break your day. Clinically, I think that you can prove that that does not make or break your day. But he was very insistent. So, for his mental sanity, he kind of needed that extra fifteen minutes.

AUTUMN: [laughing] I'm that way, too.

BEN: On the bus, I don't mind. Everyone is able to do their own thing. If Jason wants to get up at nine in the morning and take a cab to a drum shop and get antique drums or whatever, or go to a record store, that's fine. You lose a little bit of the camaraderie going from the van to a bus, but what you gain is so much more valuable in return.

AUTUMN: It's a different movie; one is not better than the other. I can think of one habit that Walla has retained, which is wandering off for hours between sound check and the show. I'm wondering when the term "Where's Walla?" was created. Was it in the van years?

BEN: We pulled over at a Wall Drug on tour in '99 and bought a couple of those *Where the Heck Is Wall Drugs?* stickers and changed them so they said "Where the Heck Is Walla?" But really, it was, "*Where the fuck is Walla?* We need to *go*. Where. The. *Fuck*. Is. Walla?"

AUTUMN: [laughing] I remember once he took a four-hour walk and came back with a Felix the Cat guitar.

BEN: Exactly.

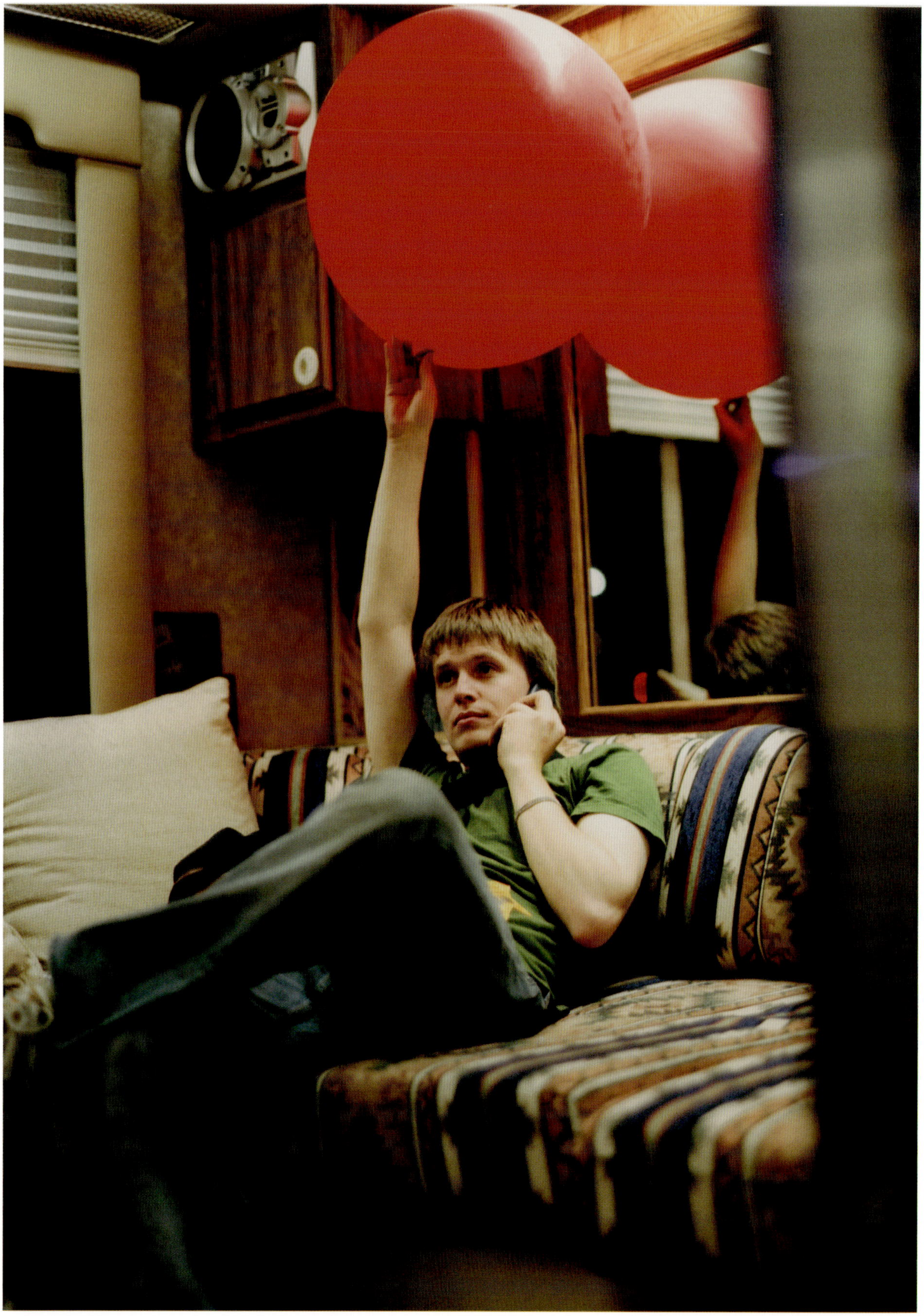

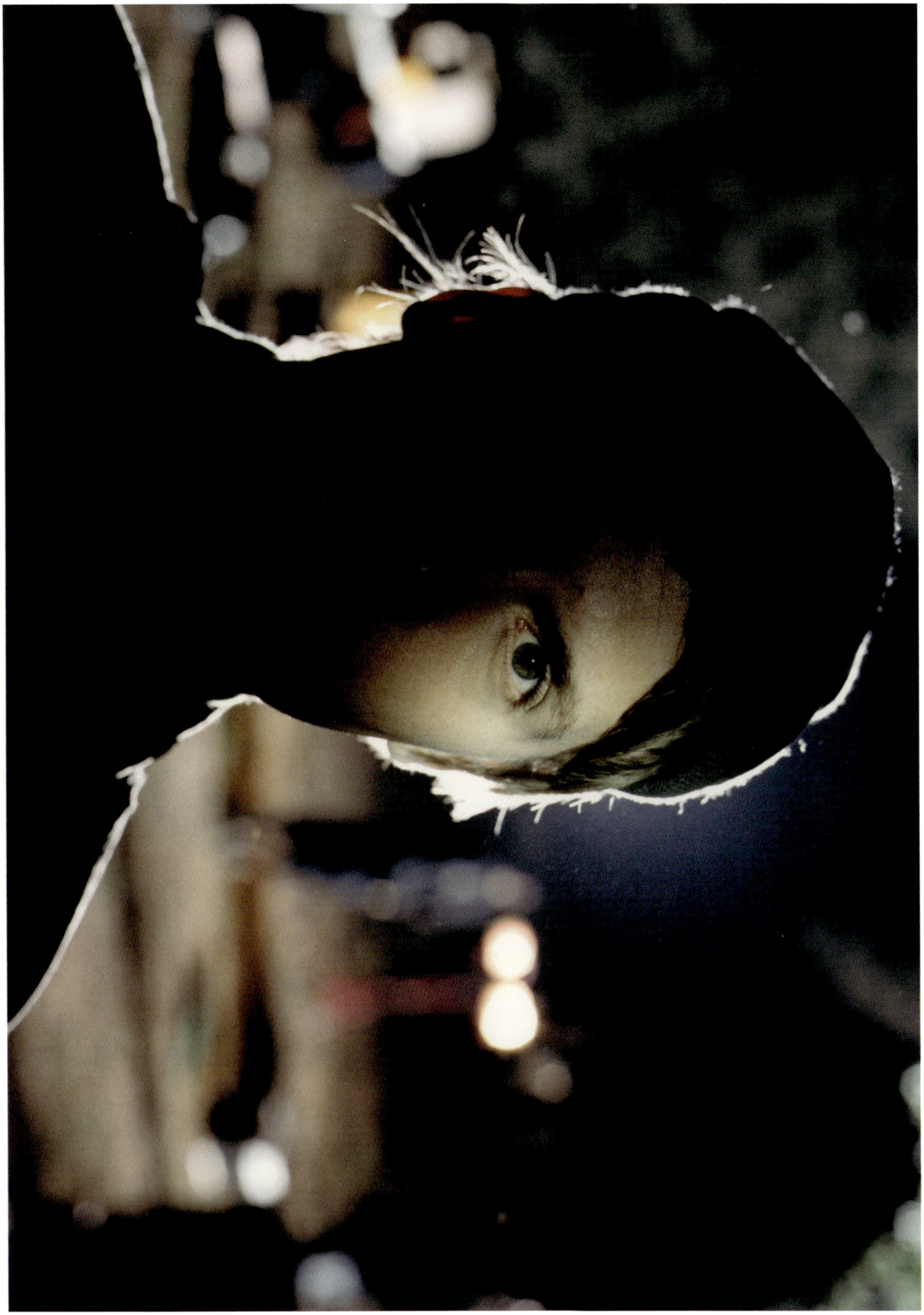

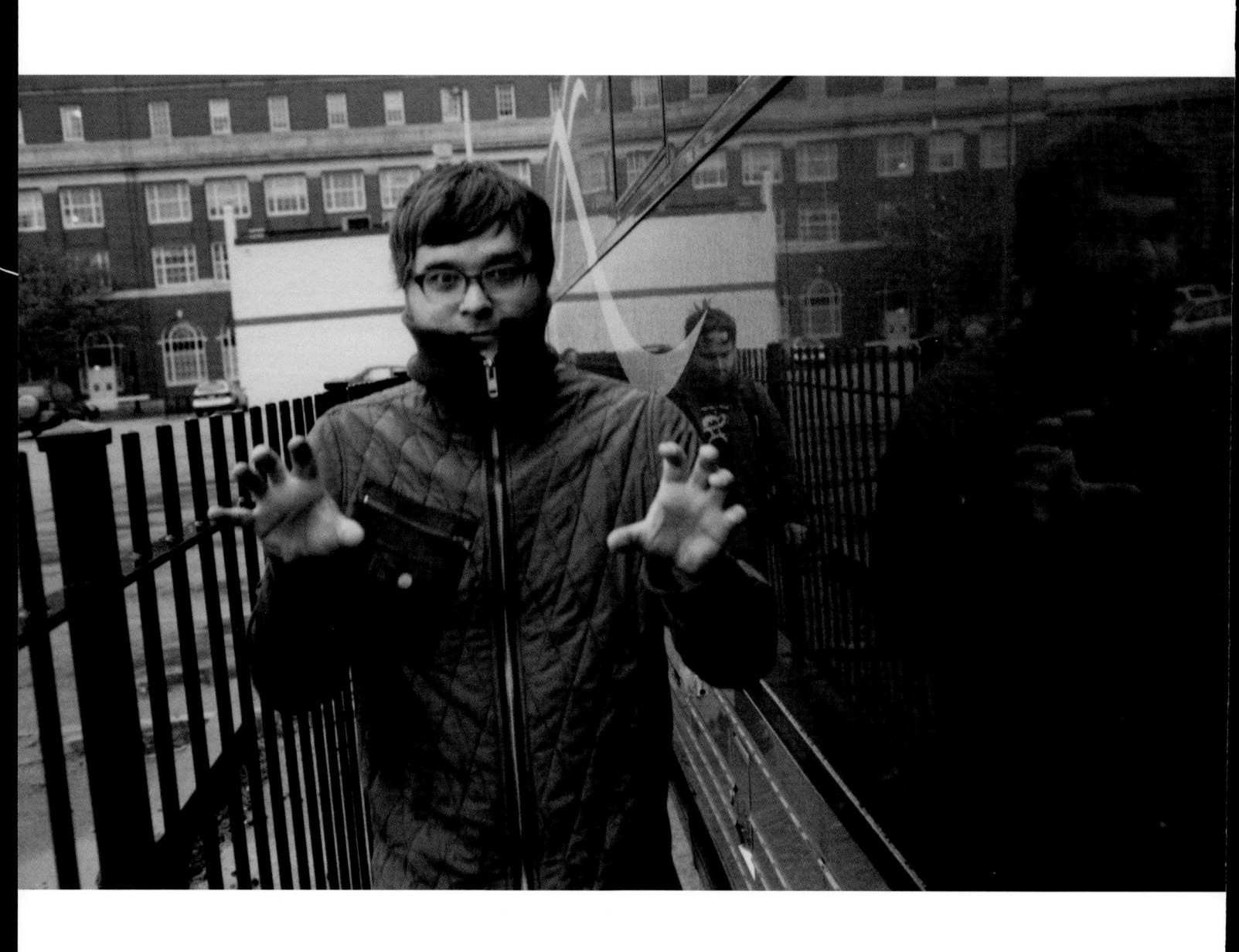

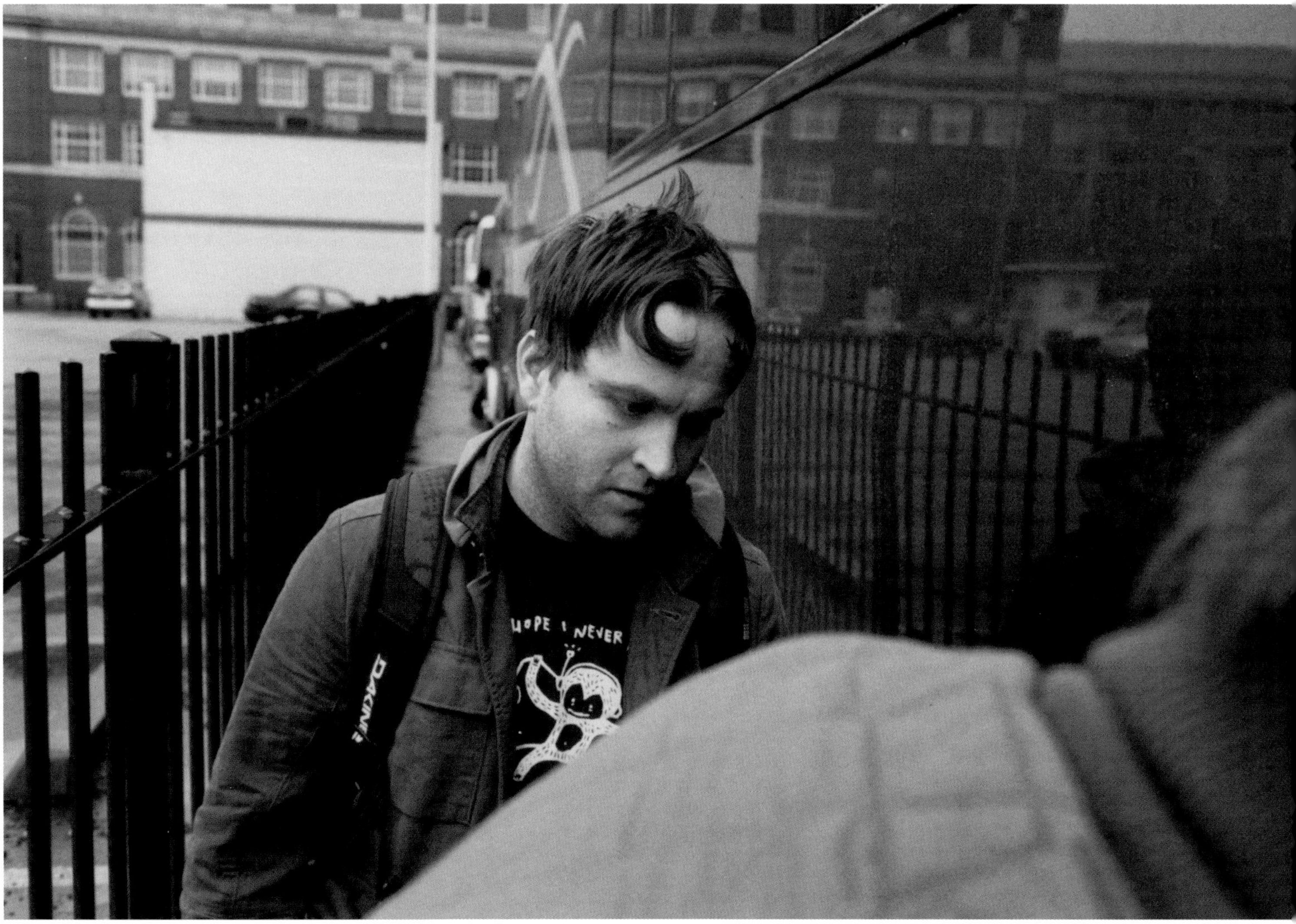

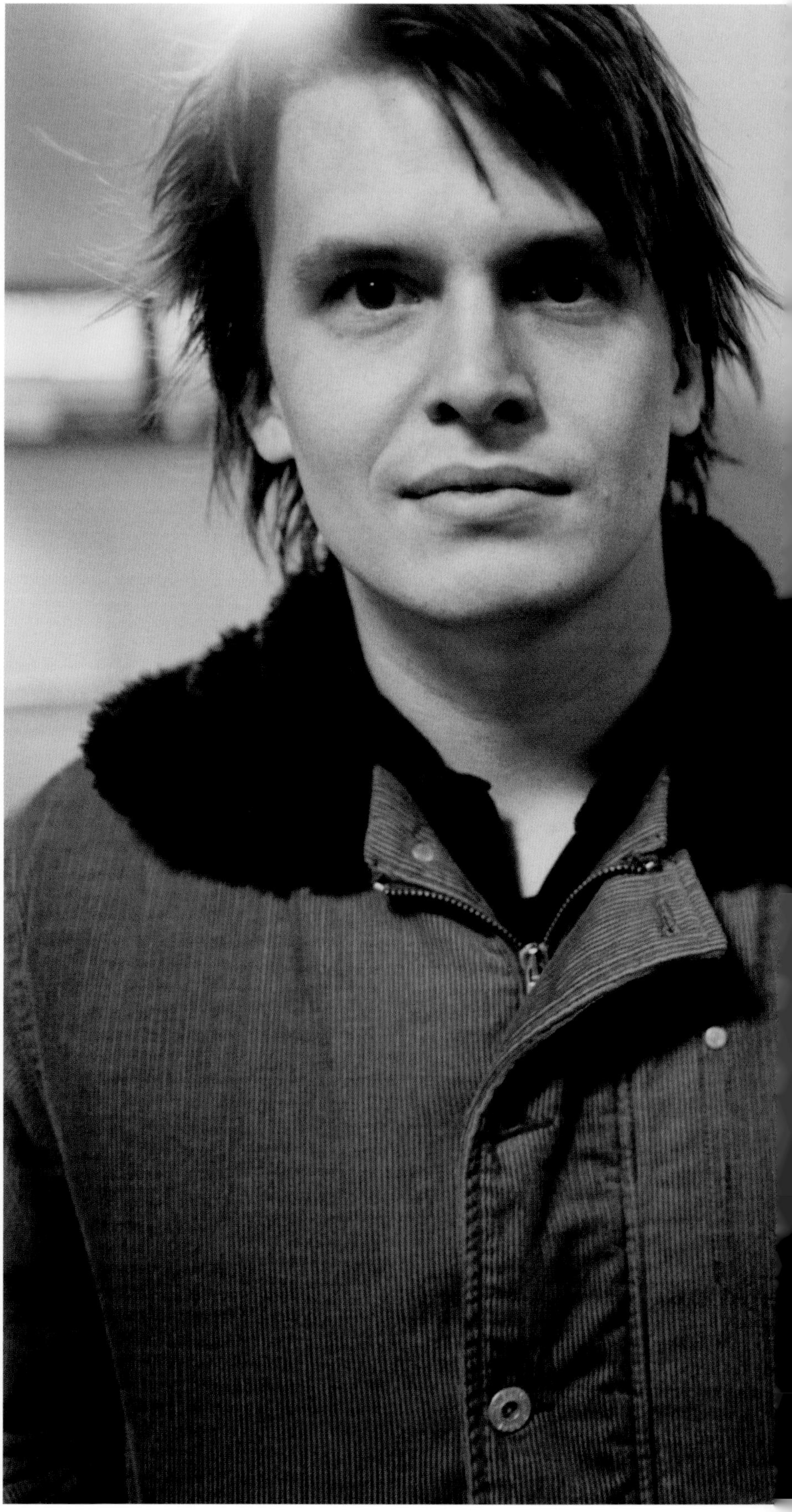

CAUTION:

REAL WORLD

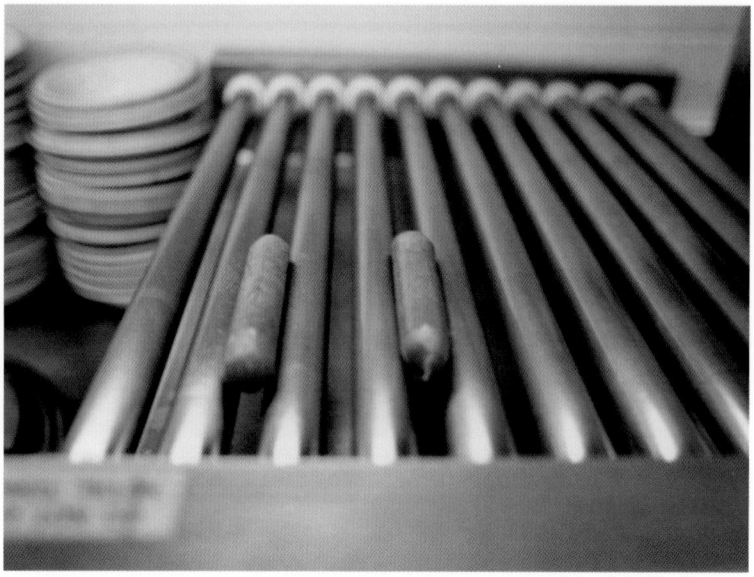

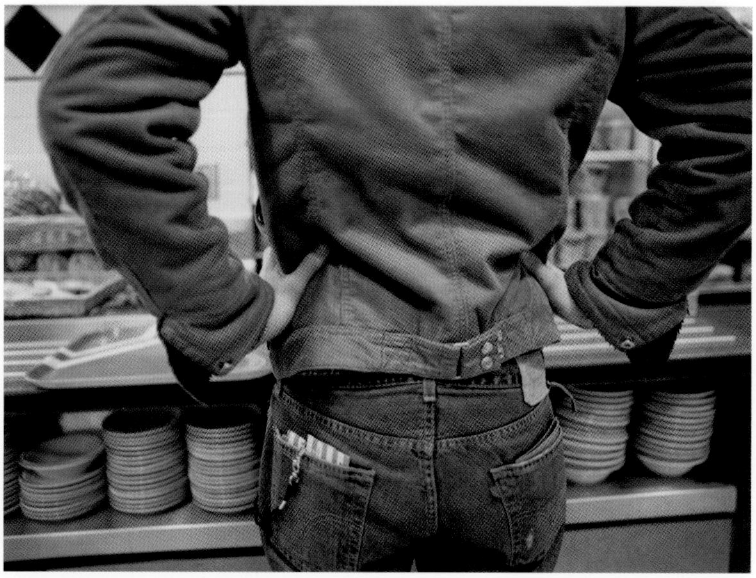

PLEASE USE the PLATES
ON top of the Salad Bar
for the SMALL Salad w/ special

Crush
Auction
Sign-ups 10/26

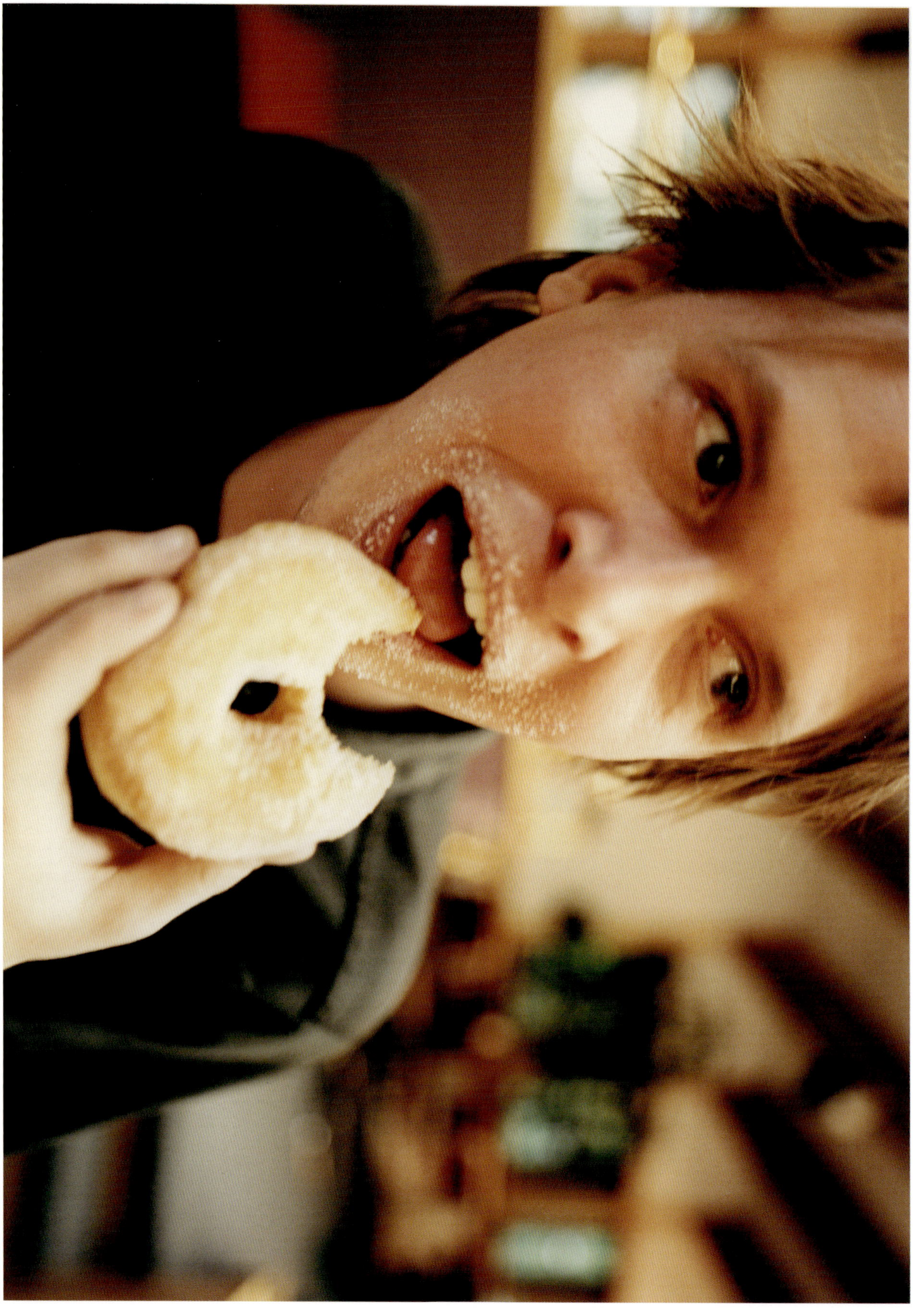

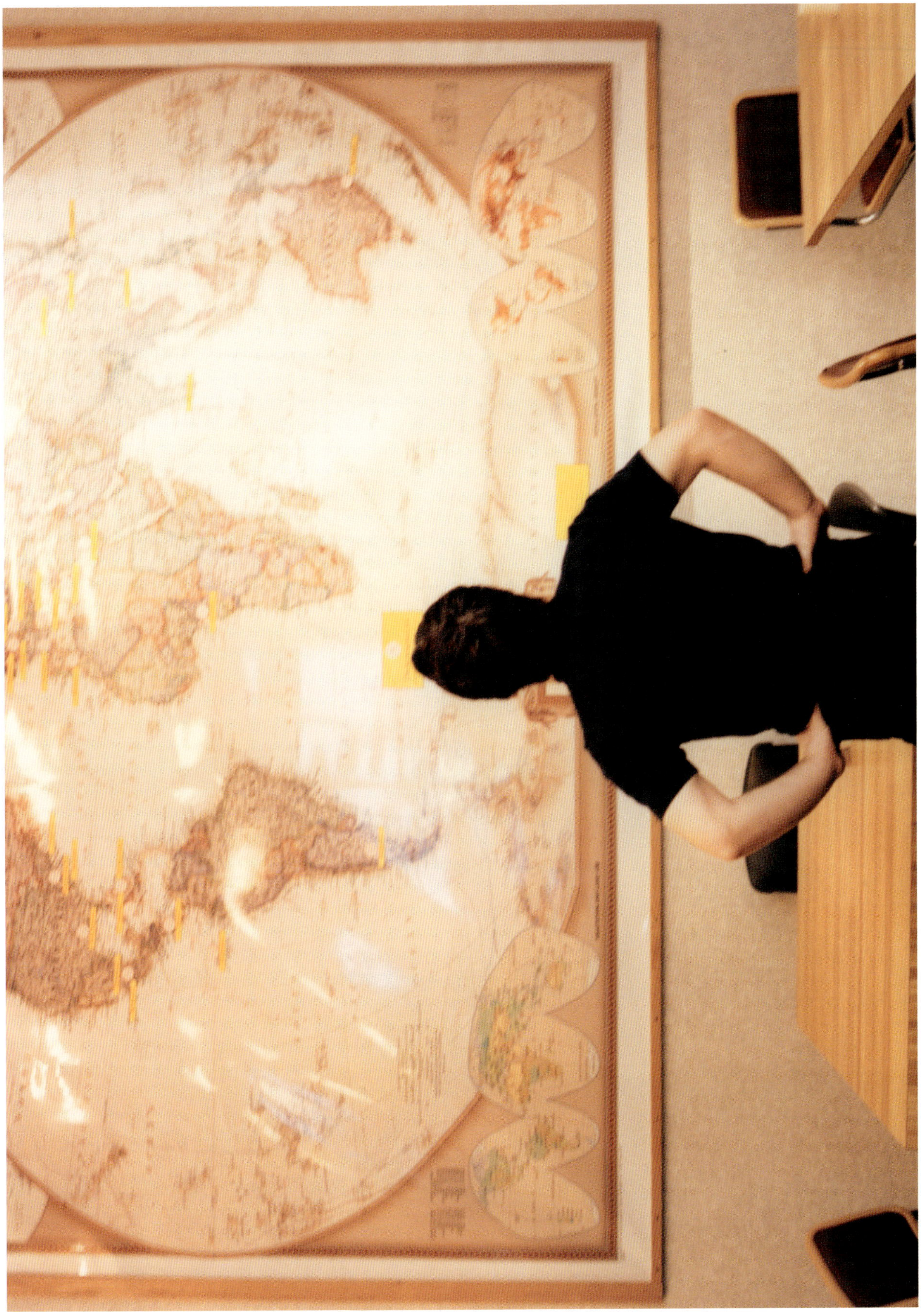

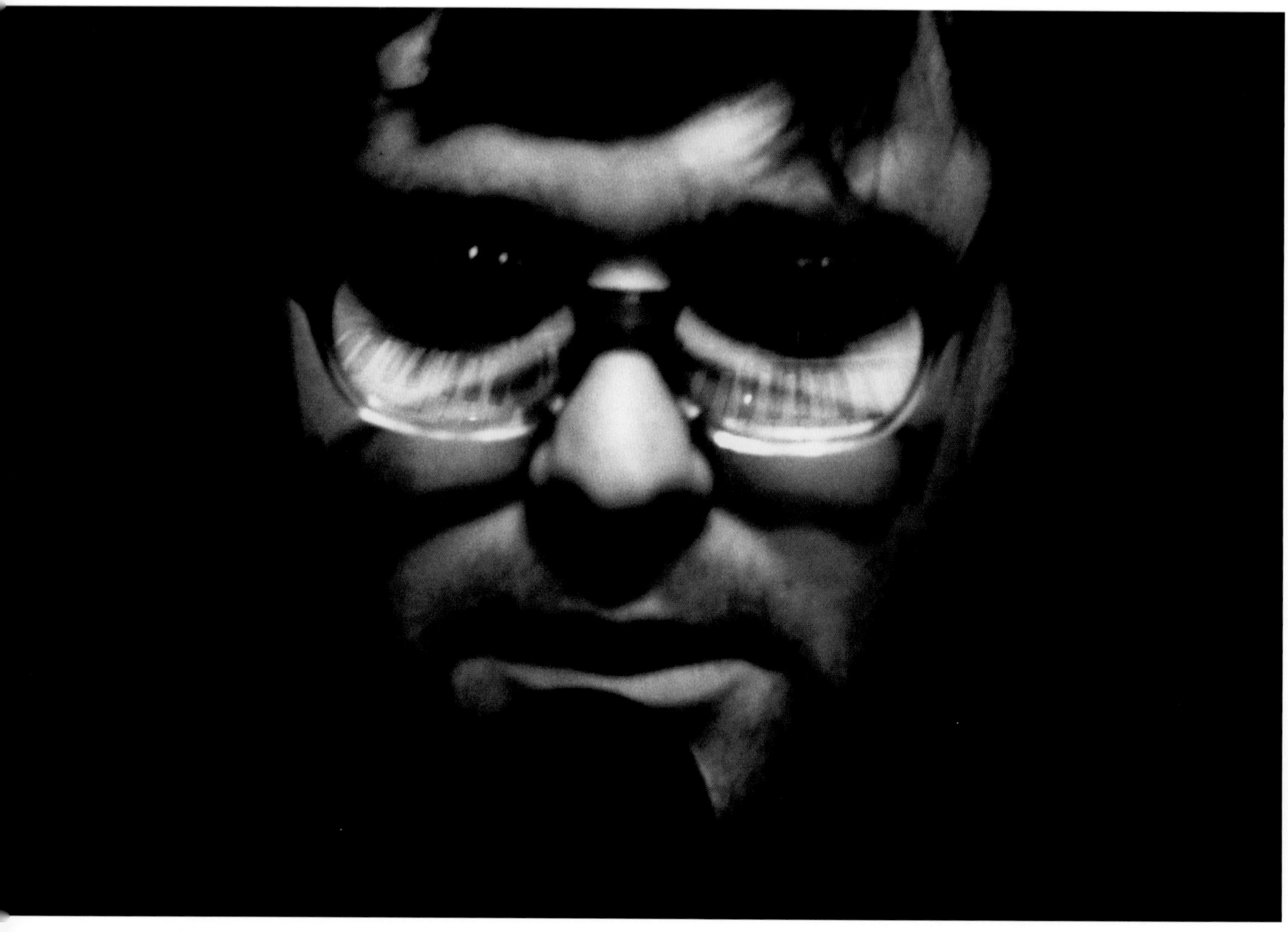

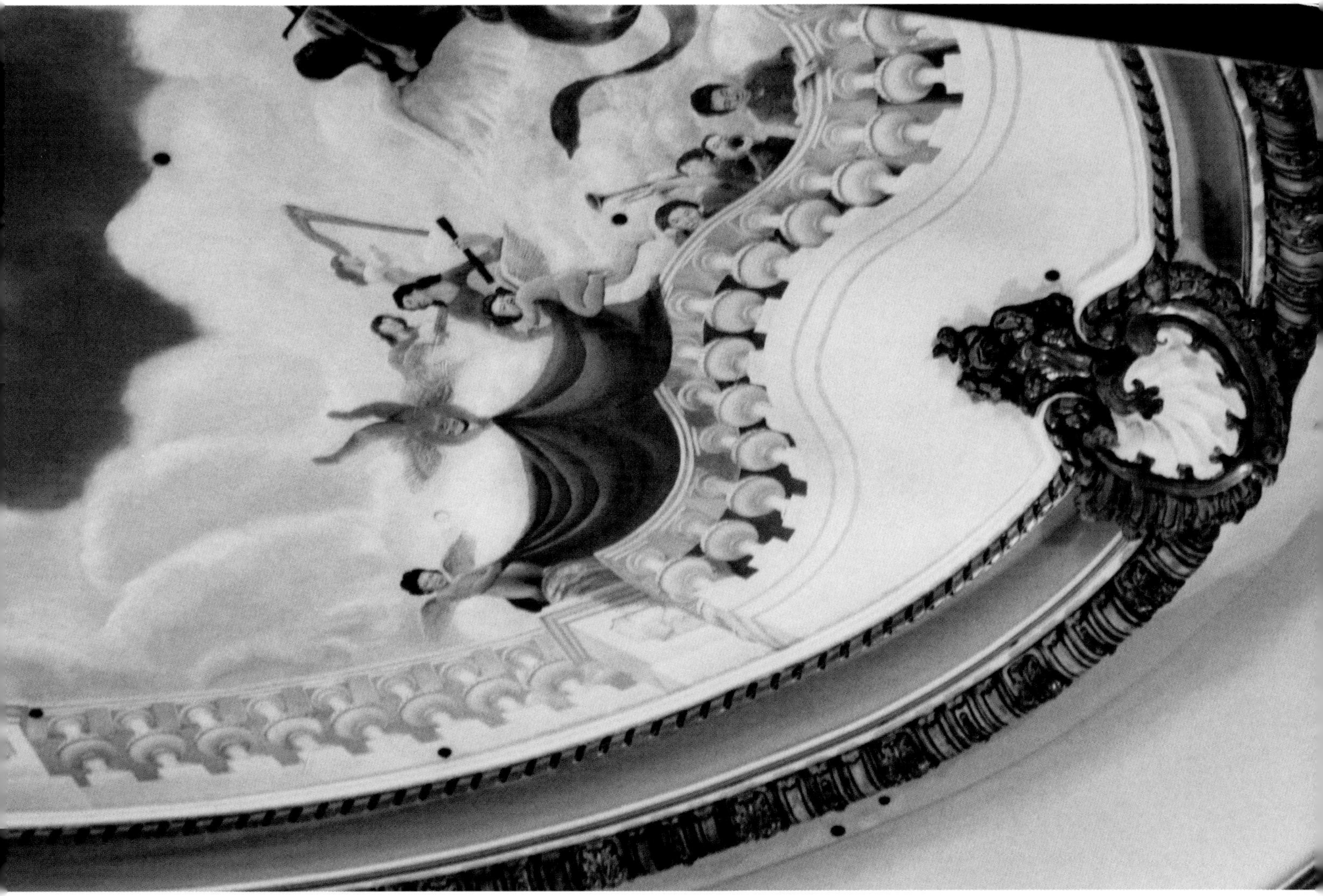

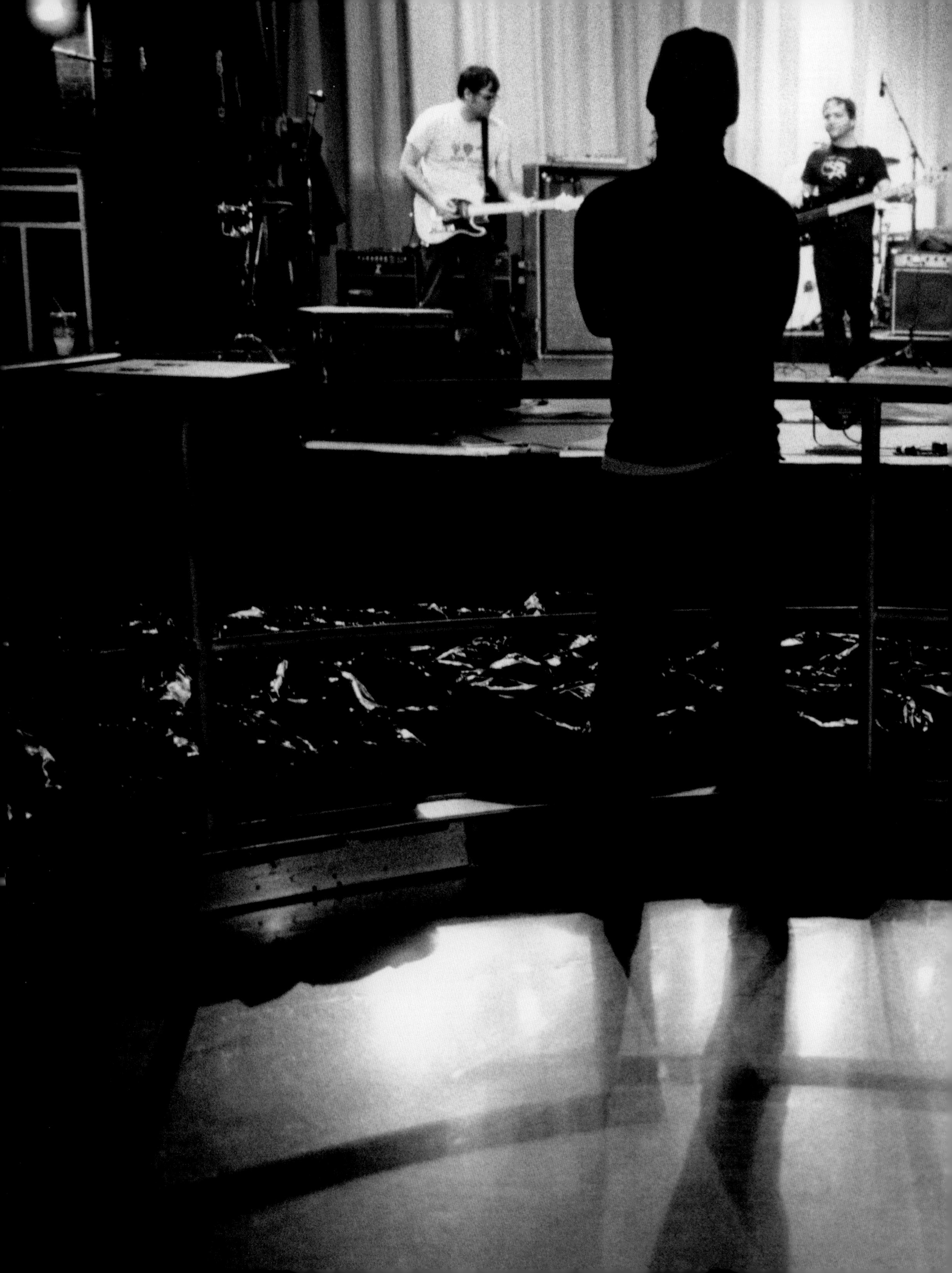

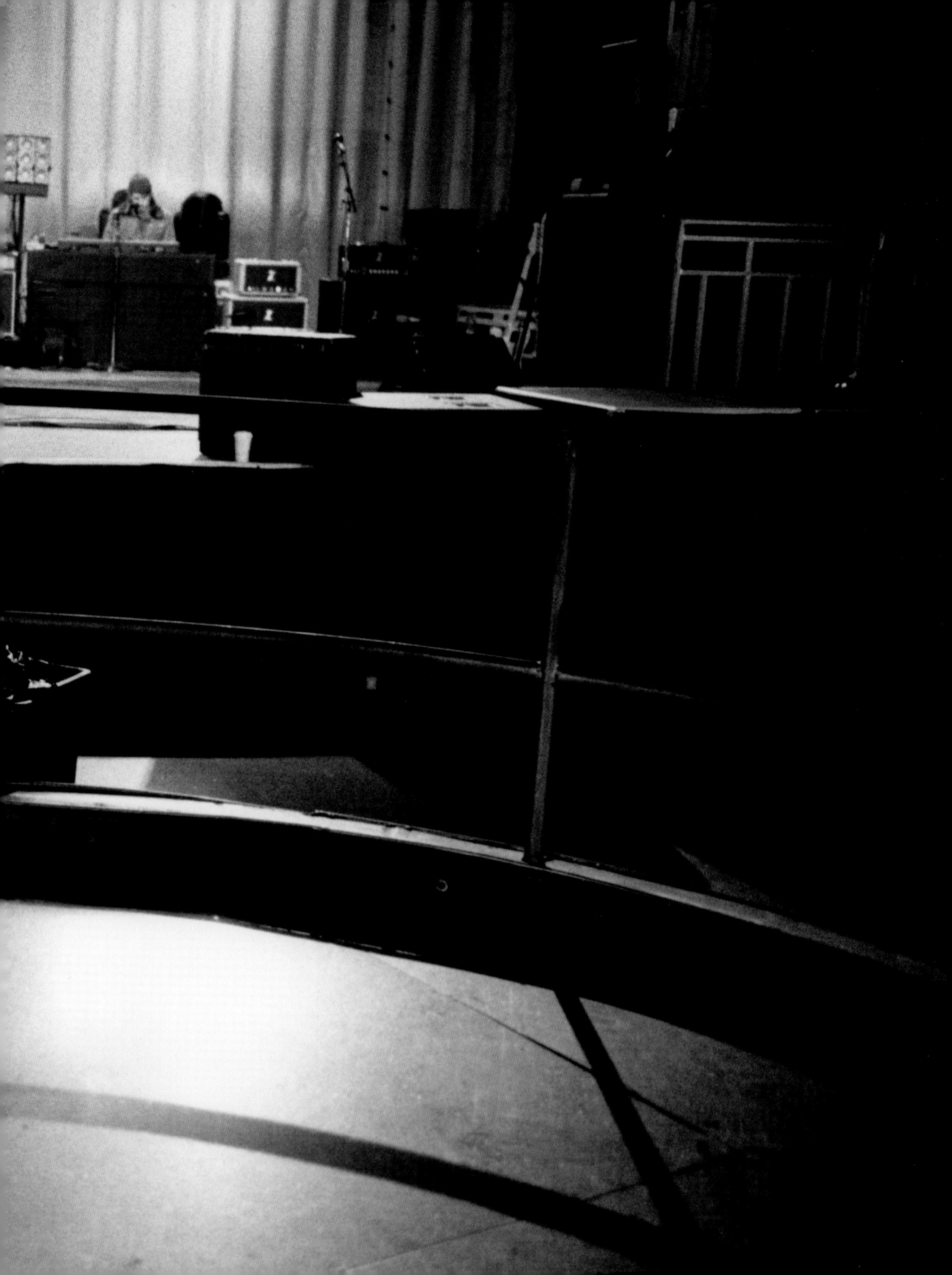

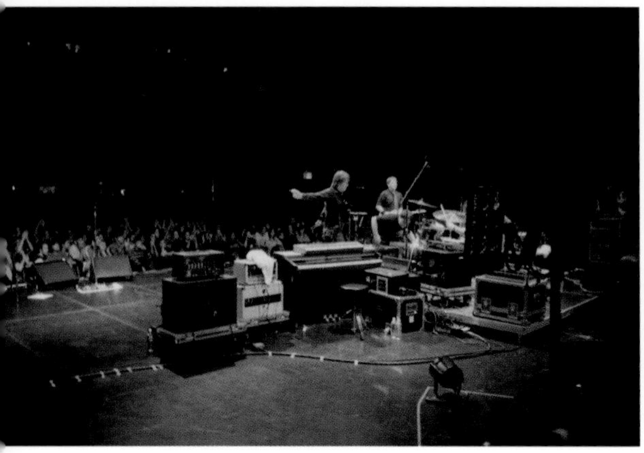
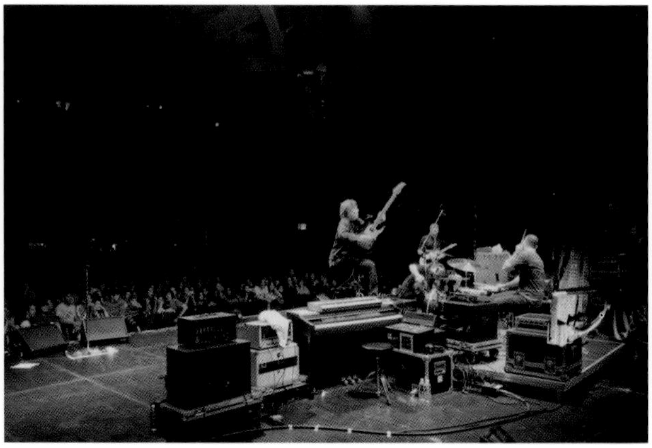
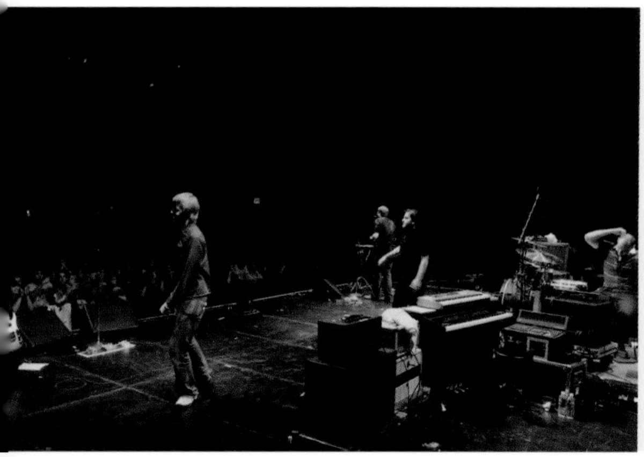
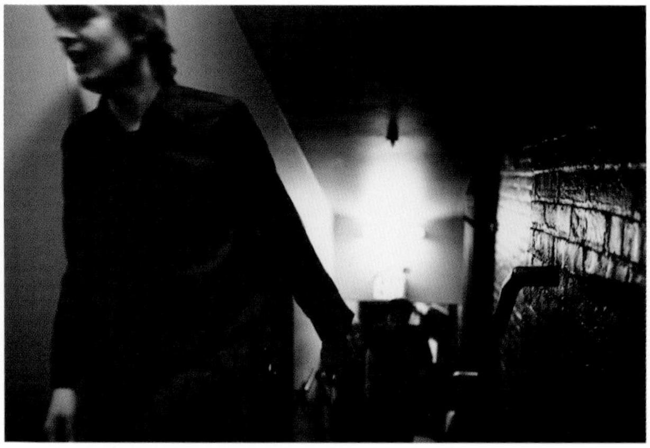
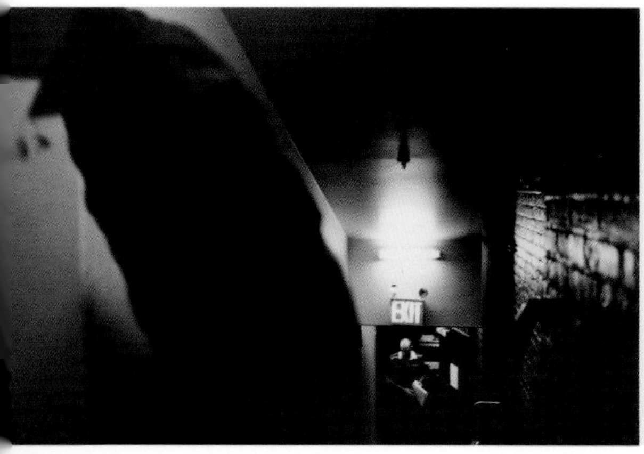
EXIT
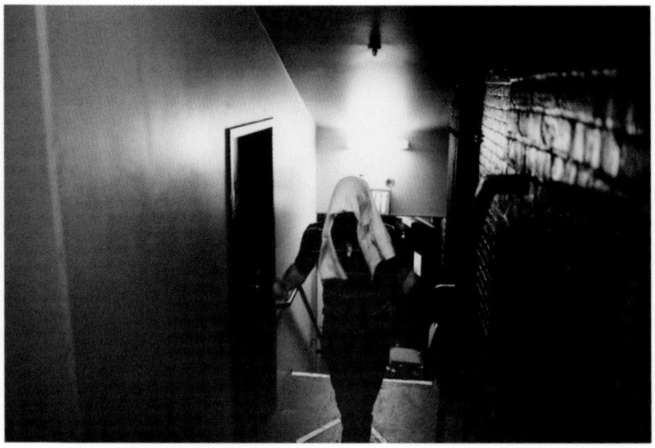

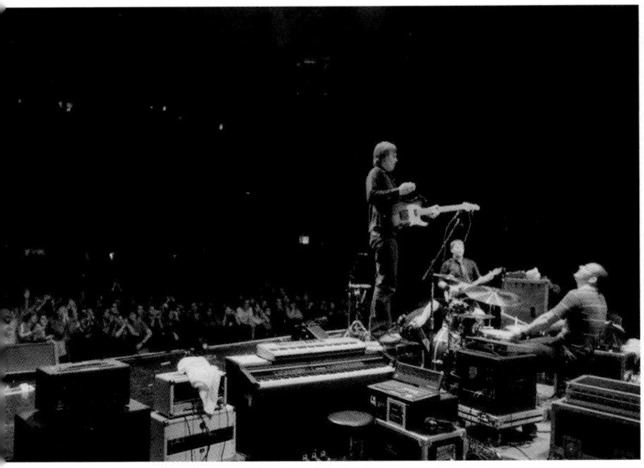

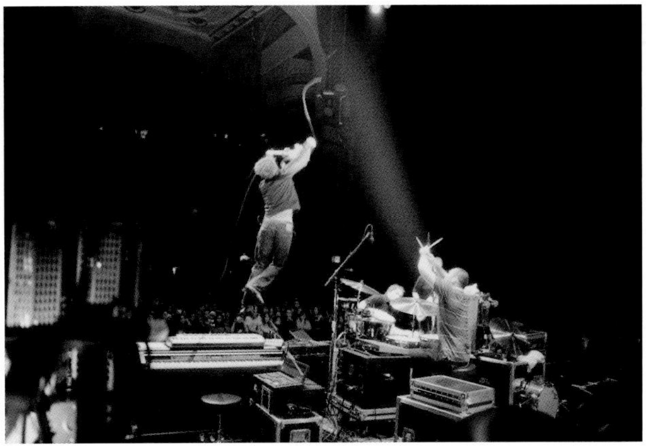

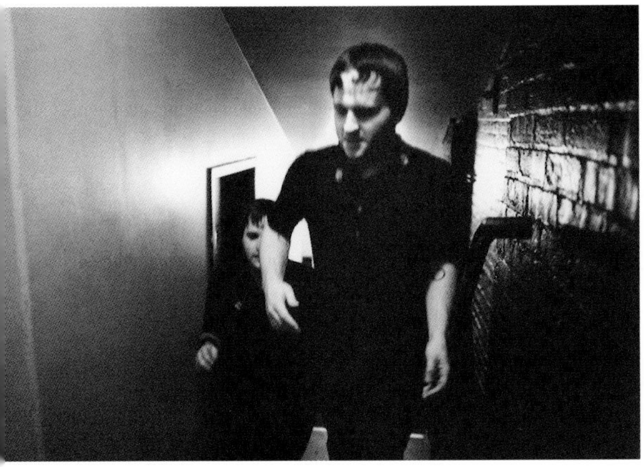

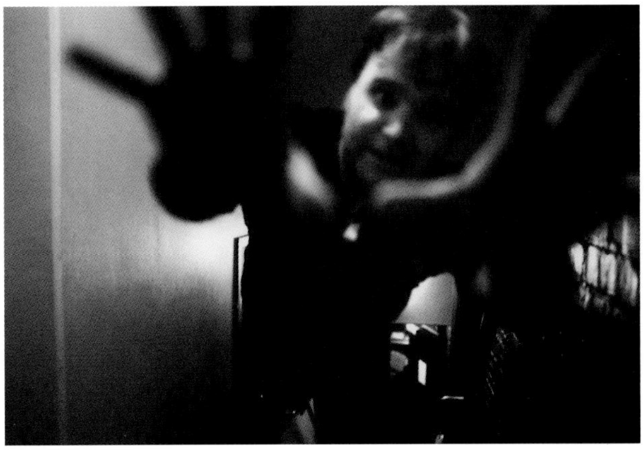

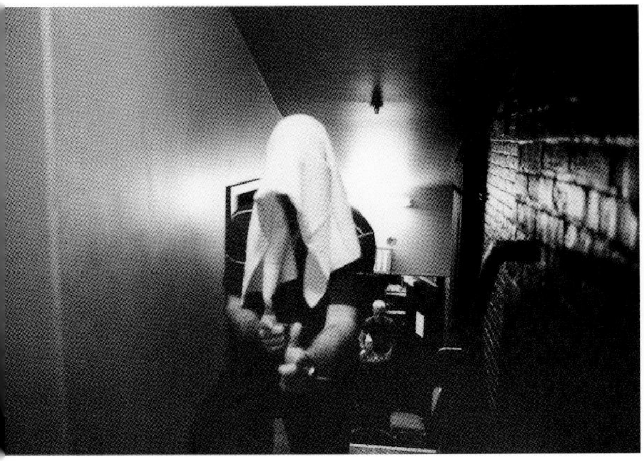

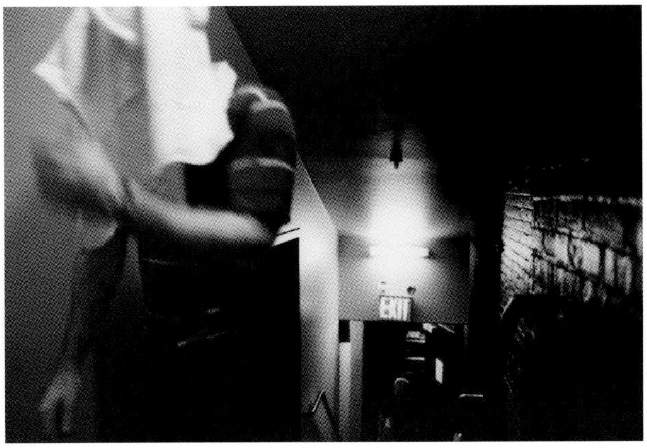
EXIT

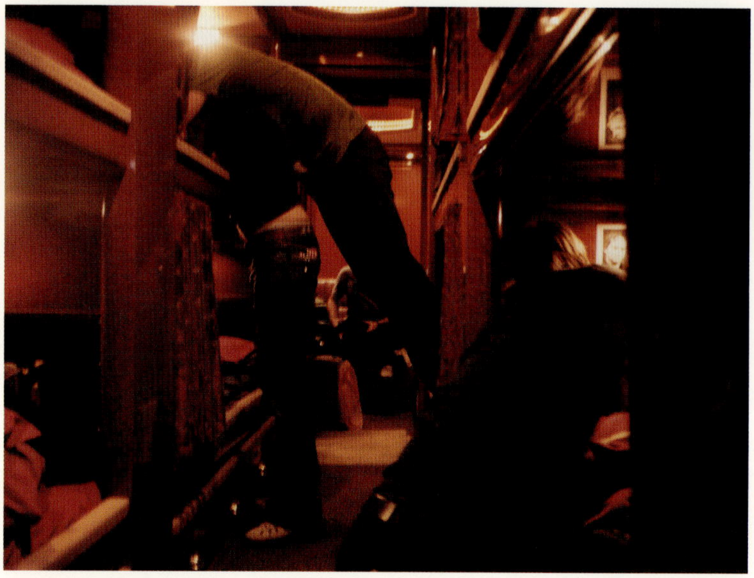

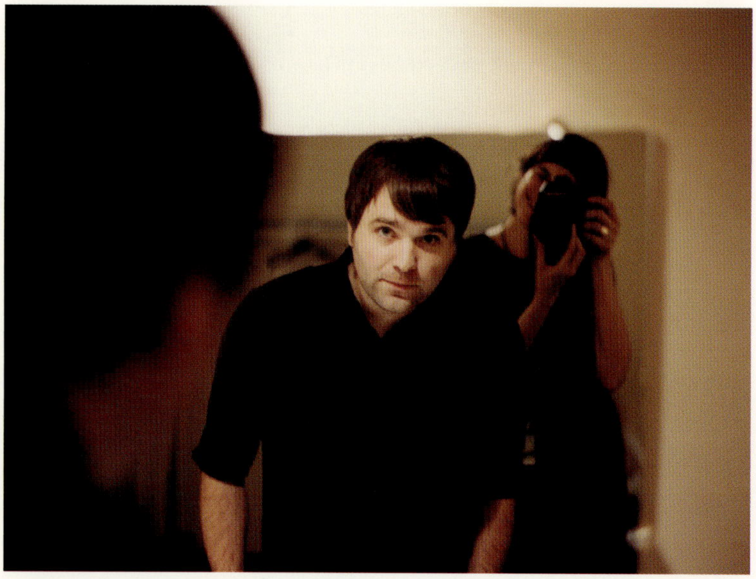

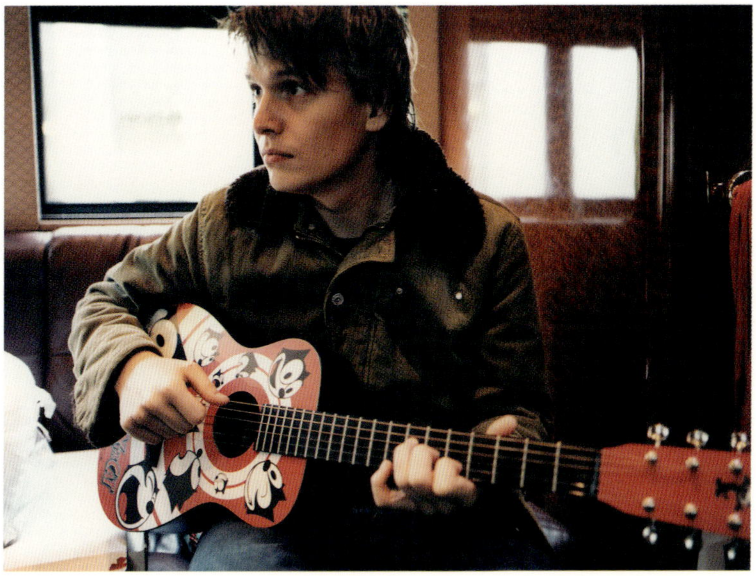

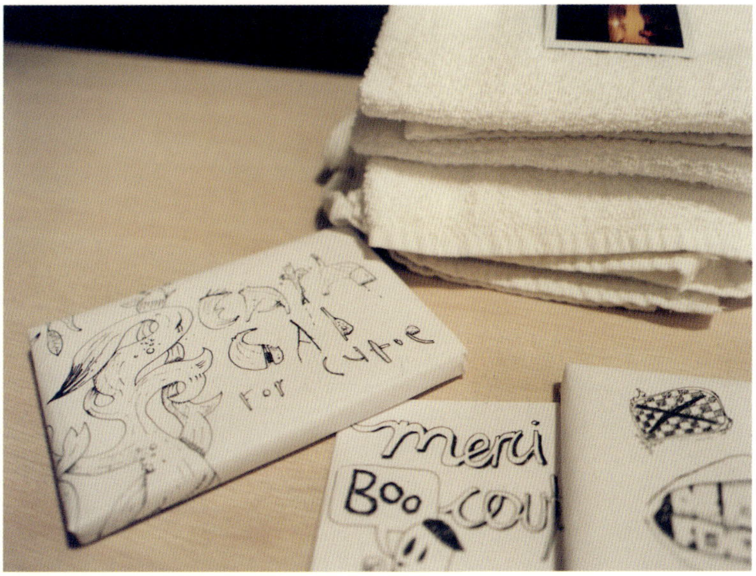
merci
Boo .cou

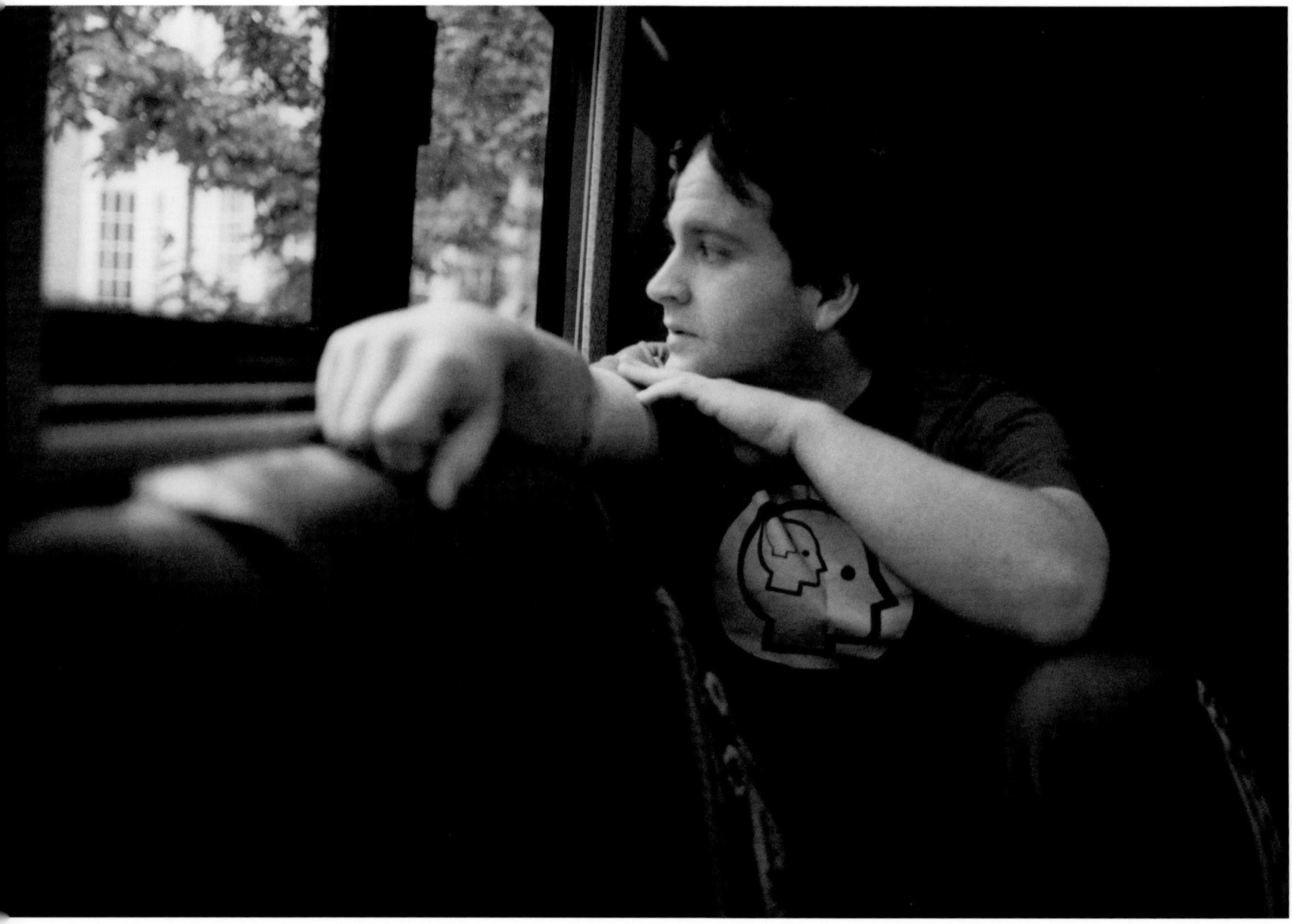

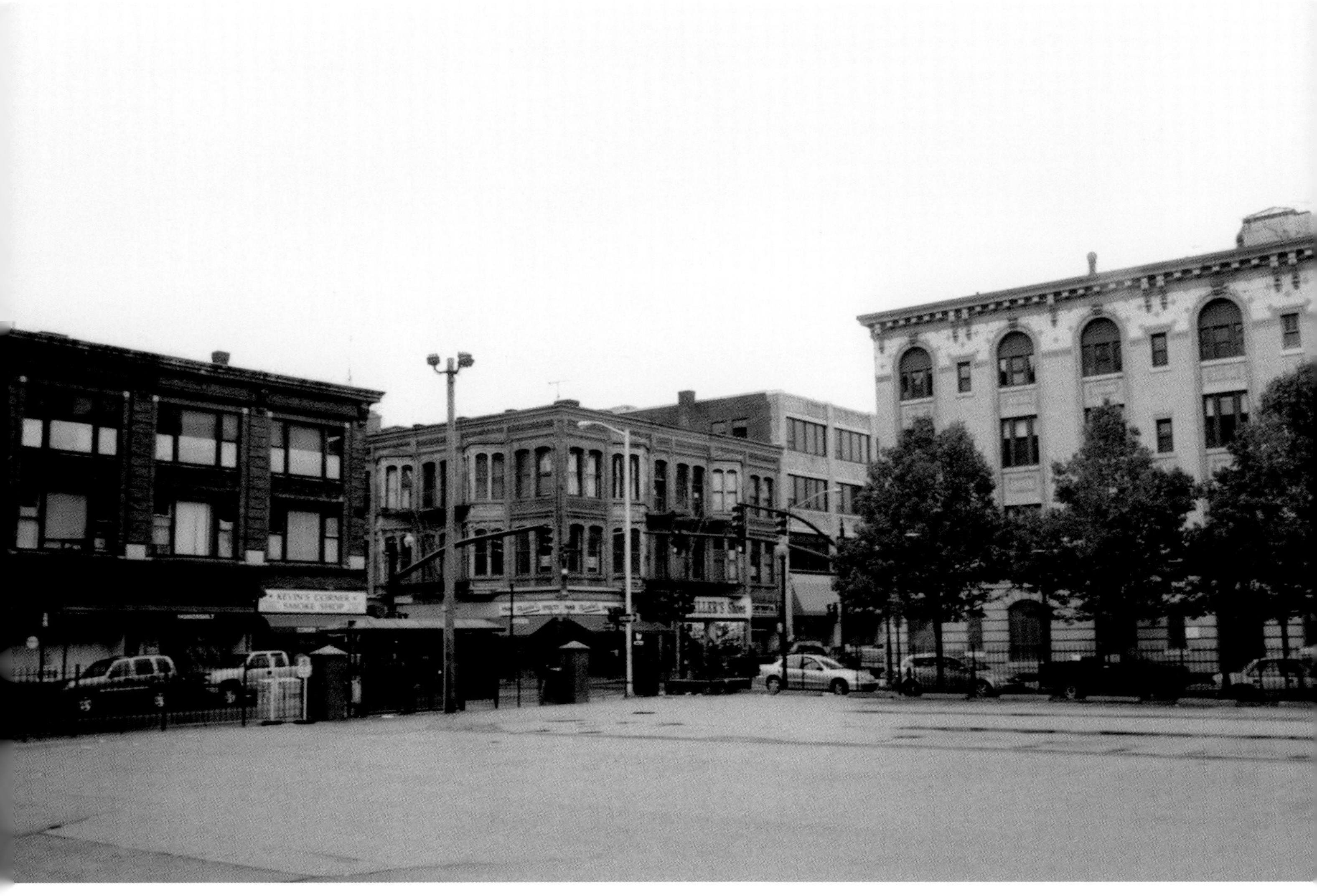
KEVIN'S CORNER
SMOKE SHOP

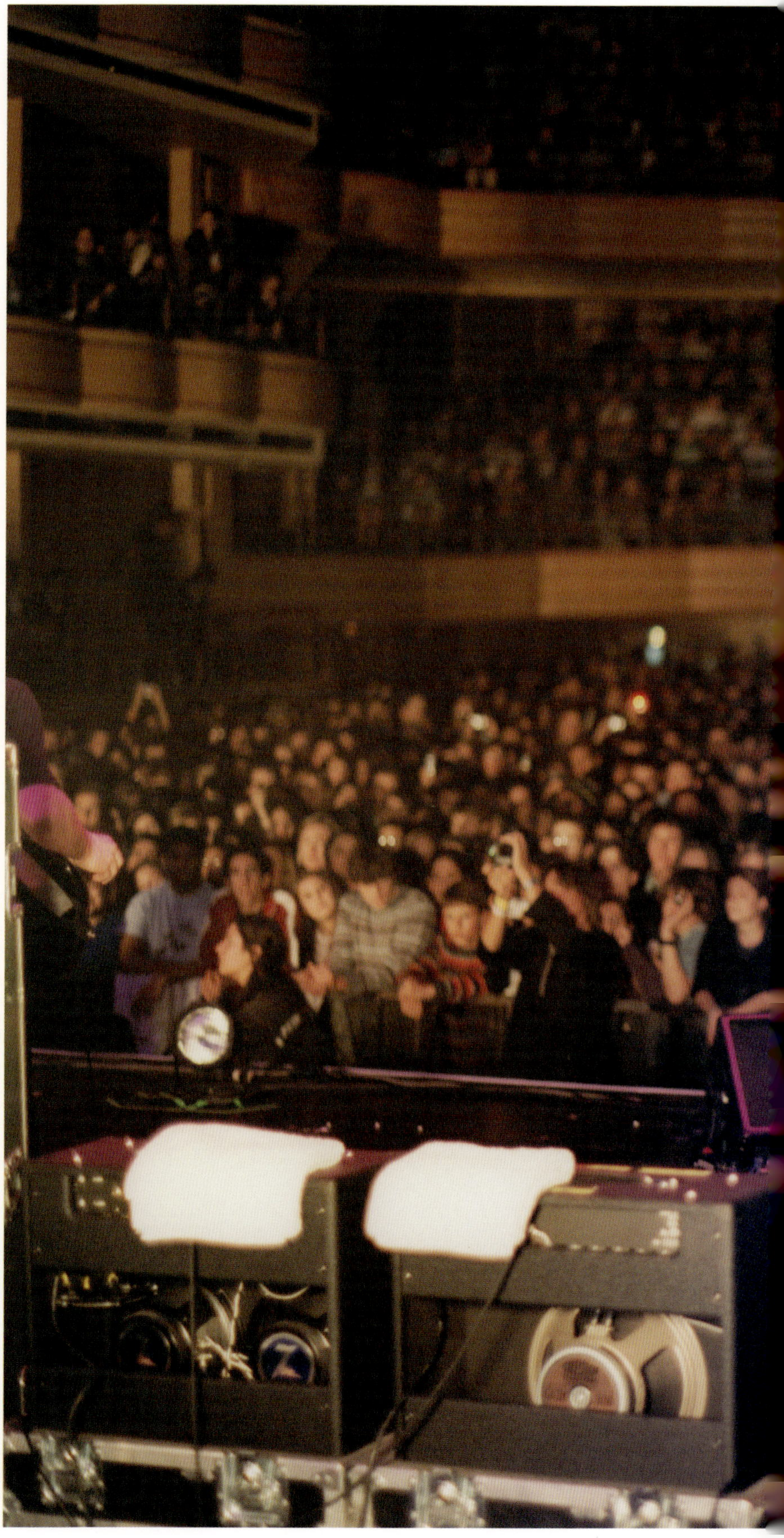

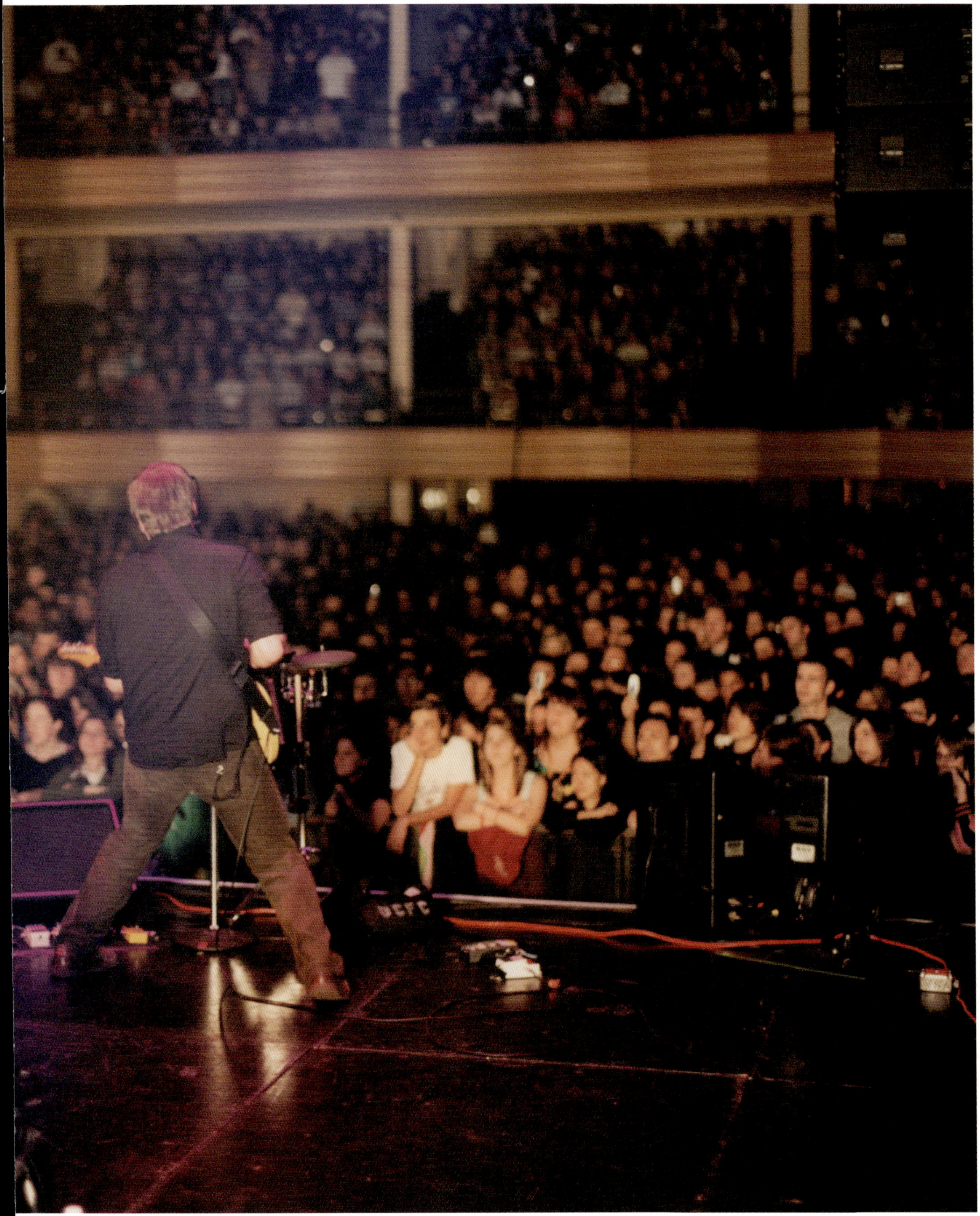

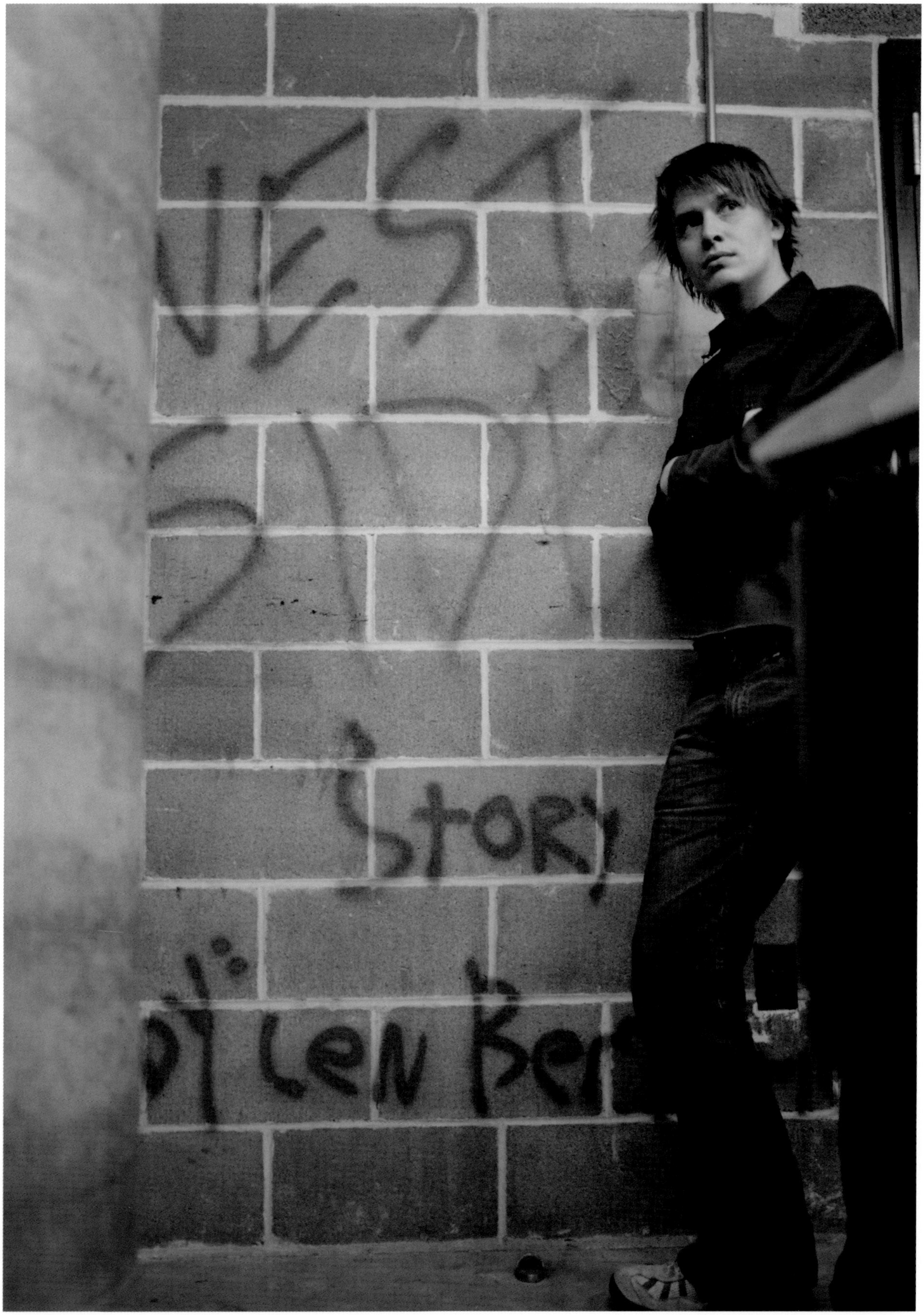
STORY

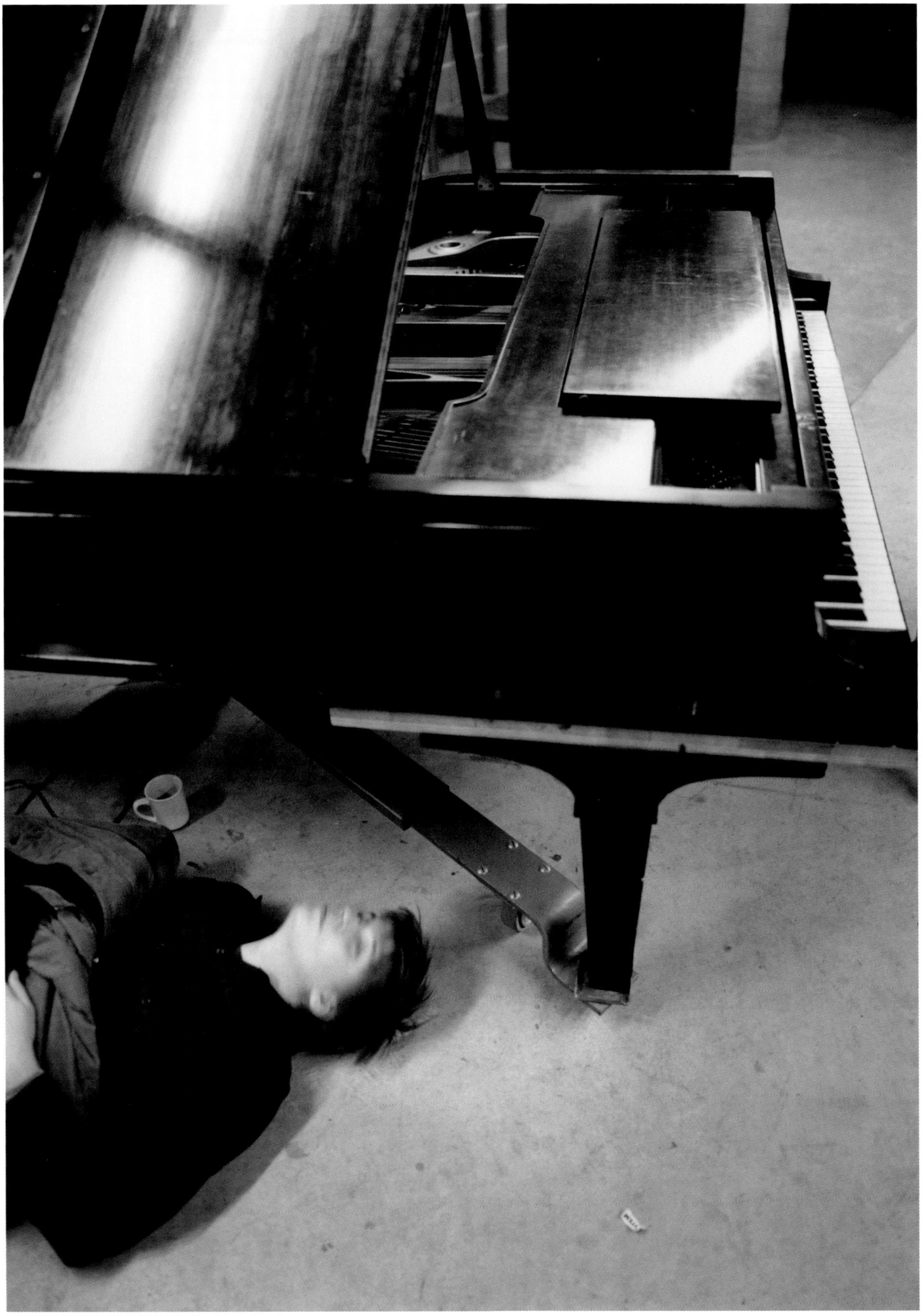

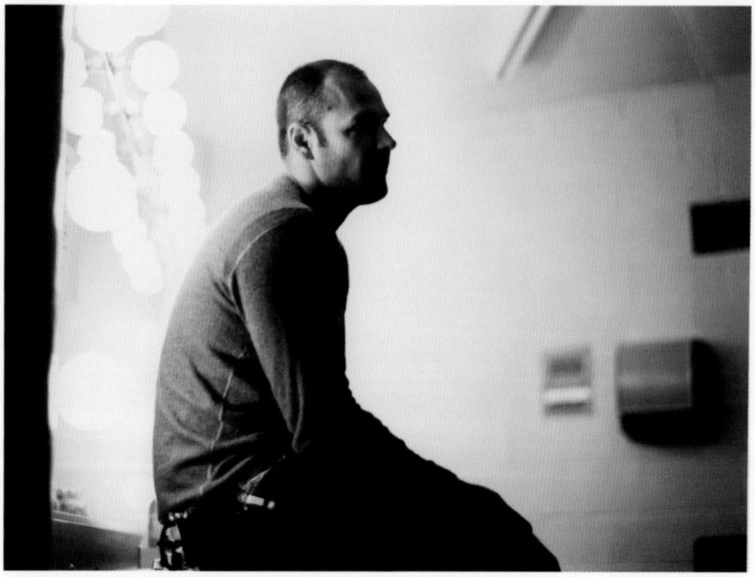

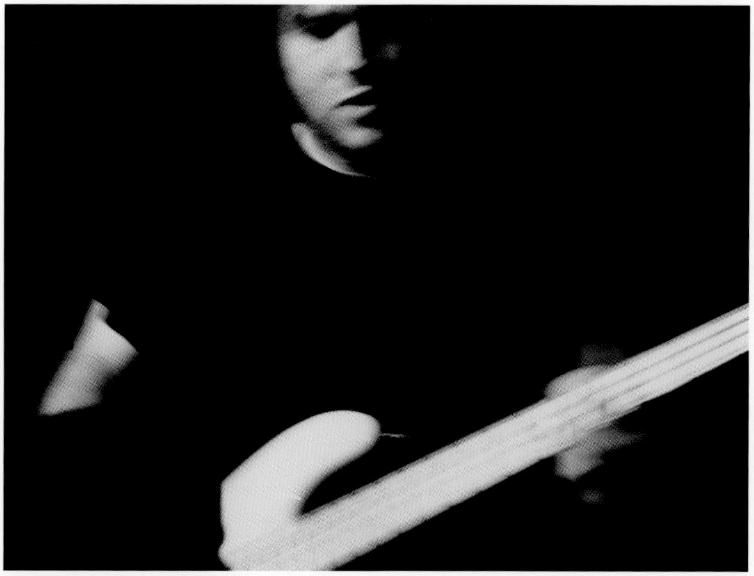

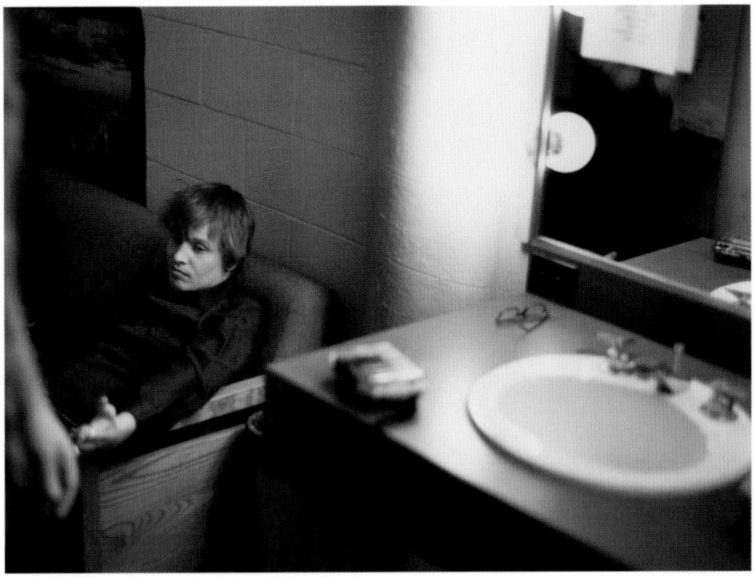

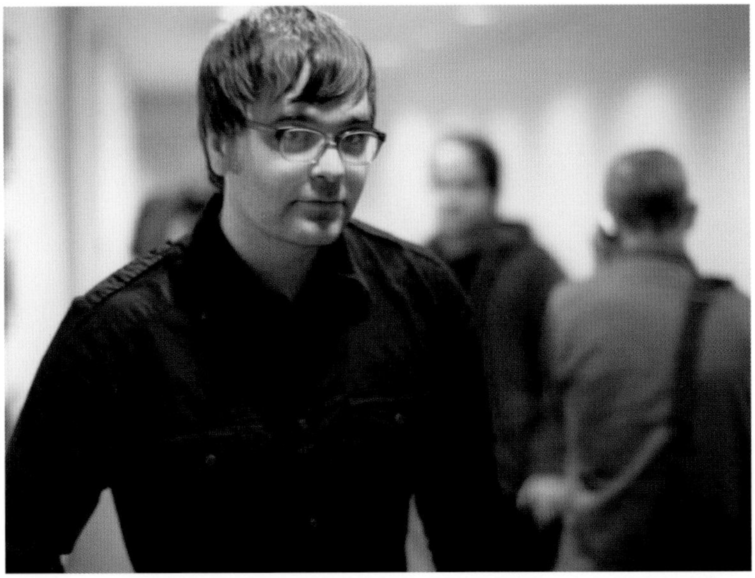

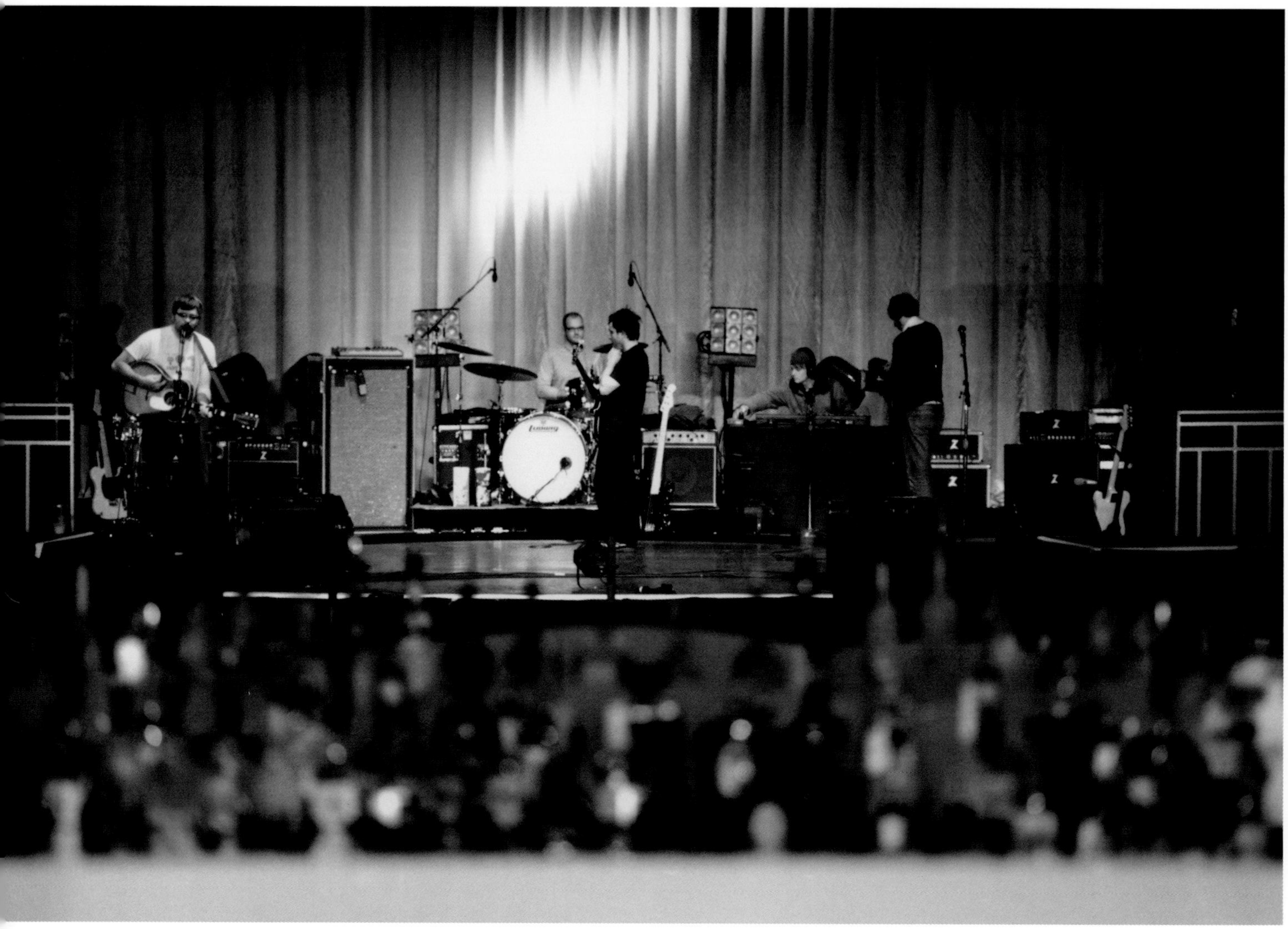

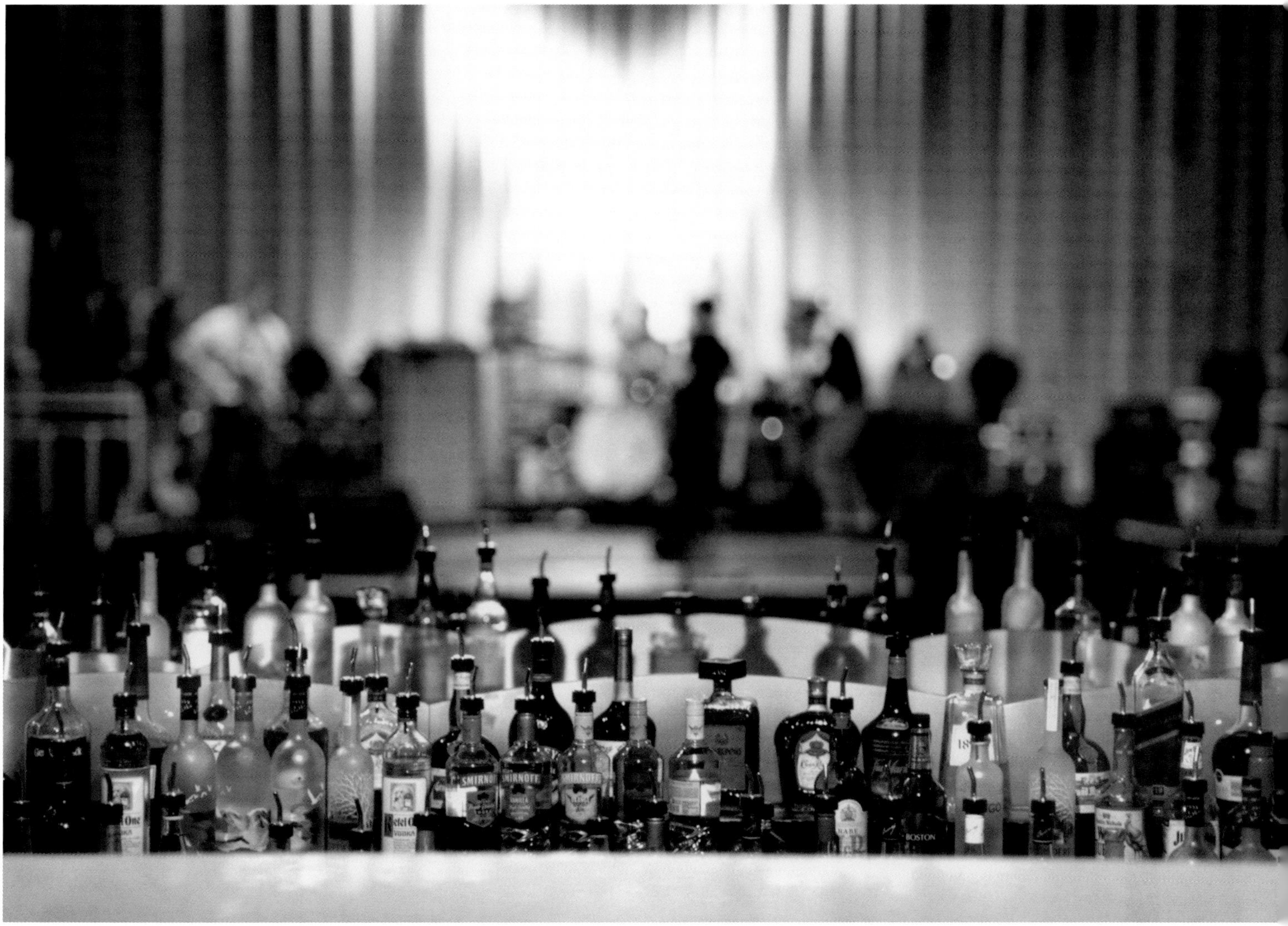

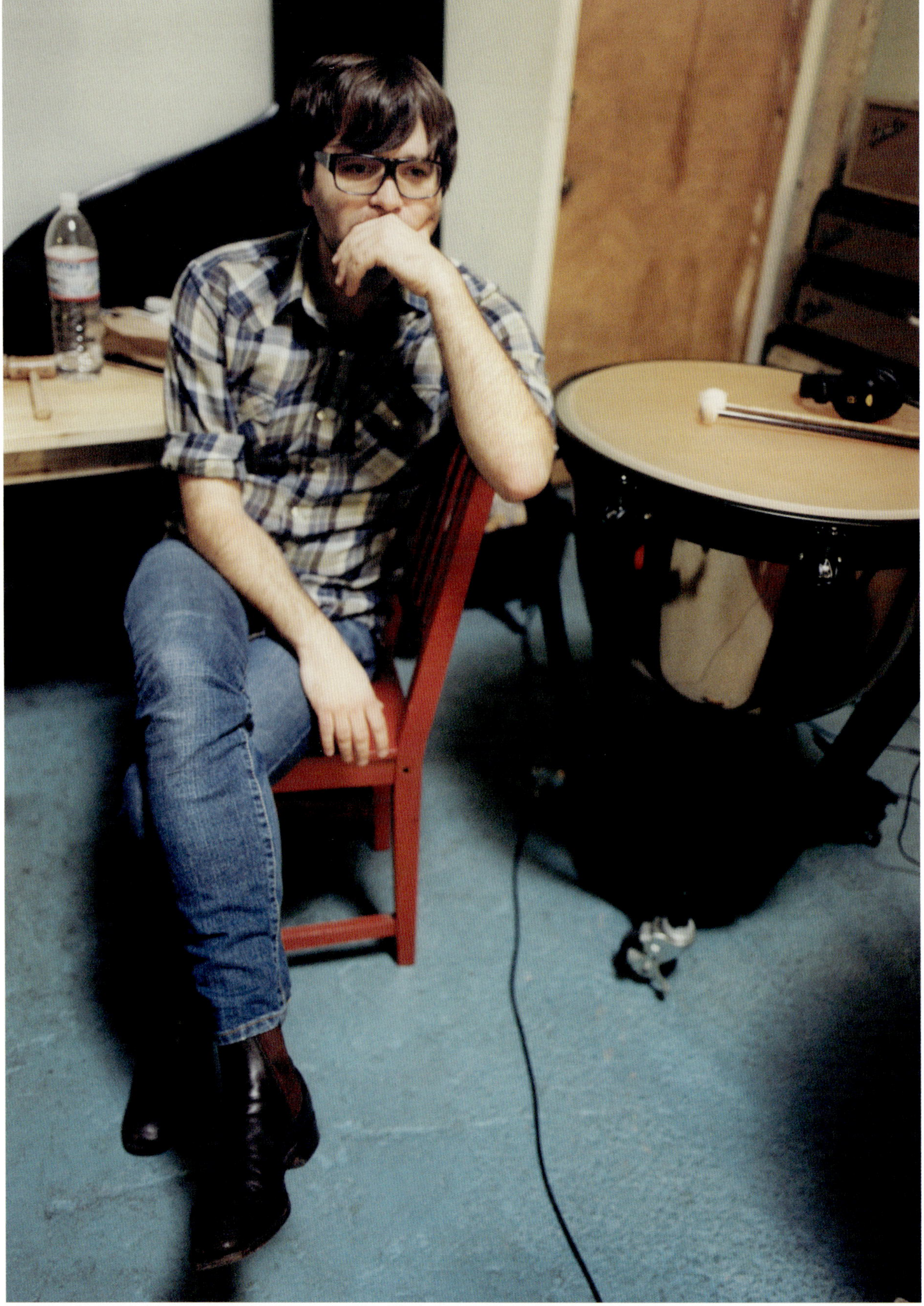

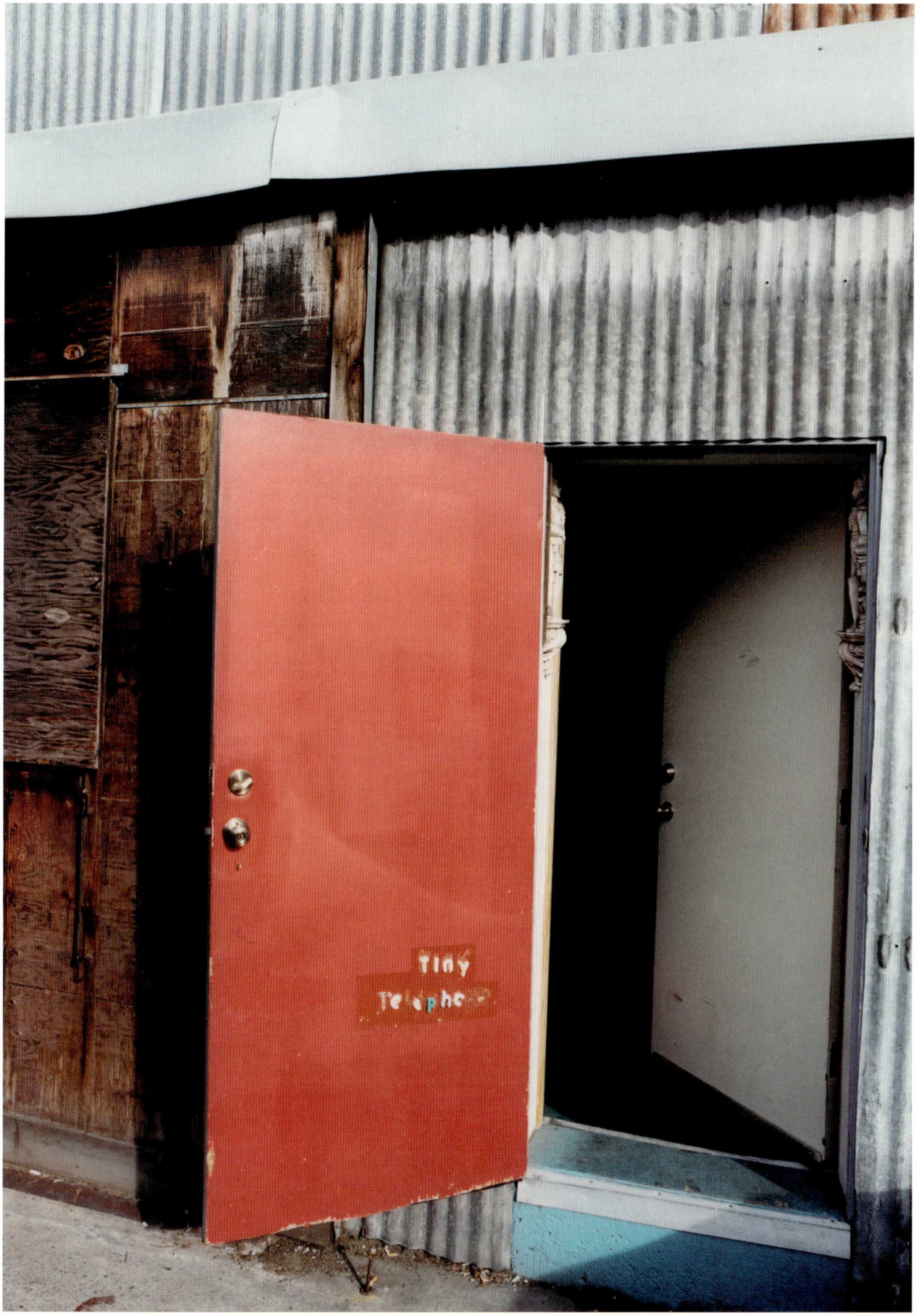
Tiny

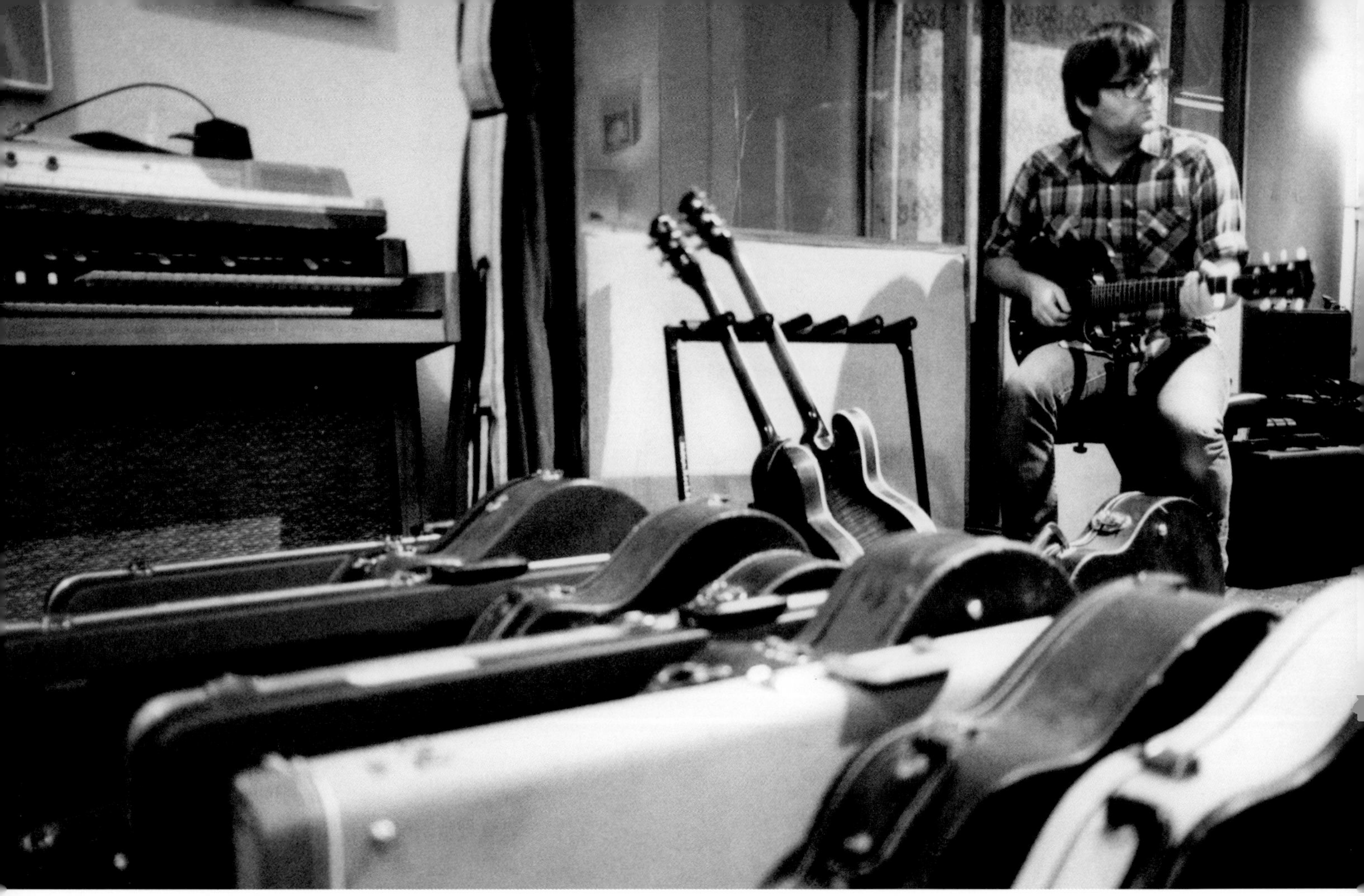

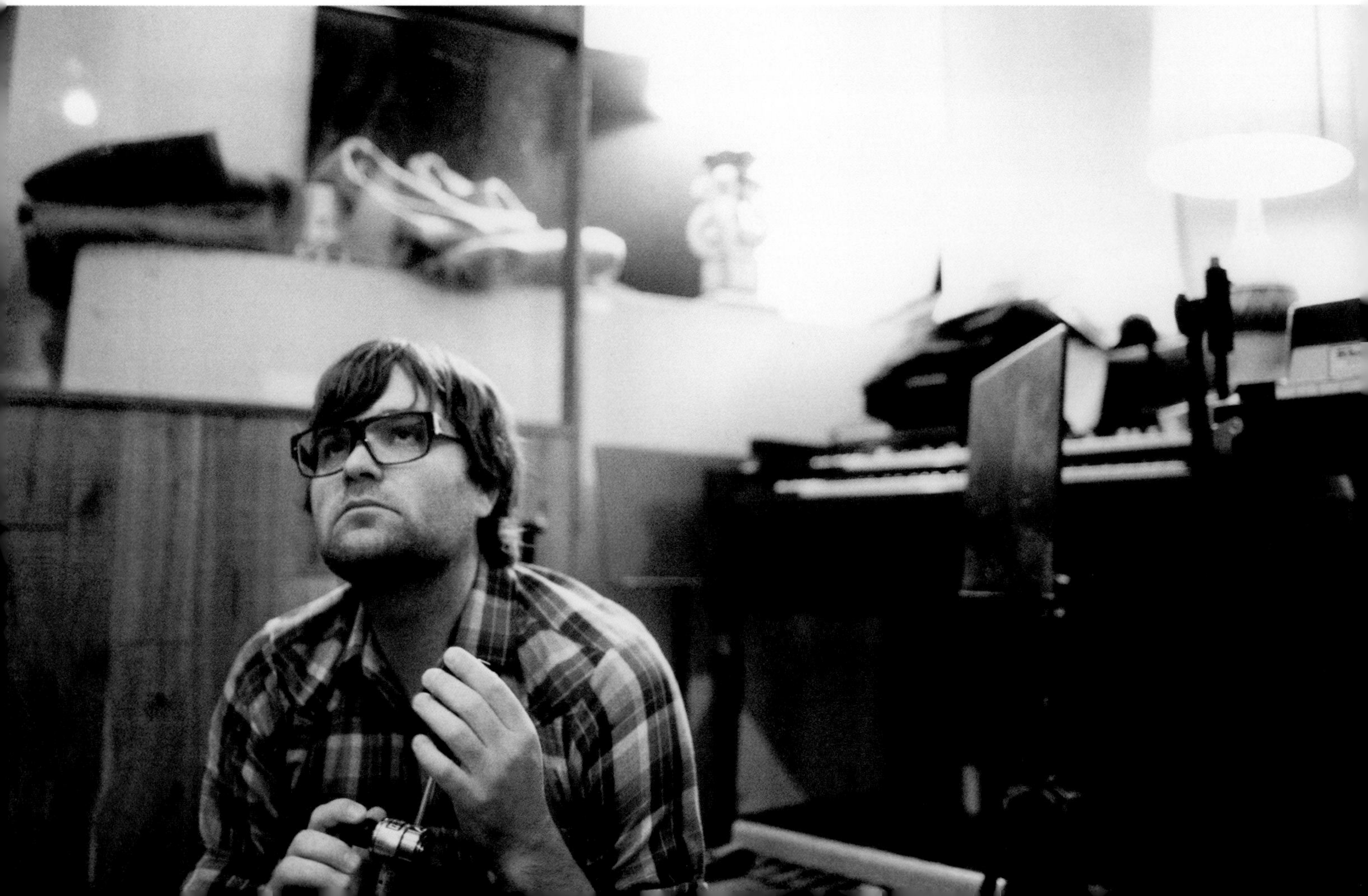

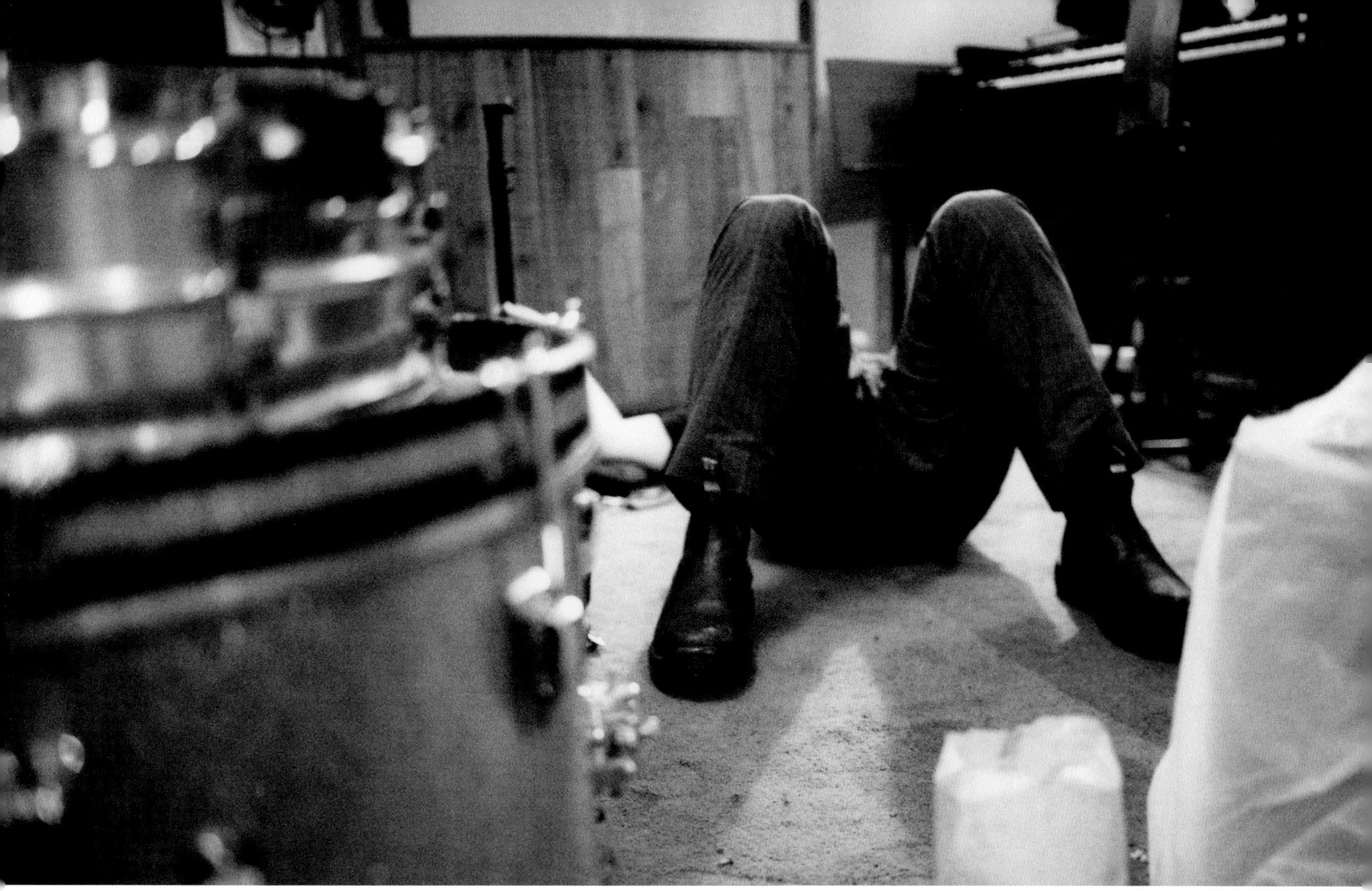

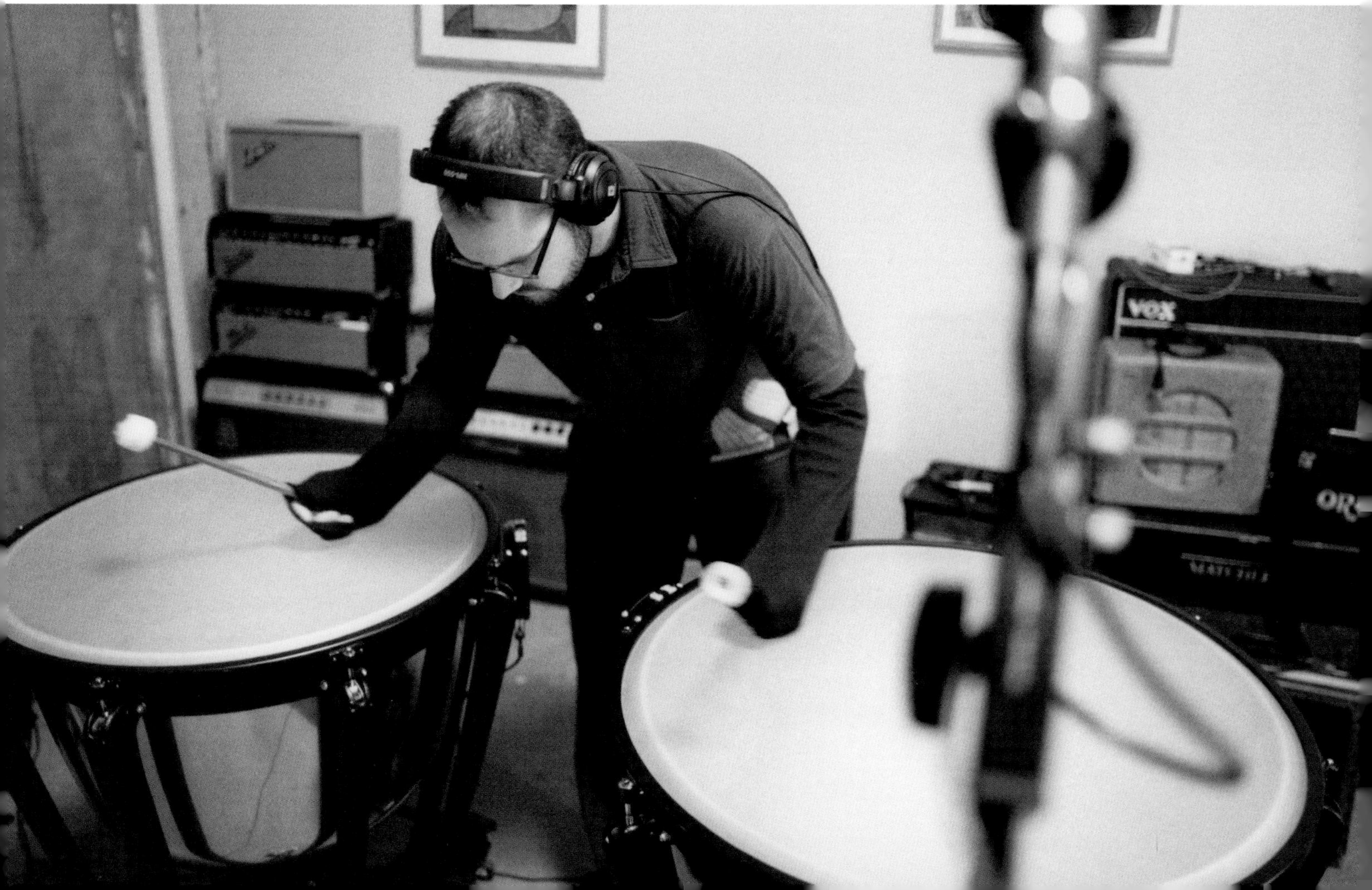
VOX

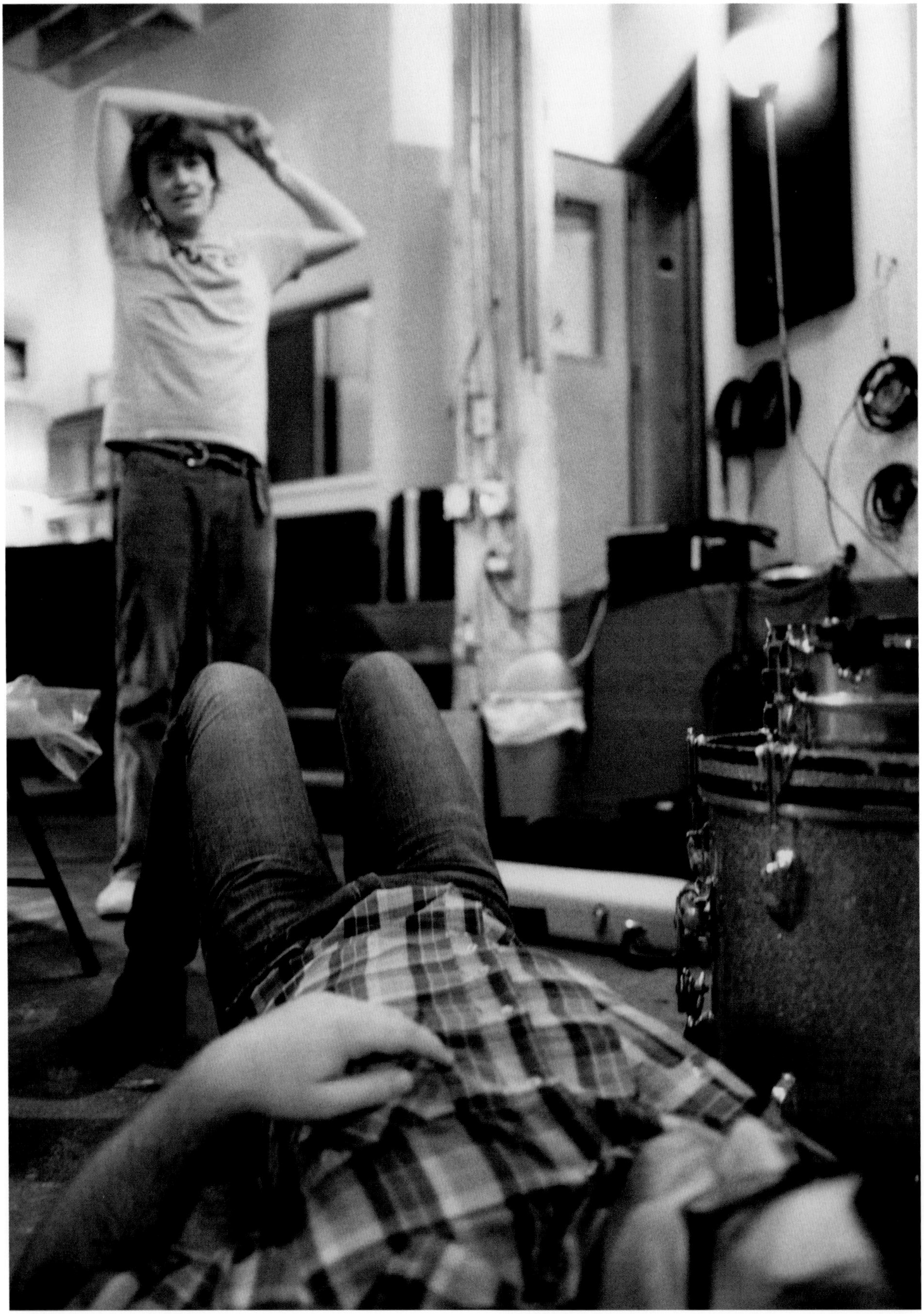

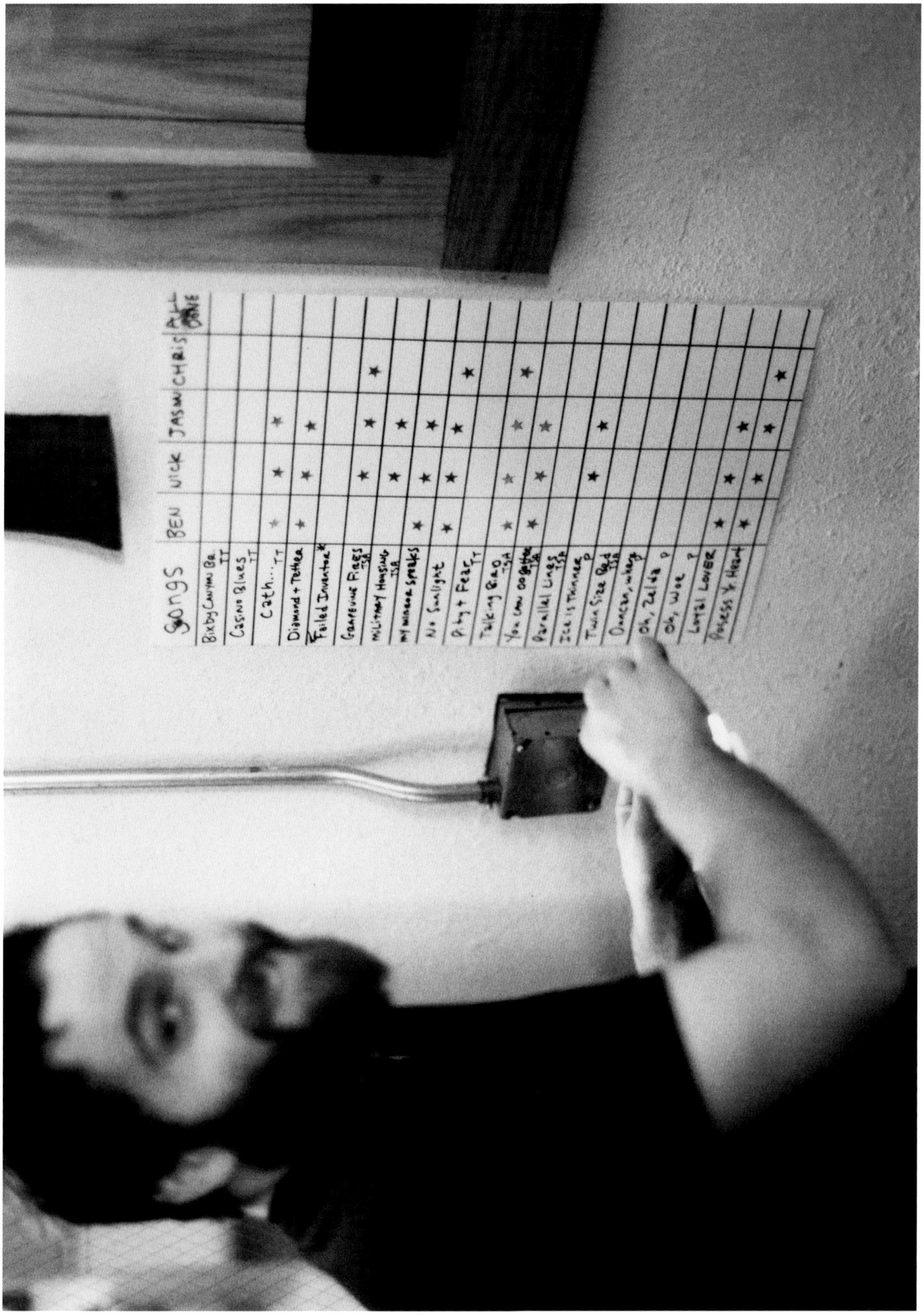
SONGS
BEN
NICK
CHRIS
Casino Blues
Diamond + Tether
Failed Inventor
Grapevine Fires
Military Housing
My Mirror Speaks
No Sunlight
Pity + Fear
Talking Bird
Parallel Lines
Ice is Thinner
Twin Size Bed
Oh, Zelda
Oh, Woe

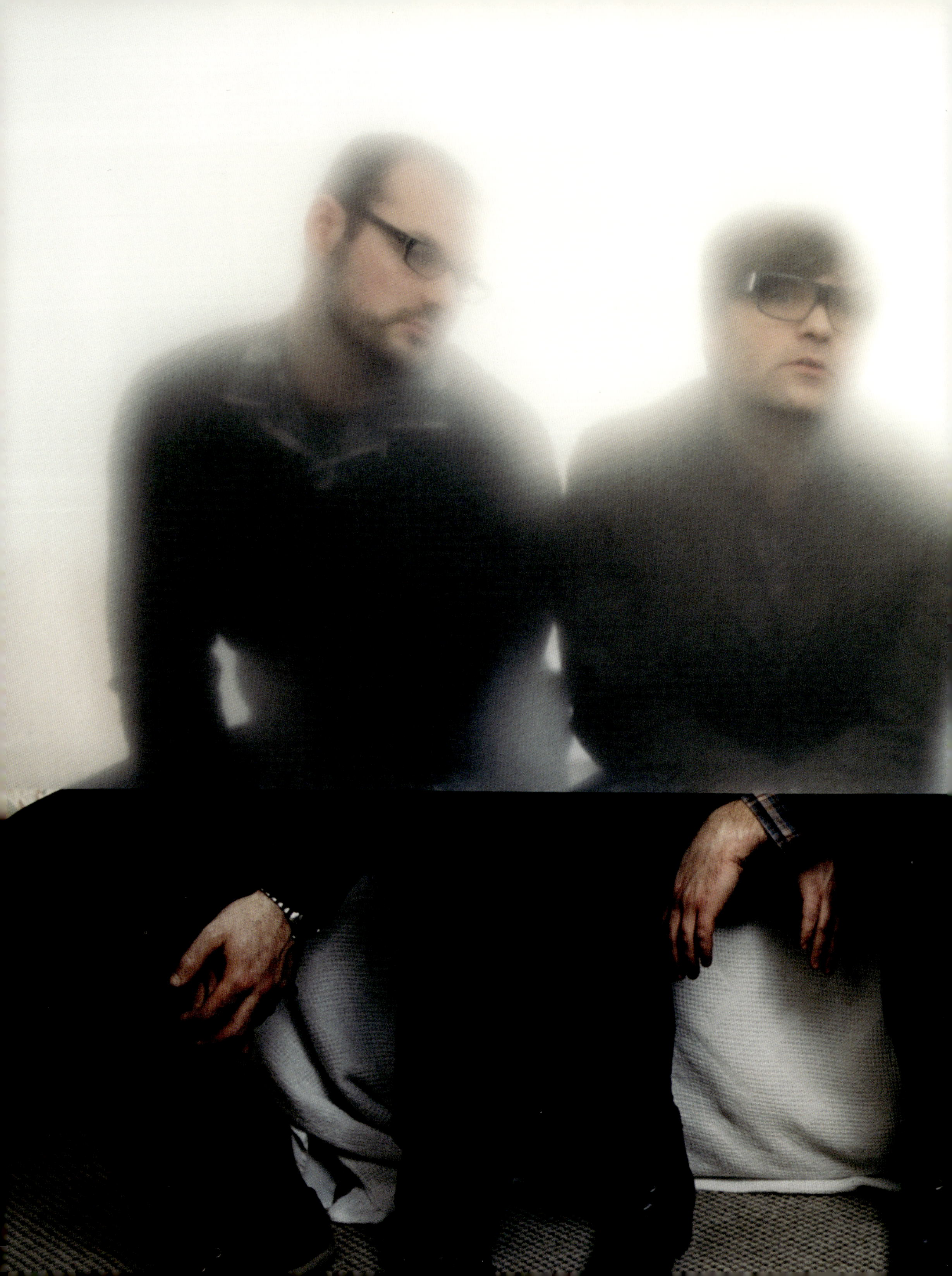

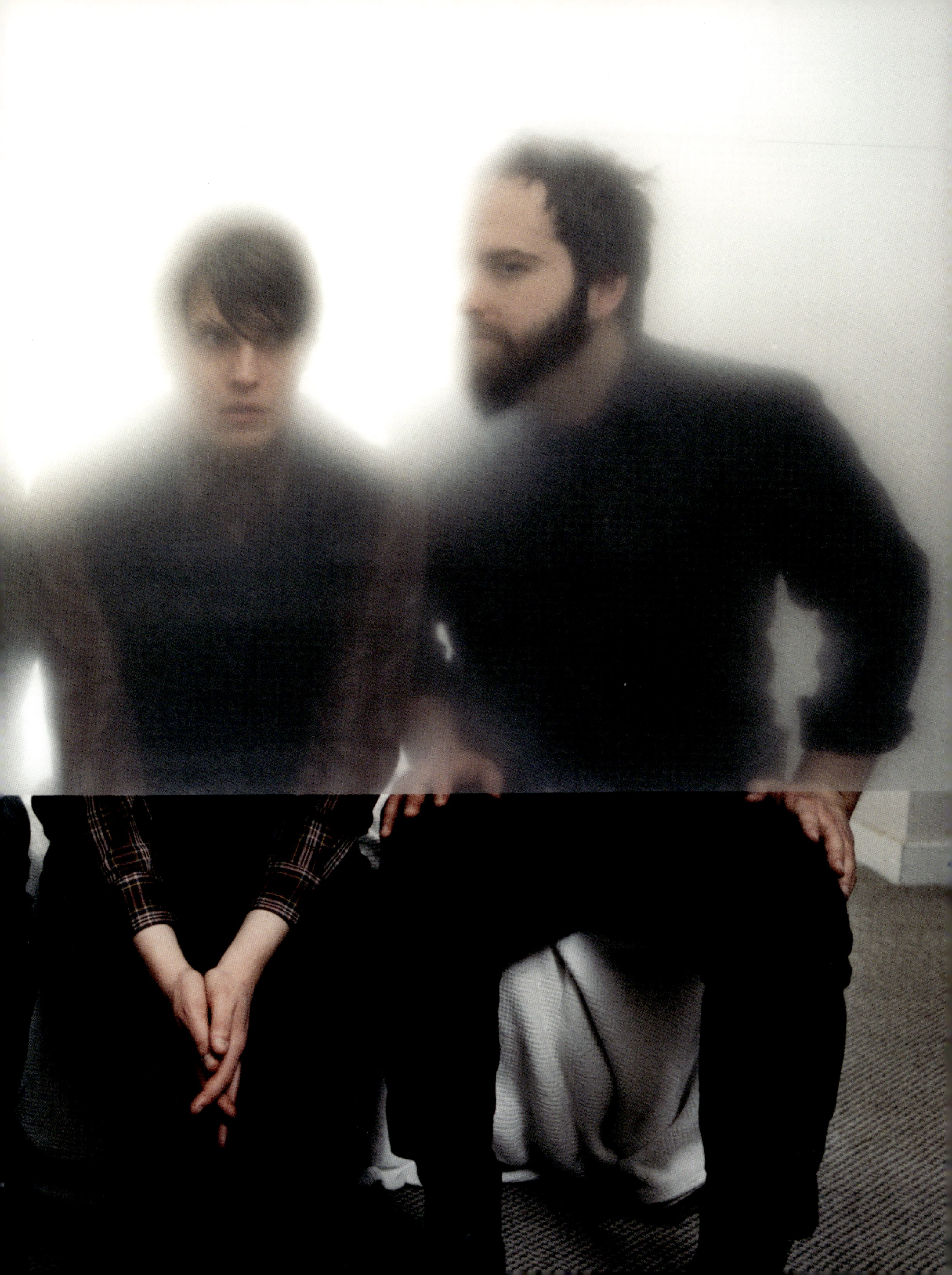

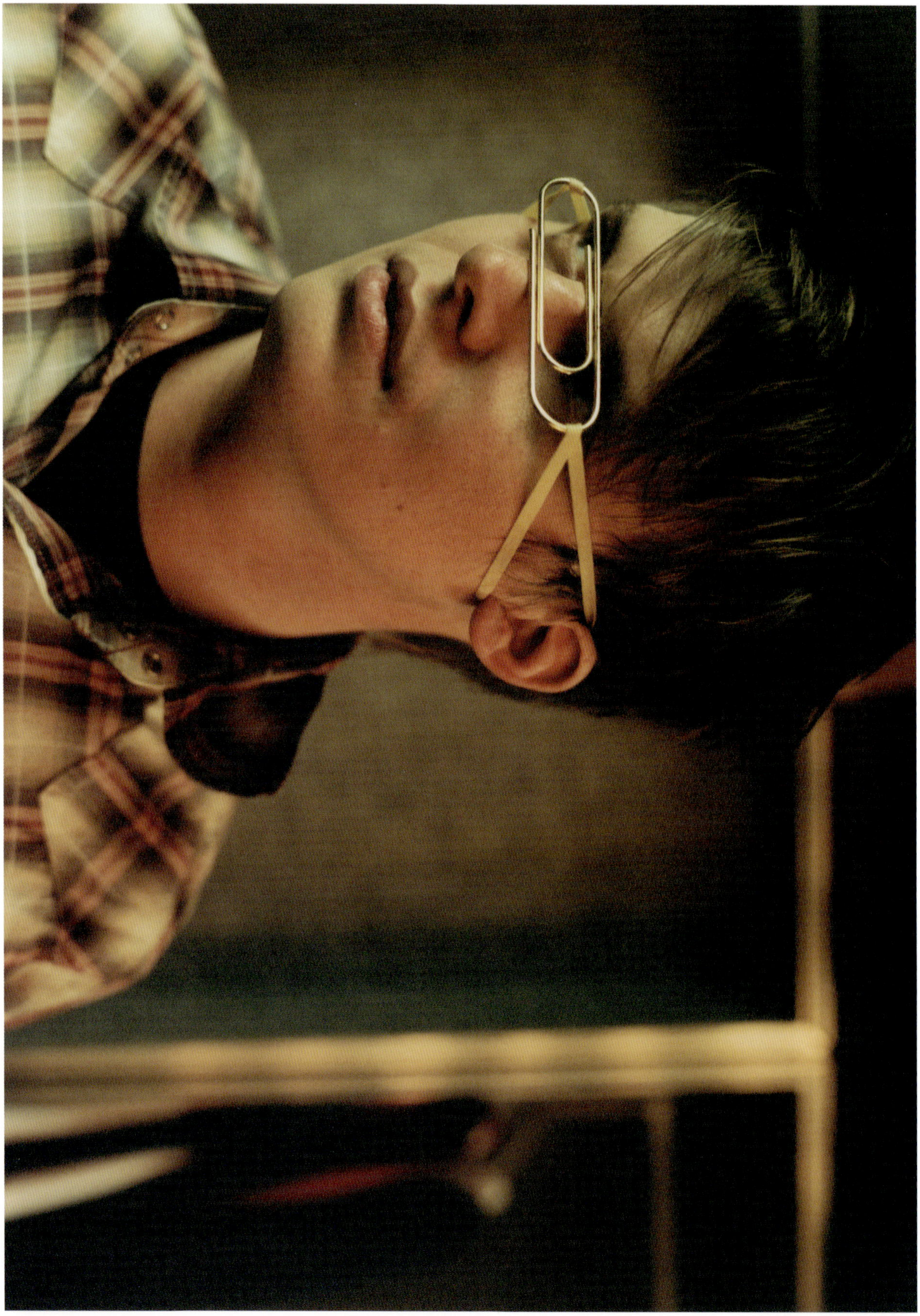

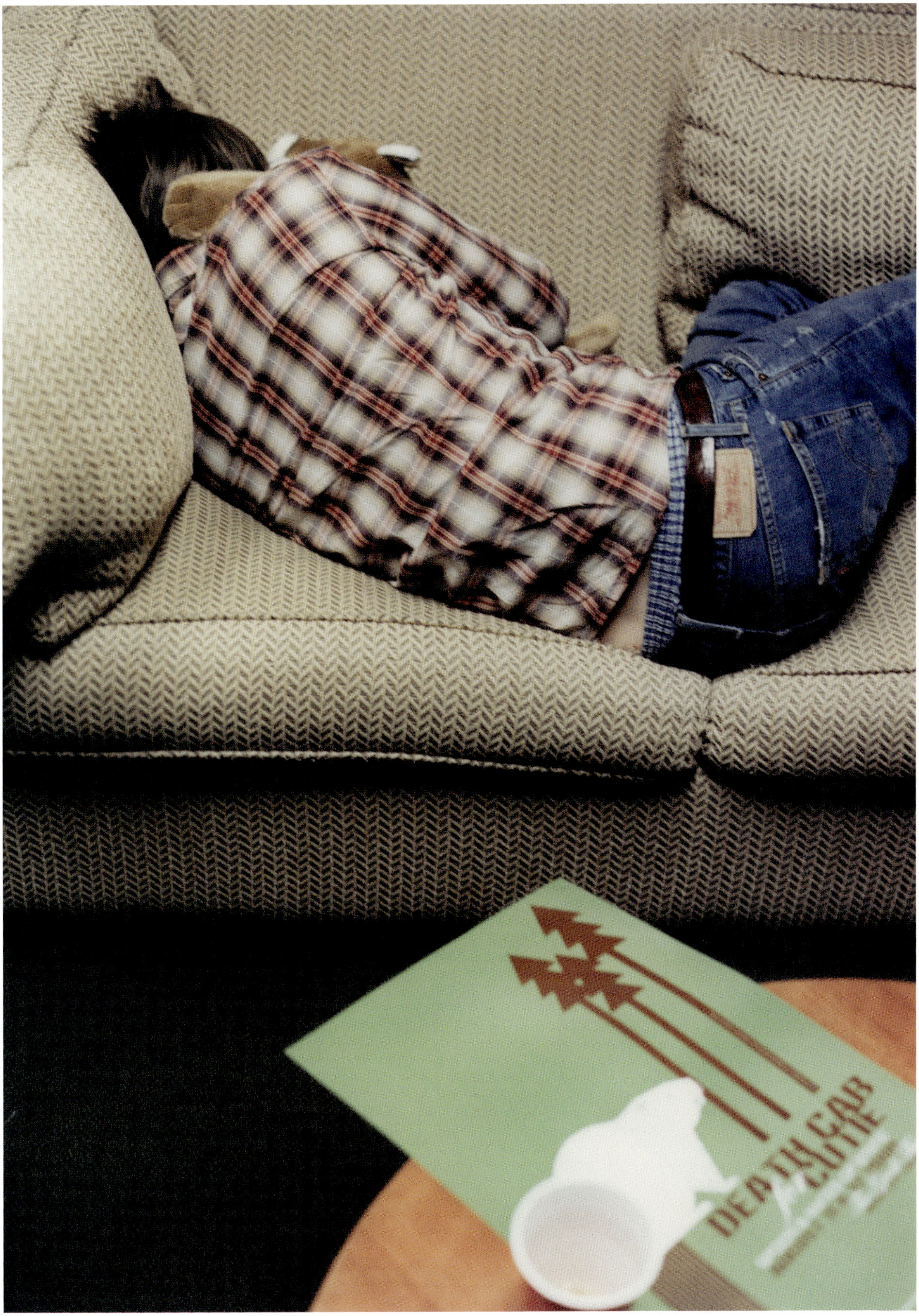
DEATH CAB

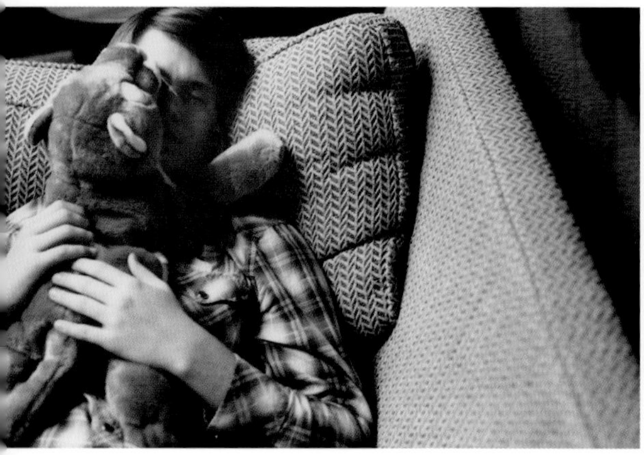

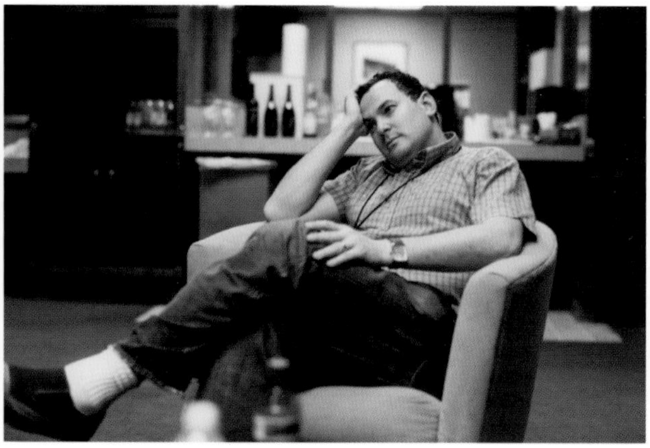

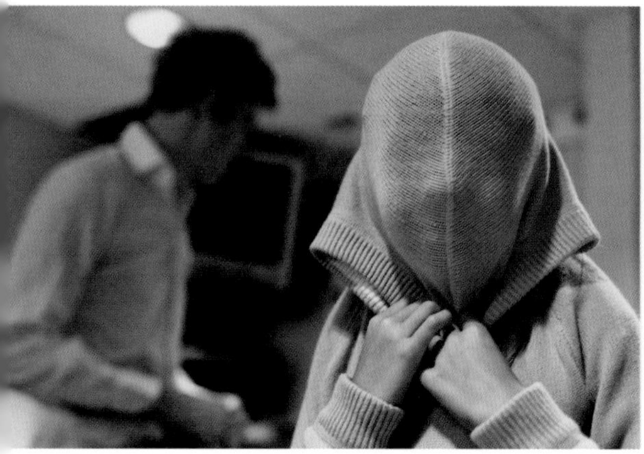

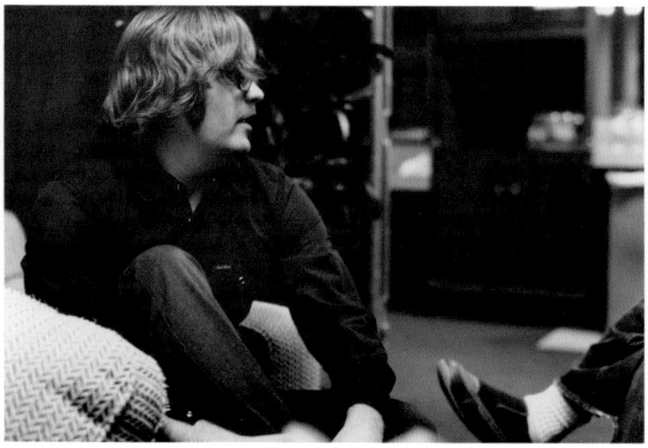

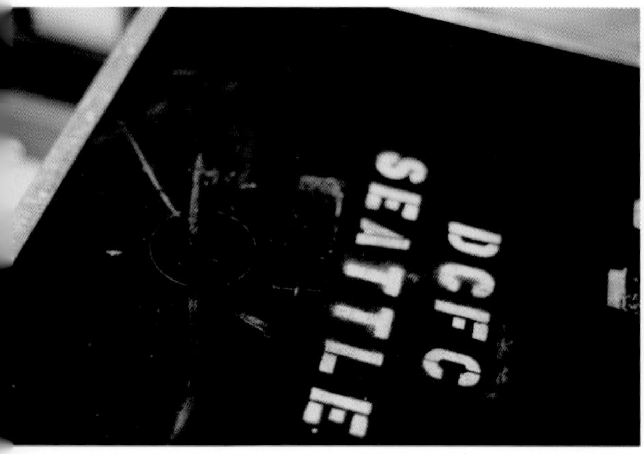
DCFC
SEATTLE.

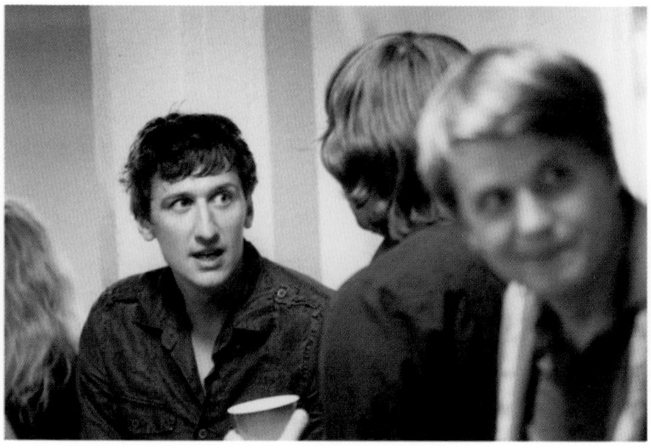

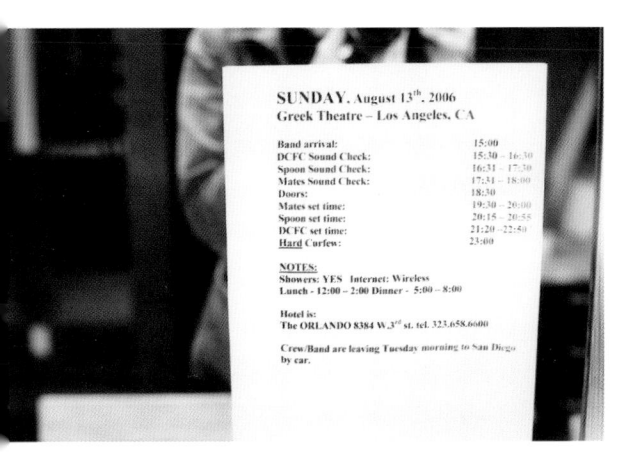

SUNDAY, August 13th, 2006
Greek Theatre – Los Angeles, CA

Band arrival:	15:00
DCFC Sound Check:	15:30 – 16:30
Spoon Sound Check:	16:31 – 17:30
Mates Sound Check:	17:31 – 18:00
Doors:	18:30
Mates set time:	19:30 – 20:00
Spoon set time:	20:15 – 20:55
DCFC set time:	21:20 – 22:50
Hard Curfew:	23:00

NOTES:
Showers: YES   Internet: Wireless
Lunch - 12:00 – 2:00 Dinner - 5:00 – 8:00

Hotel is:
The ORLANDO 8384 W 3rd st. tel. 323.658.6600

Crew/Band are leaving Tuesday morning to San Diego by car.

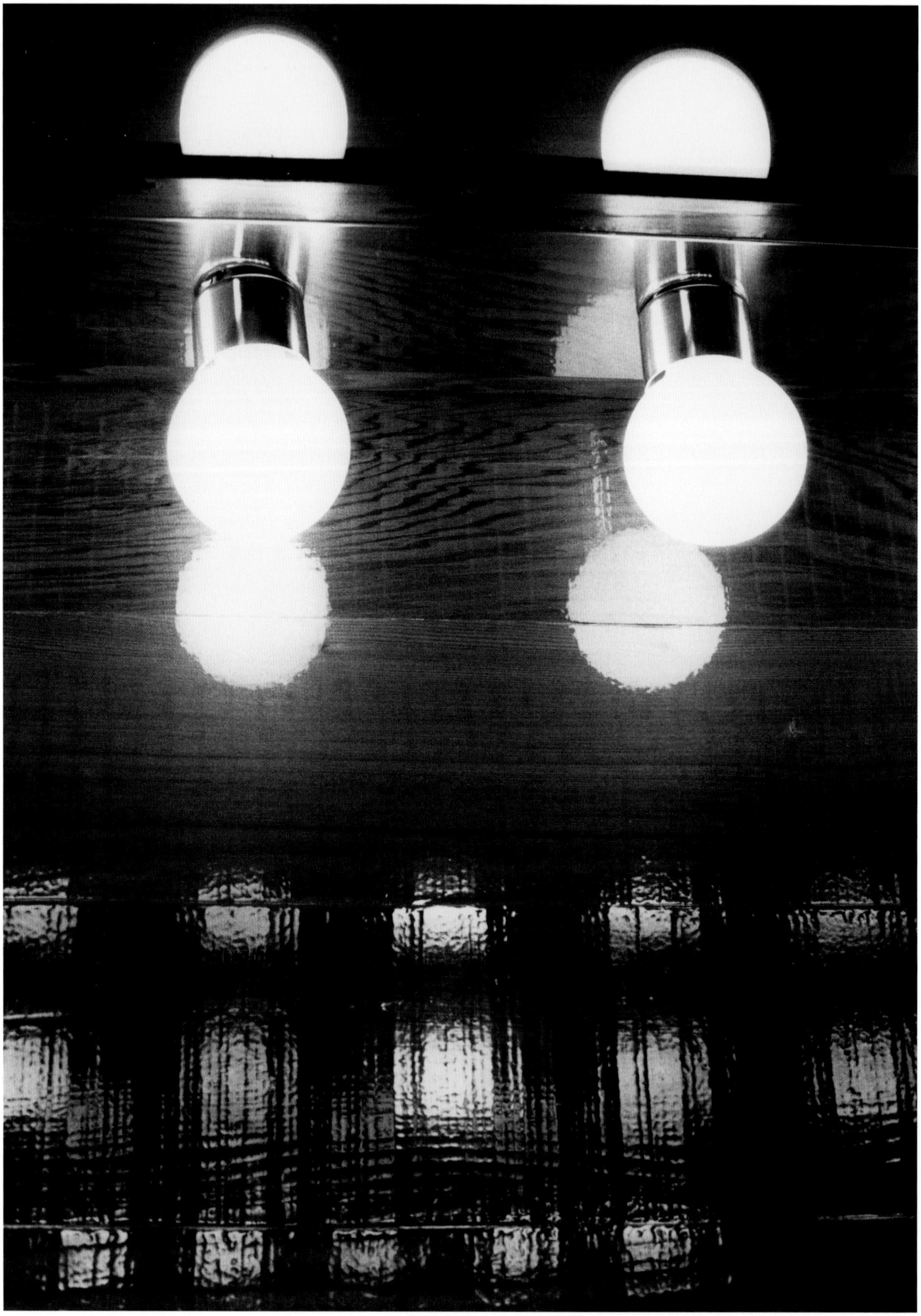

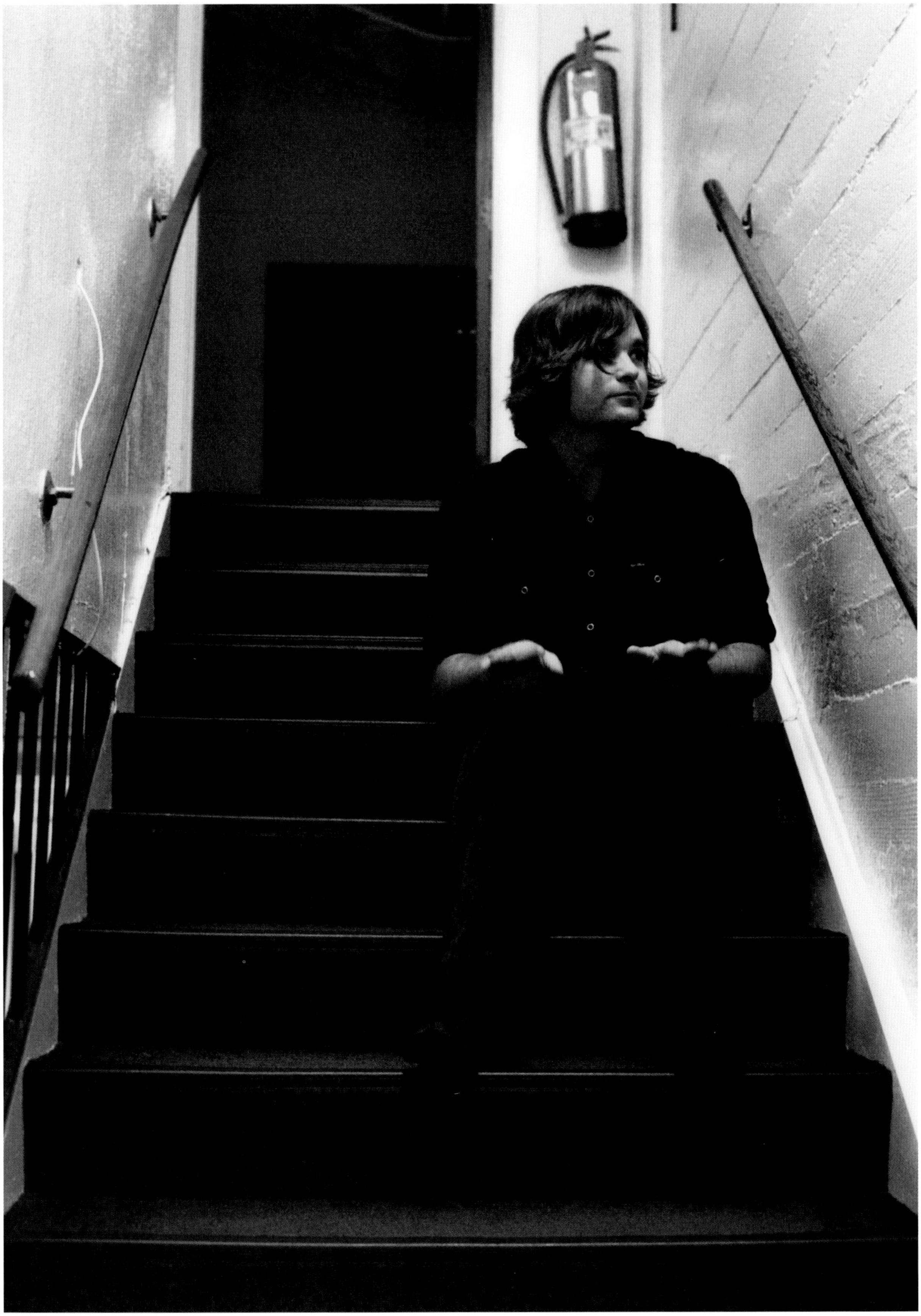

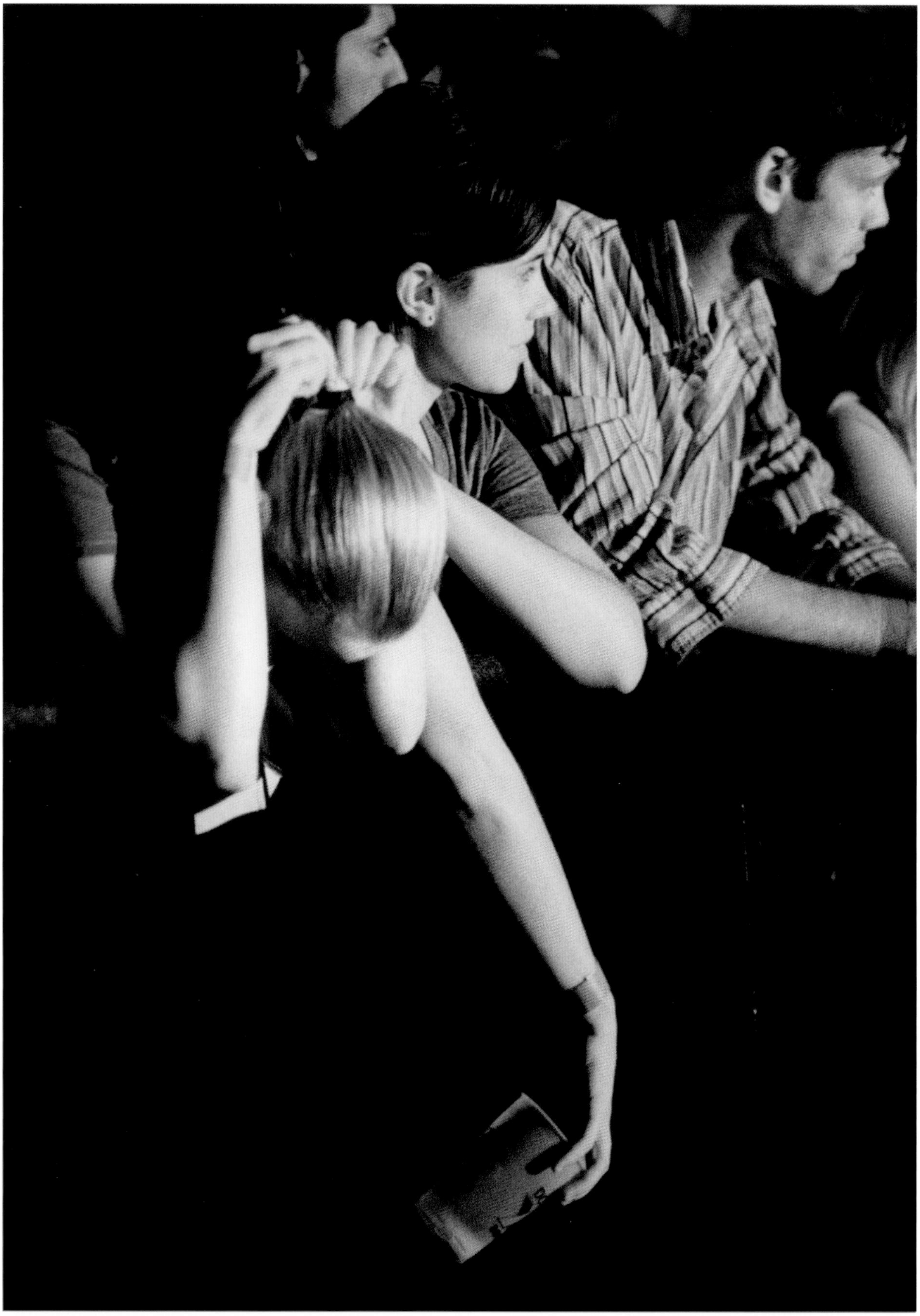

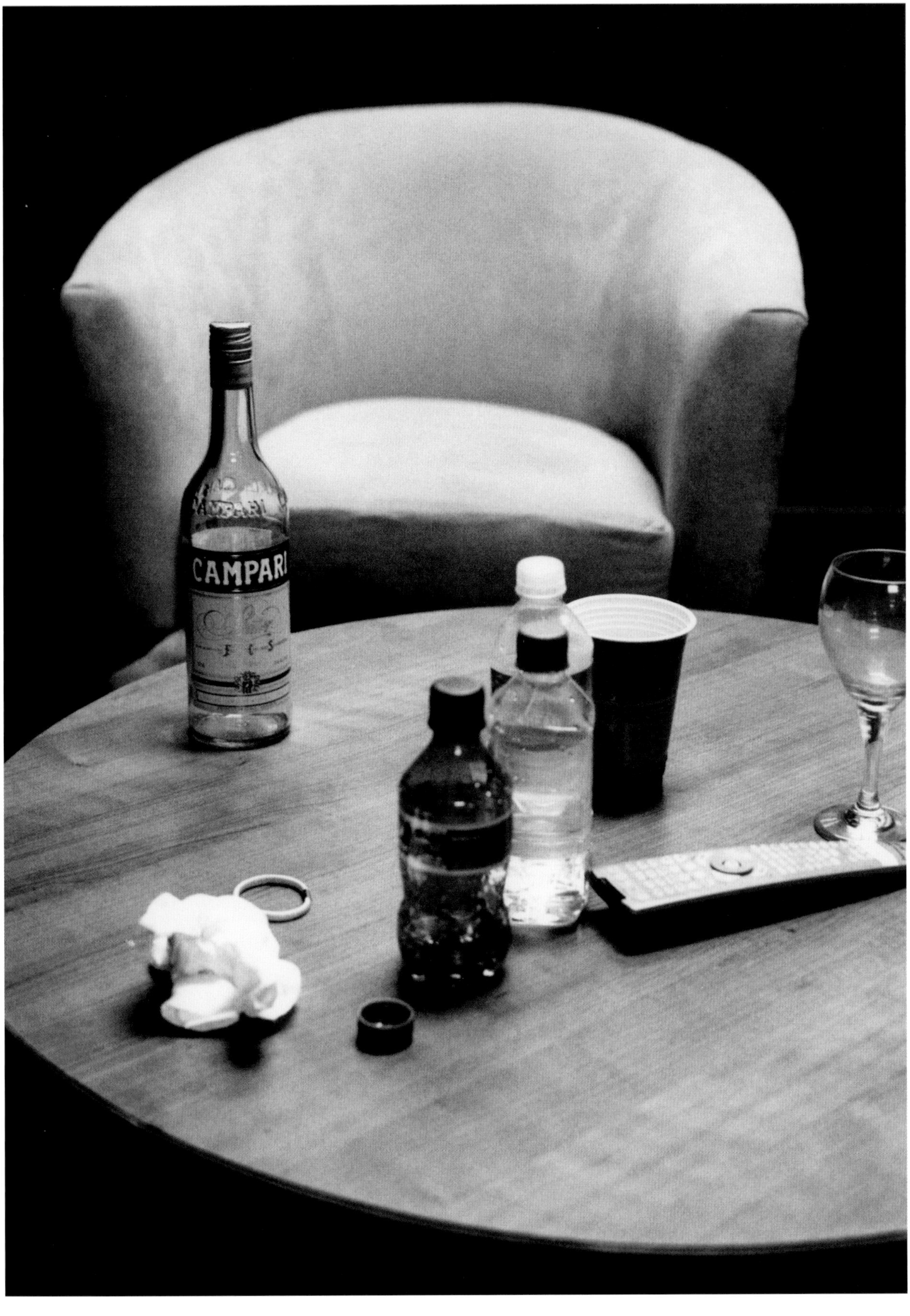
CAMPARI

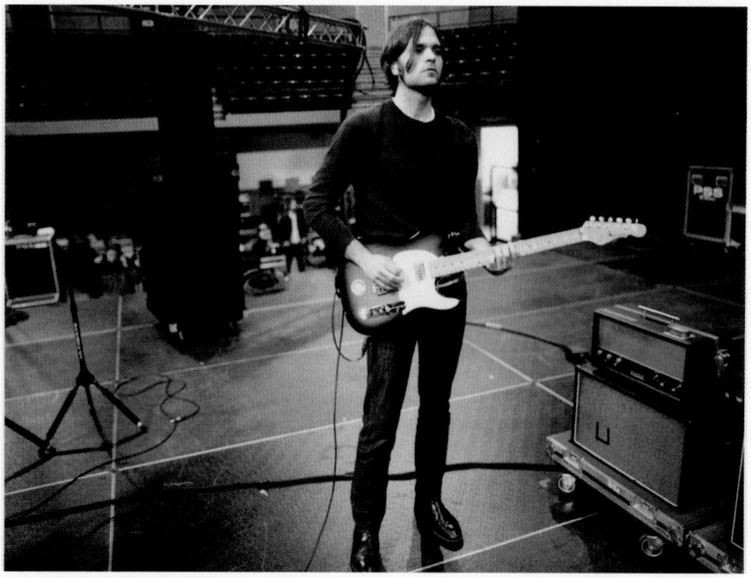

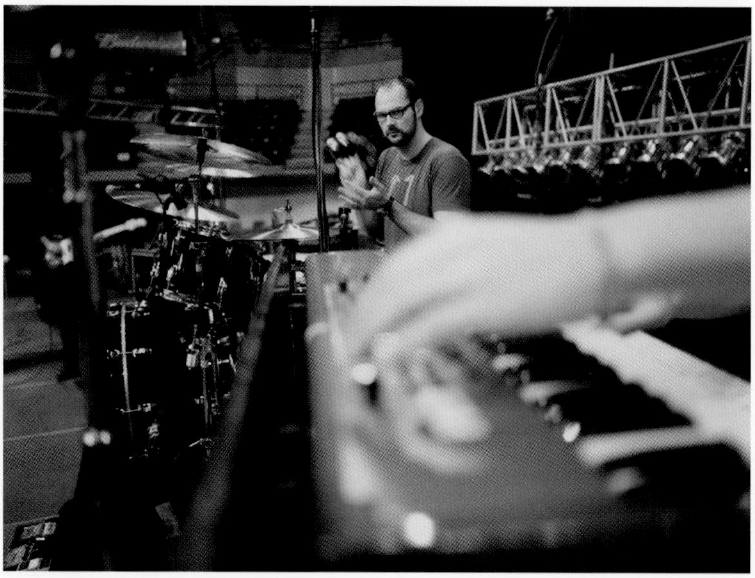

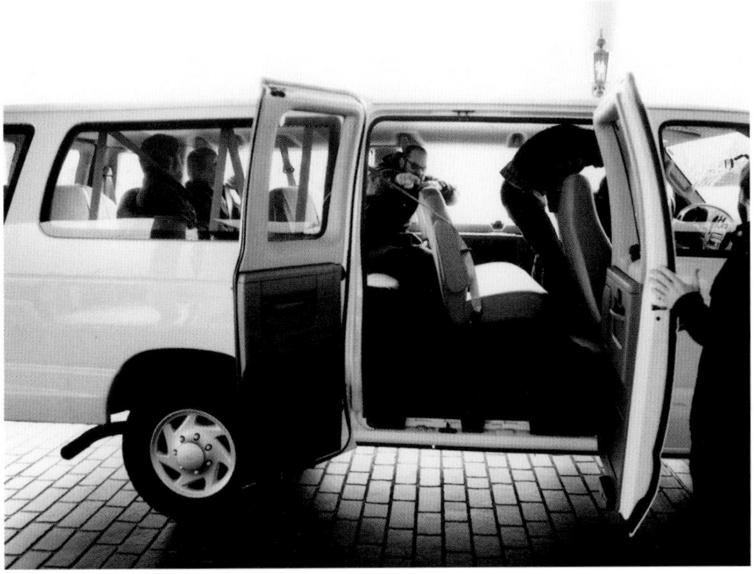

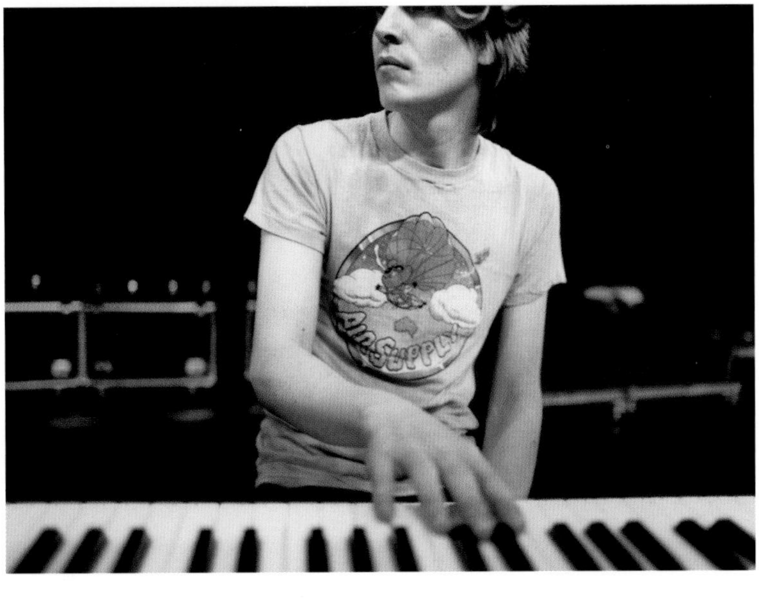

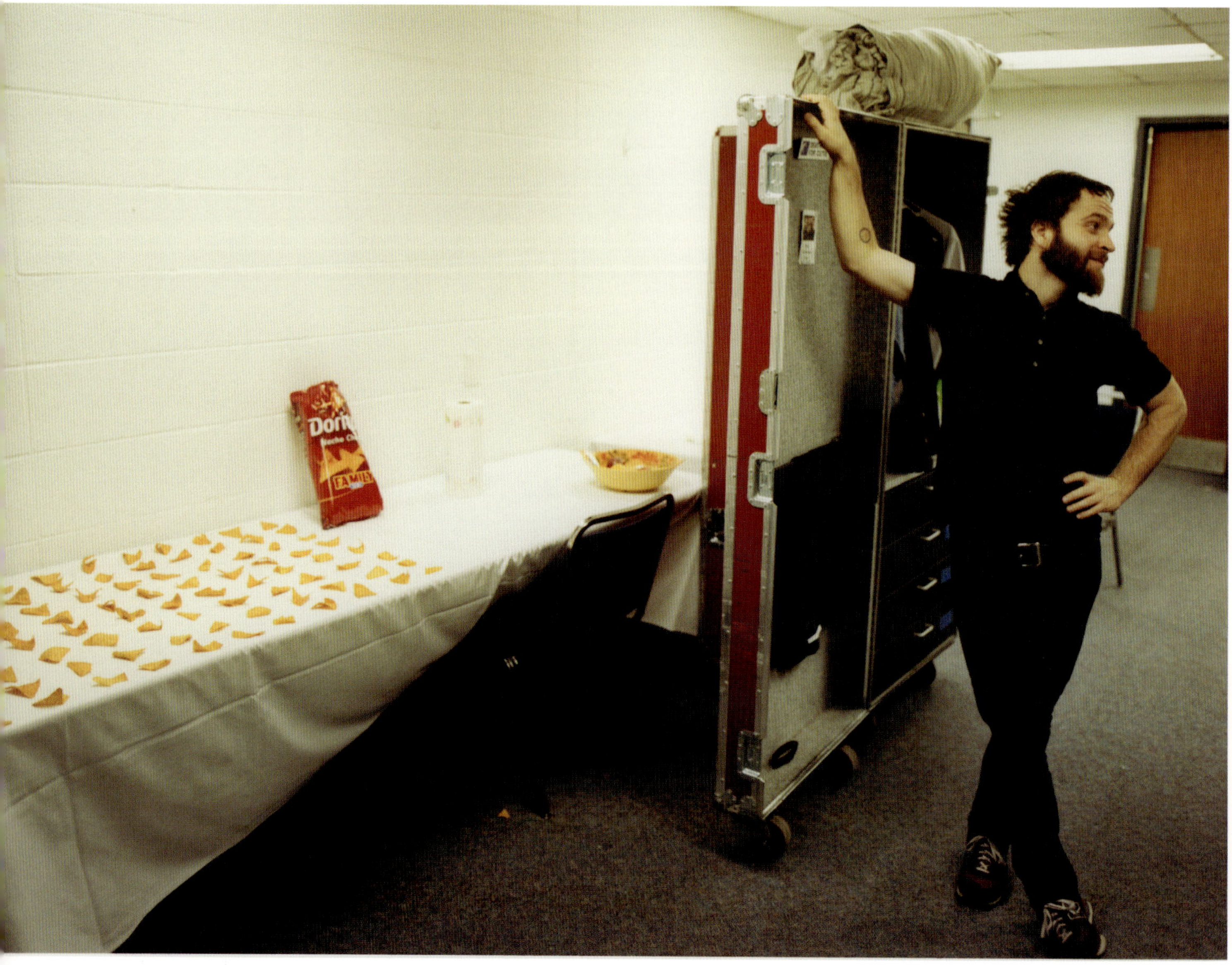

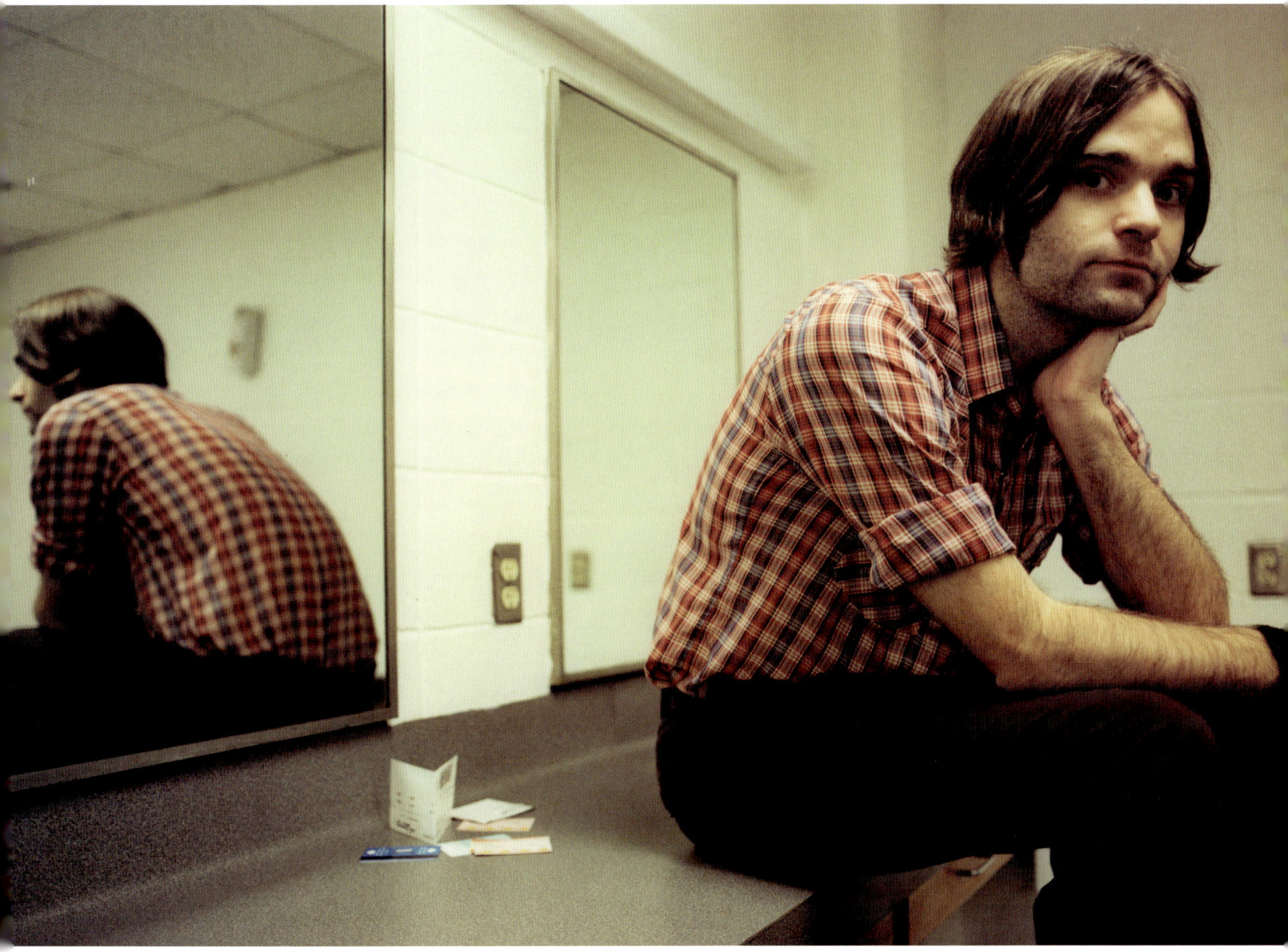

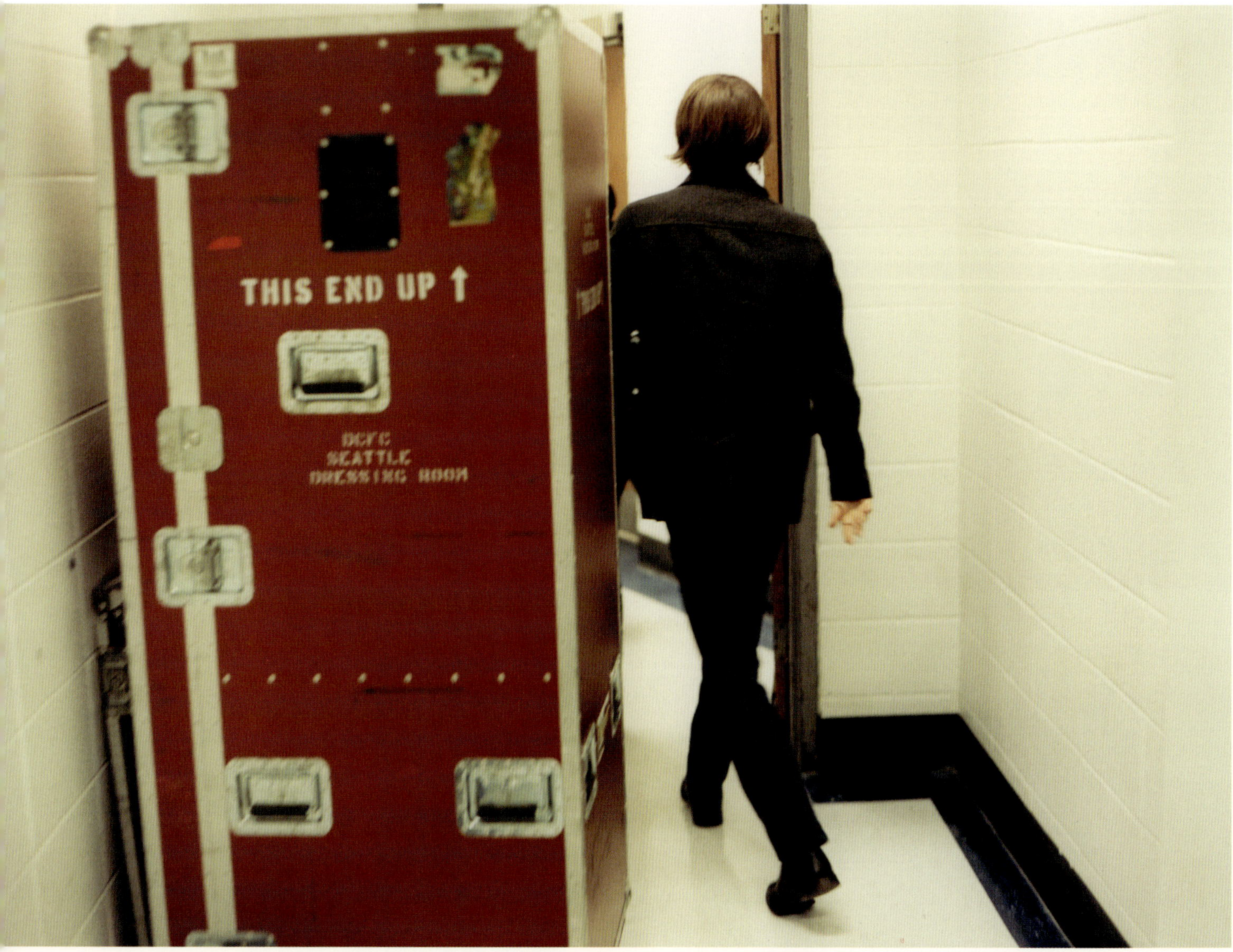
THIS END UP
SEATTLE
DRESSING ROOM

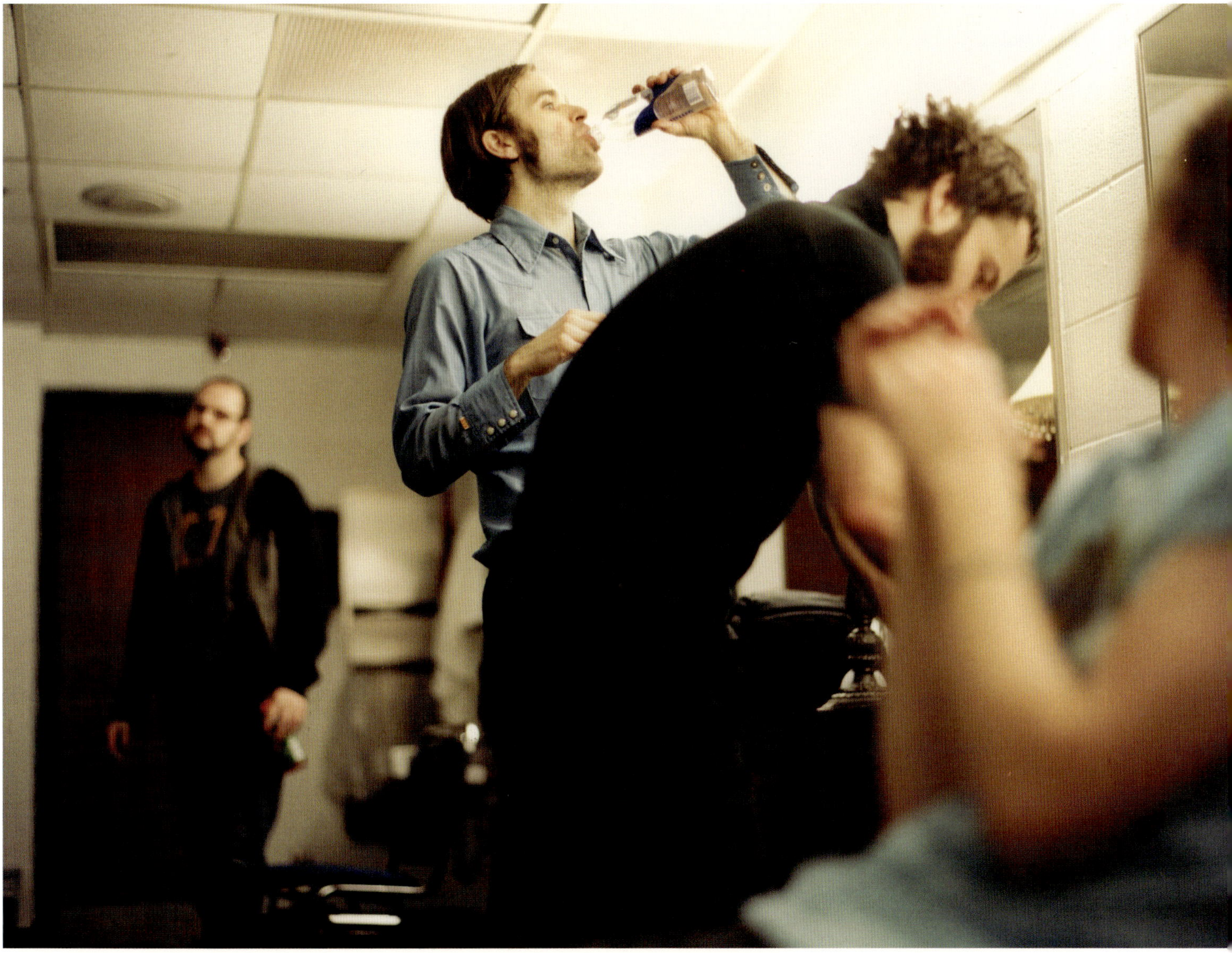

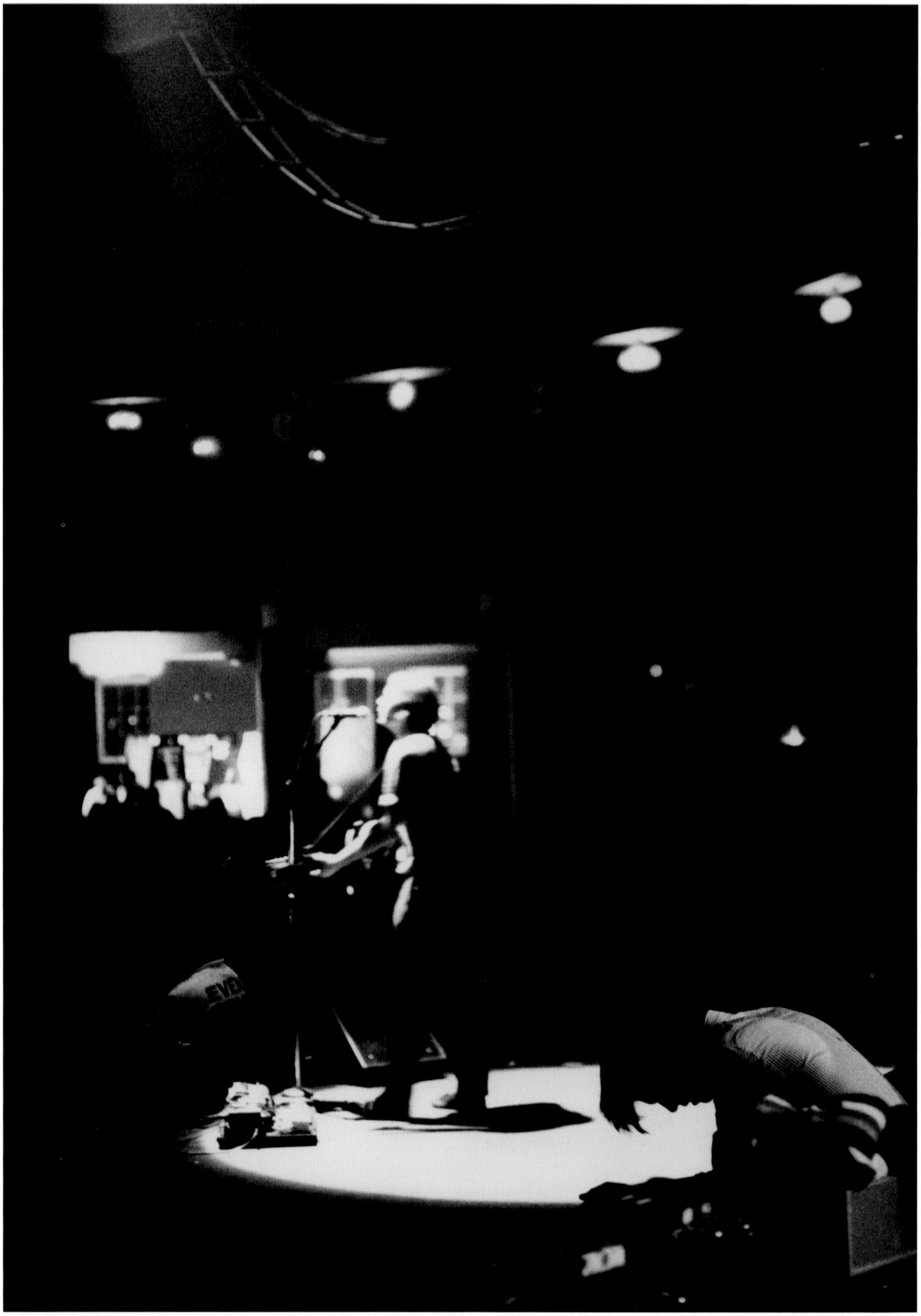

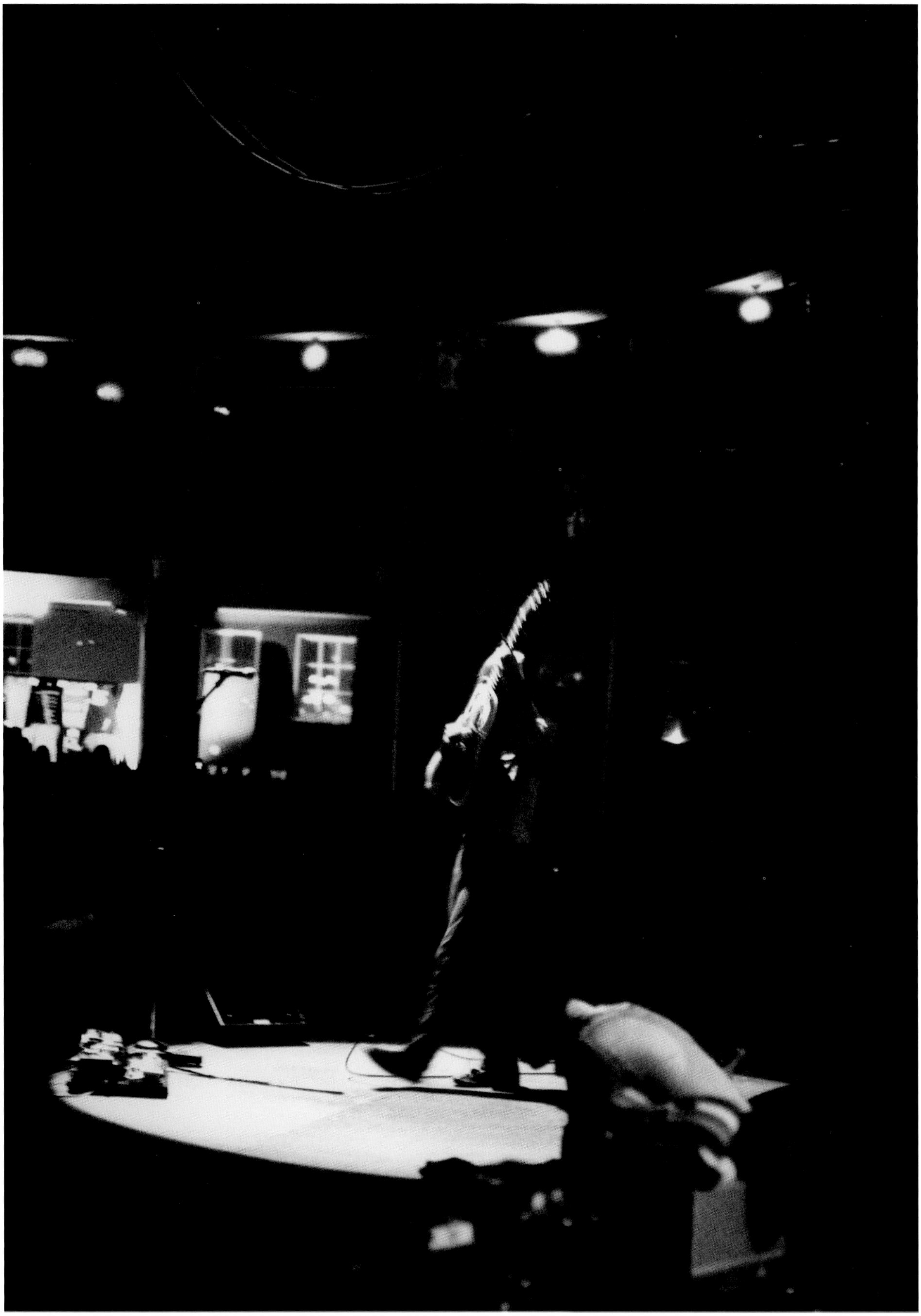

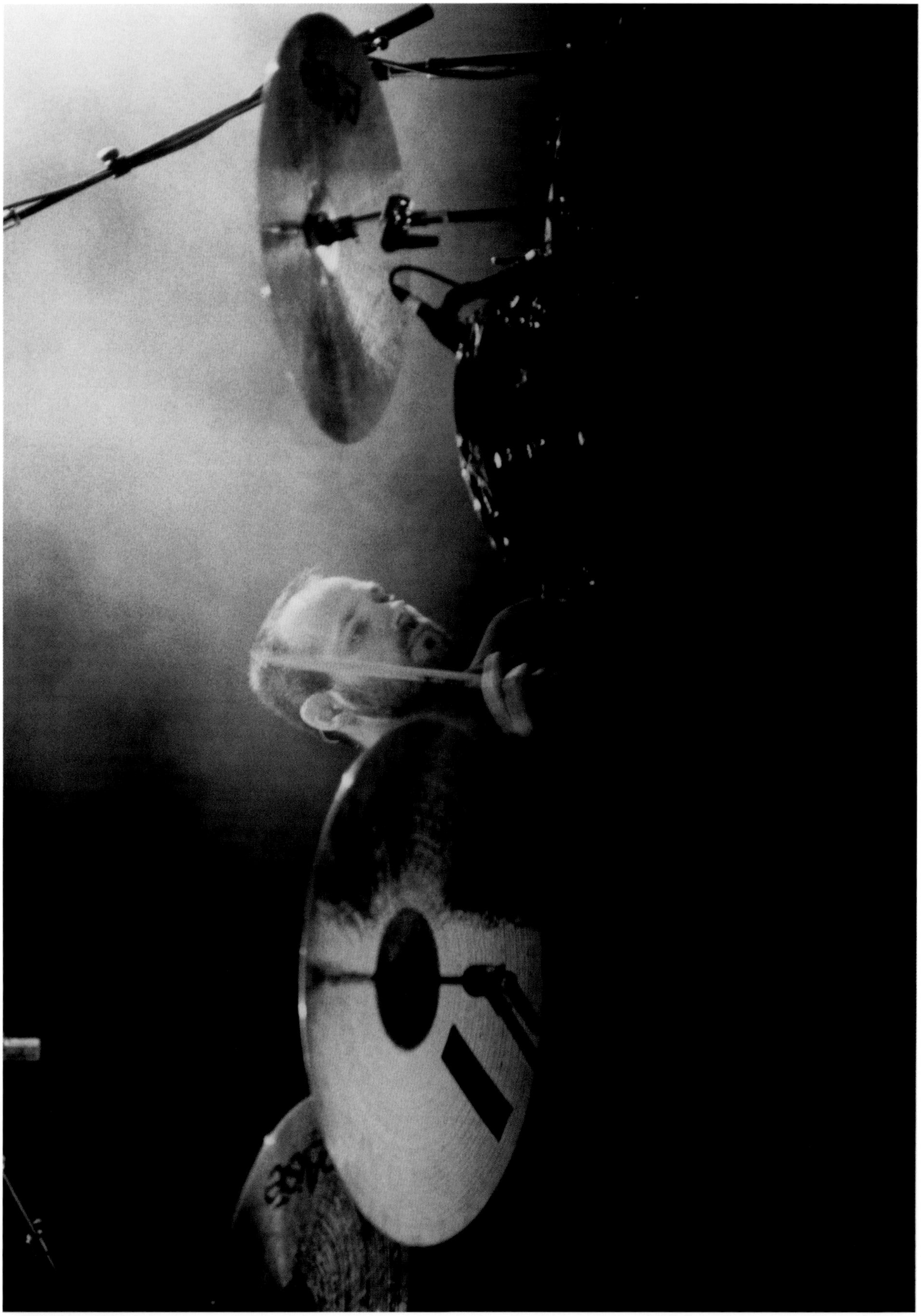

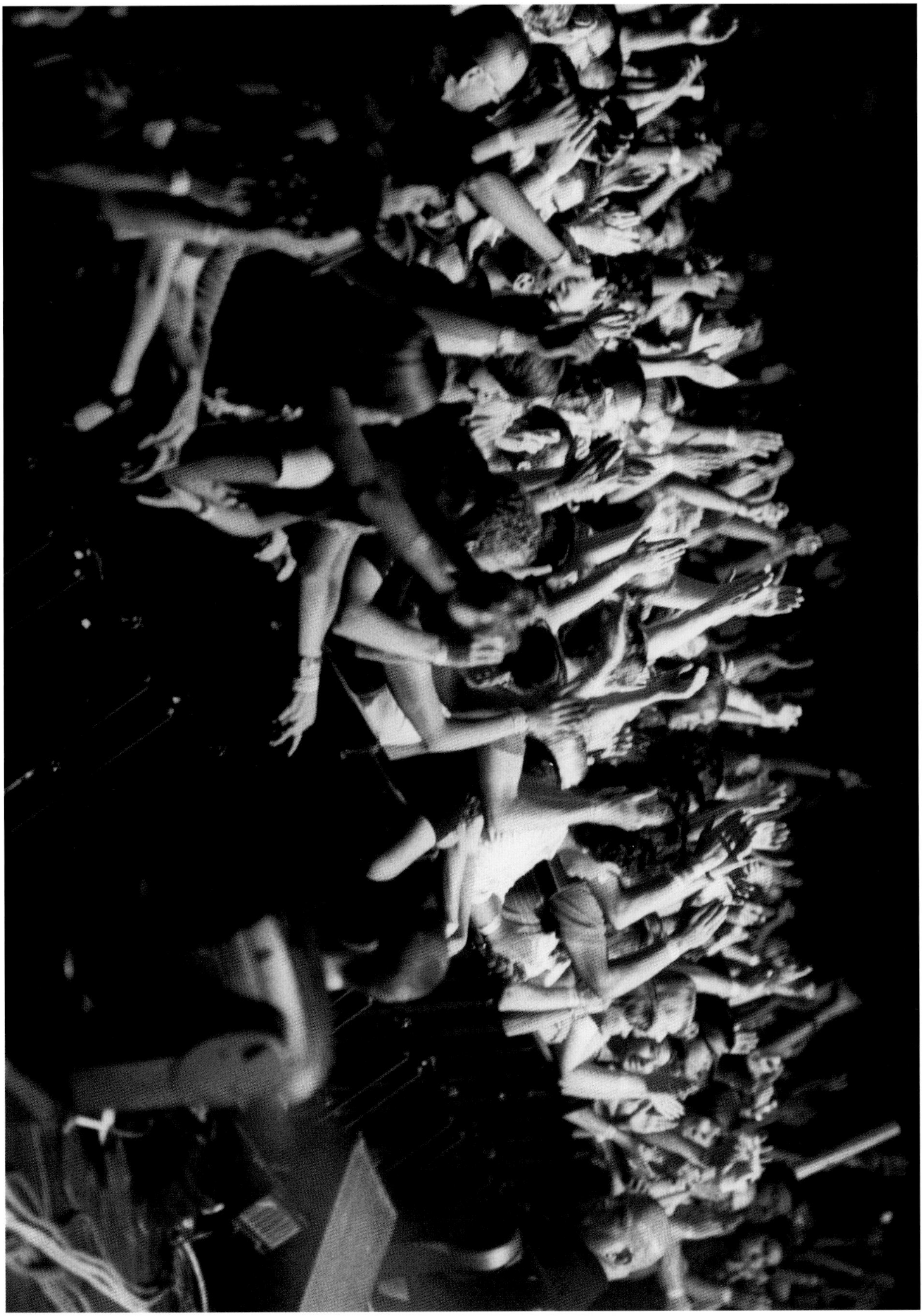

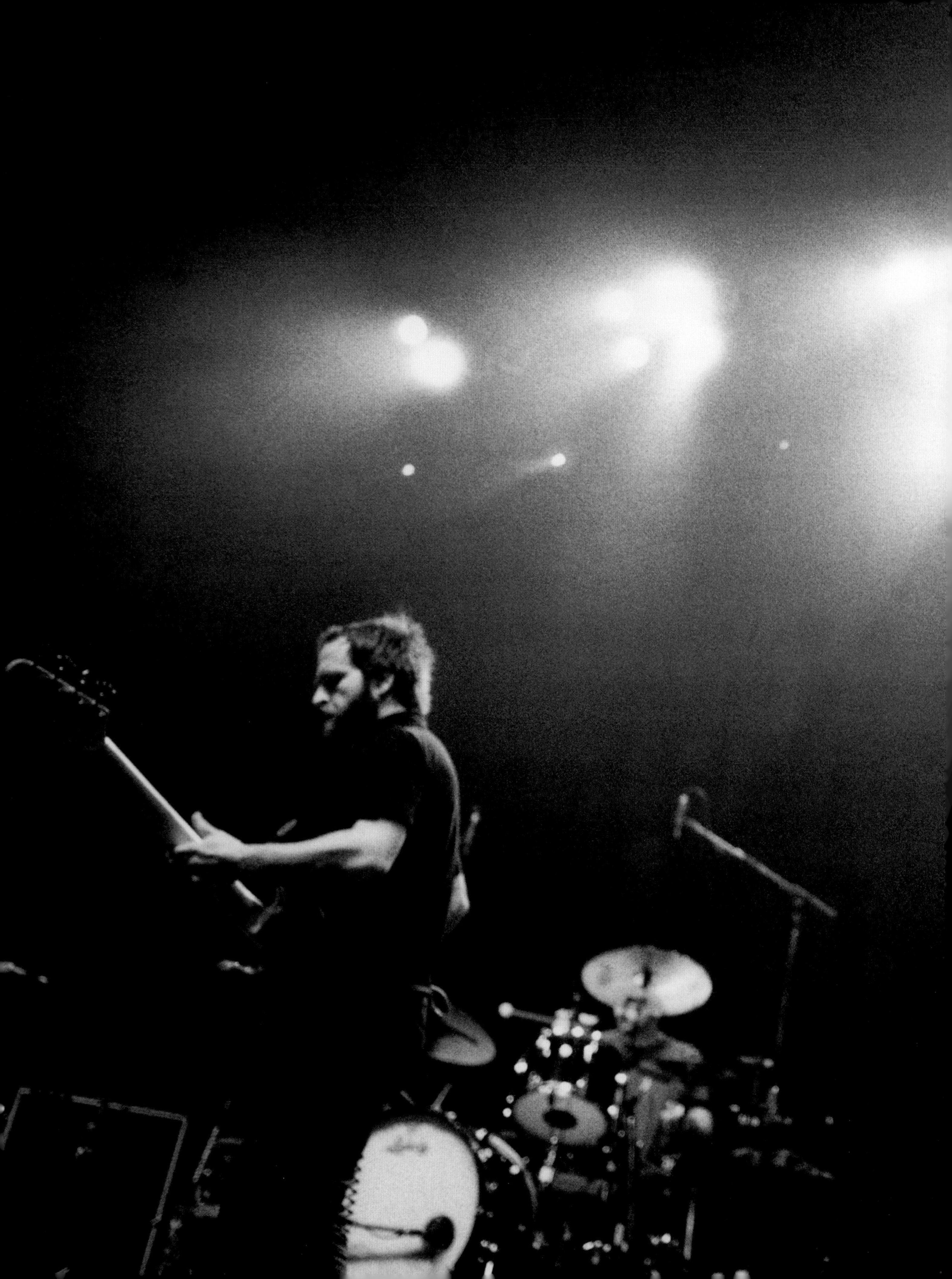

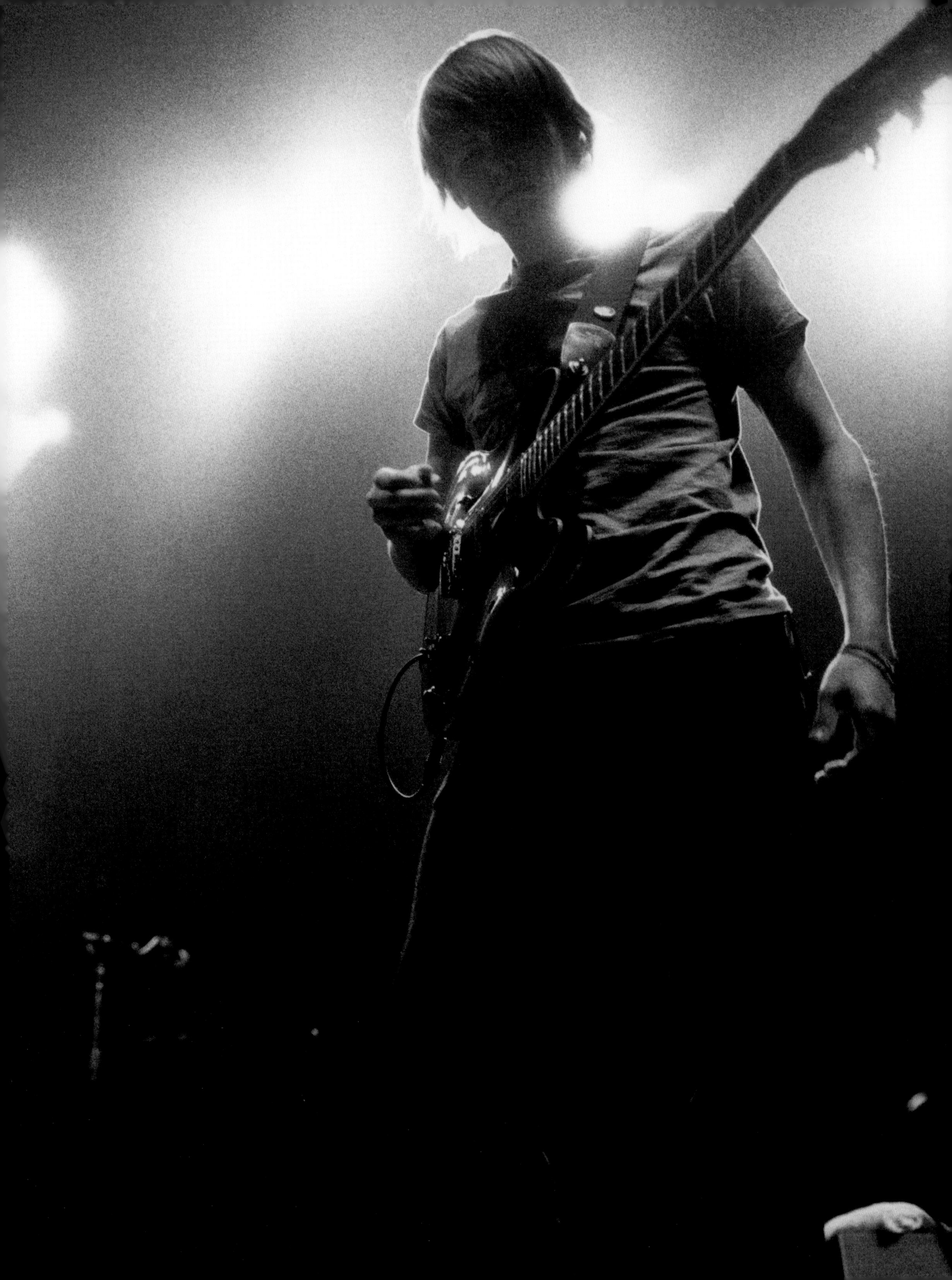

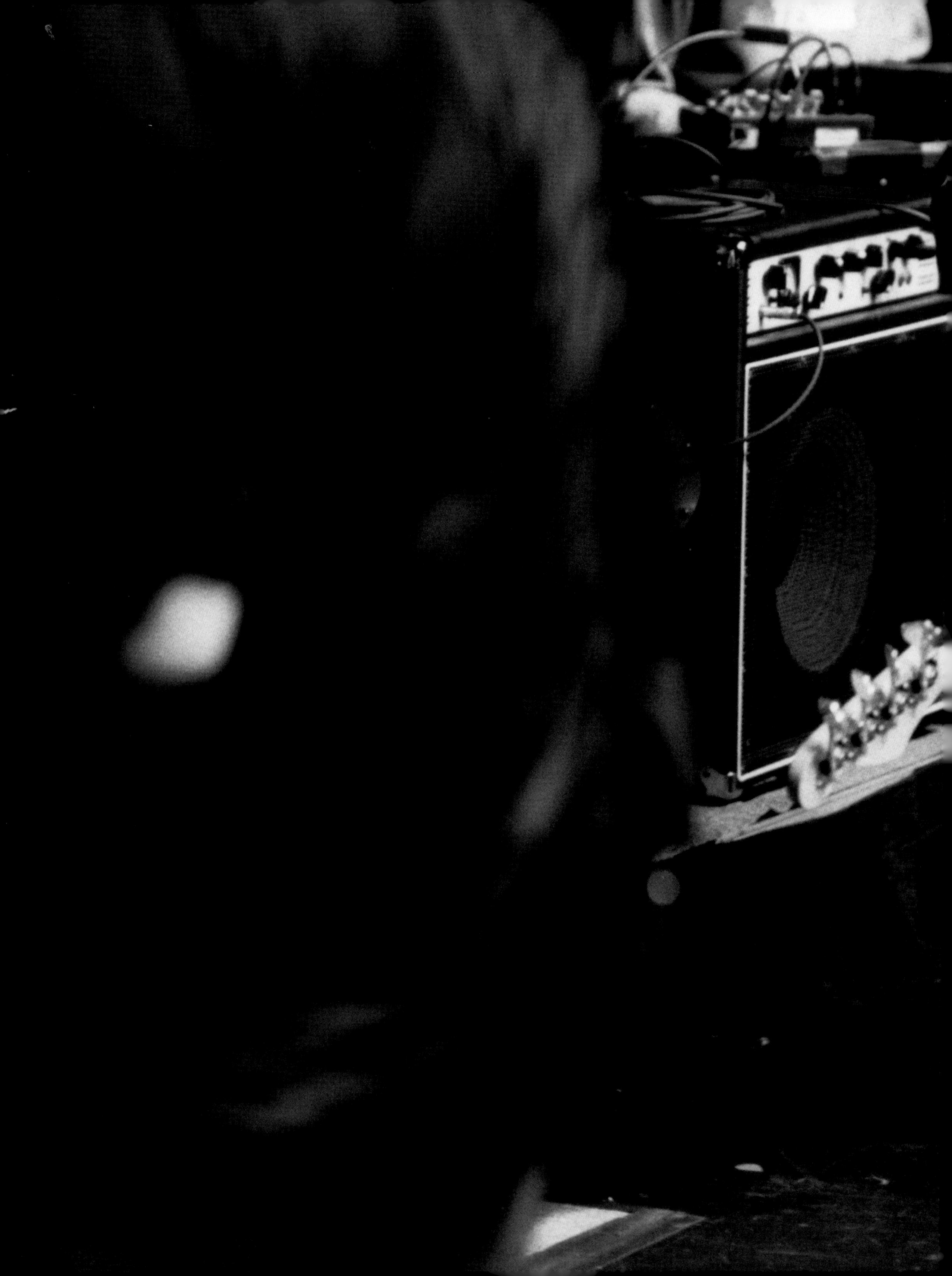

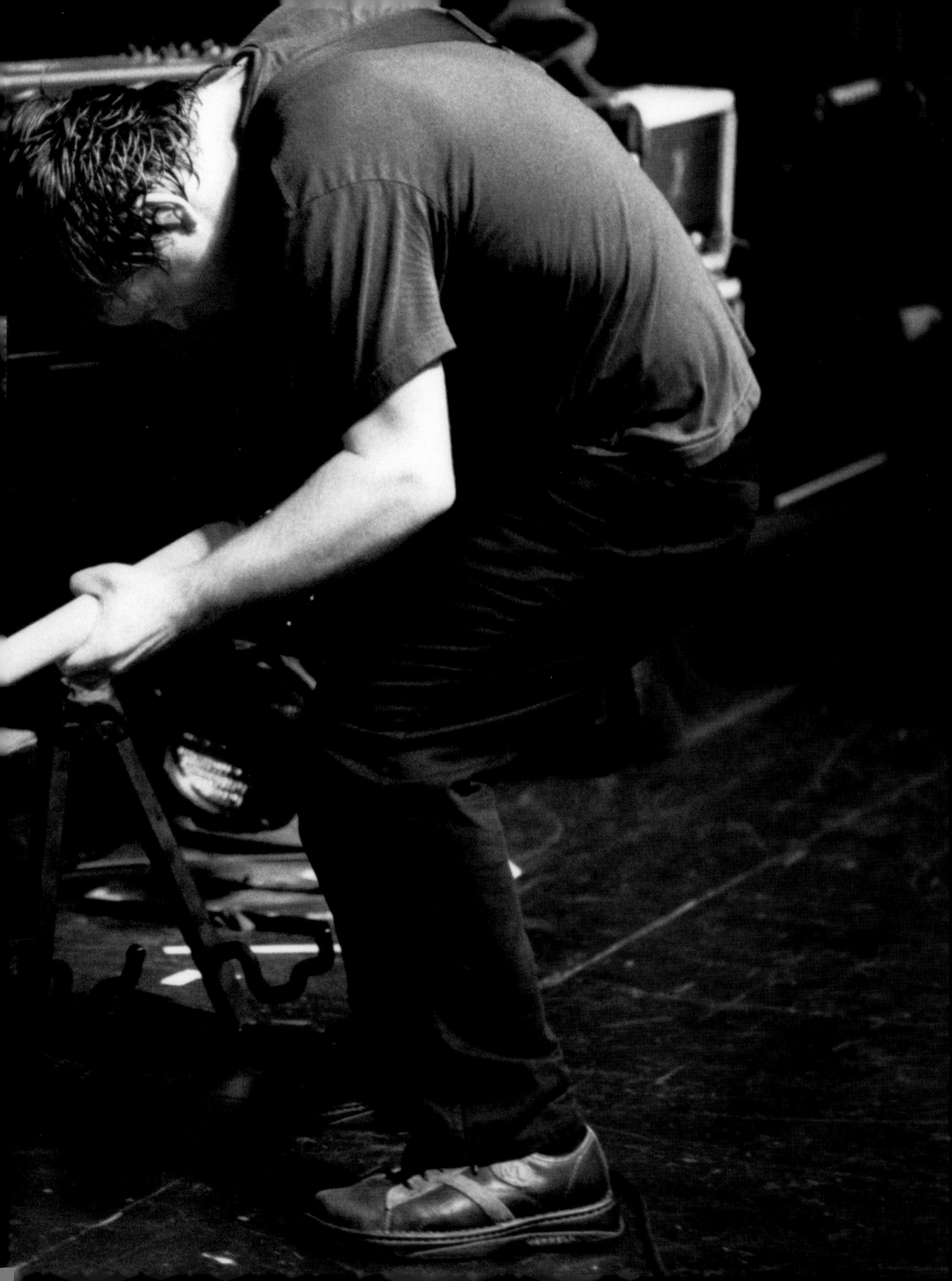

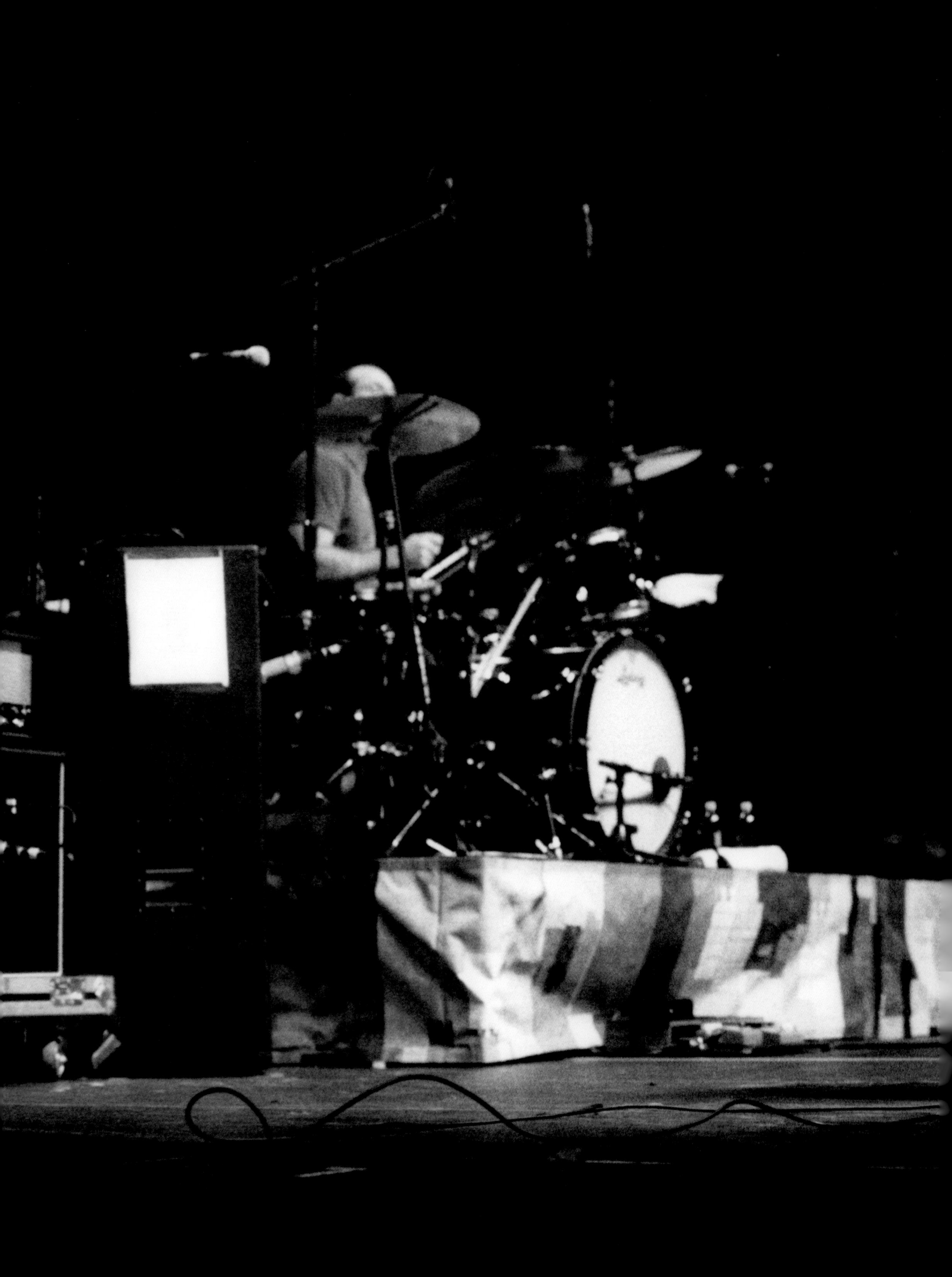

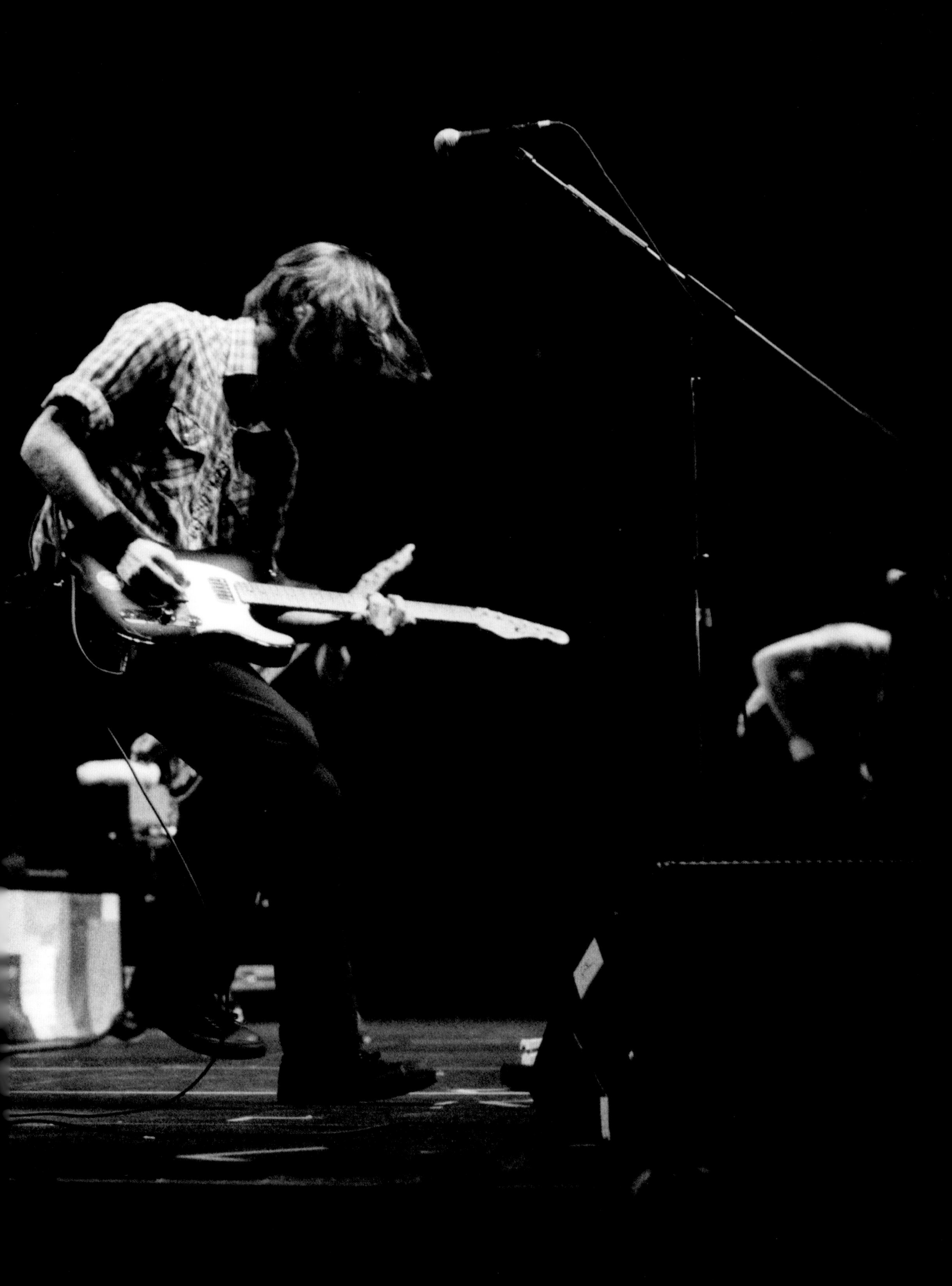

Late one night, a few days before this book was due, my friend Kate said to me on the phone, "I think a really interesting question is . . . what makes you drop everything in your life to document a subject?" She said that the instinct that drives me to do this fascinates her. I don't really know the answer, but I do know how it begins. In this case, I heard a Death Cab song called "Steadier Footing," and I listened to it about 200 times in a row. Then I listened to the rest of *The Photo Album*. Then I wanted to know more.

This kind of thing has happened a handful of times in my life. I become entirely captivated by an artist and the world they've created around themselves. Each time this happens, a strange movie plays in my head. I imagine myself walking in a circle. The subject is in the center, and we don't really know each other. I take a picture. They notice for a second, and then continue on with what they are doing. I continue circling and shooting. With each circle, we know each other a little better, and I get closer. Finally, I am shooting hands, fingers, a shoe, an eye, a mouth, the creases in their clothes. After a while, I don't notice when I take a picture, and they don't notice either.

I met Death Cab backstage at the Henry Fonda Theater in L. A. sometime in 2003. Elliott Smith had died recently, and I felt sick from going through photos, and missing him. Earlier that day I had also been looking at one of my favorite Robert Frank photos, a diptych of two 665 Polaroids he had taken. At the top is a hand shaking a small skeleton toy suspended over the ocean, and below it is a mirror and a shadow; "Sick of Goodby's" is dripping down the photo like blood. "Exactly," I thought.

I was supposed to meet Death Cab backstage that night to see how we all got along. The only camera I brought with me was my Polaroid Land Camera. Chris Walla practically hurled himself down the stairs at me when he saw my camera. "I have a Land Camera too!" We geeked out on 665 film, the black goopy mess it made, and the glorious results of that mess. We all hung out that night, and then Ben invited me down to shoot their next show at the Glass House in Pomona, which is where this book begins.

The conversations in the book were recorded over the phone and while I was on tour with them for *Narrow Stairs*. The ephemera is Walla's; he gave me the keys to his house while he was away recording and I dug through the boxes of Death Cab papers, memories, notes, letters, and scraps he had saved, and included some of my favorites here.

This is not a biography. It's my way of describing a beginning that came into my life at a time when it felt like everything was ending. I really love these guys. I circled this band, and this is what I've come up with so far. There are many more stories to be told, but for now, this is what I've got.

X Autumn de Wilde

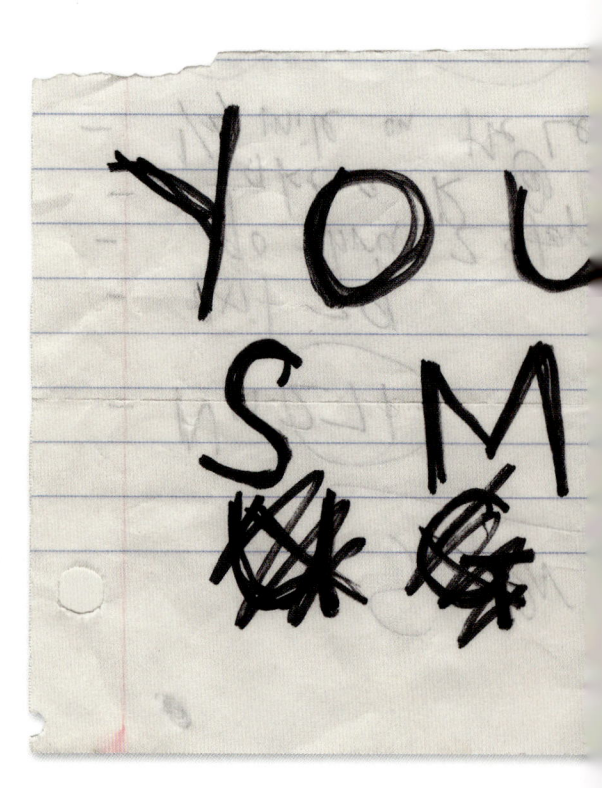

Thank you

To Death Cab for Cutie

To Kate & Laura Mulleavy
for all the late night calls at home and on the road

To my daughter Arrow, my parents Mary and Jerry, and my brother Jacob

To the Piburn family

To my studio manager Meghan Gallagher for your heart and dedication to the long days and late nights

To Lauren Dukoff for the many hours you put in when this all began

To my rep Caryn Weiss for your strength and guidance, and to the rest of the Weiss Artists team for your support

To Death Cab's tour manager Mark Duston and the entire road crew for the time you took to set me up backstage, on the bus, and on stage while I chased after the band

To Death Cab's manager Jordan Kurland and the entire team at Zeitgeist Artist Management

To Josh Rosenfeld and the entire team at Barsuk Records for your support from the very beginning of this project

To the other artists that appear in this book, Ira Elliot & Matthew Caws from Nada Surf, Amy Millan from Stars, Jenny Lewis, Jimmy Tamborello, Johnathan Rice, Britt Daniel from Spoon, and Jason Hammel from Mates of State

To my designer Jeri Heiden for your patience, vision, and friendship

To the rest of the Smog team, John, Nick, Glen & Ryan for letting me move into your studio for two books worth of chaos

To my editor Steve Mockus for your extraordinary eye and guidance

To Ben Kasman, Lindsay Sablosky, Nion McEvoy, Becca Cohen, and the entire Chronicle Books team

To Russell Adams for your beautiful darkroom prints and the talent of your team at Shulman photo lab

To Brian Greenberg, Steve Block, and Richard Photo Lab for the support that made this book possible

For many different reasons I'd also like to thank Kim and Stephanie at IO Color, Atlantic Records, Long View Farm Studios, Tiny Telephone, John Vanderslice, Justin Mitchell, Scotty Stanton, Rob Sinclair, Shirley Kurata, Charlie Staunton, Steve Cvar, Adam Siegel, Tina Pappas, Danny Gabai, Sarah Jurado, Jenny Jimenez, Anna Banana & The Pretty Parlor, Brandy St. John, Jessica Carlson, Alyssa Van Breene, Breanna Murphy, O Positive Films, Juliette Cezzar, the Farm family, the venues that have supported me, and all the Death Cab fans.

The cameras I used: Nikon FM2 Contax 645, Hassleblad 503CW, Yashica T4, Polaroid Land Camera 195, and Chris Walla's Leica.

The film I used: Kodak, Ilford, Fuji, and Polaroid.

Copyright © 2010 by Autumn de Wilde. All rights reserved.
No part of this book may be reproduced in any form without
written permission from the publisher.

Library of Congress Cataloging-in-Publication Data available.

ISBN: 978-0-8118-6951-5

Manufactured in China

Designed by Jeri Heiden, SMOG Design, Inc.

Photographic print production overseen by Meghan Gallagher,
studio manager for Autumn de Wilde.

Photographs on pp. 190–191 and back cover by Chris Walla.

10 9 8 7 6 5 4 3 2 1

Chronicle Books LLC
680 Second Street
San Francisco, CA 94107
www.chroniclebooks.com